Multiple Choice Questions in Library and Information Science

For Competitive Examinations

Biswajit Das
Madhusree Basak

Ess Ess Publications
New Delhi

MULTIPLE CHOICE QUESTIONS IN LIBRARY AND INFORMATION SCIENCE
For Competitive Examinations

ISBN: 978-81-936074-0-4

First Published 2018

Published by:
Ess Ess Publications
4831/24, Ansari Road,
Darya Ganj,
New Delhi-110 002.
INDIA
Phones: 23260807, 41563444
Fax: 41563334
E-mail: info@essessreference.com
www.essessreference.com

Cover Design by *Patch Creative Unit*

Printed and bound in India at Yash Printographics.

Contents

Acknowledgements

The successful completion of this book could not have been possible without the assistance and cooperation of many people whose names may not all be enumerated. Their contributions are sincerely appreciated and gratefully acknowledged. However we would like to express our heartfelt appreciation to Smt. Susmita Das and Mr. Nabendu Basak who has given us motivation to complete this assignment. We would like to praise God for good health and strength that was necessary in order for us to complete this book. We are thankful to our parents, friends and relatives for their constant support. We humbly extend our thanks to all the concerned persons who co-operated with us in this regard.

Biswajit Das
Madhusree Basak

Preface

'Multiple Choice Questions in Library and Information Science : For Competitive Examinations' is a book for UGC-NET (both LS and JRF), SET, Ph.D & MLIS Entrance Test & other competitive exams. It is prepared after continuous and rigorous efforts of several years. It is based on 'All in One' approach because it will be helpful for LIS students, scholars, professionals and teachers as well as for NET/SET examinees, Library and Information Science (LIS) job oriented examinations and interviews.

There are Ten Chapters in this book which contain each and every answer of Paper II questions covering NET question paper with an addition of Paper III.

The key feature of this book is incorporation of a large number of questions and answers of assertion and reasoning, chronological arrangements and matching type. There are almost 4000 multiple choice questions and their answers recorded in this book.

This is a unique effort in a way that this book contains all the questions covering several competitive exams in the field of library and information science. All answers are given at the end of each chapter.

We hope this book will be helpful for the readers. Any comments and suggestions from users' community are most welcome.

Dr. Biswajit Das
Madhusree Basak

1
Information and Communication

1. The Intellectual Property Right is related to
   (A) IT Act of 2000
   (B) Censorship
   (C) Right to Information Act
   (D) Copy Right Act
2. Patents are classified under
   (A) Primary source
   (B) Secondary source
   (C) Tertiary source
   (D) None of the above
3. Arrange the following components of communication in correct sequence of information flow.
   (i) Message (ii) Source
   (iii) Medium (iv) Receiver

   Codes:
   (A) (i) (iii) (iv) (ii) (B) (ii) (iv) (iii) (i)
   (C) (ii) (i) (iii) (iv) (D) (iv) (i) (ii) (iii)
4. The term "Information Retrieval" was coined by-
   (A) H. P. Luhn (B) Calvin Mooers
   (C) Mortimer Taube (D) Derek Austin

5. The correct sequence of information flow is-
   (A) Message → Source → Channel → Receiver
   (B) Source → Message → Channel → Receiver
   (C) Message → Channel → Source → Receiver
   (D) Message → Channel → Receiver → Source
6. The term 'Information Product' was coined by
   (A) Paul Zurkowski (B) Fritz Machlup
   (C) William Martin (D) George J. Stigler
7. Information, as a commodity, is used for
   (A) National integration
   (B) Treatment of diseases
   (C) Flood problem
   (D) Decesion making process
8. The empirical rule that describes the frequency of words in a piece of text is known as the
   (A) Heaps' Law (B) Bradford's Law
   (C) Mooers' Law (D) Zipf's Law
9. Who is the author of 'Traite de Documentation'?
   (A) S. C. Bradford (B) B. C. Vickery
   (C) Paul Otlet (D) S. R. Ranganathan
10. Which of the following is not covered in Intellectual Property Rights
   (A) Copy Right (B) Patents
   (C) Trademark (D) Thesaurus
11. Who coined the name "Information Society"?
   (A) Derek Austin (B)Daniel Bell
   (C) Allen Kent (D) E. J. Coates
12. Arrange the following writing materials in the order of their evolution
   (i) Iron (ii) Stone
   (iii) Papyrus (iv) Paper
   Codes:
   (A) ii, iii, i, iv (B)iv, ii, i, iii
   (C)iii, i, iv, ii (D)ii, i, iii, iv

13. The early work on modeling of information communication was based on :
    (A) Lasswell model
    (B) Shannon and Weaver model
    (C) Bradford and Prince model
    (D) Goode and Hatt model
14. The process of flow of Information from the generator to the user is :
    (A) Information search (B) Information transfer
    (C) Information need (D) Information system
15. "Information is piecemeal, fragmented and particular." Who said ?
    (A) Daniel Bell (B) Fritz Machlup
    (C) Brookers (D) Belkin
16. The three core processes i.e. opening, orientation and consolidation have been explained in which information seeking behavior model ?
    (A) Kuhlthou's Model
    (B) Wilson's Model
    (C) Foster's Non-linear Model
    (D) Krikela's Model
17. Which Information Retrieval Model studies the properties of the languages as well as artificial language ?
    (A) Mathematical Model (B) Economic Model
    (C) Psychological Model (D) Linguistics Model
18. Which organisation is working on intellectual property rights at international level ?
    (A) WIPO (B) UNESCO
    (C) IFLA (D) ANSI
19. The concept of 'invisible college' was first used by :
    (A) Derek Desola Price (B) F.W. Lancaster
    (C) Eugene Garfield (D) S.R. Ranganathan
20. The retrieval technique designed to find terms that are spelled incorrectly at data entry or query input is known as

(A) term masking (B) case sensitive searching
(C) fuzzy searching (D) proximity searching

21. An invisible college is a typical example of
(A) informal channel of communication
(B) formal channels of communication
(C) both (A) and (B)
(D) none of the above

22. When did Shannon and Weaver put forth the mathematical model of communication?
(A) 1938 (B) 1942
(C) 1945 (D) 1949

23. The correct order of steps involved in digital conversion of print materials is
(A) encoding, scanning, searching, display
(B) scanning, encoding, searching, display
(C) scanning, encoding, display, searching
(D) encoding, scanning, display, searching

24. Who was the Chairman of 'National Policy on Library & Information Systems' (1986)?
(A) D. N. Banerjee (B) D. P. Chattopadhyay
(C) Sam Pitroda (D) Kalpana Dasgupta

25. What are the major driving forces behind an 'Information society'?
(i) R T I (ii) I. C. T.
(iii) Internet (iv) I. T. ACT
Codes :
(A) (ii) & (i) are correct (B) (ii) & (iv) are correct
(C) (i) & (iv) are correct (D) (ii) & (iii) are correct

26. Major problems of 'Information Communication Technology' are
(i) Information overload
(ii) Information insecurity
(iii) Lack of innovative technologies
(iv) Lack of control over communication

Codes:

(A) (ii) and (iv) are correct

(B) (i) and (iv) are correct

(C) (i), (ii) and (iv) are correct

(D) (i), (ii) and (iii) are correct

27. Arrange the following according to their year of enactment in India :

(i) Freedom of Information Act

(ii) Right to Information Act

(iii) Copyright Act (Revised)

(iv) Information Technology Act

Codes :

(A) (iv), (ii), (i), (iii) (B) (iii), (iv), (i), (ii)

(C) (ii), (iii), (iv), (i) (D) (i), (iv), (ii), (iii)

28. Arrange the following according to their year of origin:

(i) Bradford's Law

(ii) Lotka's Law

(iii) Statistical Bibliography

(iv) Zipf's Law

Codes :

(A) (i), (iii), (iv), (ii) (B) (i), (ii), (iv), (iii)

(C) (iv), (iii), (i), (ii) (D) (iii), (ii), (iv), (i)

29. According to Machlup the difference between information and knowledge is:

(A) Information increases with use, whereas knowledge is constant.

(B) Information is stimulatory, whereas knowledge is practical.

(C) Information is shareable, whereas knowledge is one's property.

(D) Information is piecemeal, fragmented, particular, whereas knowledge is structured, coherent and universal.

30. Jubilee Project is associated with what?

(A) Evaluation of electronic information services
(B) Public library survey
(C) Strategic management of libraries
(D) Scale development

31. In 1974, Zurkowski used for the first time which of the following term?
(A) Digital Literacy (B) Media Literacy
(C) Computer Literacy (D) Information Literacy

32. Inference Engine is a part of which information system?
(A) Management information System
(B) Decision Support System
(C) Expert System
(D) Open System

33. Blair and Maron evaluation study on retrieval effectiveness of full text search is called
(A) Uniform Indexing (B) Citation Indexing
(C) Chain Indexing (D) Keyword Indexing

34. Which of the following is not the prerequisite for a National Information Policy?
(A) Legislative Frame work
(B) Production of National Bibliography
(C) Advisory and Administrative body
(D) ICT infrastructure facilities

35. World Intellectual Property Organization is related to
(A) UNESCO
(B) United Nations
(C) U.S. Organization
(D) International Law Organization

36. Redundancy of information is
(A) Unnecessary and should be eliminated
(B) Unnecessary but cannot be avoided
(C) Necessary and some times useful
(D) Necessary and always desirable

37. Radio Frequency Identification is used in library for :

(i) Circulation of Documents
(ii) Cataloguing of Documents
(iii) Security of Documents
(iv) Acquisition of Documents

Codes :

(A) (i) and (ii) are correct
(B) (ii) and (iv) are correct
(C) (iii) and (ii) are correct
(D) (i) and (iii) are correct

38. In 1990's 4Ps were translated into 4Cs of marketing. Here promotion (P) represents:

(A) Cost of users.
(B) Customer needs and wants
(C) Communication
(D) Convenience.

39. Index Translationum is a world bibliography of translations of

(A) Periodical articles
(B) Books
(C) Books & Periodical articles.
(D) Patents.

40. Who categorized the user studies into the following three categories ?

(i) Behaviour Studies
(ii) Use studies
(iii) Information flow studies

Codes :

(A) Maurice B Line (B) Menzel
(C) Cronin (D) Voigt

41. Which of the factor is not helping in limiting the external validity ?

(A) Reactive effect
(B) Ecological validity
(C) Interaction between selection bias of experimental variables
(D) Ecological effect

42. National Knowledge Network is to be implemented by
    (A) National Knowledge Commission
    (B) Information and Library Network
    (C) National Information Centre
    (D) Department of Information Technology
43. ISO 9000 standard denotes the
    (A) Consistence confirmance of a product or service to a given set of standard or expectations
    (B) Total customer satisfaction
    (C) Representation of stakeholders issues.
    (D) Detailed list of measuring techniques
44. Who used the phrase 'control-access directional type sources'?
    (A) R.E. Bopp (B) B.C. Wynar
    (C) W.A. Katz (D) R. Balay
45. Which State Public Library Act has the provision to collect library fund through land tax ?
    (A) Tamil Nadu (B) Karnataka
    (C) Andhra Pradesh (D) Maharashtra
46. Association of College and Research Libraries (ACRL) (USA) is a
    (A) Division of American Library Association
    (B) Independent Association for Academic & Research Libraries
    (C) Division of Special Libraries Association (USA)
    (D) Division of IFLA
47. Which one of the following is not a recommendation of National Knowledge Commission (India)?
    (A) Preparation of a National Census of Library
    (B) Encourage greater community participation in library management
    (C) Raja Rammohan Roy library foundation to act as the National co-ordination agency
    (D) Facilitate donation and maintenance of private collection

48. Which of the following are the scientists' approach according to Melvin J. Voigt (1961)?
(i) Current Approach
(ii) Everyday Approach
(iii) Exhaustive Approach
(iv) 'Catching up' or 'brushing up' approach.
Codes :
(A) (ii), (iii) and (iv) (B) (i), (iii) and (iv)
(C) (i), (ii) and (iv) (D) (i), (ii) and (iii)

49. Magazines are suitable for
(i) Leisure and entertainment
(ii) Scholarly information
(iii) Popular information
(iv) Subject information
Codes :
(A) (i), (ii) and (iii) are correct.
(B) (ii), (iii) and (iv) are correct.
(C) (i) and (iii) are correct.
(D) (ii) and (iv) are correct.

50. Which of the following are the fundamental conditions for a subject to be protected by IPR ?
(i) The work must be original
(ii) The work must be man made
(iii) The work must be intelligible
(iv) The work must be recorded/ fixed
Codes :
(A) (i), (ii) and (iii) are correct.
(B) (i), (iii) and (iv) are correct.
(C) (ii), (iii) and (iv) are correct.
(D) (i), (ii) and (iv) are correct.

51. Which of the following are the problems of present information environment ?
(i) Information indiscipline
(ii) Information literacy
(iii) Information overload
(iv) Information technology

Codes :

(A) (i), (iii) are correct

(B) (i) and (iv) are correct

(C) (ii) and (iv) are correct

(D) (i) and (ii) are correct

52. Which of the following are not partners of National Programme on Technology Enhanced Learning (NPTEL) ?

(i) IIT Madras (ii) IIT Delhi

(iii) IIIT Bangalore (iv) NIT Rourkela

Codes :

(A) (iii) and (iv) (B) (i) and (iv)

(C) (ii) and (iii) (D) (i) and (ii)

53. What is the correct order of SCONUL's "Seven Pillar Model of Information Skills"?

(i) Recognise information need

(ii) Construct strategies for locating

(iii) Compare and evaluate

(iv) Locate and access

Codes :

(A) (i), (ii), (iii), (iv) (B) (ii), (iii), (iv), (i)

(C) (i), (ii), (iv), (iii) (D) (ii), (iii), (i), (iv)

54. METS stands for

(A) Machine Encoded Transmission System

(B) Metadata Encoded for Textual Sources

(C) Machine Encoded Textual Standard

(D) Metadata Encoding Transmission Standard

55. The 12 rules for relational database were given by

(A) E.F. Codd (B) Charles Babbage

(C) James Weyer (D) Tim Berners Lee

56. WIPO is located at

(A) New York (B) London

(C) Geneva (D) Paris

57. The National Mission on Libraries, India was established in which year ?

(A) 2009 (B) 2010
(C) 2011 (D) 2012

58. The production of mental reflection and imagination is known as
(A) Information (B) Idea
(C) Data (D) Knowledge

59. Who is the propounder of the term 'Information Transfer' ?
(A) Ranganathan (B) J. Martin
(C) Calvin Moores (D) Beesman

60. Which organisation was joined with 'Library Association' to form CILIP in 2002 ?
(A) Institute of Bibliography
(B) Institute of Information Scientists
(C) Institute of Documentation
(D) Institute of Librarianship

61. Dictionary of National Biography (DNB) contains biography of prominent people of
(A) All nations (B) Europeans
(C) Americans (D) Britishers

62. Which among the following is free Audio book site ?
(A) Ebrary (B) Virtua
(C) Librivox (D) Google Books

63. Library Ethics is a combination of what ?
(i) Responsibility (ii) Accountability
(iii) Commitment (iv) Decision Making

Codes :
(A) (i), (ii) and (iii) are correct.
(B) (ii), (iii) and (iv) are correct.
(C) (i), (iii) and (iv) are correct.
(D) (i), (ii) and (iv) are correct.

64. Starting, Chaining, Browsing, Differentiating, Monitoring, Extracting, Verification and Ending are important stages of which information seeking behavior model?

(A) Dervin's Model (B) Ellis Model
(C) Marchionnini Model (D) Kuhlthan Model

65. Indian National Advisory Board for Libraries was setup in 1966 by
    (A) Association of Indian Universities
    (B) Ministry of Education
    (C) Planning Commission
    (D) University Grants Commision

66. Whose model of communication of knowledge suggests that communication as an open system may be regarded as subjective, selective, variable and yet unpredictable?
    (A) G. Gerbner (B) Juger Hebermans
    (C) E Shanon & Weaver (D) M. Foucault

67. Which Committee/Commission recommended that Imperial Library be designated as Copyright Library?
    (A) Fayzee Commission, 1939
    (B) Riche Committee, 1926
    (C) Statham Committee, 1932
    (D) Sadler Committee, 1916

68. Who said that information is both a product and process?
    (A) S.R. Ranganathan (B) J. Martin
    (C) D.J. Foskett (D) S.C. Bradford

69. One of the authorized users makes bulk downloading of a Journal using robots and consequently licensor blocks access of the journal. What may be the most appropriate action(s) that librarian should initiate?
    (i) Cancelation of authentication of the said user.
    (ii) Asking the licensor for blocking up the access without prior information.
    (iii) Investigate and take corrective measures.
    (iv) Notify user community of user restrictions.

    Codes:
    (A) (ii), (iv) are correct (B) (ii), (iii) are correct
    (C) (i), (iii) are correct (D) (i), (ii), are correct

70. What is/are common feature/s between RFID & Barcode Technology?
   (i) Read more than one item at a time
   (ii) Able to locate specific items on shelves
   (iii) Programmable
   (iv) Read while item is moving

   Codes:
   (A) (i), (ii) are correct
   (B) (iii), (iv) are correct
   (C) (ii), (iv) are correct
   (D) All the above are correct

71. Which of the bibliometric law describes the frequency of publications by author ?
   (A) Zipf's law (B) Bradford's law
   (C) Lotka's law (D) None of the above

72. Indian patents on all areas are published in
   (A) India : A reference annual
   (B) Indian chemical patent index
   (C) Gazette of India, Part-III
   (D) None of the above

73. Which of the following does not protect intellectual property ?
   (A) Encryption of data
   (B) Digital watermark
   (C) Uniquely encoded licences
   (D) Plug-ins

74. "World directory of sources of Patents" is published by
   (A) Bowker-Saur, U.S.A.
   (B) WIPO
   (C) Patent Information System, India
   (D) Derwent, London

75. Which of the following identifies user by a login permission to a licensed site.
   (A) Authorization (B) Authentication
   (C) Digital signature (D) All of the above

76. Papyras was used as a writing material by
    (A) Summarians (B) Italians
    (C) Egyptians (D) Assyrians
77. The intrinsic value of information lies in its
    (A) Procurement
    (B) Processing and Storage
    (C) Communication and Retrieval
    (D) Usage
78. "Pro Quest" is -
    (A) Traditional Commercial Publisher
    (B) Scholarly Society Publisher
    (C) Electronic Aggregator
    (D) Publisher of Higher Learning Institutions
79. The main components of an RFID system include
    (A) Handheld Reader, RFID label printer, server and External book return
    (B) RFID tags, readers or sensors, Antenna and server
    (C) RFID label printer, sensors, antenna and server
    (D) RFID tags, server, external book return, sensors
80. 'Communities' is a component of following digital library software-
    (A) GSDL (B) D space
    (C) Fedora (D) i-core
81. The term 'Literary warrant' for book classification was introduced by
    (A) W.C.B. Sayers (B) Wyndham Hulme
    (C) J.D. Brown (D) H.E. Bliss
82. Under which approach of Wersig-Neveling's information theory, information is seen as static relations between physical objects which may be perceived or not?
    (A) The meaning approach
    (B) The structural approach
    (C) The process approach
    (D) The knowledge approach

83. Which information theory focuses on the purpose of communication is, to inform, instruct or motivate the receiver?

(A) Shannon's Theory (B) Weaver's Theory

(C) Ackoff's Theory (D) Yovit's Theory

84. 'Noise' in Information retrieval is due to

(A) Precision (B) Recall

(C) Relevant Information (D) Redundant Information

85. Whose model of communication of knowledge suggests that communication is an open system?

(A) G. Garbner (B) Juger Hebermans

(C) Shannon & Weaver (D) M. Foucault

86. 'Trans Border Data Flow' means

(A) Exchange of documents between countries

(B) Free flow of information between countries

(C) Flow of information between countries

(D) Exchange of electronic information between countries

87. Which of the following are not the Models of communication?

(i) Vintage Model (ii) Lasswell's Model

(iii) Epidemic Model (iv) Garbner's Model

Codes:

(A) (i) & (iv) are correct.

(B) (ii) & (iii) are correct.

(C) (i) & (iii) are correct.

(D) (iii) & (iv) are correct.

88. Who introduced the concept of 'knowledge industry' ?

(A) Peter Drucker (B) Fritz Machlup

(C) Marc Porat (D) William Saffady

89. The mode of displaying graphic informationpixel by pixel with bits in main memory is

(A) Bit handling (B) Bit mapping

(C) Bit pattern (D) Bit matrix

90. The important methods of measuring impact factor of any information retrieval system are :

(i) Expression Rate (ii) Precision Rate
(iii) Recall Rate (iv) Depression Rate

Codes :

(A) (i) and (iii) are correct.
(B) (ii) and (iv) are correct.
(C) (ii) and (iii) are correct.
(D) (iii) and (iv) are correct.

91. A non-linear model of information seeking behaviour was presented by
(A) T.D. Wilson (B) Ellis
(C) Kulthou (D) Allen Foster

92. A systematic method and process of studying and evaluating whether the expenditure for products, materials, or services is justified by the benefits is
(A) Break Even Analysis
(B) Cost-Effective Analysis
(C) System Analysis
(D) Administrative Analysis

93. Cost recovery and profit making aspects in relation to gathering information, organization, services and usage, etc. refer to
(A) Economy evaluation
(B) Coverage evaluation
(C) Workforce evaluation
(D) User evaluation

94. A situation where a digital resource is no longer readable is called
(A) Digital Divide (B) Digital Representation
(C) Digital Rendering (D) Digital Obsolescence

95. EUAL stands for
(A) E-monitoring library for Academics
(B) End User Logistics Association
(C) Electronic Usage of Library Acquisitions
(D) End User License Agreement

96. The three leadership styles identified by Koontz and others are

(i) Autocratic (ii) Democratic
(iii) Trait approach (iv) Free-reign

Codes:

(A) i, ii and iii are correct.
(B) ii, iii and iv are correct.
(C) iii, iv and i are correct.
(D) i, ii and iv are correct.

97. Which of the following are not the features of ISDN?
(i) Simultaneous Digital Transmission
(ii) Set of communication standards
(iii) Creates and combines packets
(iv) Program to visit web pages

Codes:

(A) i & ii are correct. (B) ii & iii are correct.
(C) iii & iv are correct. (D) i & iv are correct.

98. Which of the following methods are adopted for offering information literacy?
(i) Stand alone course
(ii) Integrated with curriculum
(iii) Online course
(iv) Internship

Codes:

(A) i and ii (B) i, ii and iii
(C) ii and iv (D) i, ii and iv

99. Shannon's model of information theory is criticized for which of the following reasons?
i. Concern on semantic issues
ii. Engineering bias
iii. Concern for technical transmission
iv. Emphasis on effectiveness

Codes:

(A) i and ii are correct.
(B) ii and iii are correct.
(C) iii and iv are correct.
(D) i and iii are correct.

100. Arrange the following stages of knowledge representation in order:

i. Gather data
ii. Knowledge database
iii. Codification
iv. Content mapping

Codes:

(A) iv, iii, i, ii
(B) iii, i, iv, ii
(C) ii, iv, i, iii
(D) i, iii, ii, iv

101. Name the characteristics of information in which the more information we have, the more we use, the more it becomes useful.

(A) Synergetic Characteristics
(B) Diffusive Characteristics
(C) Compressible Characteristics
(D) Shareable Characteristics

102. MIS provides all sorts of information required for :

(A) Management of Organisation
(B) Preparation of Budget
(C) Administration
(D) Decision making

103. Identify the correct sequence of elements of communication :

(A) Channel-Decoder-Destination-Encoder-Message-Source
(B) Decoder-Channel-Destination-Message- Source-Encoder
(C) Source-Encoder-Message-Channel-Decoder-Destination
(D) Encoder-Decoder-Source-Message-Channel-Destination

104. Who advocated the seven basic statistical tools for quality control ?

(A) Joseph Juran
(B) Phillip Crosby
(C) Kauro Ishikawa
(D) C.A. Cutter

105. LOCKSS (Lots of Copies Keep Stuff Safe) project was launched by :

(A) Mellon Foundation
(B) Stanford University
(C) University of California
(D) OCLC

106. Identify the abilities of an information literate person:
   i. the ability to find information
   ii. the ability to prepare bibliographic description of information
   iii. the ability to use information
   iv. the ability to evaluate information

   Codes :

   (A) i, ii, iii are correct. (B) i, iii, iv are correct.
   (C) i, ii, iv are correct. (D) ii, iii, iv are correct.

107. Which of the following are threats to information security ?
   i. Personal firewalls ii. Compromise to IPR
   iii. Anti-spyware iv. Acts of espionage

   Codes :

   (A) i, ii, iii are correct. (B) ii, iii are correct.
   (C) ii, iv are correct. (D) ii, iii, iv are correct.

108. Technological Gatekeeper is :
   (A) A formal method of giving current awareness service
   (B) A method of technology assessment and evaluation
   (C) A process of transfer of technology
   (D) An informal mechanism of keeping user informed of relevant development

109. Who among the following honoured with 'Nobel Prize' for his substantial contribution in Documentation ?
   (A) S. C. Bradford (B) Loosjes
   (C) Eric De Grolier (D) Henri La Fontaine

110. The office of patent information system in India is at
   (A) Mumbai (B) New Delhi
   (C) Kolkata (D) Nagpur

111. 'Noise' in Information Retrieval is due to

(A) Precision
(B) Recall
(C) Relevant information
(D) Redundant information

112. The concept "Invisible College" first used by :
(A) Eugene Garfield (B) Derek Solla Price
(C) Allent Kent (D) Carl Savage

113. "Fair use" is a term most relevant to :
(A) Intellectual Property Right
(B) Books borrowed for home reading
(C) Copyright
(D) Use of reference books

114. Ontology is
(A) An Indexing Method
(B) Classification of Internet based documents
(C) Cataloguing of Internet based documents
(D) Documentation service

115. Chairman of National Knowledge Commission is.
(A) Pranab Mukherjee (B) Nandan Nilekani
(C) P. Chidambaram (D) Sam Pitroda

116. The transmission of receiver's reaction back to the sender is known as
(A) Noise (B) Feedback
(C) Medium (D) Source

117. How is stochastic equation of information solved ?
(A) By statistical rules
(B) By dynamic rules
(C) By statistical and dynamic rules
(D) None of these.

118. Information Science is a discipline that investigates
(A) the properties and behaviour of information
(B) the forces governing the flow of information
(C) the means for processing of information for optimal uses
(D) all of these.

119. Information may be categorised into
   (A) logical, analytical and statistical
   (B) statistical, descriptive and analytical
   (C) analytical, statistical and systematic
   (D) systematic, analytical and descriptive.
120. IPR stands for
   (A) Indian Press Registration
   (B) Intellectual Property Right
   (C) International Property Right
   (D) Indian Property Regulations.
121. 'Fair use' is the norm for determining the legality of
   (A) producing the second edition of a book
   (B) photocopying an entire book
   (C) making available a book to another library on inter-library loan
   (D) prescribing a book as a text book.
122. There are a few basic factors which may be applied in winning the hearts of the readers. They are
   (A) psychological factor, environmental factor, social factor
   (B) self factor, psychological factor, service factor
   (C) service factor, philosophical factor, self factor
   (D) technological factor, service factor, self factor.
123. The marketing concepts in Library Service include
   (A) analysis, planning, implementation and control
   (B) advertising, planning, analysis and control
   (C) distribution, control, analysis, implementation
   (D) indexing, planning, control and implementation.
124. Linear model of communication in knowledge based on Aristotles' model of communication was proposed by
   (A) Juger Heberman
   (B) A.J. Wells
   (C) C.E. Shannon & W. Weaver
   (D) G. Gerbner

125. Arrange the following in chronological sequence :
   (i) Digital Millennium Copyright Act
   (ii) Right to Information Act. (India)
   (iii) Information Technology Act (India)
   (iv) Indian Copyright Act

   Codes :

   (A) (IV), (I), (III), (II) (B) (IV), (II), (III), (I)
   (C) (I), (IV), (II), (III) (D) (II), (III), (I), (IV)

126. Which one is the most important problem being faced by Institutional Repositories for archiving the documents ?
   (A) Availability (B) Rarity
   (C) Copyright issues (D) Author's resistance

127. As per Indian Copyright Law, copyright is granted for
   (A) Fifty years after the book is published
   (B) Fifty years after the death of the author
   (C) Sixty years after the book is published
   (D) Sixty years after the death of the author

128. NAAC stands for
   (A) National Accreditation and Authority Council
   (B) Northern Accreditation and Authorities Committee
   (C) National Assessment and Accreditation Council
   (D) Northern Assessment and Accreditation Council

129. The term 'Exponential growth' refers to
   (A) Linear growth
   (B) Normal mode of distribution
   (C) Geometric Progression
   (D) Arithmetic Progression

130. Who expressed knowledge in a simple mathematical equation k(s) + _ 1 = k (s + _ s) ?
   (A) Fritz Machlup (B) B.C. Brooks
   (C) N.J. Belkin (D) C.E. Shannon

131. Which is not a near synonym term to information ?
   (A) Ideas (B) Data
   (C) Catalogue (D) Facts

132. Arrange the following according to chronological order:
    (i) Universal Copyright convention
    (ii) Berne Convention
    (iii) Indian Copyright Act
    (iv) WIPO Copyright Act
    Codes :
    (A) (ii), (iv), (iii), (i) (B) (iii), (ii), (iv), (i)
    (C) (i), (iii), (ii), (iv) (D) (ii), (i), (iii), (iv)
133. BERNE CONVENTION is concerned with :
    (A) Translations (B) Copyright
    (C) Patents (D) Standards
134. Information Technological year was adopted in
    (A) 1980 (B) 1982
    (C) 1983 (D) 1984
135. Information is ...
    (A) Raw data (B) Raw knowledge
    (C) Input data (D) Organized data
136. Handling of Information in the sense of production is called :
    (A) Information Marketing
    (B) Information Industry
    (C) Information Production
    (D) Information Revolution
137. SAARC documentation centre was established at
    (A) Dhaka (B) Kathmandu
    (C) New Delhi (D) Karachi
138. Informal communication among knowledgeable person is known as :
    (A) Invisible College
    (B) Information Gatekeeper
    (C) Communication Gatekeeper
    (D) Knowledge Management
139. Who was the chairman of National Library Committee of India.
    (A) B.S. Jha (B) K.P. Sinha
    (C) S. Mudaliar (D) C.D. Deshmukh

140. Where is the head quarter of Patent Information System in India.

(A) Pune (B) Mumbai

(C) Nagpur (D) Delhi

141. The act enacted in India in 1856 on Intellectual Property Right was based on .

(A) American Patent Law 1810

(B) British Patent Law 1852

(C) The Patent Bill

(D) The Design Act of 1911

142. Whether intellectual property can be sold.

(A) No (B) Sale is possible

(C) Yes (D) None of these

143. The term communication came from which language?

(A) Greek (B) Latin

(C) German (D) French

144. Who is the propounder of the term information transfer?

(A) Ranganathan (B) J.Martin

(C) Beesman (D) Calvin Moores

145. To which country the credit is given to coin the term information society ?

(A) USA (B) France

(C) Japan (D) India

146. Today information is regarded as which of the following?

(A) Wealth (B) Commodity

(C) Products (D) All the above

147. Now a days what is a most important vital resource for societal development of a country ?

(A) Books (B) Kowledge

(C) Information (D) Data

148. What is the unit of information ?

(A) Bit (B) Byte

(C) Gram (D) Hertz

149. When was the International institute of Documentation established?

(A) 1931 (B) 1934
(C) 1940 (D) 1945

150. Who said that "Librarianship is not a profession"?
(A) Madden, Moon, Moore, Mc Pheron
(B) Goode, Rossi, Shaffer, Gullis
(C) Dewey, Rundey, Reeves, Aishen
(D) Ranganathan, Dewey, Cutter

151. The author who familiarized and popularized the term cyberspace?
(A) coats? (B) William Gibson.
(C) T.S.Elliot (D) Robert Frost

152. The term "Information Service" is an improvised name ....
(A) Administration (B) Documentation
(C) Bibliography (D) Reference service

153. Information Gatekeepers come under which sources?
(A) documentary (B) human
(C) institutional (D) neo-conventional

154. Which legal document can be used as a source of industrial information ?
(A) Report (B) Law Review
(C) Patent (D) Specification

155. Raw, unevaluated, unprocessed and unorganized facts is known as:
(A) Data (B) Information
(C) Knowledge (D) Wisdom

156. Information retrieval is fastest from
(A) Floppy Disk (B) Magnetic Tape
(C) Hard Disk (D) None of the above

157. "It is a library with little or no physical presence of books, periodicals, reading space or support staff, but are that disseminate disseminate selective information directly to distribute library customers, usually electronically". Said by whom?
(A) Kay Gapen (B) Powell
(C) Sherwell (D) H. G. Wells

158. "A library is a public institution or establishment charged with the care of collection of books, the duty of making them accessible to those who require the use of them and the task of converting every person in its neighborhood into a habitual library goers and reader of books."Quoted by whom?
(A) Dr S R Ranganathan (B) K.N.Raj
(C) C.A.Cutter (D) W.C.Sayers

159. Classification of all types of libraries has been made by-
(A) IFLA (B) UNISIST
(C) UNESCO (D) INSDOC

160. "Special libraries serve a specialist clientele, located within a single establishment or group and all engaged in working towards one common purpose." Who said this
(A) R.Astall (B) UNESCO
(C) J.D.Brown (D) E.C.Richardson

161. The real name of 'Mark Twain' is
(A) Milton
(B) Keats
(C) Samuel Longhorne Clemens
(D) William Wordsworth

162. In a communication model, noise refers to
(A) loudness of signal
(B) lack of understanding between sender and receiver
(C) any disturbance which affects the transmission
(D) irrelevant information

163. The following is not an example of re-packaging of information
(A) Trend report (B) Catalogue
(C) Summary (D) Digest

164. Invisible colleges are
(A) networks of people interested in the same subject
(B) help in communication
(C) neither (1) nor (2)
(D) both (1) and (2)

165. Information is a part of ...
(A) Information Science (B) Scientific achievement
(C) Knowledge (D) Communication

166. Eureka is a powerful and easy to use research service by
(A) RLG (B) RLIN
(C) ERIC (D) USA IN

167. What does "Communication of Information" means?
(A) Process of transmitting information
(B) Process of disseminating information
(C) Process of retrieval of information
(D) Process of scanning information

168. What is Intellectual Property?
(A) Books (B) All reading material
(C) Intellectual thoughts (D) All of the above

169. The term "Information Service" is an improvised name ....
(A) Administration (B) Documentation
(C) Bibliography (D) Reference service

170. What is a process of Information ?
(A) Books (B) CD-ROM
(C) Computers (D) None of the above

171. What is the essential aspect of information service?
(A) Retrieval of information
(B) Storage of information
(C) Collection of information
(D) Communication of information

172. What is a Patent
(A) An agreement to the Government
(B) Document of the library
(C) An agreement between the inventor and the Government
(D) An agreement between library and Publisher

173. Desirableness of personal contact between reader and library material was stressed by

(A) H.P. Luhn
(B) Derek Austin
(C) Samuel H. Green(FATHER OF REFERENCE WORK)
(D) S.C. Broadford

174. 'Informatics' is a term which was first used for documentation in
(A) Britain (B) USA
(C) USSR/Russia (D) India

175. Intellectual Property Rights are recognized by
(A) Copyright (B) Patent
(C) Both (D) Neither

176. NATIS stands for
(A) National Information System
(B) National Technical Information System
(C) National Team for Information Science
(D) None of the above

177. How is stochastic equation of information solved ?
(A) By statistical rules
(B) By dynamic rules
(C) By statistical and dynamic rules
(D) None of these.

178. Information Science is a discipline that investigates
(A) the properties and behaviour of information
(B) The forces governing the flow of information
(C) The means for processing of information for optimal uses
(D) all of these.

179. User education may be provided in four interrelated areas which are
(A) user's awareness, user studies, library orientation, bibliographic instruction
(B) user's awareness, library orientation, inter-profiling, bibliographic instruction
(C) aptitude test of the users, use of cataloguing, inter-profiling, user's awareness
(D) bibliographic instruction, library orientation, computer literacy, user's awareness.

180. The marketing concepts in Library Service include
    (A) analysis, planning, implementation and control
    (B) advertising, planning, analysis and control
    (C) distribution, control, analysis, implementation
    (D) indexing, planning, control and implementation.

181. WIPO stands for :
    (A) World Information and Patents Organisation
    (B) World Intellectual Property Organisation
    (C) World International Property Organisation
    (D) World Information Protection Organisation

182. Technological Gatekeeper is :
    (i) An informal channel
    (ii) A term coined by T.J. Allen
    (iii) A formal channel
    (iv) A term coined by Derek De J. Solla Price

    Code :
    (A) (i) and (ii) are correct
    (B) (i) and (iii) are correct
    (C) (ii) and (iii) are correct
    (D) (iii) and (iv) are correct

183. Informal Communication among knowledgeable persons is known as :
    (A) Invisible College
    (B) Information Gatekeeper
    (C) Communication Gatekeeper
    (D) Knowledge Management

184. Which of the following are produced by Institute of Scientific Information :
    (i) Science Citation Index
    (ii) Current Contents
    (iii) Index Medicus
    (iv) Atom Index

    Code :
    (A) (i), (ii) and (iii) (B) (i) and (ii) only
    (C) (ii) and (iii) only (D) (i) and (iv) only

185. The name of S. C. Bradford is associated with
    (A) occurrence of terms in a paragraph
    (B) number of articles written by anauthor
    (C) law of scattering
    (D) citation of an article.
186. 'Recall' and 'Precision' are the terms used in
    (A) reference service
    (B) information retrieval system
    (C) library management
    (D) book selection.
187. PRECIS has been developed by
    (A) E. J. Coates (B) Derek Austin
    (C) S. R. Ranganathan (D) Mortimer Taube.
188. POPSI is a
    (A) post co-ordinate indexing system
    (B) keyword based indexing system
    (C) preco-ordinate indexing system
    (D) citation indexing.
189. Controlled vocabulary in indexing is called
    (A) a thesaurus
    (B) a language dictionary
    (C) a dictionary of synonyms
    (D) a list of subject headings.
190. The concept of 'Paperless Society' was first given by
    (A) Derek Austin (B) F. W. Lancaster
    (C) Jesse H. Shera (D) Maurice F. Taube.
191. The effect of reduction in the level of specificity of indexing on information retrieval is that it
    (A) increases precision and decreases recall
    (B) increases recall and decreases precision
    (C) increases recall and precision both
    (D) decreases recall and precision both.
192. The process of retrieving detail / document relevant to a query from a catalogue/database adequately defines

(A) documentation
(B) acquisition
(C) information retrieval services
(D) cataloguing services.

193. The term 'recall' is used in information retrieval to refer to
(A) recollect the documents
(B) the ability of a system to retrieve relevant documents
(C) to recollect the irrelevant documents
(D) to retrieve irrelevant documents.

194. 'Truncation' is a technique used in
(A) cataloguing
(B) classification
(C) reference service
(D) online information retrieval.

195. The logic 'And', 'Or', and 'Not' was devised by
(A) F. W. Lancaster (B) George Boole
(C) S. R. Ranganathan (D) M. A. Gopinath.

196. Lotka's law is concerned with
(A) single number of paper per author
(B) two papers per author
(C) three papers per author
(D) average number of papers per author.

197. The mathematical theory of communication is associated with
(A) S. Ramanujan (B) S. R. Ranganathan
(C) I. N. Sengupta (D) Shannon and Weaver.

198. 'Bibliometrics' is a study of
(A) quantitative analysis of publications
(B) qualitative analysis of publications
(C) macro analysis of publications
(D) micro analysis of publications.

199. The Shanon –Weaver Model of Information as criticized for

(A) being too mathematical
(B) being unidirectional
(C) being primarily suited to electronic commission
(D) all of the above.

200. There are a total number of 50 relevant documents in a collection response to a query, only 30 documents are retrieved of these only 10 were relevant. What is the recall percentage?
(A) 20% (B) 33%
(C) 40% (D) 60%.

201. The concept of 'Librametry' was developed by
(A) S. C. Bradford (B) J. D. Bernal
(C) D. J. Foskett (D) S. R. Ranganathan.

202. A retrieval system retrieves a total of 50 documents. Out of these 40 are irrelevant. Another 10 documents which were relevant but not retrieved. The precision percentage for that query would be
(A) 40% (B) 20%
(C) 60% (D) 80%.

203. The query on "Use of Audio Visual Aids in teaching Science at Primary Schools" can be framed as
(A) Audio Visual aids and Science and Primary Schools
(B) Audio Visual aids or Science or Primary Schools
(C) Audio Visual aids or Science and Primary schools
(D) Audio Visual aids and Science or Primary Schools.

204. Which of the following can be considered as formal channels of communication?
(A) Conferences, Research Reports, Theses
(B) Research Reports, Correspondence, Books
(C) Short Communication, Journals, E-Mail, Theses
(D) Conversations, Electronic Journals, Research Reports.

205. A device for searching through a fragment of the search term so that it can match related terms starting with the same term is known as
(A) Boolean Search (B) Truncation
(C) Thesaurus (D) Indexing Language.

206. Venn diagram was developed by
(A) John Venn (B) Peter Venn
(C) Alfred Venn (D) Marlos Venn.

207. The merit of what type of searching is to offer the using of Boolean logic which allows limiting or expanding the search, as required?
(A) manual searching (B) online searching
(C) literature searching (D) reference searching.

208. Brenda Dervin and M.Kochen have researched on
(A) Information retrieval
(B) Information needs
(C) Computerized library system
(D) Classification

209. In a communication model noise refers to
(A) Loudness of signal
(B) Lack of understanding between sender and receiver
(C) any disturbances which affect the transmission
(D) irrelevant information

210. The following is not an example of repackaging of information
(A) Trend report (B) Catalogue
(C) Summary (D) Digest

211. The relationship between the terms 'Ships' and "Boat" is
(A) Syntactic relation (B) Semantic relation
(C) Both of them (D) Neither

212. Invisible colleges
(A) Networks of people interested in the same subject
(B) Help in communication
(C) neither (I) nor (ii).
(D) both (i) and (ii)

213. 'Informatics' is a term which was first use for documentation in
(A) Britain (B) USA (M.F.Collen, 1994)
(C) USSR/Russia (D) India

214. Intellectual Property Rights are recognised by
   (A) Copyright (B) Patent
   (C) Both (D) neither

215. The fundamental equation of Information Science has been put forward by:
   (A) Michael Buckland (B) Robert Brooks
   (C) Marc Porat (D) Wersig Gernot

216. Source, Message, Transmitter and Receiver are the components of communication model
   (A) Shannon-Weaver (B) Schramm
   (C) Lasswell (D) George Gerbner

217. Who said that Knowledge is of two kinds. We know a subject ourselves or we know where we can find information about it?
   (A) S.R.Ranganathan (B) W.C.Berwick Sayers
   (C) Samuel Johnson (D) H.E.Bliss

218. Data about data is known as:
   (A) Micro data (B) Database
   (C) Metadata (D) Databank

219. Which among the following is considered as an informal channel of Information Communication?
   (A) Journals (B) Textbooks
   (C) Invisible Colleges (D) Technical Reports

220. The smallest unit of data in a database is:
   (A) Record (B) File
   (C) Field (D) Table

221. Shannon and Weaver are associated with:
   (i) Mathematical theory of communication
   (ii) Models of communication
   (iii) Theories of Management
   (iv) Library software packages

   Code :

   (A) (i) and (ii) are correct
   (B) (i) and (iii) are correct
   (C) (ii) and (iii) are correct
   (D) (ii) and (iv) are correct

222. Technological Gatekeeper is:
   (i) An informal channel
   (ii) A term coined by T.J.Allen
   (iii) A formal channel
   (iv) A term coined by Derek De Solla Price
   Code :
   (A) (i) and (ii) are correct
   (B) (i) and (iii) are correct
   (C) (ii) and (iii) are correct
   (D) (iii) and (iv) are correct
223. Informal communication among knowledgeable persons is known as:
   (A) Invisible college
   (B) Information gatekeeper
   (C) Communication gatekeeper
   (D) Knowledge management
224. "God has chosen me as an instrument, the honour done to me should act as an incentive to the younger generation to devote their lives whole heartedly to library science and service". Whose quotation is this?
   (A) B.S.Kesavan (B) Melvil Dewey
   (C) S.R.Ranganathan (D) W.C.B.Sayers
225. One of the following has designed models of communication:
   (A) Shannon and Weaver
   (B) Ranganathan and Neelameghan
   (C) Losswell and Gerbher
   (D) Blake and Mouton
226. OAI stands for:
   (A) Open Access Initiatives
   (B) Open Archives Initiatives
   (C) On-line Archives Initiatives
   (D) On-line Access Initiatives
227. The term "Information Science" came into existence in this year:

(A) 1988 (B) 1959
(C) 1961 (D) 1975

228. Industrial environment in India is making a quantum jump because:
(A) Information is a resource whose generation consumes time
(B) Information is a resource whose generation is money
(C) Information is a resource that consumes money and time
(D) Information absorptions and innovation in the field of the technology

229. Monopoly in business is coming to an end because of a:
(A) Information (B) Money flow
(C) Competitiveness (D) Lack of information

230. Information is a major resource which:
(A) helps company to lose money
(B) helps company to have an edge in competition
(C) helps company to gain better manpower
(D) Knowledge Management

231. Electronics industry is both an important and competent industry as it:
(A) is growing at the rate of fifteen percent
(B) is growing at the rate of five hundred percent
(C) is growing at the rate of fourteen percent
(D) is not growing at all

232. The types of information usually sought by companies are:
(A) economic and legal information
(B) information on personnel relation
(C) information on technology and market trends
(D) all the above

233. Which is the correct logical sequence of the following:
(A) Information, knowledge, data, wisdom
(B) Knowledge, Information, wisdom, data

(C) Data, knowledge, information, wisdom

(D) Data, information, knowledge, wisdom

234. Arrange the following Act according to year of enactment:

(A) Copyright Act, The Patent Act, Information Technology Act, IPR Act

(B) The Patent Act, Copyright Act, Information Technology Act, IPR Act

(C) Copyright Act, IPR Act, The Patent Act, Information Technology Act

(D) Copyright Act (1957), The Patent Act (1970), IPR Act, Information Technology Act (2006)

235. The quotation "Where is the Wisdom, We Lost in Knowledge.." is by

(A) John Keats (B) M.P.Carter

(C) T.S.Eliot (D) Marshall McLuhan

236. Entropy is a measure of

(A) Degree of relevance of information

(B) Quantity of irrelevant information

(C) Degree of uncertainty in information

(D) Degree of certainty in information

237. 'Libraries as Gateways to Knowledge' is the title of the document

(A) National Information Policy, 1986

(B) Information Technology Act, 2000

(C) National Knowledge Commission on Libraries, 2007

(D) None of the above

238. Rolland Munro described accountability as

(A) Classified documentary artifacts

(B) Formal artifacts only

(C) Unpublished and published documents

(D) Informal, formal and documentary records

239. The phrase 'record keeping' is associated with

(A) Computer programmers

(B) Archivists

(C) Chartered Accounts

(D) Office Managers

240. What integral components Munro has identified for accounting in the business?
   (A) Records and Codes
   (B) Documentary archives
   (C) Materials and devices
   (D) Legal Regulations

241. In general usage accountability means
   (A) Something done informally
   (B) Something achieved
   (C) Something done continuously
   (D) All of the above

242. Accountability, which is represented by an artefact, includes
   (A) Process, Records, People
   (B) Theory, Practice, Records
   (C) Theory, Practice, People
   (D) People, Records, Accounts

243. Which is not a near synonym term to information?
   (A) Ideas (B) Data
   (C) Catalogue (D) Facts

244. Arrange the following according to chronological order:
   (i) Universal Copyright convention (1952)
   (ii) Berne Convention (1886)
   (iii) Indian Copyright Act (1957)
   (iv) WIPO Copyright Act (1996)

   Code :
   (A) (ii), (iv), (iii), (i) (B) (iii), (ii), (iv), (i)
   (C) (i), (iii), (ii), (iv) (D) (ii), (i), (iii), (iv)

245. Linear model of communication in knowledge based on Aristotles' model of communication was proposed by
   (A) Juger Heberman
   (B) A.J.Wells
   (C) C.E.Shannon & W.Weaver
   (D) G.Gerbner

246. Arrange the following in chronological sequence:
   (I) Digital Millennium Copyright Act
   (II) Right to Information Act (India)
   (III) Information Technology Act (India)
   (IV) Indian Copyright Act

   Codes:

   (A) (IV), (I), (III), (II) (B) (IV), (II), (III), (I)
   (C) (I), (IV), (II), (III) (D) (II), (III), (I), (IV)

247. The headquarters of World Trade Organisation is located in :
   (A) Geneva (B) Paris
   (C) Washington (D) New York

248. Which have the following occuupied the basic resources of an information society?
   (A) Educational and Culture
   (B) Agriculture and Industries
   (C) Information and Knowledge
   (D) Academic and Public Libraries

249. Which Law of Library Science implies Right information to the right user ?
   (A) Second (B) Third
   (C) First (D) Fourth

250. The term "Information Service" is an improvised name ....
   (A) Administration (B) Documentation
   (C) Bibliography (D) Reference service

251. In communication, a major barrier to reception of messages is
   (A) audience attitude (B) audience knowledge
   (C) audience education (D) audience income

252. Didactic communication is
   (A) intra-personal (B) inter-personal
   (C) organisational (D) relational

253. In communication, the language is
   (A) the non-verbal code (B) the verbal code
   (C) the symbolic code (D) the iconic code

254. Identify the correct sequence of the following:
    (A) Source, channel, message, receiver
    (B) Source, receiver, channel, message
    (C) Source, message, receiver, channel
    (D) Source, message, channel, receiver

255. Now days what is a most important vital resource for societal development of a country?
    (A) Books (B) Kowledge
    (C) Information (D) Data

256. What is the unit of information?
    (A) Bit (B) Byte
    (C) Gram (D) Hertz

257. The term "Information Service" is an improvised name?
    (A) Administration (B) Documentation
    (C) Bibliography (D) Reference service

258. Which is a legal document and can be used as a source of industrial information ?
    (A) Report (B) Law Review
    (C) Patent (D) Specification

259. Information Gatekeepers come under which sources?
    (A) documentary (B) human
    (C) institutional (D) neo-conventional

260. Generally the information sources are divided mainly in to following categories?
    (A) Primary and secondary.
    (B) Reference and information sources
    (C) Documentary and non-documentary
    (D) Books and periodicals

261. The act enacted in India in 1856 on Intellectual Property Right was based on?
    (A) American Patent Law 1810
    (B) British Patent Law 1852
    (C) The Patent Bill
    (D) The Design Act of 1911

262. Which of the following is a specialized information organization online tool?

(A) Mamma (B) Dogpile
(C) Vivisimo (D) Entireweb

263. Sometimes the terms 'data' and 'knowledge' are synonymously used for
(A) wisdom (B) intelligence
(C) news (D) information.

264. A state with its organs of executive, legislature and judiciary, business generates vast amount of
(A) knowledge (B) wisdom
(C) information (D) facts.

265. When data is processed, interpreted and presented in an organised form, it becomes
(A) news (B) facts
(C) knowledge (D) information.

266. Growth of information beyond a manageable limit characterises the explosion of
(A) books (B) libraries
(C) information (D) news.

267. The forecast note on weather conditions, based on processed and interpreted atmospheric data is
(A) data (B) news
(C) facts (D) information.

268. Which are the building block of knowledge and all three are handled in libraries offering different types of services?
(A) Wisdom and information
(B) Data and information
(C) News and information
(D) Intelligence and information.

269. Just as, cotton can be loomed into yarns which can be weaved into cloth, data can be weaved into information which can be used to form an organised body of
(A) knowledge (B) information
(C) wisdom (D) facts.

270. Large scale use of information in all countries by a wide cross section of people has resulted in coining of terms like

(A) information explosion
(B) mass production of information
(C) information society
(D) information use.

271. Match the following:

List I	**List II**
(i) Sense-Making Approach	(w) B. Dervin
(ii) Anomalous State of Knowledge	(x) S. R. Ranganathan
(iii) Spiral of Scientific Method	(y) Michael Casey
(iv) Library 2.0	(z) N. J. Belkin

Codes: (i)(ii) (iii) (iv)
(A)(w)(z)(x)(y)
(B)(x)(w)(z)(y)
(C)(y)(w)(x)(z)
(D)(z)(y)(w)(x)

272. Match the following :

List – I	**List – II**
a. Statistical Quality/ Process Control (SQC/SPC	i. Identify the intensity of each problem in the production process
b. Check Shets	ii. Selected variables checked
c. Pareto Chart	iii. Identify the relationship between problems and cause
d. Fish Bone Diagram	iv. Record variables in the production process

Codes:	**(a)**	**(b)**	**(c)**	**(d)**
(A)	ii	iv	i	iii
(B)	iv	ii	iii	i
(C)	iii	iv	i	ii
(D)	i	ii	iv	iii

273. Match the following :

List – I	**List – II**
a. Sinha Committee	i. Library staff strength
b. Dr. S.R. Ranganathan Committee	ii. Central Medical Library
c. Report of Dr. Shaw and Panchayat, Dr. D. B. Krishna Rao	iii. Libraries at Block, District and State level
d. Dr. J. Bhore Committee	iv. National Agricultural System of Agriculture Libraries

Codes:	**(a)**	**(b)**	**(c)**	**(d)**
(A)	iii	i	ii	iv
(B)	iv	iii	ii	i
(C)	iii	i	iv	ii
(D)	i	iii	ii	iv

274. Match the following :

List – I	**List – II**
a. Classical Models	i. Ruesch and Bateson's Functional Model
b. Linear Model	ii. Aristotle
c. Non-linear Model	iii. Lasswell
d. Multi dimensional	iv. Westley and Mackan's Conceptual Model

Codes:	**(a)**	**(b)**	**(c)**	**(d)**
(A)	ii	iii	iv	i
(B)	ii	iv	i	iii
(C)	i	ii	iii	iv
(D)	iii	ii	iv	i

275. Match the following:

List – I	**List – II**
a. Introduction to Modern information Retrieval	i. H. Borko & C. Bernier (McGraw Hill)
b. Indexing Concepts and Methods	ii. G. Salton & M.J. McGill (Academic Press)

c. Thesaurus Construction: A Practical Manual (Aslib) — iii. J.E. Rowley & R. Hartley

d. Organizing Knowledge; An introduction to Managing Access to Information (Ashgate) — iv. J. Aitchison & A. Gilchrist

Codes:	**(a)**	**(b)**	**(c)**	**(d)**
(A)	i	ii	iii	iv
(B)	ii	i	iv	iii
(C)	iv	i	ii	iii
(D)	iii	i	iv	ii

276. Match the following:

List – I	**List – II**
a. Information over load	i. Indexing and abstracting
b. Variation in quality and reliability	ii. Translation
c. Multiplicity of language	iii. Reviews and digests
d. Information scatter	iv. Alert services

Codes:	**(a)**	**(b)**	**(c)**	**(d)**
(A)	i	ii	iii	iv
(B)	iv	iii	ii	i
(C)	ii	iv	iii	i
(D)	iii	i	ii	iv

277. Match the following :

List – I	**List – II**
a. Coding	i. Received signal not the one transmitted
b. Noise	ii. Measure of closeness of relationship
c. Entropy	iii. Message to a signal
d. Equivocation	iv. Measure of uncertainty

Codes:	(a)	(b)	(c)	(d)
(A)	iv	ii	iii	i
(B)	ii	iii	iv	i
(C)	i	ii	iii	iv
(D)	iii	i	iv	ii

278. Match the following :

List – I	List – II
a. Information Theory	i. Ogden and Richards
b. Theory of Signs	ii. Locke
c. Triadic Relationships	iii. Shannon
d. Doctrine of Signs	iv. Morris

Codes:	(a)	(b)	(c)	(d)
(A)	ii	iii	iv	i
(B)	iii	iv	i	ii
(C)	i	iii	iv	ii
(D)	ii	i	iii	iv

279. Match the following :

List – I	List – II
a. Organisational chart	i. Identification of responsibility for specific tasks
b. Flow charts	ii. Examine specific detailed procedure
c. Activity charts	iii. Division of responsibility & functions
d. Decision table	iv. Diagrams composed of symbols and directional lines

Codes:	(a)	(b)	(c)	(d)
(A)	i	iv	ii	iii
(B)	ii	iii	iv	i
(C)	iii	iv	i	ii
(D)	iv	ii	iii	i

280. Match the following :

List – I	List – II
a. Information should be as accurate as possible	i. Broadus
b. Get the best title on any subject but add midiocres that are well read.	ii. Haines
c. Know the community's character and interest	iii. McColvin
d. Consider the duration as well as intensity of the demand	iv. Drury

Codes:	(a)	(b)	(c)	(d)
(A)	iii	iv	ii	i
(B)	ii	iii	i	iv
(C)	i	ii	iv	iii
(D)	iv	i	iii	ii

281. Match the functions performed by different layers of OSI model :

List – I	List – II
a. Delivery of Packets from source of destination	i. Application layer
b. Data transmission rate	ii. Data link layer
c. Access to network resources	iii. Network layer
d. Provide hop-topop delivery	iv. Physical layer

Codes:	(a)	(b)	(c)	(d)
(A)	i	iii	ii	iv
(B)	ii	iv	i	iii
(C)	iii	iv	i	ii
(D)	iii	i	iv	ii

282. Match the following :

List – I	List – II
a. Gender	i. Dependent variable
b. Information Technology	ii. Variable
c. Usership in libraries	iii. Binomial variable
d. Logical set of attributes	iv. Independent variable

Codes:	**(a)**	**(b)**	**(c)**	**(d)**
(A)	i	iv	ii	iii
(B)	iii	iv	i	ii
(C)	ii	i	iv	iii
(D)	iv	iii	ii	i

283. Match the following:

List – I	**List – II**
a. The assessment device that appears to measure the subject matter it purports to	i. Content validity
b. Thc assessment device in which individual's test score predicts the probable behavior on a second variable	ii. Construct validity
c. The assessment device which adequately measures the major dimensions of the behavior under consideration	iii. Criterionrelated validity
d. The assessment device which appears to measure the generalelements it purports tomeasure	iv. Face validity

Codes:	**(a)**	**(b)**	**(c)**	**(d)**
(A)	i	ii	iv	iii
(B)	ii	i	iii	iv
(C)	iv	iii	i	ii
(D)	iii	i	ii	iv

284. Match the following :

List – I	List – II
a. Behaviour studies	i. Extent of use of facilities/ service
b. Use studies	ii. Pattern of Science communicatio
c. User studies	iii. Interaction of user with communication system
d. Information flow	iv. Use of communication studies medium

Codes:	(a)	(b)	(c)	(d)
(A)	i	iv	ii	iii
(B)	iii	iv	i	ii
(C)	ii	iii	i	iv
(D)	ii	iv	iii	i

285. Match the following:

List – I	List – II
a. National Library of the World	i. Wilfred Ashworth
b. Special Libraries	ii. L.J. Strauss
c. Scientific and Technical Libraries	iii. A. Esdaile
d. Handbook of Special Libraries	iv. C.M. Lewis

Codes:	(a)	(b)	(c)	(d)
(A)	i	iv	iii	ii
(B)	ii	iii	iv	i
(C)	iii	iv	ii	i
(D)	iv	ii	iii	i

286. Match the following :

List – I	List – II
a. Halftone	i. Translate instructions from original software to new platforms
b. Threshold	ii. Imaging with varying densities
c. Emulation	iii. Transfer of digital materials
d. Migration	iv. Minimum level to detect a signal

Codes:	**(a)**	**(b)**	**(c)**	**(d)**
(A)	i	iii	iv	ii
(B)	iii	ii	iv	i
(C)	ii	iv	i	iii
(D)	ii	i	iii	iv

287. Match the following:

List – I	**List – II**
a. Theory of Hygiene & Motivation	i. Likerts
b. Maturity Theory	ii. Vroom and Lawler
c. Expectancy Theory	iii. Herzberg
d. Analysis Theory	iv. Argyris

Codes:	**(a)**	**(b)**	**(c)**	**(d)**
(A)	ii	iii	iv	i
(B)	iii	iv	ii	i
(C)	ii	i	iii	iv
(D)	iv	i	ii	iii

288. Match the following:

List – I	**List – II**
a. Harrold Koontz	i. MBO
b. Rensis Likert	ii. Three leadership styles
c. Peter Drucker	iii. Four systems management
d. George Haber	iv. Problem solving Vs. Decision making

Codes:	**(a)**	**(b)**	**(c)**	**(d)**
(A)	i	ii	iii	iv
(B)	iii	iv	i	ii
(C)	iv	iii	ii	i
(D)	ii	iii	i	iv

289. Match the following:

List – I	**List – II**
a. Information Literacy Competency Standards for Higher Education	i. IFLA
b. Seven Pillars of Information literacy	ii. CAUL

c. Guidelines on Information Literacy for Life Long Learning — iii. ACRL

d. Information Literacy Working Group — iv. SCONUL

Codes:	**(a)**	**(b)**	**(c)**	**(d)**
(A)	iii	iv	i	ii
(B)	iv	ii	iii	i
(C)	iii	i	ii	iv
(D)	ii	iii	i	iv

290. Match the following theories with the respectively profounders:

List – I	**List – II**
a. Cybernetics	i. Charles Osgood (1916)
b. Human information processing	ii. Marshal C. Yovits
c. Psychological approach to message transmission	iii. Nobert Wiener (1894 – 1964)
d. General Information System	iv. R.L. Ackoff

Codes:	**(a)**	**(b)**	**(c)**	**(d)**
(A)	i	iii	ii	iv
(B)	i	ii	iv	iii
(C)	iii	i	iv	ii
(D)	iii	ii	i	iv

291. Match the following:

List – I	**List – II**
a. N. Grogan	i. Scientific & Technical Libraries
b. J. Saha	ii. Scientific & technical libraries; an introduction to literature
c. Nilfred Ashworth	iii. Handbook of special librarianship & information work
d. L.J. Strauss	iv. Special libraries and information services in India & USA

Codes:	(a)	(b)	(c)	(d)
(A)	ii	iv	iii	i
(B)	i	ii	iv	iii
(C)	ii	i	iii	iv
(D)	iv	ii	i	iii

292. Match the following:

List – I	List – II
a. Behaviour Science	i. Cognitive Process of Information
b. Philosophical Studies	ii. Studies on Epistomology
c. Ontology	iii. Information processing in living things
d. Biological Science	iv. Study of nature of existence

Codes:	(a)	(b)	(c)	(d)
(A)	iv	iii	i	ii
(B)	iii	ii	iv	i
(C)	ii	i	iii	iv
(D)	i	ii	iv	iii

293. Match the following:

List – I	List – II
a. Informing about best books	i. Support service
b. Guidance to use citation manual	ii. Bibliography
c. Providing prints for downloads	iii. Readers advisory
d. Providing list of URLs	iv. Users education

Codes:	(a)	(b)	(c)	(d)
(A)	ii	iii	i	iv
(B)	iii	iv	i	ii
(C)	iv	ii	iii	i
(D)	ii	iv	iii	i

294. Match the following national organizations with their relevant mission :

List – I	List – II
a. National Mission on Libraries	i. Digitization of AYUSH literature
b. National Mission for Manuscripts	ii. Nurturing of talent
c. T.K.D.L.	iii. Capacity building
d. NME-ICT	iv. Connects India's past with present

Codes:	**(a)**	**(b)**	**(c)**	**(d)**
(A)	i	ii	iii	iv
(B)	iii	iv	i	ii
(C)	iv	iii	ii	i
(D)	ii	i	iii	iv

295. Match the following :

List -I	List - II
(1) Bradford's Law	(a) Author's productivity
(2) Lotkas Law	(b) Citation indexing
(3) Eugene Garfield	(c) Word frequency
(4) Zip's Law	(d) Law of scattering

Answer:

(A) 1 (a), 2 (b), 3 (d), 4 (c) (B) 1 (c), 2 (d), 3 (b), 4 (a)

(C) 1 (d), 2 (b), 3 (a), 4 (c) (D) 1 (d), 2 (a), 3 (b), 4 (c)

296. Match the following :

List – I	List – II
(a) The Right to Information Act of India	(i) 2000
(b) Universal Declaration of Human Rights	(ii) 2005
(c) Information Technology Act. (India)	(iii) 1948
(d) Digital Millennium Act	(iv) 1998

Codes:	**(a)**	**(b)**	**(c)**	**(d)**
(A)	(i)	(ii)	(iii)	(iv)
(B)	(ii)	(iii)	(i)	(iv)
(C)	(iii)	(ii)	(iv)	(i)
(D)	(iv)	(iii)	(ii)	(i)

297. Match the following :

List-I (Terms)	**List-II (Forms of Communication)**
(A) Invisible College	1. Physical carrier
(B) Noise	2. Formal channel
(C) Medium	3. Barreir
(D) Document	4. Informal channel

Codes:	**(a)**	**(b)**	**(c)**	**(d)**
(A)	1	2	3	4
(B)	2	1	3	4
(C)	4	3	2	1
(D)	4	3	1	2

298. Match the following items given in List – I and List – II

List-I	**List-II**
(A) Informatique	(i) English
(B) Informatik	(ii) Italian
(C) Informatica	(iii) French
(D) Informatics	(iv) German

Codes:	**(a)**	**(b)**	**(c)**	**(d)**
(A)	(iii)	(iv)	(ii)	(i)
(B)	(ii)	(i)	(iv)	(iii)
(C)	(iv)	(iii)	(i)	(II)
(D)	(iii)	(i)	(ii)	(iv)

299. Match the following:

List-I	**List-II**
(a) Actand	(i) Weaver
(b) Action	(ii) Cotton
(c) Actor	(iii) Machine
(d) Tool	(iv) Spinning

Codes:	**(a)**	**(b)**	**(c)**	**(d)**
(A)	i	iii	iv	ii
(B)	iii	iv	ii	i
(C)	ii	iv	i	iii
(D)	iv	iii	i	iv

(C) (A) is true but (R) is false

(D) (A) is false but (R) is true

306. **Assertion (A) :** Information literacy is necessary for the users.

Reason (R) : It promotes the use of libraries and information centres.

Codes:

(A) Both (A) and (R) are true

(B) Both (A) and (R) are false

(C) (A) is true but (R) is false

(D) (A) is false but (R) is true

307. **Assertion (A) :** Evaluation of information is necessary.

Reason (R) : Anybody can write on internet.

Codes:

(A) Both (A) and (R) are false

(B) Both (A) and (R) are true

(C) (A) is true but (R) is false

(D) (A) is false but (R) is true

308. **Assertion (A) :** Information systems support promotion of research, development and innovation relating to the national development of a country.

Reason (R) : Information is the basic input to the development.

Code:

(A) Both (A) and (R) are true and (R) is not the correct explanation

(B) Both (A) and (R) is the correct explanation

(C) (A) is true but (R) is false

(D) (A) is false but (R) is true

309. **Assertion (A) :** In contemporary digital environment, IPR become the focal point.

Reason (R) : Many fold increase of unfair use of I.P.

Codes:

(A) (A) and (R) are true.

(B) (A) and (R) are false.

(C) (A) is true and (R) is false.

(D) (A) is false and (R) is true.

310. **Assertion (A) :** Libraries are changing in the wake of emerging ICT environment.

Reason (R) : Libraries are adopting new competencies to operate services in the environment of information super highways.

(A) Both (A) and (R) are true
(B) (A) is true but (R) is false
(C) (A) is false but (R) is true
(D) Both (A) and (R) are false

311. **Assertion (A) :** Information can be obtained from several sources other than libraries.

Reason (R) : The scope of library science is narrower than information science.

Codes:

(A) (A) is false and (R) is true
(B) (A) is true and (R) is false
(C) Both (A) and (R) are true
(D) Both (A) and (R) are false

312. **Assertion (A) :** Knowledge is growing exponentially.

Reason (R) : Number of researchers have increased.

Codes :

(A) Both (A) & (R) are true.
(B) Both (A) and (R) are false.
(C) (A) is false but (R) is true.
(D) (A) is true but (R) is false.

313. **Assertion (A) :** Library & Information centres are knowledge/management centres.

Reason (R) : Libraries handle tacit knowledge.

Codes :

(A) Both (A) and (R) are true.
(B) (A) is partially true, but (R) is false.
(C) (A) is false, but (R) is true.
(D) Both (A) and (R) are false.

314. **Assertion (A) :** Information Literacy is a basic skill essential for work environment in 21st century.

Reason (R) : Information iteracy helps to train the users to make use of ICT.

Codes :

(A) Both (A) and (R) are true.

(B) Both (A) and (R) are false.

(C) (A) is true, but (R) is false.

(D) (A) is false, but (R) is true.

315. **Assertion (A) :** Qualitative measures must be made quantifiable in order to be convincing.

Reason (R) : Qualitative measures are a necessary complement to quantitative measures.

Codes :

(A) (A) is true, (R) is false.

(B) (A) is false, (R) is true.

(C) Both (A) & (R) are true.

(D) Both (A) & (R) are false.

316. **Assertion (A) :** Informative abstracts provide a concise summary of the subject content of an article.

Reason (R) : These are title-oriented than finding-oriented.

Codes :

(A) Both (A) and (R) are true.

(B) (A) is true but (R) is false.

(C) (A) is false but (R) is true.

(D) Both (A) and (R) are false.

317. **Assertion (A) :** E-publications have added enormous quantity of literature but adversely affected the quality of literature.

Reason (R) : Present decade has accepted E-publication as channels of fast communication.

Codes :

(A) (A) is true (R) is false.

(B) (A) is false, but (R) is correct.

(C) Both (A) & (R) are false.

(D) Both (A) & (R) are true.

318. **Assertion (A) :** The exclusive rights conferred by Intellectual property rights can generally be transferred / licenced to third parties.

Reason (R) : The creators want to make monetary benefits out of their intellectual product.

Codes :

(A) (A) is true but (R) is false.

(B) (A) is false but (R) is true.

(C) Both (A) & (R) are true.

(D) Both (A) & (R) are false.

319. **Assertion (A) :** The encouraging environment of all time, full reading halls with the students in the libraries is diminishing day by dav.www.netugc.in

Reason (R) : All the reading material is easily available and accessible on Internet to all the students.

Codes:

(A) Both (A) and (R) true.

(B) Both (A) and (R) are false.

(C) (A) is true, but (R) is false.

(D) (A) is false, but (R) is true.

320. **Assertion (A) :** There is a tremendous increase in number of doctoral degrees being awarded in library and information science.

Reason (R) : Any academician in LIS holding a Ph.D degree is entitled to supervise research programme.

Codes:

(A) (A) is true and (R) is partially true.

(B) Both (A) and (R) are true.

(C) Both (A) and (R) are false.

(D) (A) is false and (R) is true.

321. **Assertion (A) :** The information seeking behavior research at the current times is on the social and cultural context of human interaction with information.

Reason (R) : Attempt is being made to interpret social and cultural experiences of individuals with respect to their information seeking and searching experiences.

Codes :

(A) (A) is true and (R) is false.

(B) Both (A) and (R) are false.

(C) (A) is false and (R) is true.

(D) Both (A) and (R) are true.

322. **Assertion (A) :** With the emergence of Internet, there is no need for reference service in this technology-based era.

Reason (R) : Internet has allowed access to every one to seek his/her information from anywhere, any time.

Codes:

(A) Both (A) and (R) are true.

(B) Both (A) and (R) are false.

(C) (A) is false but (R) is partially true.

(D) (A) is true, but (R) is false.

323. **Assertion (A) :** Micrographic services have lost acceptance for preservation and dissemination of archival material.

Reason (R) : ICT has brought in cost effective alternatives and replaced micrographic services.

Codes :

(A) (A) is true and (R) is partially true.

(B) Both (A) & (R) are false.

(C) (A) is true, (R) is false.

(D) (A) is false, (R) is true.

324. **Assertion (A) :** Institutions generate information through research and development activities.

Reason (R) : All such generated information forms the grey literature.

Codes :

(A) Both (A) and (R) are true.

(B) Both (A) and (R) are false.

(C) (A) is true, (R) is partially true.

(D) (A) is false, (R) is true.

325. **Assertion (A) :** Maximizing the access to information in higher education is the motto of UGC-INFONET project.

Reason (R) : The financial grants of UGC-INFONET are not being fully utilized by all University Libraries for the assigned purpose.

Codes :

(A) Both (A) and (R) false.

(B) (A) is true and (R) is partially true.

(C) (A) is true and (R) is false.

(D) (A) is false and (R) is true.

326. **Assertion (A) :** The effective reprographic service in libraries indirectly demotivates the user for tearing/ theft of reading material.

Reason (R) : The user gets the photocopy of reading materials free of cost.

Codes :

(A) (A) is false and (R) is true.

(B) Both (A) and (R) are true.

(C) (A) is true and (R) is false.

(D) Both (A) and (R) are flase.

327. **Assertion (A) :** RFID technology is still not widely installed in Indian Library Environment.

Reason (R) : The standardization, application and innovation are constantly changing.

Codes:

(A) Both (A) & (R) true and (R) is the correct explanation of (A).

(B) Both (A) & (R) are true, but (R) is not the correct explanation of (A).

(C) (A) is true, but (R) is false.

(D) (A) is false, but (R) is true.

328. **Assertion (A) :** Proliferation of LIS schools in India produced mediocre professionals.

Reason (R) : Curriculum and teaching techniques have not been upgraded at university level.

Codes :

(A) Both (A) and (R) are partially true.

(B) Both (A) and (R) are false.

(C) (A) is true and (R) is false.

(D) (A) is false and (R) is true.

329. **Assertion (A) :** Several Library Science departments in India have shifted to integrated MLIS program.

Reason (R) : MLIS Program (integrated) is a right solution to knowledge explosion in the field.

Codes :

(A) Both (A) and (R) are false.

(B) (A) is true and (R) is false.

(C) Both (A) and (R) are true.

(D) (A) is false and (R) is true.

330. **Assertion (A) :** UGC is financially supporting all academic libraries.

Reason (R) : UGC is primarily responsible for the overall development of libraries of higher education in India.

Codes :

(A) (A) is false and (R) is true.

(B) (A) is true and (R) is false.

(C) Both (A) and (R) are true.

(D) Both (A) and (R) are false.

331. **Assertion (A) :** The entire scholarly publishing system is in danger of eroding due to increasing influence of predatory publishing.

Reason (R) : Many prey on Junior researchers and graduate students with personalized messages praising their earlier work and inviting them to submit a new manuscript.

Codes :

(A) (A) is true but (R) is false.

(B) (A) is false but (R) is true.

(C) Both (A) and (R) are false.

(D) Both (A) and (R) are true.

332. **Assertion (A) :** Metrics based evaluation is not suitable for assessing research performance of individual.

Reason (R) : Construction of citation profiles depend upon the databases used.

Codes :

(A) Both (A) and (R) are true.

(B) Both (A) and (R) are false.

(C) (A) is true, but (R) is false.

(D) (A) is false, but (R) is true.

333. **Assertion (A) :** Effective methods of communicating in H.R. Management of libraries still remains elusive.

Reason (R) : The management do not have the needed direction of approach, precision of thoughts and their expression and empathy.

Codes :

(A) (A) is truc, (R) is false.

(B) Both (A) and (R) are false.

(C) (A) is true, (R) is partially true.

(D) (A) is false, (R) is true.

334. **Assertion (A) :** MARC should never be used outside the context of the cataloguing rules.

Reason (R) : MARC is simply a coding scheme for entering bibliographic information into computer records.

Codes :

(A) Both (A) and (R) are true.

(B) (A) is true but (R) is false.

(C) (A) is false but (R) is true.

(D) Both (A) and (R) are false.

335. **Assertion (A) :** It is a time to separate the copyright issues for scholarly works from entertainment works.

Reason (R) : The scholarly works are public funded fact based, collaborative and intellectual heritage of the institution.

Codes :

(A) (A) is false and (R) is true.

(B) Both (A) and (R) are true but (R) is not the correct explanation of (A).

(C) Both (A) and (R) are false.

(D) (A) is true but (R) is false.

336. **Assertion (A) :** With quick and comprehensive availability of informative through internet resources, need for reference service with a human touch is decreasing.

Reason (R) : Internet resources can satisfy all types of information needs of information seekers.

Codes :

(A) (A) is true and (R) is false.

(B) Both (A) and (R) are false.

(C) (A) is false and (R) is true.

(D) (A) and (R) are true.

337. **Assertion (A) :** Scholar frequency to visit academic libraries has decreased tremendously over the period of last two decades.

Reason (R) : E-scholarly resources are easily accessible to everyone from anywhere anytime.

Codes :

(A) Both (A) and (R) are true.

(B) Both (A) and (R) are false.

(C) (A) is true, but (R) is false.

(D) (A) is false, but (R) is true.

338. **Assertion (A) :** H-index lacks sensitivity to performance changes.

Reason (R) : It can never decrease and is insensitive to number of citations received.

Codes :

(A) Both (A) and (R) are false.

(B) Both (A) and (R) are true.

(C) (A) is true but (R) is false.

(D) (A) is false, but (R) is true.

339. **Assertion (A) :** Z 39.50 standard protocol enables communication among networked computers through a single search interface.

Reason (R) : Z 39.50 application in library consortia environment can enhance resource sharing.

Codes :

(A) Both (A) and (R) are true.

(B) Both (A) and (R) are false.

(C) (A) is true and (R) is false.

(D) (A) is false and (R) is true.

340. **Assertion (A) :** Though information is considered as a commodity, Libraries are not sound in finances.

Reason (R) : All types of Libraries have failed in promoting information as a commodity.

Codes :

(A) (A) is true, but (R) is false.

(B) (A) is false, but (R) is true.

(C) Both (A) and (R) are true.

(D) Both (A) and (R) are false.

341. **Assertion (A) :** Intellectual Property Rights facilitate free flow of information.

Reason (R) : Effective free flow of information is the pre-requisite for knowledge society.

Codes:

(A) (A) is true, but (R) is false.

(B) (A) is false, but (R) is true.

(C) Both (A) and (R) are true.

(D) Both (A) and (R) are false

342. **Assertion (A) :** Library legislation is not a pre-requisite for providing free library service.

Reason (R) : There are states/union territories that are advanced in public library services without library legislation.

Codes :

(A) (A) is true, but (R) is false.

(B) (A) is false, but (R) is true.

(C) Both (A) and (R) are true.

(D) Both (A) and (R) are false.

343. **Assertion (A) :** Data stored in bibliographic database comprise inputs of bibliographic details of a document for identification, storage and retrieval purpose.

Reason (R) : Most of the bibliographic databases consist of indexing and abstracting series.

Codes :

(A) (A) is false, but (R) is true.

(B) Both (A) and (R) are true.

(C) (A) is true, but (R) is false.

(D) Both (A) and (R) are false.

344. **Assertion (A) :** Knowledge organisation and knowledge management are conceptually one and the same.

Reason (R) : Simple Knowledge Organisation System (SKOS) is designed for knowledge management.

Codes :

(A) (A) is true, but (R) is false.

(B) (R) is true, but (A) is false.

(C) Both (A) and (R) are true.

(D) Both (A) and (R) are false.

345. **Assertion (A) :** Social networking tools are very effective for marketing of Library products and services.

Reason (R) : They help to reach out the patrons anywhere and at any time.

Codes:

(A) Both (A) and (R) are true.

(B) Both (A) and (R) are false.

(C) (A) is true, but (R) is false.

(D) (A) is false, but (R) is true.

346. **Assertion (A) :** Information Literacy is a technique and skill known by the information literate for utilizing the wide range of information sources and tools.

Reason (R) : It discourages the use of libraries and information centres and makes the patron independent in identifying, locating and using information sources without depending upon an intermediary.

Codes:

(A) Both (A) and (R) true.

(B) Both (A) and (R) are false.

(C) (A) is true, but (R) is false.

(D) (A) is false, but (R) is true.

347. **Assertion (A) :** Inverse document frequency is the logarithm of the reciprocal of the number of documents in a collection that contains a given term.

Reason (R) : Inverse document frequency measure is computed from term frequency and inverse document frequency.

Codes:

(A) Both (A) and (R) are true.

(B) Both (A) and (R) are false.

(C) (A) is true, but (R) is false.

(D) (A) is false, but (R) is true.

348. **Assertion (A) :** Subject gateways are suitable for all types of users for finding their information.

Reason (R) : Subject gateways are developed by subject and computer experts.

Codes:

(A) (A) is true, but (R) is false.

(B) (A) is false, but (R) is true.

(C) Both (A) & (R) are true.

(D) Both (A) & (R) are false.

349. **Assertion (A) :** Acceptance of First Law of library Science "Books are for Use" has brought forth far reaching change in the present digital environment.

Reason (R) : Online access, open access, virtual reference are the results of this acceptance.

Codes:

(A) (A) is true, but (R) is false.

(B) (A) is false, but (R) is true.

(C) Both (A) and (R) are false.

(D) Both (A) and (R) are true.

350. **Assertion (A) :** A database can be searched with a query language.

Reason (R) : A database can store a large amount of data.

Codes :

(A) Both (A) and (R) are true, but (R) is not the correct explanation of (A).

(B) Both (A) and (R) are true and (R) is correct explanation of (A).

(C) (A) is true, but (R) is false.

(D) (A) is false, but (R) is true.

351. **Assertion (A) :** To increase accessibility to information for differently abled users we need to accept assistive technologies.

Reason (R) : Information for all.

Codes :

(A) Both (A) and (R) are true, but (R) is not. the correct explanation of (A)

(B) Both (A) and (R) are true and (R) is the correct explanation of (A).

(C) (A) is true, but (R) is false.

(D) (A) is false, but (R) is true.

352. **Assertion (A) :** According to National Knowledge Commission, 'the library and information services sector in India has not kept pace with the paradigmatic changes taking place in society'. Reason (R) : There is no proportionate growth in library resources.

Codes :

(A) Both (A) and (R) are true.

(B) (A) is true, but (R) is false.

(C) Both (A) and (R) are false.

(D) (A) is false, but (R) is true.

353. **Assertion (A) :** Information Literacy provides training to use maximum resources available in a library.

Reason (R) : Information Literacy always aims at specific group of users.

Codes :

(A) (A) is false, but (R) is true.

(B) Both (A) and (R) are false.

(C) Both (A) and (R) are true.

(D) (A) is true, but (R) is false.

354. **Assertion (A) :** Performance measurement is necessary to support decision making in libraries and information centres.

Reason (R) : Right decision at a right time helps libraries and information centres to achieve goals.

Codes :

(A) Both (A) and (R) are true and (R) is the correct explanation of (A).

(B) Both (A) and (R) are false.

(C) Both (A) and (R) are true, but (R) is not a correct explanation of (A).

(D) (A) is false, but (R) is true.

355. **Assertion (A) :** Internet access provides information in abundance.

Reason (R) : Information available on internet always lacks authenticity.

Codes :

(A) Both (A) and (R) are true and(R) is the correct explanation of (A).

(B) (A) is false, but (R) is true.

(C) Both (A) and (R) are true, but (R) is not a correct explanation of (A).

(D) (A) is true but (R) is false.

356. **Assertion (A) :** Copyright Act safeguards the interest of the author.

Reason (R) : The Act is essential to maximise the circulation of documents

(A) Both A and R are true and R is the correct explanation

(B) A and R are true and R is not the correct explanation

(C) A is true but R is false

(D) A is false but R is true

357. **Assertion (A) :** Information can be obtained from several sources other than the libraries.

Reason (R) : Library science is narrower in scope than information science

Codes:

(A) (A) is false and (R) are true

(B) (R) is false and (A) is true

(C) Both (A) and (R) are false

(D) Both (A) and (R) are true

358. **Assertion (A) :** RDF supports the use and exchange of metadata on the web.

Reason (R) : Bibliographic standards are the means to create and disseminate secondary information.

Codes :

(A) (A) is true, (R) is false.

(B) (A) is false, (R) is true.

(C) Both (A) & (R) are correct.

(D) Both (A) & (R) are false.

ANSWERS

1. (D)	2. (A)	3. (C)	4. (B)
5. (B)	6. (A)	7. (D)	8. (D)
9. (C)	10. (D)	11. (B)	12. (D)
13. (A)	14. (B)	15. (B)	16. (C)
17. (D)	18. (A)	19. (A)	20. (C)
21. (A)	22. (D)	23. (B)	24. (B)
25. (D)	26. (C)	27. (B)	28. (D)
29. (D)	30. (A)	31. (D)	32. (C)
33. (D)	34. (B)	35. (B)	36. (A)
37. (D)	38. (C)	39. (B)	40. (B)
41. (D)	42. (C)	43. (A)	44. (C)
45. (D)	46. (A)	47. (C)	48. (D)
49. (C)	50. (D)	51. (A)	52. (A)
53. (C)	54. (D)	55. (A)	56. (C)
57. (D)	58. (B)	59. (D)	60. (B)
61. (D)	62. (C)	63. (A)	64. (B)
65. (B)	66. (A)	67. (A)	68. (B)
69. (D)	70. (D)	71. (C)	72. (C)
73. (D)	74. (B)	75. (B)	76. (C)
77. (D)	78. (C)	79. (B)	80. (B)
81. (B)	82. (B)	83. (C)	84. (D)
85. (A)	86. (D)	87. (C)	88. (B)
89. (B)	90. (C)	91. (D)	92. (B)
93. (A)	94. (D)	95. (D)	96. (D)
97. (C)	98. (B)	99. (B)	100. (D)

101. (D)	102. (C)	103. (C)	104. (C)
105. (B)	106. (B)	107. (D)	108. (D)
109. (D)	110. (D)	111. (D)	112. (B)
113. (C)	114. (B)	115. (D)	116. (B)
117. (C)	118. (D)	119. (B)	120. (B)
121. (B)	122. (A)	123. (D)	124. (C)
125. (A)	126. (D)	127. (D)	128. (C)
129. (D)	130. (B)	131. (C)	132. (D)
133. (B)	134. (A)	135. (D)	136. (A)
137. (C)	138. (A)	139. (B)	140. (C)
141. (B)	142. (C)	143. (B)	144. (C)
145. (C)	146. (D)	147. (C)	148. (A)
149. (A)	150. (A)	151. (B)	152. (D)
153. (B)	154. (C)	155. (A)	156. (C)
157. (B)	158. (A)	159. (C)	160. (A)
161. (C)	162. (B)	163. (B)	164. (D)
165. (A)	166. (A)	167. (B)	168. (D)
169. (D)	170. (B)	171. (D)	172. (C)
173. (C)	174. (D)	175. (C)	176. (A)
177. (A)	178. (D)	179. (A)	180. (A)
181. (B)	182. (D)	183. (A)	184. (B)
185. (C)	186. (B)	187. (B)	188. (C)
189. (A)	190. (B)	191. (B)	192. (C)
193. (B)	194. (D)	195. (B)	196. (D)
197. (D)	198. (A)	199. (D)	200. (B)
201. (D)	202. (B)	203. (A)	204. (A)
205. (B)	206. (A)	207. (B)	208. (B)
209. (B)	210. (B)	211. (A)	212. (D)
213. (B)	214. (C)	215. (B)	216. (A)
217. (C)	218. (C)	219. (C)	220. (A)
221. (A)	222. (A)	223. (A)	224. (C)
225. (A)	226. (A)	227. (B)	228. (D)
229. (C)	230. (B)	231. (B)	232. (D)
233. (D)	234. (D)	235. (C)	236. (C)
237. (C)	238. (D)	239. (B)	240. (C)
241. (B)	242. (A)	243. (C)	244. (D)
245. (C)	246. (A)	247. (A)	248. (C)
249. (B)	250. (D)	251. (A)	252. (B)
253. (B)	254. (A)	255. (C)	256. (A)
257. (D)	258. (A)	259. (D)	260. (C)
261. (B)	262. (C)	263. (D)	264. (C)
265. (D)	266. (C)	267. (D)	268. (D)
269. (A)	270. (C)	271. (A)	272. (A)

273. (C)	274. (A)	275. (D)	276. (B)
277. (D)	278. (B)	279. (C)	280. (A)
281. (C)	282. (B)	283. (C)	284. (B)
285. (C)	286. (C)	287. (B)	288. (D)
289. (A)	290. (C)	291. (A)	292. (D)
293. (D)	294. (B)	295. (D)	296. (B)
297. (C)	298. (A)	299. (C)	300. (B)
301. (C)	302. (B)	303. (C)	304. (B)
305. (B)	306. (A)	307. (C)	308. (B)
309. (A)	310. (A)	311. (B)	312. (A)
313. (B)	314. (C)	315. (C)	316. (B)
317. (D)	318. (C)	319. (C)	320. (A)
321. (D)	322. (C)	323. (A)	324. (C)
325. (B)	326. (C)	327. (B)	328. (A)
329. (B)	330. (A)	331. (D)	332. (A)
333. (C)	334. (A)	335. (B)	336. (A)
337. (C)	338. (B)	339. (A)	340. (A)
341. (B)	342. (C)	343. (B)	344. (D)
345. (A)	346. (C)	347. (A)	348. (B)
349. (D)	350. (A)	351. (B)	352. (A)
353. (D)	354. (A)	355. (A)	356. (C)
357. (D)	358. (C)		

2
Library Society

1. The Public Library Manifesto was issued by
   (A) IFLA (B) UNESCO
   (C) ILA (D) RRRLF
2. The Books and Newspaper Delivery Act in India was enacted in the year
   (A) 1879 (B) 1867
   (C) 1905 (D) 1851
3. The main objective of Raja Ram Mohan Roy Library Foundation is to promote
   (A) School Libraries (B) College Libraries
   (C) Public Libraries (D) Prison Libraries
4. Arrange the following professional associations according to the year of establishment.
   (i) IFLA (ii) ASLIB
   (iii) ALA (iv) SLA (USA)

   Codes:

   (A) (i) (iii) (ii) (iv) (B) (iv) (ii) (iii) (i)
   (C) (iii) (iv) (i) (ii) (D) (iii) (iv) (ii) (i)
5. With which agency did UNESCO collaborate to establish UNISIST ?
   (A) ICSU (B) FID
   (C) IFLA (D) ILA

Codes:

(A) (i) and (ii) are correct

(B) (ii) and (iii) are correct

(C) (i) and (iv) are correct

(D) (iii) and (iv) are correct

19. Arrange the following ancient libraries in order of their origin

(i) Alexandria library (ii) Nalanda library

(iii) Ashurbanipal library (iv) Takshila library

Codes:

(A) i, iv, iii, ii (B) ii, i, iv, iii

(C) iv, i, iii, ii (D) iv, ii, iii, i

20. "Annual Review of Information Science and Technology" was first published in 1966 by :

(A) Institute for Scientific Information

(B) American Society of Information Science (ASIS)

(C) IFLA

(D) Canadian Association of Information Science

21. 'Annals of Library and Information Studies' journal is published by :

(A) ILA (B) DRTC

(C) NISCAIR (D) IASLIC

22. Who is the Member Secretary of University Library Committee as per Maharashtra Universities Act, 1994?

(A) BCUD Director (B) Librarian

(C) Dy. Librarian (D) Registrar

23. The first Ph.D. in India in Library Science was awarded to :

(A) B.S. Keshvan (B) D.B. Krishna Rao

(C) P.N. Kaula (D) S.R. Ranganathan

24. Which of the following Universities was the pioneer to appoint a Reference Librarian for the first time in India?

(A) Banaras Hindu University

(B) Delhi University

(C) Madras University

(D) Aligarh Muslim University

25. Which of the following organisations in India is responsible for assigning the thirteen digit International Standard Book Number?
    (A) NISCAIR
    (B) Raja Ram Mohun Roy National Agency for ISBN
    (C) Raja Rammohun Roy Library Foundation
    (D) The National Library, Kolkata
26. According to IFLA's FRBR, the objectives of an information system can be expressed by the following tasks:
    (A) locate, select, obtain and collocate
    (B) find, select, obtain and navigate
    (C) identify, find, obtain and collocate
    (D) find, identify, select and obtain
27. Raja Rammohun Roy Library Foundation is basically responsible for development of
    (A) Academic library (B) National library
    (C) Special library (D) Public library
28. Library legislation generally ensures smooth management of
    (A) Academic libraries (B) Documentation centres
    (C) Public libraries (D) Special libraries
29. The book entitled 'Five laws of Library Science' was first published in
    (A) 1925 (B) 1930
    (C) 1931 (D) 1933
30. Which of the following organisations is not established under the aegis of the Ministry of Culture?
    (A) National Mission of Manuscripts
    (B) National Library of India
    (C) India Office Library
    (D) Raja Rammohun Roy Library Foundation
31. The RFID technology is used in the library to perform
    (A) Information retrieval
    (B) Serial management
    (C) Circulation operations
    (D) SDI service

32. 'Dware-Dware Gyan Sampada' is a
    (A) Public Library Initiative
    (B) Digital Library Initiative
    (C) Virtual Library Initiative
    (D) UNESCO Initiative
33. 'Melvil Dewey Medal' is an annual award given by
    (A) IFLA Award Committee
    (B) ALA Award Committee
    (C) ILA Award Committee
    (D) ASLIB Award Committee
34. The significance of the year 2011 for LIS education in India is
    (A) Golden Jubilee year
    (B) Platinum Jubilee year
    (C) Diamond Jubilee year
    (D) Centenary year
35. 'RRRLF' falls under the:
    (A) Ministry of Human Resource Development
    (B) Ministry of Information & Broadcasting
    (C) Ministry of Culture
    (D) Ministry of Science & Technology
36. "Internet Public Library" is being maintained by
    (A) MIT, Massachusettes
    (B) University of Michigan
    (C) University of Arizona
    (D) Drexal University
37. Which libraries are functioning as depository libraries?
    (i) Delhi Public Library
    (ii) Connemara Public Library
    (iii) British Council Library
    (iv) Central Reference Library

    Codes :

    (A) (i), (iii), (iv) are correct
    (B) (i) & (iii) are correct
    (C) (i) & (ii) are correct
    (D) (ii) & (iii) are correct

38. Arrange the following associations according to their year of establishment :

(i) IASLIC (ii) ASLIB
(iii) ALA (iv) SLA

Codes :

(A) (iv), (ii), (iii), (i) (B) (ii), (iii), (iv), (i)
(C) (iii), (iv), (ii), (i) (D) (i), (iv), (ii), (iii)

39. Arrange the following Public Library Acts according to their year of enactment :

(i) Uttar Pradesh PL Act
(ii) Arunachal Pradesh PL Act
(iii) Orissa PL Act
(iv) Gujarat PL Act

Codes :

(A) (iv), (iii), (i), (ii) (B) (ii), (iii), (i), (iv)
(C) (ii), (i), (iv), (iii) (D) (iii), (ii), (i), (iv)

40. Who were involved in Public Library Movement in India?

(i) Sayaji Rao Gaekwad II
(ii) C.D. Deshmukh
(iii) S. Radhakrishnan
(iv) S.R. Ranganathan

Codes :

(A) (i) & (iii) are correct (B) (ii) & (iv) are correct
(C) (i) & (iv) are correct (D) (ii) & (iii) are correct

41. Which is the correct sequence of the national libraries in the order of their year of establishment?

(i) British Library (formerly British Museum Library)
(ii) Library of Congress (Washington D.C.)
(iii) Lenin Library (Moscow)
(iv) Bibliotheque Nationale (Paris)

Codes :

(A) (i), (ii), (iii), (iv) (B) (ii), (iii), (i), (iv)
(C) (iii), (ii), (iv), (i) (D) (iv), (iii), (ii), (i)

42. Arrange the following State Library Acts in chronological order :
    (i) Karnataka Public Library Act
    (ii) Uttar Pradesh Public Library Act
    (iii) Goa Public Library Act
    (iv) Bihar Public Library Act

    Codes :

    (A) (i), (iii), (ii), (iv) (B) (i), (ii), (iii), (iv)
    (C) (ii), (iii), (iv), (i) (D) (iii), (i), (iv), (ii)

43. National Knowledge Network is to be implemented by
    (A) National Knowledge Commission
    (B) Information and Library Network
    (C) National Information Centre
    (D) Department of Information Technology

44. Raja Rammohan Roy Library Foundation (RRRLF) was established by
    (A) Indian Library Association
    (B) Department of Culture, Govt. of India
    (C) Govt. of West Bengal
    (D) Ministry of Home Affairs, Govt. of India

45. A remarkable feature of Mysore Public Library Act, 1965 is the provisional library service to the ?
    (A) Deaf (B) Blind
    (C) Dumb (D) Lame

46. Association of College and Research Libraries (ACRL) (USA) is a
    (A) Division of American Library Association
    (B) Independent Association for Academic & Research Libraries
    (C) Division of Special Libraries Association (USA)
    (D) Division of IFLA

47. Which of the following is not an implication of Fourth Law of Library Science ?
    (A) Classified arrangement
    (B) Stack-room-guides
    (C) Issue Methods
    (D) Rural Library Services

48. Which one of the following is not a recommendation of National Knowledge Commission (India)?
    (A) Preparation of a National Census of Library
    (B) Encourage greater community participation in library management
    (C) Raja Rammohan Roy library foundation to act as the National co-ordination agency
    (D) Facilitate donation and maintenance of private collection

49. Where the first M. Phil programme in Library and Information Science was started in India ?
    (A) University of Madras (B) University of Delhi
    (C) University of Mysore (D) University of Bombay

50. Corollary for Second Law of Library Science is
    (A) Books for all (B) Free Books Service
    (C) Free Library Service (D) Books every where

51. The National Mission on Libraries, India was established in which year ?
    (A) 2009 (B) 2010
    (C) 2011 (D) 2012

52. Which organisation was joined with 'Library Association' to form CILIP in 2007 ?
    (A) Institute of Bibliography
    (B) Institute of Information Scientists
    (C) Institute of Documentation
    (D) Institute of Librarianship

53. The concept of 'Ask Library Anything' was originally initiated by
    (A) Indian Library Association
    (B) ASLIB
    (C) Special Library Association
    (D) American Library Association

54. TKDL is developed and managed by
    (A) National Library and RRRLF
    (B) CSIR and RRRLF
    (C) CSIR and AYUSH
    (D) AYUSH and National Library

55. Arrange the following State Library Acts according to their year of establishment:

(i) Goa (ii) West Bengal
(iii) Orissa (iv) Karnataka

Codes :

(A) iv ii iii i (B) iv ii i iii
(C) ii i iii iv (D) iii ii i iv

56. Which department of the Government of India deals with Public Libraries?

(A) Department of Archaeology
(B) Department of Culture
(C) Department of Primary Education
(D) Department of Science and Technology

57. Which of the following states don't have library legislation?

(i) Haryana (ii) Delhi
(iii) J & K (iv) Manipur

Codes:

(A) (i) and (ii) are correct
(B) (ii) and (iii) are correct
(C) (i) and (iv) are correct
(D) (ii) and (iii) are correct

58. Give in sequence, the following in order of their origin:

i. National Library ii. Calcutta Public Library
iii. Imperial Library Act iv. Imperial Library

Codes:

(A) ii iii iv i (B) i ii iii iv
(C) iii i iv ii (D) ii iv iii i

59. "Information Literacy Competency Standards for Higher Education" is prepared by

(A) AASL (B) IFLA
(C) SCONUL (D) ACRL

60. Which Committee/Commission recommended that Imperial Library be designated as Copyright Library?

(A) Fayzee Commission, 1939
(B) Riche Committee, 1926
(C) Statham Committee, 1932
(D) Sadler Committee, 1916

61. Who said that information is both a product and process?
(A) S.R. Ranganathan (B) J. Martin
(C) D.J. Foskett (D) S.C. Bradford

62. Which of the following activities are supported by UGC?
(i) Facilitating increased access to information.
(ii) Monitoring the implementation of revised curriculum.
(iii) Making policies for human resource development
(iv) Funding all academic libraries.

Codes:
(A) (i) and (ii) are correct
(B) (i) and (iii) are correct
(C) (ii) and (iii) are correct
(D) (i) and (iv) are correct

63. Which of the following methods are suitable to achieve quality of teaching, learning in LIS?
(i) Research-led teaching
(ii) State of the art computer lab
(iii) Problem-based learning
(iv) Introducing the course at degree level

Codes:
(A) (ii) and (iv) (B) (i), (iii) and (iv)
(C) (i) and (iii) (D) (iii) and (iv)

64. What is/are common feature/s between RFID & Barcode Technology?
(i) Read more than one item at a time
(ii) Able to locate specific items on shelves
(iii) Programmable
(iv) Read while item is moving

Codes:

(A) (i), (ii) are correct

(B) (iii), (iv) are correct

(C) (ii), (iv) are correct

(D) All the above are correct

65. When a librarian has to show the rationale for the purchase of more e-resources, which of the following's will help to support his/her stand?

(i) Collection development policy

(ii) Indent from users

(iii) Book selection tools

(iv) All the above

Codes:

(A) (i) and (ii) are correct

(B) (i) and (iii) are correct

(C) (ii) and (iii) are correct

(D) (iv) is correct

66. Who said, "Public Library is the responsibility of Local and National Authorities. It must be supported by specific legislation and financed by National and Local Govnerments" ?

(A) S.R. Ranganathan (B) Gopala Rao Ekbote

(C) Sinha Committee (D) UNESCO Manifesto

67. 'Library Technology Project (LTP) Reports' are published by –

(A) ILA (B) ALA

(C) CILIP (D) SLA

68. Which Education Commission observed "Nothing can be more damaging to a growing department than to neglect its library or give it a low priority" ?

(A) Kothari Education Commission

(B) Radhakrishnan Education Commission

(C) Calcutta University Commission

(D) Mudaliar Commission on Secondary Education

69. International Advisory Committee on Documentation, Libraries and Archives (UNESCO) was established in

(A) 1966 (B) 1967

(C) 1968 (D) 1969

70. Which law of Library Science states that information is basic input to human growth and development?

(A) Fourth Law (B) Third Law

(C) Second Law (D) Fifth Law

71. The main components of an RFID system include

(A) Handheld Reader, RFID label printer, server and External book return

(B) RFID tags, readers or sensors, Antenna and server

(C) RFID label printer, sensors, antenna and server

(D) RFID tags, server, external book return, sensors

72. Arrange in sequence the following committees in order of that year of commencement :

(i) Library Committee

(ii) Committee on national network system for university libraries

(iii) Review committee on Library Science

(iv) Curriculum Development Committee on Library and Information Science

Codes :

(A) i ii iii iv (B) iii iv ii i

(C) iii ii i iv (D) i iii ii iv

73. Arrange the following Library Acts according to the year of their enactment:

(i) Arunachal Pradesh (ii) Bihar

(iii) Lakshadweep (iv) Rajasthan

Codes:

(A) (ii), (iv), (iii), (i) (B) (iv), (i), (ii), (iii)

(C) (ii), (iii), (i), (iv) (D) (iv), (iii), (ii), (i)

74. Identify the place where IFLA was first found.

(A) The Hague, Netherlands

(B) Edinburgh, Scotland

(C) Helsinki, Finland

(D) London

75. Information For All Programme (IFAP) was launched by

(A) IFLA (B) Library of Congress

(C) OCLC (D) UNESCO

76. Skill Development Programme (SDP) for public librarians in India is initiated by

(A) Ministry of Human Resource Development, Govt. of India

(B) Directorate of Library Services, Govt. of West Bengal

(C) Raja Ram Mohan Roy Library Foundation

(D) Indian Library Association

77. Arrange the following Public Library Acts according to their year of enactment :

(i) Chhattisgarh Public Library Act

(ii) Gujarat Public Library Act

(iii) Orissa Public Library Act

(iv) Uttar Pradesh Public Library Act

Codes :

(A) (ii) (iii) (iv) (i) (B) (iii) (ii) (iv) (i)

(C) (iv) (ii) (i) (iii) (D) (iii) (iv) (ii) (i)

78. Arrange the following according to their year of establishment :

(i) Khuda Bakhsha Oriental Public Library

(ii) Sahitya Akademi Library, Delhi

(iii) Rampur Raza Library

(iv) The Asiatic Society

Codes :

(A) (ii) (iv) (i) (iii) (B) (iii) (i) (iv) (ii)

(C) (i) (iv) (ii) (iii) (D) (iv) (i) (ii) (iii)

79. Public Library Association (PLA) is a division of

(A) ALA (B) ILA

(C) IFLA (D) IASLIC

80. The oldest and largest library Association in the World is;

(A) LA (B) ILA

(C) ALA (D) IASLIC

81. Which of the following organizations are involved in providing translation services in India?

i. NISCAIR ii. National Library of India

iii. IASLIC iv. IATLIS

Codes:

(A) ii and iv are correct. (B) ii and iii are correct.

(C) i and iv are correct. (D) i and iii are correct.

82. Which of the following are the works related to IFLA's Committee on Freedom of Access to Information and Freedom of Expression (FAIFE)?

i. Publish reports, participate in national and international conferences and organize workshops.

ii. Monitor the state of intellectual freedom within the library community world-wide and publish newsletters and online news.

iii. Respond to violations of free access to information and freedom of expression and make press releases.

iv. Cross-association activities, to bring participants together.

Codes:

(A) i, iii and iv are correct.

(B) ii, iii and iv are correct.

(C) i, ii and iv are correct.

(D) i, ii and iii are correct.

83. Arrange the following Library Acts according to their year of enactment:

i. Uttarakhand ii. Orissa

iii. Manipur iv. Goa

Codes:

(A) iv, i, ii, iii (B) i, ii, iii, iv

(C) iii, iv, ii, i (D) ii, iii, i, iv

84. Arrange the following libraries according to their year of origin:

i. Asiatic Society Library, Bombay
ii. Connemara Public Library, Madras
iii. Delhi Public Library, Delhi
iv. National Library of India, Calcutta

Codes:

(A) i, ii, iv, iii (B) i, iii, iv, ii
(C) ii, iv, iii, i (D) iv, iii, ii, i

85. Arrange in sequence the following committees workshop in order of their year of constitution:
i. UGC Committee for Development of University and College Libraries (S.R. Ranganathan)
ii. UGC Committee on National Network System for University Libraries (Dr. Yashpal)
iii. UGC Review Committee on Library Science (S.R. Ranganathan)
iv. UGC Workshop on Standards for College Libraries

Codes:

(A) iii, iv, i, ii (B) iii, ii, i, iv
(C) i, iii, iv, ii (D) i, ii, iv, iii

86. Who has recommended the establishment of district, taluka, town and village libraries ?
(A) S.R. Ranganathan
(B) Velaga Venkatappayya
(C) Fyzee Report
(D) Library Advisory Committee

87. Arrange the following in chronological order :
i. Delivery of Books and Newspapers Act
ii. RTI Act
iii. Imperial Library Act
iv. IT (Amendment) Act

Codes :

(A) i, iv, ii, iii (B) iii, i, ii, iv
(C) iii, ii, i, iv (D) iv, iii, i, ii

88. Arrange the following in chronological order :
i. UNESCO Public Library Manifesto
ii. A.A.A. Fyzee Report

iii. Library Advisory Committee Report

iv. Raja Ram Mohan Roy Library Foundation

Codes :

(A) i, ii, iii, iv (B) ii, iii, iv, i

(C) i, iv, ii, iii (D) iii, i, ii, iv

89. Identify the association that has changed its original name

(A) ILA (B) SLA

(C) LA (D) ALA

90. The Farmington plan is associated with :

(A) Library Legislation

(B) Library Cataloguing

(C) Library Cooperation

(D) Library Indexing Service

91. UNESCO assisted Model Public Library in India is located at :

(A) Kolkata (B) Delhi

(C) Mumbai (D) Chennai

92. IFLA took up the "Universal Availability of Publication" program in the year

(A) 1973 (B) 1976

(C) 1972 (D) 1970

93. International Information System on Research in Documentation (ISORID) was established by :

(A) IFLA (B) UNESCO

(C) SLA (D) ALA

94. The journal "Knowledge Organization" is published by:

(A) IFLA (B) ISKO

(C) LA (D) LC

95. The oldest and the largest Library Association in the world is-

(A) ALA (B) LA

(C) IFLA (D) IASLIC

96. Which of the following is an 'Acronym' ?

(A) UNESCO (B) UNO

(C) UNDP (D) UGC

97. Match the following and choose the correct answer from the codes given below :

List A	List B
(1) Asiatic Society Library	a. Kolkata
(2) Connemara Public Library	b. Chennai
(3) Khuda Bux Oriental Library	c. Patna
(4) Saraswati Mahal Library	d. Tanjore.

Codes :	**1**	**2**	**3**	**4**
(A)	a	b	c	d
(B)	d	a	b	c
(C)	c	d	a	b
(D)	b	d	a	c

98. Whether Library is a system ?
    (A) Yes, it has various sections as sub-systems coordinating each other forming a system
    (B) No, it cannot be a system
    (C) It is quite impossible
    (D) Library is separate from a system.

99. In which year did A. W. Borden start a refresher course for librarians in India ?
    (A) 1905 (B) 1910
    (C) 1912 (D) 1913

100. In which year was the International Book Year celebrated by UNESCO ?
    (A) 1931 (B) 1947
    (C) 1952 (D) 1972

101. What is the full form of IATLIS ?
    (A) International Association of Trade Unions of Library Science
    (B) Indian Association of Teachers in Library & Information Science
    (C) Indian Airlines Technical Lower Intelligence Services
    (D) Indian Air Traffic Light, Information and Signal.

102. IIA founded in U.S.A. in 1968 stands for

(A) Integrated Industry Association
(B) Information Industry Association
(C) Integrated Illiteracy eradication Association
(D) Institute of Information Association.

103. The book 'Library Administration' was brought out by Ranganathan in
(A) 1925 (B) 1933
(C) 1931 (D) 1935

104. LA is the Library Association of
(A) Manipur (B) Andhra Pradesh
(C) Great Britain (D) Canada

105. Three great achievements in U.S.A. were noticed i.e. enunciation of DDC classification scheme, formation of American Library Association and the publication of 1 st Journal of the librarianship in the year
(A) 1857 (B) 1859
(C) 1876 (D) 1901

106. Of the following libraries in India, which one is the oldest library ?
(A) Asiatic Society Library, Bombay
(B) Connemara Public Library, Madras
(C) Delhi Public Library, Delhi
(D) National Library of India, Calcutta.

107. Calcutta Public Library was established during
(A) 15th Century (B) 16th Century
(C) 19th Century (D) 20th Century

108. Library Legislation refers to the development of
(A) Academic Libraries (B) Special Libraries
(C) Public Libraries (D) None of the above

109. IASLIC was founded in the year
(A) 1955 (B) 1965
(C) 1975 (D) 1985

110. Number of States in India which have enacted Public Library Legislation till date is
(A) Seven (B) Ten
(C) Thirteen (D) Nineteen

111. Which publication was not authored by S.R. Ranaganathan ?
    (A) Prolegomena to libraryclassification
    (B) Reference Service
    (C) Ramanujan : The man and the Mathematician
    (D) Living with Books
112. 'Five Laws of Library Science' was first published in
    (A) 1925 (B) 1930
    (C) 1931 (D) 1933
113. Arrange the following States according to the year of enactment of library legislation :
    (i) Pondicherry (ii) Orissa
    (iii) Rajasthan (iv) Karnataka
    Codes :
    (A) (iv), (i), (iii), (ii) (B) (iv), (ii), (iii), (i)
    (C) (iv), (iii), (i), (ii) (D) (i), (iii), (ii), (iv)
114. Arrange the following chronologically according to their year of Birth :
    (i) S.R. Ranganathan (ii) Melvil Dewey
    (iii) C.A. Cutter (iv) B.S. Kesvan
    Codes :
    (A) (ii), (i), (iv), (iii) (B) (i), (iii), (iv), (ii)
    (C) (iii), (ii), (i), (iv) (D) (iv), (i), (ii), (iii)
115. Who is the Father of Library Movement in USA ?
    (A) F. W. Lancaster (B) Paul Wasserman
    (C) Melvil Dewey (D) Allen Kent
116. Which library is authorized to receive books under 'Delivery of Books Act'?
    (A) National Science Library, Delhi
    (B) Central Library, Delhi
    (C) State Central Library, Mumbai
    (D) Parliament Library, Delhi
117. All Union Institute for Scientific and Technical Information (VINITI) was established in
    (A) 1952 (B) 1953
    (C) 1954 (D) 1956

118. Identify the correct order as per year of establishment

(i) ASLIB (ii) IATLIS

(iii) SLA (iv) ALA

Codes :

(A) (iv), (iii), (i), (ii) (B) (iv), (ii), (i), (iii)

(C) (ii), (i), (iv), (iii) (D) (i), (ii), (iii), (iv)

119. Arrange the following Laws of Library Science as given by Ranganathan :

(i) Save the time of the reader

(ii) Books are for use

(iii) Every book has its reader

(iv) Every Reader has his book

Codes :

(A) (ii), (iv), (iii), (i) (B) (iv), (ii), (i), (iii)

(C) (ii), (i), (iv), (iii) (D) (iii), (ii), (i), (iv)

120. Arrange the following Public Library Acts according to their year of enactment :

(i) Pondicherry (ii) Madras

(iii) Haryana (iv) Orissa

Codes :

(A) (iv), (iii), (i), (ii) (B) (ii), (iii), (i), (iv)

(C) (ii), (i), (iv), (iii) (D) (iii), (ii), (i), (iv)

121. Arrange the following in chronological order :

(i) Fayzee Committee

(ii) K. P. Sinha Committee

(iii) Chattopadhyaya Committee

(iv) Radhakrishnan Committee

Codes :

(A) (i), (ii), (iii), (iv) (B) (iv), (iii), (i), (ii)

(C) (i), (iv), (ii), (iii) (D) (iii), (i), (ii), (iv)

122. The Library Association (UK) is now the component of

(A) ASLIB (B) CILIP

(C) ALA (D) None of the above

123. Which of the following professional Associations does not exist now ?

(A) IFLA (B) FID
(C) ALA (D) IASLIC

124. Arrange the following professional Associations according to the year of their establishment :
(i) ILA (ii) IASLIC
(iii) ALA (iv) ASLIB
Codes :
(A) (i), (ii), (iii), (iv) (B) (iii), (iv), (i), (ii)
(C) (iv), (iii), (ii), (i) (D) (i), (iii), (ii), (iv)

125. The University which telecasts interaction educational programmes through its own channel is
(A) Osmania University
(B) University of Pune
(C) Annamalai University
(D) Indira Gandhi National Open University (IGNOU)

126. Who has signed an MOU for Accreditation of Teacher Education Institutions in India?
(A) NAAC and UGC (B) NCTE and NAAC
(C) UGC and NCTE (D) NCTE and IGNOU

127. National Library Week in India is being celebrated annually since :
(A) 1914 (B) 1933
(C) 1950 (D) 1968

128. Maulana Abul Kalam Azad, the then Union Education Minister formally declared one of the following libraries open to the public on 2nd February, 1953 :
(A) Connemara Public Library
(B) Delhi Public Library
(C) National Library, Calcutta
(D) Saraswathi Mahal Library, Tanjore

129. Library Literature is a :
(A) Primary source of information
(B) Secondary source of information
(C) Tertiary source of information
(D) Literary source of information

130. The Indian State which enacted the library legislation in the year 1948 is :

(A) Kerala (B) Meghalaya

(C) Tamil Nadu (Madras) (D) Rajasthan

131. A.Issac Collijin was the first president of IFLA B."Tree of porphyry" is formed as a result of Polychotonomy

(A) A only Correct (B) B only correct

(C) A&B are correct (D) None is correct

132. Who designated Dr.Ranganathan as "father of library science" ?

(A) Jawaharlal Nehru (B) Sir Radhakrishnan

(C) Rajendra Prasad (D) Sir.Maurice Gwoyer

133. A.Borden introduced Open Access System in India B.The concept of "anamolous state of knowledge " was proposed by Dr.Ranganathan

(A) A only Correct (B) B only correct

(C) A&B are correct (D) None is correct

134. How many national library in Italy ?

(A) 4 (B) 8

(C) 12 (D) 16

135. A.UGC was founded in 1953 B.UNESCO was founded in 1951

(A) A only Correct (B) only correct

(C) A&B are correct (D) None is correct

136. Which is the largest University Library in the World?

(A) Harvard University Library, USA

(B) New York University Library, USA

(C) Delhi University Library, India.

(D) Madras University Library

137. A.India Office Library is situated in New Delhi B. "Library is the heart of an institution" said by S.R.Ranganathan

(A) A only Correct (B) B only correct

(C) A&B are correct (D) None is correct

138. When was Dr.S. R. Ranganathan was appointed as a National research professor of Library science

(A) 1942 (B) 1962
(C) 1972 (D) 1952

139. Which Indian University first started M.Lib.Sc. & M.Phil courses
    (A) University of Delhi
    (B) University of Madras
    (C) S.N.D.T. Women University, Bombay
    (D) Aligar Muslim University

140. Which Commission recommended 10% of the total college budget for development of Libraries
    (A) Dr. S. R. Ranganathan Committee
    (B) Mehrotra Committee
    (C) Kothari committee
    (D) Curriculum development committee in LIS

141. UNISIST is a
    (A) Software (B) A Programme
    (C) Welfare association (D) A committee

142. Where did Dr. S. R. Ranganathan put forth his five laws of library science?
    (A) Meenakshi college, Annamalainagar
    (B) Hindu College, New Delhi
    (C) City College, Bangalore
    (D) Christ College, Bangalore

143. When did ILA became the member of IFLA?
    (A) 1952 (B) 1955
    (C) 1957 (D) 1965

144. Which association's tagline is "managing information"?
    (A) IFLA (B) Aslib
    (C) ALA (D) LC

145. Which association's tagline is "connecting people and information"?
    (A) SLA (B) IFLA
    (C) ALA (D) COMLA

146. When was the International institute of Documentation established?

(A) 1931 (B) 1934
(C) 1940 (D) 1945

147. Which organization has introduced the concept of "Sister libraries" for children`s and young adults reading?
(A) UNESCO (B) IFLA
(C) LC (D) LA

148. Who said that "Librarianship is not a profession"?
(A) Madden, Moon, Moore, Mc Pheron
(B) Goode, Rossi, Shaffer, Gullis
(C) Dewey, Rundey, Reeves, Aishen
(D) Ranganathan, Dcwcy, Cutter

149. Who has introduced Advancement of Librarianship Programme?
(A) IFLA (B) UNESCO
(C) FID (D) ICSU

150. In which year International institute of Documentation changed to International federation of Documentation?
(A) 1931 (B) 1937
(C) 1945 (D) 1948

151. In which year headquarter of FID was shifted from Brussels to The Hague?
(A) 1925 (B) 1928
(C) 1930 (D) 1934

152. Who gave the sixth law of library science "Every reader his/her freedom"?
(A) Walt Crawford (B) Michael Gorman
(C) James R. Rettig (D) Lenart Bjorneborn

153. Where was the first library noticed in India?
(A) Taxila (B) Nalanda
(C) Vallabhi (D) Sravasti

154. When was the curriculam development committee on LIS instituted?
(A) 1988-89 (B) 1990-93
(C) 1994-97 (D) 1999-02

155. Who published the journal International classification?
(A) IFLA (B) UNESCO
(C) ISKO (D) ALA

156. Which association in India awards teachers in LIS?
(A) IATLIS (B) ILA
(C) IASLIC (D) SIS

157. Where is the headquarter of SLA?
(A) New York (B) Lagos
(C) Shimla (D) New Delhi

158. Which law of library Science relates to the growth of libraries
(A) Forth law (B) First law
(C) Second law (D) Fifth law

159. UAP stands for what of the following
(A) United Academy of publication
(B) Universal Association of Publishers
(C) Universal Availability of Publications.
(D) Universal Association of Publishers

160. Resource sharing is a part of
(A) Library cooperation
(B) Library Administration
(C) Library Management
(D) Library Cataloging

161. Library Techology Report is a publication of
(A) ALA (B) IASLIC
(C) LA (D) ILA

162. ABGILA is a quarterly publication of
(A) Assam Library Association
(B) Andhra Desa Library Association
(C) Indian Library Association
(D) Raja Ram Mohun Roy Foundation

163. Which term was coined by Dr.S.R.Ranganathan for mobile libraries
(A) Moving Library (B) Library on Wheels
(C) Library Machine (D) All of above

164. The Librarian Day celebrated on
   (A) 15th Sep (B) 24th Nov
   (C) 11th Dec (D) 12th Aug
165. Forms of Extension service
   (A) Library Websites
   (B) Library Orientation
   (C) Book fair and Exhibition
   (D) All
166. The first library school was started by
   (A) Melvin Dewey
   (B) Charles Williamson
   (C) John Macfarlane
   (D) William Allenson Borden
166. Who was Published the monthly Journal "The Library World'
   (A) Krishan kumar (B) J. D. Brown
   (C) H. W. Wilson (D) K. Navlavi
167. Who is the first editor of "Modern Librarian"?
   (A) F.Monbrary Volte (B) Dr. S. R. Ranganathan
   (C) J. D. Brown (D) Krishan Kumar
168. Mobile library is a kind of which service?
   (A) Reference service
   (B) Extension service
   (C) Ready reference service
   (D) Long range reference service
169. Reading centre, story hours, exhibition and reading to literature are form of
   (A) Extension service
   (B) Service of Public library
   (C) Both
   (D) None
170. Study carrels are exclusive areas meant for-
   (A) students (B) public
   (C) women (D) researchers
171. Who has prescribed certain standards for library binding?

(A) ILA (B) ALA
(C) BLA (D) NBT

172. Resource sharing is a part of ...
(A) Library cooperation (B) Library administration
(C) Library management (D) Library cataloguing

173. Which one is Library and Information Science Journal name?
(A) Reference Reviews incorporating ASLIB Book Guide
(B) Reference Reviews incorporating ASLIB Book journals
(C) Reference Reviews incorporating ASLIB Book Review
(D) Reference Reviews incorporating ASLIB E-Book

174. "Shodhganga" is a national level repository of:
(A) E-Books (B) E-Journals
(C) E-Theses (D) Journal Articles

175. When RRRLF was established?
(A) 1970 (B) 1971
(C) 1972 (D) 1974

176. Where is the headquarter of RRRLF?
(A) Banglore (B) Delhi
(C) Calcutta (D) Lucknow

177. Who provides the ISBN?
(A) Niscair (B) Nissat
(C) Insdoc (D) RRRLF

178. RRRLF provides the?
(A) ISSN (B) ISBN
(C) CCF (D) MARC

179. "It is a library with little or no physical presence of books, periodicals, reading space or support staff, but are that disseminate disseminate selective information directly to distribute library customers, usually electronically". Said by whom?
(A) Kay Gapen (B) Powell
(C) Sherwell (D) H. G. Wells

180. "A library is a public institution or establishment

charged with the care of collection of books, the duty of making them accessible to those who require the use of them and the task of converting every person in its neighborhood into a habitual library goers and reader of books."Quoted by whom?

(A) Dr S R Ranganathan (B) K.N.Raj
(C) C.A.Cutter (D) W.C.Sayers

181. Classification of all types of libraries has been made by-
(A) IFLA (B) UNISIST
(C) UNESCO (iv) INSDOC

182. "Special libraries serve a specialist clientele, located within a single establishment or group and all engaged in working towards one common purpose." Who said this
(A) R.Astall (B) UNESCO
(C) J.D.Brown (D) E.C.Richardson

183. Informal self education is possible in what kind of library?
(A) National Library (B) Public Library
(C) Specific Library (D) College Library

184. The headquarters of Raja Ram Mohan Roy Library Foundation is situated at
(A) Delhi (B) Calcutta
(C) Chennai (D) Nagpur

185. The first library Act in India was passed and implemented in
(A) Maharashtra (B) Andhra Pradesh
(C) Madras (D) Karnataka

186. The concept of UBC was introduced by
(A) UNESCO (B) LC
(C) FID (D) IFLA

187. NATIS stands for
(A) National Information System
(B) National Technical Information System
(C) National Team for Information Science
(D) None of the above

188. C.L.R.I (Central Leather Research Institute) is located at
 (A) Chennai (B) Calicut
 (C) Cochin (D) Cuttack
189. Information about Indian research studies on bakery and milling is input to IFIS through
 (A) The Central Rice Research Institute
 (B) Indian Agricultural Research Institute
 (C) National Institute of Nutrition
 (D) Central Food Technological Research Institute
190. UNESCO's information programme is known as
 (A) NATIS (B) GIP
 (C) UAP (D) UBC
191. Extension services to the blind by a public library is justified by
 (A) the fourth law of library science
 (B) the fifth law of library science
 (C) the first law of library science
 (D) all the laws of library science
192. Which of the following is not a national library?
 (A) Library of Congress
 (B) British Library
 (C) Bibliotheque Nationale
 (D) Smithsonian Institute
193. UNESCO's Public Library Manifesto was last revised in
 (A) 1990 (B) 1998
 (C) 1997 (D) 1994
194. Which law of library Science relates to the growth of libraries...
 (A) Forth law (B) First law
 (C) Second law (D) Fifth law
195. The Five laws of library science are a set of good norms to good practice in...
 (A) Society (B) Libraries
 (C) Librarianship (D) Library science

196. Reading centre's, story hours, exhibitions and reading to literature are forms of ...
   (A) Extension service
   (B) Service of a public library
   (C) Both
   (D) None
197. Informal self education is possible in what kind of library?
   (A) National Library (B) Public Library
   (C) Specific Library (D) College Library
198. The word Library is made of the word
   (A) Liber (B) Libra
   (C) Libre (D) Liberae
199. Books for all is the same according to which law of library Science
   (A) Books are for use
   (B) Every reader and his/her book
   (C) Every book and its reader
   (D) Save the time of the reader
200. Saraswathi Mahal Library is at
   (A) Tanjore (B) Bhubaneswar
   (C) Jaipur (D) Thiruvanathapuram
201. Association is a
   (A) Personal Author (B) Pseudonymous Author
   (C) Periodical publication (D) Corporate Author
202. Library of Congress is located at
   (A) Washington D.C (B) Chicago
   (C) New York (D) London
203. Connema Public Library was established after the name of the then
   (A) Governor (B) Judge
   (C) King (D) Philanthropist
204. Of the following libraries in India, which one is the oldest library ?
   (A) Asiatic Society Library, Bombay
   (B) Connemara Public Library, Madras

(C) Delhi Public Library, Delhi

(D) National Library of India, Calcutta.

205. In which year did A. W. Borden start a refresher course for librarians in India ?

(A) 1905 (B) 1910

(C) 1912 (D) 1913.

206. In which year was the International Book Year celebrated by UNESCO ?

(A) 1931 (B) 1947

(C) 1952 (D) 1972.

205. The author who defined Reference Service as the "Process of establishing contact between a reader and his documents in a personal way" is :

(A) WA. Katz (B) L. Shores

(C) M. Hutchins (D) S. R. Ranganathan

206. The National Library for the visually handicapped is located at :

(A) Allahabad (B) Indore

(C) Dehradun (D) Nainital

207. Identify the correct chronological order in which the following were established :

(A) National Library of India (Kolkata), Delhi Public Library, Documentation Research and Training Centre, Raja Ram Mohan Roy Library Foundation

(B) Delhi Public Library, Documentation Research and Training Centre, Raja Ram Mohan Roy Library Foundation, National Library of India (Kolkata)

(C) Documentation Research and Training Centre, Raja Ram Mohan Roy Library Foundation, National Library of India (Kolkata), Delhi Public Library

(D) Raja Ram Mohan Roy Library Foundation, National Library of India (Kolkata), Delhi Public Library, Documentation Research and Training Centre

208. The state which does not provide for library cess is

(A) Tamil Nadu (B) Andhra Pradesh

(C) West Bengal (D) Karnataka.

209. Parry Committee Report (UK) relates to
   (A) Public Libraries (B) University Libraries
   (C) National Libraries (D) Special Libraries.
210. The ILA was founded in the year
   (A) 1924 (B) 1933
   (C) 1950 (D) 1952.
211. The state that enacted library legislation in 1965 is
   (A) Karnataka (B) Haryana
   (C) Goa (D) Manipur.
212. William A. Borden, the first librarian in Baroda state, came from
   (A) UK (B) USA
   (C) France (D) Australia.
213. Library of Congress is
   (A) National Library of the USA
   (B) The Library of Indian Congress
   (C) The Library of the Parliament of India
   (D) National Library of Australia
214. 'Library Literature' is published by
   (A) DESIDOC (B) H. W. Wilson
   (C) INSDOC (D) R. C. Bowker
215. Science Information Centre of the UGC is located at
   (A) INSDOC
   (B) Indian Institute of Science, Bangalore
   (C) DESIDOC
   (D) DRTC.
216. The centre which is not a Sectoral Information Centre of NISSAT is
   (A) Central Food Technological Research Institute (Mysore)
   (B) Central Drug Research Institute (Lucknow)
   (C) Central Machine Tools Institute (Bangalore)
   (D) Central Road Research Institute (New Delh(i).
217. The Headquarters of INFLIBNET is located at
   (A) Delhi (B) Mumbai
   (C) Bangalore (D) Ahmedabad.

218. UNISIST is
   (A) World Science Information Programme
   (B) documentation centre in the US
   (C) type of special information service in science & technology
   (D) an indexing system.
219. INIS stands for
   (A) Information Network in Nuclear Science & Technology
   (B) Library Development Programme in Nuclear Science
   (C) Information Network in Naval Science
   (D) Information Network in Information Science.
220. 'Right book to the right reader at right time' is a principle enumerated by
   (A) Ranganathan (B) Dewey
   (C) Drury (D) Haines.
221. The professional organization concerned mainly with teachers of library science in India is
   (A) IASLIC (B) ILA
   (C) BLA (D) IATLIS
222. Andrew Carnegie was concerned with
   (A) Library and Information Science
   (B) Information Technology
   (C) Mathematics
   (D) Philanthrophy.
223. Kenyan Committee of UK was concerned with
   (A) school libraries (B) university libraries
   (C) research libraries (D) public libraries.
224. Obligation of state to provide library services to masses is related with
   (A) 1st law of Library Science
   (B) 2nd law of Library Science
   (C) 3rd law of Library science
   (D) 4th law of Library Science.

225. The first Library Science school was started by Melvil Dewey in
   (A) Yale University (B) Chicago University
   (C) Harvard University (D) Columbia University
226. The first act of Parliament to provide free public library service was passed in Great Britain in
   (A) 1860 (B) 1834
   (C) 1850 (D) 1856.
227. General Information Programme (PG(i) is connected with
   (A) ALA (B) IFLA
   (C) ILA (D) UNESCO.
228. 'Child growth' and 'adult growth' has been discussed by S. R. Ranganathan is concerned with
   (A) 2nd law of Library Science
   (B) 3rd law of Library Science
   (C) 4th law of Library Science
   (D) 5th law of Library Science.
229. The Library Association (Great Britain) was founded in
   (A) 1876 (B) 1878
   (C) 1877 (D) 1879.
230. Library extension activity is not related with
   (A) mobile library service
   (B) book fair and exhibition
   (C) lecture on library matters
   (D) inter library loan.
231. IFLA was founded in the year
   (A) 1937 (B) 1927
   (C) 1928 (D) 1929
232. British Library is a
   (A) University Library (B) Research Llibrary
   (C) College Library (D) National Library.
233. The Advisory Committee for libraries appointed by the Government of India is also known as

(A) Chattopadhyay Committee
(B) Sinha Committee
(C) Ranganathan Committee
(D) Parry Committee.

234. The first librarian of National Library was
(A) M. A. Gopinath (B) I. K. Ravichandra Rao
(C) S. R. Ranganathan (D) B. S. Kesavan.

235. The Library Legislation was not passed in the state of
(A) West Bengal (B) Orissa
(C) Andhra Pradesh (D) Punjab.

236. The third law of Library Science is
(A) every reader his/her book
(B) every book its reader
(C) books are for use
(D) save the time of the user.

237. The first university which offered Ph. D. in Library Science in India is
(A) Madras University (B) Jadavpur University
(C) Punjab University (D) Delhi University.

238. The person associated with library movement in India is
(A) F. W. Lancaster (B) Blaise Cronin
(C) W. A. Borden (D) Thomas Childers.

239. The person associated with library movement in the erstwhile state of Baroda
(A) Balaji Baji Rao
(B) Shibaji
(C) Shambhaji Rao
(D) Maharaja Sayaji Rao Gaikward.

240. UNESCO came into existence in the year
(A) 1947 (B) 1956
(C) 1946 (D) 1948.

241. The particular law of Library Science makes it obligatory on the part of the state to enact library legislation is
(A) 1st law of Library Science
(B) 3rd law of Library Science

(C) 4th law of Library Science

(D) 2nd law of Library Science.

242. The year was declared as international year of literacy in

(A) 1992 (B) 1991

(C) 1990 (D) 1993.

243. Mobile library service is mainly a tool for

(A) inter-library loan (B) reference service

(C) referral service (D) library extension work.

244. In the enactment of the British Public Library Act of 1850, a major played by

(A) Edward Robinson (B) Edward Edwards

(C) Edward Marshall (D) Edward Samuelson.

245. The present name of ASLIB is

(A) Association of Library and Information Bureaux

(B) Association of Special Library and Information Bureaux

(C) Association of Special Information Bureaux

(D) Association for Information Management.

246. The first librarian of Imperial Library was

(A) John McDonald (B) John Maxmuller

(C) John Abraham (D) John McFarlane.

247. Indian Library Association takes into its fold to

(A) public libraries (B) university libraries

(C) research libraries (D) all types of libraries.

248. The National Library, Calcutta Act came into force in

(A) 1949 (B) 1950

(C) 1952 (D) 1951.

249. First Master's degree programme in Library Science in India was started by

(A) Jawaharlal Nehru University

(B) The University of Delhi

(C) Madras University

(D) Gulberga University.

250. The number of Indian states has passed library legislation up to 2003

(A) 10 (B) 11
(C) 12 (D) 13.

251. Delhi Public Library was established in the year
(A) 1955 (B) 1957
(C) 1950 (D) 1960.

252. The IFLA Annual General Conference, 1992 was held in
(A) London (B) Paris
(C) New York (D) India.

253. Library Week in India is organised during the month of
(A) September (B) October
(C) November (D) December.

254. Library movement in the erstwhile state of Baroda started in the year
(A) 1911 (B) 1912
(C) 1910 (D) 1913.

255. Ranganathan Committee Report on development of university and college libraries was published by
(A) DESIDOC (B) DRTC
(C) UGC (D) ILA.

255. The latest library act was passed by
(A) Mizoram (B) Kerala
(C) Goa (D) Orissa.

256. The activity does not fall under purview of library extension
(A) mobile library service
(B) book fair
(C) exhibition on library matters
(D) extending the library building.

257. According to Education Commission, 1964-66, the percentage of university budget should be earmarked for its library expenditure is
(A) 5.5% (B) 7.5%
(C) 6.5% (D) 8.5%.

258. Second library school was started in

(A) Kakatiya University
(B) Bundelkhand University
(C) Osmania Unversity
(D) Punjab University.

259. First library training school was started in
(A) Hyderabad University
(B) The University of Calcutta
(C) Anna University
(D) Madras University.

260. Which committee/commission described Public Libraries as 'Stagnating Pools of Books'?
(A) Ranganathan Committee
(B) Sinha Committee
(C) Fyzee Committee
(D) Kothari Committee.

261. A Professional Association should primarily
(A) function as a trade union
(B) work for the development of its members
(C) undertake research in professional techniques
(D) serve as an employment exchange.

262. The National Library, Kolkata receives books on deposit under
(A) The Registration of Books Act, 1887
(B) The Delivery of Books Act, 1954
(C) The Copyright Act, 1935
(D) all of the above.

263. Library Legislation supports the Public Library Movement by
(A) ensuring that funds are made available
(B) establishing local library authorities
(C) making library services mandatory
(D) all of the above.

264. Library orientation, bibliographic instruction and user education are related in the following way
(A) all mean the same thing

(B) user education is wider and encompasses the other two
(C) library orientation is wider and encompasses the other two
(D) none of these.

265. Which of the following should be the primary objective of a college library?
(A) to promote research activities
(B) to encourage reading habits
(C) to support teaching programmes of the college
(D) to provide for the recreational needs of the students.

266. Zero growth libraries that
(A) libraries must not buy books
(B) libraries do not get more space
(C) libraries must need but many books as they aid
(D) libraries do not get more funds.

267. With which agency did UNESCO collaborate to establish UNISIST?
(A) ICSU (B) FID
(C) IFLA (D) ALA.

268. Public libraries support which type of education?
(A) formal (B) vocational
(C) non-formal (D) technical.

269. In which society Information and knowledge are considered as principal resources?
(A) agricultural society
(B) information society
(C) eastern society
(D) industrial society.

270. The laws of Library Science contribute to good librarianship enunciated by
(A) Melvil Dewey
(B) American Library Association
(C) Prof. B. S. Kesavan
(D) Dr. S. R. Ranganathan.

271. The first law of Library science has implication on which location of library?
   (A) stack
   (B) building
   (C) furniture and equipment
   (D) records and registers.
272. The third law of Library Science works in full conformity with
   (A) resource sharing (B) closed access
   (C) obligation of staff (D) open access.
273. "Library is a growing organism" means library grows by the number of books, readers and
   (A) audio visuals (B) computers
   (C) staff (D) budget.
274. While planning and designing a library building there should be adequate provision of expansion both horizontally and
   (A) breadth (B) vertically
   (C) length (D) radius.
275. Which Report made a number of recommendations for the development of public libraries?
   (A) J. S. Mill
   (B) McColvin
   (C) Prof. S. Radha Krishnan
   (D) Melvil Dewey.
276. Mercantile libraries were established to foster educational and recreational reading among their employees in
   (A) USA (B) France
   (C) India (D) U. K.
277. Deptt. Of Culture, Govt. of India took initiative for the development of libraries in the country through a draft document namely
   (A) National Education Policy
   (B) NAPLIS
   (C) National Information Policy
   (D) IASLIC.

278. The National Library, Kolkata was earlier known as
   (A) The Imperial Library
   (B) The Asiatic Society Library
   (C) The National PublicLibrary
   (D) Connemera Public Library.

279. The biggest library in the world is
   (A) Delhi Public Library
   (B) The Library of Congress
   (C) The British Library
   (D) National Library, Kolkata.

280. For maintenance and development of the library, Prof. K. N. Raj Committee recommended
   (A) 10% (B) 25%
   (C) 20% (D) 15%.

281. One of the important functions of a national library is preparation of
   (A) Union Catalogue
   (B) National Catalogue
   (C) National Bibliography
   (D) National Index.

282. The British Library is responsible for publishing
   (A) British National Bibliography
   (B) UK Public Libraries Act
   (C) Books in Print
   (D) Wales Bibliography.

283. School, College and University libraries constitute
   (A) public libraries (B) academic libraries
   (C) research libraries (D) special libraries.

284. Which has taken a number of steps to organize and improve the services of school libraries in India?
   (A) NCERT (B) KVS
   (C) CBSE (D) ILA.

285. Which of the following state enacted Public Libraries Act in 1989?
   (A) Andhra Pradesh (B) Gujrat
   (C) Haryana (D) Goa.

286. Mizoram Public Libraries Act was enacted in the year of
   (A) 1993 (B) 1990
   (C) 1978 (D) 1991.

287. The state central library of Tamil Nadu is
   (A) Madras University Library
   (B) Connemara Public Library
   (C) Ranganathan's Public Library
   (D) IIT Library.

288. Which Public Libraries Act provides reservation of woman and one ST members to all Library Committees?
   (A) Goa (B) West Bengal
   (C) Kerala (D) Mizoram.

289. Which of the following state does not have the provision of library cess?
   (A) Tamil Nadu (B) West Bengal
   (C) Karnataka (D) Andhra Pradesh.

290. Which type of programmes are conducted in order to know the information requirements of the readers?
   (A) Orientation Programmes
   (B) Workshops
   (C) User Studies
   (D) Training Programmes.

291. Making users acquainted with the library's usage and services is known as
   (A) User Orientation (B) User Analysis
   (C) User Studies (D) Feed back.

292. Which is concerned with providing instructions to the users how to make use of the information resources available in the libraries?
   (A) User Orientation
   (B) User Education
   (C) Learner Integration
   (D) Bibliographic Instruction.

293. The information policy objectives of which institution lay stress on user education?

(A) IFLA (B) FID
(C) UNESCO (D) UNISIST.

294. In India, which institution was organized a number of seminars and workshops for promotion of user education?
(A) NASSDOC (B) DRTC
(C) INSDOC (D) PARLE.

295. At which institution the British Library has established a Centre for Research on User Studies (CRUX)?
(A) University of Leads (B) Oxford College
(C) University of Wales (D) University of Sheffield.

296. CALIBNET and DELNET were established with the support of
(A) RRRLF (B) INSDOC
(C) NISSAT (D) NISTAD.

297. The Headquarters of FID are located at
(A) Washington (B) Paris
(C) The Hague (D) London.

298. In librarianship, building a good image of the library and information profession in society is known as
(A) National Policy (B) professional ethics
(C) library rules (D) library economics.

299. ILA has developed a database of libraries called
(A) NALANDA (B) Granthalaya
(C) SOUL (D) Suchika.

300. American Library Association has instituted an award for creative professional achievement in the name of
(A) John Daniel (B) Melvil Dewey
(C) J. H. Shera (D) J. S. Mills.

301. Journal of Librarianship is a serial publication of
(A) The Library Association
(B) Indian Library Association
(C) American Library Association
(D) Canada Library association.

302. IFLA has developed an internationally acceptable bibliographic record format named as

(A) UNIMARC (B) CCF
(C) CANMARC (D) UKMARC.

303. The 49th FID Congress and Conference was held at
(A) London (B) New Delhi
(C) Paris (D) Kolkata.

304. UGC provides major financial support to which libraries?
(A) National (B) Public
(C) University (D) Technical.

305. UGC Information Centre in Social Sciences is established at
(A) Dr. B. R. Ambedkar University, Lucknow
(B) Utkal University, Bhubaneswar
(C) Osmania University, Hyderabad
(D) M. S. University.

306. A national body which provides major financial support to public libraries is
(A) UGC (B) RRRLF
(C) NML (D) NBT.

307. INIS is sponsored by
(A) IAEA (B) IDRC
(C) FID (D) IFLA.

308. Which institution serves as a national centre for India to AGRIS?
(A) BARC (B) ARIC
(C) NIC (D) NISTAD.

309. NISSAT is under the administrative control of
(A) Dept. of S & T
(B) DSIR
(C) Deptt. Of Education
(D) National Informatics Centre.

310. NISSAT brings out a newsletter namely
(A) IT Bulletin
(B) Information Bulletin
(C) Information Today and Tomorrow
(D) Modern IT.

311. Information relating to Defence Studies are provided by

(A) INSDOC (B) DESIDOC

(C) NASSDOC (D) NML.

312. RRRLF is a

(A) Library association

(B) A public library

(C) A public trust for supporting libraries

(D) A Government body to support public libraries

313. The Chairman of the Advisory Committee for Libraries appointed by Government of India in 1957 to investigate the state of libraries in India was

(A) S.R.Ranganathan (B) K.P.Sinha

(C) D.P.Chattopadhyay (D) A.A.A.Fyzee

314. Which of the following is not a national library?

(A) Library of Congress

(B) British Library

(C) Bibliotheque Nationale

(D) Smithsonian Institute

315. UNESCO Public Library manifesto was last revised in

(A) 1990 (B) 1998

(C) 1997 (D) 1994 <latest 2001>

316. Library week is celebrated on

(A) 10th November (B) 14th November

(C) 14th December (D) 25th December

317. The study of Epistomology deals with:

(A) Modes of formation of subjects

(B) Classification of knowledge

(C) Cataloguing of composite books

(D) Origin, source and nature of knowledge

In the type of items, there may be more than one answer. Identify the correct combination:

(A) I and II are correct

(B) II and III are correct

(C) I, II and III are correct

(D) II and IV are correct

318. Based on the years of establishment arrange the following in chronological order. Use the code given below:

I. ASLIB (1924) II. ALA (1876)

III. ILA (1933) IV. IFLA (1927)

Codes:

(A) III, IV, II, I (B) I, IV, III, II

(C) II, I, IV, III (D) IV, I, III, II

319. Identify the correct order in which the commission were set up. Use the code given below:

I. Roy Committee on StateUniversities Review

II. Radhakrishnan Commission on Education (1948)

III. Kothari Commission on Education (1964)

IV. Mudaliar Commission of Secondary Education (1953)

Codes:

(A) I, IV, III, II (B) IV, III, I, II

(C) III, II, I, IV (D) II, IV, III, I

320. The first All India Conference of Librarians in 1918 was held at:

(A) Baroda (B) Calcutta

(C) Madras (D) Lahore

321. The first library science school in the world was started

(i) By Melvil Dewey

(ii) At Columbia University, New York (USA)

(iii) By W.C.Berwick Sayers

(iv) At London University, London (UK)

Code :

(A) (i) and (ii) are correct

(B) (i) and (iv) are correct

(C) (ii) and (iii) are correct

(D) (iii) and (iv) are correct

322. "God has chosen me as an instrument, the honour done to me should act as an incentive to the younger generation to devote their lives whole heartedly to library science and service". Whose quotation is this?

(A) B.S.Kesavan (B) Melvil Dewey
(C) S.R.Ranganathan (D) W.C.B.Sayers

323. CALIBER is sponsored by:
(A) INFLIBNET (B) DELNET
(C) AGRINET (D) CALIBNET

324. Headquarters of UNESCO
(A) Washington (B) Paris
(C) London (D) The Hague

325. "Search strategy is the mirror in the dark". Whose quotation is this?
(A) Kartz (B) Ranganathan
(C) Bliss (D) Cutter

326. INDEST is a
(A) Bibliography (B) Consortium
(C) Directory (D) Dictionary

327. This particular law of library science gives emphasis on the delegation of the government to enact library legislation in their respective states:
(A) First Law (B) Second Law
(C) Third Law (D) Fourth Law

328. Identify the correct chronological order in which they were set up:
(A) ILA, IASLIC, APLA, IATLIS
(B) APLA, ILA, IASLIC, IATLIS
(C) IASLIC, ILA, IATLIS, APLA
(D) IATLIS, IASLIC, ILA, APLA

329. Library as a living system "takes a new matter, casts off old matter, changes in size and takes new shapes and term". Whose quotation is this?
(A) B.S.Kesavan (B) Melvil Dewey
(C) S.R.Ranganathan (D) W.C.B.Sayers

330. UNISIST, a project of UNESCO was launched in this year:
(A) 1994 (B) 1972
(C) 1958 (D) 2001

331. "The Wheat loan Educational Exchange Programme" was initiated in:

(A) 1951 (B) 1972
(C) 1981 (D) 1999

332. Identify the chronological order of the following Public Libraries Acts.

(i) Andhra Pradesh Public Libraries Act
(ii) Karnataka Public libraries Act
(iii) Haryana Public Libraries Act
(iv) Maharashtra Public Libraries Act

Codes:

(A) (ii), (iv), (iii), (i) (B) (iii) (i), (ii), (iv),
(C) (iii) (iii), (ii), (i), (D) (iv) (iv), (iii), (i), (ii)

333. Who has not change its name?

(A) Library Association, U.K.
(B) ALA
(C) ASLIB
(D) IFLA

334. NISCAIR is a part of:

(A) DST (B) ISRO
(C) DSIR (D) CSIR

335. 'Best is the enemy of the Good' is said by:

(A) Drury (B) Urquart
(C) Foskett (D) Shera

336. Arrange the following associations in the order of year of establishment:

(A) SIS, IASLIC, IATLIS, ILA
(B) IASLIC, ILA, SIS, IATLIS
(C) ILA, SIS, IASLIC, IATLIS
(D) ILA (1933), IASLIC (1956), IATLIS (1970), SIS (1976)

337. IATLIS is an association of:

(A) Library Science Faculty
(B) Special Librarians
(C) Librarians of Public Libraries
(D) Librarians of Teachers' Training Colleges

338. With which agency did UNESCO collaborate to establish UNISIST?
(A) ICSU (B) FID
(C) IFLA (D) ILA

339. Which university appointed the first full time university librarian?
(A) Delhi University (B) Punjab University
(C) Madras University (D) Calcutta University

340. The quotation "Where is the Wisdom, We Lost in Knowledge.." is by
(A) John Keats (B) M.P.Carter
(C) T.S.Eliot (D) Marshall McLuhan

341. CONPOLIS (India) was set up in the year
(A) 1985 (B) 1986
(C) 1987 (D) 1988

342. First time efforts for the development of libraries in India were made
(A) S.R.Ranganathan (B) S.Radhakrishnan
(C) Sayaji Rao Gaekwad I (D) Sayaji Rao Gaekwad II

343. Public Library Law has already been passed in the following States. Identify the correct chronological order in which they were enacted.
(i) Uttaranchal (Uttarakhand)
(ii) Orissa
(iii) Gujarat
(iv) Haryana

Codes:
(A) (i), (ii), (iii), (iv) (B) (ii) (iv), (ii), (i),
(C) (iii) (ii), (iii), (iv), (D) (iii), (ii), (i), (iv)

344. Arrange the following events of Public Library movement in chronological order:
(i) Enact of Press and Registration of Books Act (1867)
(ii) Establishment of the Punjab Library, Lahore
(iii) Constitution of Fyzee Committee
(iv) Declaration of Imperial Library (Calcutta) as National Library of India (1948)

Codes:

(A) (i) (iii) (iv) (ii) (B) (i) (ii) (iii) (iv)

(C) (ii) (iii) (iv) (i) (D) (iv) (i) (iii) (ii)

345. Arrange the following principles and canon according to their levels as enunciated by Dr. S.R.Ranganathan

(i) Principles of Cataloguing

(ii) General Normative Principles

(iii) Laws of Library Science

(iv) Canons of Cataloguing

Codes:

(A) (i) (iv) (iii) (ii) (B) (ii) (iii) (iv) (i)

(C) (ii) (i) (iv) (iii) (D) (i) (iv) (ii) (iii)

346. Resources sharing among libraries was prompted by the factors

(A) Price escalation (B) Information explosion

(C) Both (i) and B) (D) None of the above

347. The Library Association (UK) is now the component of

(A) ASLIB (B) CILIP

(C) ALA (D) None of the above

348. Which of the following professional Associations does not exist now?

(A) IFLA (B) FID

(C) ALA (D) IALSIC

349. Arrange the following States chronologically according to year of enactment of Library Legislation

(i) Tamil Nadu (1948) (ii) U.P. (2006)

(iii) Gujarat (2000) (iv) Mizoram (1994)

Codes:

(A) (iv), (iii), (i), (ii) (B) (ii), (iv), (iii), (i)

(C) (i), (iv), (iii), (ii) (D) (i), (ii), (iv), (iii)

350. Number of States in India which have enacted Public Library Legislation till date is

(A) Seven (B) Ten

(C) Thirteen (D) nineteen

351. Which publication was not authored by S.R.Ranganathan?

(A) Prolegomena to library classification
(B) Reference Service
(C) Ramanujan: The man and the Mathematician
(D) Living with Books

352. Arrange the following States according to the year of enactment of library legislation:

(i) Pondicherry (ii) Orissa
(iii) Rajasthan (iv) Karnataka

Codes:

(A) (iv), (i), (iii), (ii) (B) (iv), (ii), (iii), (i)
(C) (iv), (iii), (i), (ii) (D) (iv) (i), (iii), (ii), (iv)

353. Arrange the following chronologically according to their year of Birth:

(i) S.R.Ranganathan (1892-1972)
(ii) Melvil Dewey
(iii) C.A.Cutter (1837-1903)
(iv) B.S.Kesavan

Codes:

(A) (ii), (i), (iv), (iii) (B) (i), (iii), (iv), (ii)
(C) (iii), (ii), (i), (iv) (D) (iv), (i), (ii), (iii)

354. Library play an important role in supporting educational, cultural and ......activities of a society.

(A) Technical (B) Research
(C) Vocational (D) Industrial

355. Which have occuupied the basic resources of an information society ?

(A) Educational and Culture
(B) Agriculture and Industries
(C) Information and Knowledge
(D) Academic and Public Libraries

356. Which among the following are the first law of library science is restated for use?

(A) Library/Information
(B) Books/Readers/
(C) Information/Knowledge
(D) Documents/Information.

357. The third law of Library Science works in full conformity with
(A) Resourch Sharing (B) Closed Access
(C) Open Access (D) Obligation of Staff

358. The basic components of a library are i] books ii] Readers and ii]-
(A) Staff (B) Budget
(C) Building (D) Furniture

359. Which library was another form of Book Club or reading society ?
(A) Monastic (B) Subscription
(C) Correlation (D) Commercial

360. Who is other personalities except William Ewart responsible for library legislation in U.K.?
(A) Joseph Brotherlon (B) George Biraback
(C) Allan Ramsay (D) W.K. Smith

361. The first general library law in USA was enacted in
(A) 1950 (B) 1956
(C) 1964 (D) 1970

362. The acronym for Assocation for Information Management is-
(A) IAMA (B) AIM
(C) ASLIB (D) IIM

363. The earlier name of National Library, Calcutta was
(A) Natiional Information Centre
(B) National Public Library
(C) Calcutta Public Library
(D) The Imperial Library

364. Name of the Department of Govt. of India under which NAPLIS document was prepared by a committee ?
(A) Education
(B) Information and Broadcasting
(C) Culture
(D) Information Technolgy

365. ALA Glossary of Library Terms defines the National Library as 'a library maintained by a

(A) Province (B) Nation

(C) County (D) State.

366. Who has been declared as an institution of national importance by Govt. of India
   (A) National Library, Calcutta
   (B) Delhi Public Library, Delhi
   (C) Connemera Public Library, Chennai
   (D) Asiatic Society Library, Mumbai
367. Who appointed Librarian of Library of Congress ?
   (A) President of USA
   (B) Chairman, Congress
   (C) Chief Executive, Library Affairs
   (D) President of Library of Congress
368. A School library inculcates.......children among the school
   (A) Saving habits (B) competing habits
   (C) reading habits (D) writing habits.
369. Which committee recommended 20% of the college budget for the maintenance and development of the library?
   (A) Prof. S.R. Ranganathan
   (B) Prof. S. Radhakrishnan
   (C) Prof. Lakshanaswamy
   (D) Prof. K. N. Raj
370. Information and Library Network (INFLIBNET) centre is established by.........
   (A) UGC (B) RRRLF
   (C) NBT (D) NISSAT
371. Enactment of Public Library Act is otherwise known as
   (A) Right to Information
   (B) Intellectual Property Right
   (C) Copy Right
   (D) Library Legislation

372. Which one of the following enable to create a cadre of Public Library acts ?
   (A) All India Library Service
   (B) State Library Service
   (C) Indian Information
   (D) Subordinate Library

373. Which of the following cess.per rupee on house tax or property tax being recommended under Model Public Library Bill, 1963?
   (A) Six Paise (B) Four Paise
   (C) Seven Paise (D) Ten Paise

374. Haryana Public Libraries act was passed in the year........
   (A) 1987 (B) 1989
   (C) 1990 (D) 1992

375. Which state enacted public libraries act in 1993?
   (A) Mizoram (B) Sikkim
   (C) Goa (D) Nagaland

376. Which is the State Central Library of Tamil Nadu
   (A) Oriental Library
   (B) Madras University Library
   (C) Connemera Public Library
   (D) Ranganathan Insitute of Library Studies

377. Which Act provide reservation on one women and one ST members to all library Committees.
   (A) Kerala (B) Goa
   (C) Manipur (D) Gujrat

378. Administration of Public Libraries in Manipur comes under-
   (A) Panchayatiraj Department
   (B) Information and Public Relations Department
   (C) Cultural Department
   (D) Education Department

379. Which state of the following does not have the provision of library cess.

(A) Kerala (B) Maharashtra
(C) Andhra Pradesh (D) Tamil Nadu

380. Dr. S. R. Ranganathan has grouped the users in to four categories such as i] general i] ordinary iii] freshman iv]-
(A) students (B) specialist inquirer
(C) public (D) researchers

381. Which British Library has established a centre for research on user studies (CRUS).
(A) Leeds University (B) University of Oxford
(C) University of Wales (D) University of Shefield

382. Which is one of the indirect methods of knowing the user's needs.
(A) Citatioin analysis (B) Interviews
(C) Field Survey (D) Using Statics

383. A Case study of use of Delhi University Library was conducted in -
(A) 1962 (B) 1965
(C) 1968 (D) 1970

384. Motivating the potential users to use information resources is known as
(A) Bibliographic instruction
(B) User's Profile
(C) User Education
(D) User Orientation

385. Introduction the user to the general methods of library usage and service is called
(A) Orientation (B) Instruction
(C) Initiation (D) Induction

386. Calcutta Library Network, CALIBNET was sponsored by-
(A) CSIR (B) NISSTAD
(C) NISSAT (D) ICAR

387. Which is a Natioinal level Library and Information Network.
(A) INFLIBNET (B) CALIBNET
(C) MALIBNET (D) NICNET

388. ILA has developed a database of libraries called
   (A) Soul (B) Nalanda
   (C) Oasis (D) CDS/ISIS

389. Journal of Librarianship is a serial publication of-
   (A) American Librarian Association
   (B) Indian Library Association
   (C) The Library Association
   (D) ASLIB

390. Association for Information Management is located in-
   (A) Rome (B) Washington
   (C) Paris (D) London

391. IFLA has developed an internationally acceptable bibliographic standard namely
   (A) CCF (B) UNIMARC
   (C) UK Marc (D) FRBR

392. Which is an apex body for promoting Public Library Service in India?
   (A) NBT (B) NISSAT
   (C) INSDOC (D) RRRLF

393. Which serves as a national centre for India to AGRIS?
   (A) ARIC (B) ASIC
   (C) PID (D) NISTAD

394. Where did Dr. S. R. Ranganathan put forth his five laws of library science?
   (A) Meenakshi college, Annamalainagar
   (B) Hindu College, New Delhi
   (C) City College, Bangalore
   (D) Christ College, Bangalore

395. Who has prescribed certain standards for library binding?
   (A) ILA (B) ALA
   (C) BLA (D) NBT

396. In which year headquarter of FID was shifted from Brussels to The Hague?
   (A) 1925 (B) 1928
   (C) 1930 (D) 1934

397. Who gave the sixth law of library science "Every reader his/her freedom"?
(A) Walt Crawford (B) Michael Gorman
(C) James R. Rettig (D) LenartBjorneborn

398. In which year International institute of Documentation changed to International federation of D
(A) 1931 (B) 1937
(C) 1945 (iv) 1948

399. NICFOS is related to .
(A) Leather (B) Machine tools
(C) Food Science (D) Atom

400. Delivery of Book Act passed in the year?
(A) 1963 (B) 1972
(C) 1960 (D) 1954

401. When was Dr.S. R. Ranganathan was appointed as a National research professor of Library science?
(A) 1942 (B) 1962
(C) 1972 (D) 1952

402. When was the curriculam development committee on LIS instituted?
(A) 1988-89 (B) 1990-93
(C) 1994-97 (D) 1999-02

403. Who published the journal International classification?
(A) IFLA (B) UNESCO
(C) ISKO (D) ALA

404. Who gave the sixth law of library science "Every reader his/her freedom"?
(A) Walt Crawford (B) Michael Gorman
(C) James R. Rettig (D) LenartBjorneborn

405. ISO-9960 is related with?
(A) Standard for encoding data on CD-ROM
(B) Standard for Computer Hardware
(C) Standard for Information Processing
(D) Standard for Networking

406. In which year the ISBN allocation office in India shifted from Kolkatta to Delhi?

(A) 2009 (B) 2010

(C) 2011 (D) 2012

407. Which of the following is not an example of equivalence relationship?

(A) Nervous System- Central nervous system

(B) Freedom - Liberty

(C) Hunting - Hunters

(D) Wearing – Cloth.

408. Who is the first editor of "Modern Librarian"?

(A) F.Monbrary Volte (B) Dr. S. R. Ranganathan

(C) J. D. Brown (D) Krishan Kumar

409. Where is the headquarter of SLA?

(A) New York (B) Lagos

(C) Shimla (D) New Delhi

410. ABGILA is a quarterly publication of?

(A) Assam Library Association

(B) Andhra Desa Library Association

(C) Indian Library Association

(D) Raja Ram Mohun Roy Foundation

411. Which Indian University first started M.Lib.Sc. & M.Phil courses?

(A) University of Delhi

(B) University of Madras

(C) S.N.D.T. Women University, Bombay

(D) Aligar Muslim University

412. Match the following :

List 'A'	**List 'B'**
(1) Chattopadhyaya	(i) 1959 Committee Report
(2) Kothari Commission	(ii) 1942 Report
(3) Sinha Committee Report	(iii) 1986
(4) Fyzee Committee Report	(iv) 1966

Code :

(A) 1 (iii), 2 (iv), 3 (i), 4 (ii)

(B) 1 (iv), 2 (iii), 3 (ii), 4 (i)

(C) 1 (ii), 2 (iv), 3 (iii), 4 (i)

(D) 1 (iv), 2 (ii), 3 (i), 4 (iii)

413. Match the following :

List – I	**List – II**
(a) Elements of Library Classification	(i) D.J. Desolla Price
(b) Little Science Big Science	(ii) S.R. Ranganathan
(c) Documentation	(iii) D.J. Fosket
(d) Subject Approach to Information	(iv) S.C. Bradford

Codes:	**(a)**	**(b)**	**(c)**	**(d)**
(A)	(ii)	(iii)	(iv)	
(B)	(ii)	(i)	(iv)	(iii)
(C)	(iii)	(ii)	(i)	(iv)
(D)	(iv)	(ii)	(iii)	(i)
(E)	(i)	(ii)	(iii)	(iv)

414. Match the following

List – I	**List – II**
(a) Best books for the largest numbers	(i) D.B.Krishna Rao
(b) Library is the heart of all university work	(ii) B.S. Kesavan
(c) First Ph.D. in Library Science	(iii) S. Radhakrishnan
(d) First Librarian of National Library (India)	(iv) MelvilDewey

Codes:	**(a)**	**(b)**	**(c)**	**(d)**
(A)	(i)	(ii)	(iii)	(iv)
(B)	(iv)	(iii)	(ii)	(i)
(C)	(iii)	(iv)	(i)	(ii)
(D)	(iv)	(iii)	(i)	(ii)

415. Match the following :

List-I	List-II
(A) Maharashtra Public Libraries Act	(i) 2004
(B) Gujarat Public Libraries Act	(ii) 2005
(C) Orissa Public Libraries Act	(iii) 1967
(D) West Bengal Public Libraries Act	(iv) 1988
	(v) 1979

Codes:	(a)	(b)	(c)	(d)
(A)	(i)	(iii)	(ii)	(iv)
(B)	(ii)	(v)	(iv)	(iii)
(C)	(iii)	(i)	(ii)	(v)
(D)	(v)	(ii)	(iv)	(iii)

416. Match the following :

List-I	List-II
(a) Nehru Memorial Museum Library	(i) Chennai
(b) Connemara Public Library	(ii) Pune
(c) Bhandarkar Oriental Research Institute Library	(iii) Patna
(d) Khudabaksh Oriental Library	(iv) Delhi
	(v) Allahabad

Codes:	(a)	(b)	(c)	(d)
(A)	(iii)	(v)	(iv)	(ii)
(B)	(v)	(iv)	(i)	(ii)
(C)	(v)	(ii)	(iv)	(i)
(D)	(iv)	(i)	(ii)	(iii)

417. Match the following :

List-I	List-II
(a) IFLA	(i) Science Citation Index
(b) Unesco	(ii) First search
(c) OCLC	(iii) Patent Information
(d) ISI	(iv) Public Library Manifesto
	(v) Universal Availability of Publications

Codes:	**(a)**	**(b)**	**(c)**	**(d)**
(A)	(iii)	(iv)	(ii)	(i)
(B)	(iv)	(iii)	(i)	(ii)
(C)	(v)	(iv)	(ii)	(i)
(D)	(v)	(i)	(iv)	(ii)

418. Match the following:

List-I (Writing materials)	**List-II (Place of origin)**
I. Clay Tablet	a. Algeria/Babylonia
II. Palm Leaves	b. Egypt
III. Paper	c. Ninveh
IV. Papyrus	d. China
	e. India

Codes:

(A) I-c, II-b, III-a, IV-d (B) I-d, II-e, III-a, IV-c

(C) I-c, II-e, III-d, IV-b (D) I-c, II-b, III-a, IV-d

419. Match the following:

List-I	**List-II**
(a) Kothari Commission	(i) Status and Pay scales of libraries
(b) Radhakrishnan Commission	(ii) Public Library System
(c) Mehrotra Commission	(iii) Library Budget as a percentage
(d) Fyzee Commission	(iv) Importance of library in Academic Institutions
	(v) Special libraries

Codes:	**(a)**	**(b)**	**(c)**	**(d)**
(A)	(iii)	(i)	(v)	(ii)
(B)	(iii)	(iv)	(i)	(ii)
(C)	(ii)	(iii)	(i)	(v)
(D)	(iv)	(iii)	(ii)	(i)

420. Match the following:

List-I (Library Act)	**List-II (Year of Enactment)**
(a) Madras Public Libraries Act	(i) 1965
(b) West Bengal Public Libraries Act	(ii) 1960
(c) Andhra Pradesh Public Libraries Act	(iii) 1948
(d) Karnataka Public Libraries Act	(iv) 1979

Codes:	**(a)**	**(b)**	**(c)**	**(d)**
(A)	(iii)	(iv)	(ii)	(i)
(B)	(i)	(ii)	(iii)	(iv)
(C)	(iii)	(ii)	(iv)	(i)
(D)	(ii)	(i)	(iv)	(iii)

421. Match the following:

List-I	**List-II**
(a) Maharashtra Public Libraries Act	(i) 2004
(b) Gujarat Public Libraries Act	(ii) 2005
(c) Orissa Public Libraries Act	(iii) 1967
(d) West Bengal Public Libraries Act	(iv) 1988
	(v) 1979

Codes:	**(a)**	**(b)**	**(c)**	**(d)**
(A)	(i)	(iii)	(ii)	(iv)
(B)	(ii)	(v)	(iv)	(iii)
(C)	(iii)	(i)	(ii)	(v)
(D)	(v)	(ii)	(iv)	(iii)

422. Match the following:

List-I	**List-II**
(a) Nehru Memorial Museum Library	(i) Chennai
(b) Connemara Public Library	(ii) Pune
(c) Bhandkar Oriental Research Institute Library	(iii) Patna
(d) Khudabaksh Oriental Library	(iv) Delhi
	(v) Allahabad

Codes:	**(a)**	**(b)**	**(c)**	**(d)**
(A)	(iii)	(v)	(iv)	(ii)
(B)	(v)	(iv)	(i)	(ii)
(C)	(v)	(ii)	(iv)	(i)
(D)	(iv)	(i)	(ii)	(iii)

423. Match the following:

List-I	List-II
(a) IFLA	(i) Science Citation Index
(b) UNESCO	(ii) First serach
(c) OCLC	(iii) Patent information
(d) ISI	(iv) Public Library Manifesto
	(v) Universal Availability of Publications

Codes:	**(a)**	**(b)**	**(c)**	**(d)**
(A)	(iii)	(iv)	(ii)	(i)
(B)	(iv)	(iii)	(i)	(ii)
(C)	(v)	(iv)	(ii)	(i)
(D)	(v)	(i)	(iv)	(ii)

424. Match the following:

List-I	List-II
(a) MS-DOS	(i) Multi-User Operating System
(b) UNIX	(ii) DTP Software
(c) Excel	(iii) DBMS
(d) pagemaker	(iv) Single User Operating System
	(v) Spreadsheet Software

Codes:	**(a)**	**(b)**	**(c)**	**(d)**
(A)	(iv)	(v)	(i)	(ii)
(B)	(v)	(i)	(ii)	(iii)
(C)	(iii)	(i)	(ii)	(v)
(D)	(iv)	(i)	(v)	(ii)

425. Match the following:

List-I	List-II
(a) OCLC	(i) City
(b) INFLIBNET	(ii) International
(c) CALIBNET	(iii) Regional
(d) ASTINFO	(iv) National

Codes:	**(a)**	**(b)**	**(c)**	**(d)**
(A)	(ii)	(i)	(iv)	(iii)
(B)	(ii)	(iv)	(i)	(iii)
(C)	(iii)	(ii)	(iv)	(i)
(D)	(iii)	(i)	(ii)	(iv)

426. Match the following:

List-I	List-II
(a) B.S.Kesavan	(i) Cataloguing Rules
(b) W.C.B.Sayers	(ii) National Library
(c) C.A.Cutter	(iii) School of Librarianship
(d) J.D.Brown	(iv) List of Subject Headings
	(v) Subject Classification

Codes:	**(a)**	**(b)**	**(c)**	**(d)**
(A)	(v)	(iii)	(ii)	(i)
(B)	(iii)	(ii)	(iv)	(v)
(C)	(ii)	(iii)	(i)	(v)
(D)	(v)	(ii)	(iv)	(i)

427. Match the following:

List-I	List-II
(a) NISCAIR	(i) MINISIS
(b) DESIDOC	(ii) LibSys
(c) IDRC	(iii) Granthalaya
(d) INFOTEK	(iv) Sanjay
	(v) SLIM

Codes:	**(a)**	**(b)**	**(c)**	**(d)**
(A)	(ii)	(v)	(iii)	(iv)
(B)	(i)	(ii)	(v)	(iv)
(C)	(iii)	(ii)	(i)	(v)
(D)	(iii)	(iv)	(i)	(ii)

428. Match the following:

List-I	List-II
(a) Fyzee Committeee	(i) Library Budget
(b) Knowledge Commission	(ii) Status and Payscales of libraries
(c) Mahrotra Committee	(iii) Public Libraries
(d) Kothari Commission	(iv) Knowledge Society
	(v) Importance of library in academic institutions

Codes:	**(a)**	**(b)**	**(c)**	**(d)**
(A)	(i)	(iv)	(iii)	(v)
(B)	(iv)	(ii)	(v)	(iii)
(C)	(v)	(ii)	(iv)	(iii)
(D)	(iii)	(iv)	(ii)	(i)

429. Match the following:

List-I	**List-II**
(a) Library is a people's university	(i) Kothari
(b) Library is a growing organisation	(ii) Urquart
(c) Library can be useful to society	(iii) Ranganathan
(d) Library is the heart of the University	(iv) Sayajirao Gayakwad

Codes:	**(a)**	**(b)**	**(c)**	**(d)**
(A)	(iv)	(iii)	(ii)	(i)
(B)	(iv)	(i)	(iii)	(ii)
(C)	(ii)	(iv)	(iii)	(i)
(D)	(iv)	(ii)	(i)	(iii)

430. Match the following:

List-I	**List-II**
(a) P.Wassermann	(i) Line of thinking
(b) P.Atherton	(ii) Foundation of Education for Librarianship
(c) J.H.Shera	(iii) New Librarianship
(d) Maurice B.Line	(iv) Putting knowledge to work

Codes:	**(a)**	**(b)**	**(c)**	**(d)**
(A)	(i)	(ii)	(iii)	(iv)
(B)	(ii)	(i)	(iii)	(iv)
(C)	(iv)	(iii)	(i)	(ii)
(D)	(iii)	(iv)	(ii)	(i)

431. Match the following:

List-I	List-II
(a) British Library	(i) Russia
(b) Bibliotheque National	(ii) USA
(c) Lenin Library	(iii) UK
(d) Library of Congress	(iv) France

Codes:	**(a)**	**(b)**	**(c)**	**(d)**
(A)	(iv)	(iii)	(i)	(ii)
(B)	(i)	(ii)	(iii)	(iv)
(C)	(iii)	(iv)	(i)	(ii)
(D)	(iii)	(iv)	(ii)	(i)

432. Match the following:

List-I (Library Act)	List-II (Year of Enactment)
(a) Orissa	(i) 2006
(b) Goa	(ii) 2005
(c) Uttaranchal	(iii) 2001
(d) Uttar Pradesh	(iv) 1994

Codes:	**(a)**	**(b)**	**(c)**	**(d)**
(A)	(i)	(ii)	(iii)	(iv)
(B)	(iii)	(iv)	(ii)	(i)
(C)	(iv)	(iii)	(ii)	(i)
(D)	(ii)	(i)	(iii)	(iv)

433. Match the following items given in List – I and List – II

List-I	List-II
(a) Informatique	(i) English
(b) Informatik	(ii) Italian
(c) Informatica	(iii) French
(d) Informatics	(iv) German

Codes:	**(a)**	**(b)**	**(c)**	**(d)**
(A)	(iii)	(iv)	(ii)	(i)
(B)	(ii)	(i)	(iv)	(iii)
(C)	(iv)	(iii)	(i)	(ii)
(D)	(iii)	(i)	(ii)	(iv)

434. Match the following:

List-I	**List-II**
(a) Five Laws of Library Science	(i) C.D.Needham
(b) Subject approach to information	(ii) S.R.Ranganathan
(c) Organising Knowledge in Libraries	(iii) B.C.Vickery and A.Vickery
(d) Information Science in theory and practice	(iv) A.C.Foskett

Codes:	**(a)**	**(b)**	**(c)**	**(d)**
(A)	(ii)	(iv)	(i)	(iii)
(B)	(i)	(iii)	(iv)	(ii)
(C)	(iii)	(ii)	(iv)	(i)
(D)	(iv)	(ii)	(iii)	(i)

435. Match the following:

List-I	**List-II**
(a) Little Science, Big Science	(i) S.C.Bradford
(b) Documentation	(ii) William Martin
(c) The third Wave	(iii) Eric J de Solla Price
(d) The Information Society	(iv) Alwin Toffler

Codes:	**(a)**	**(b)**	**(c)**	**(d)**
(A)	(i)	(ii)	(iii)	(iv)
(B)	(iii)	(i)	(iv)	(ii)
(C)	(iv)	(iii)	(ii)	(i)
(D)	(ii)	(i)	(iv)	(iii)

436. Match the following:

List I	**List II**
(i) Danicl J. Boorstin	(w) National Library, India
(ii) Joseph Van Praet	(x) British Library
(iii) Y. M. Mulay	(y) Library of Congress
(iv) Antonio Panizzi	(z) Bibliotheque Nationale

Codes:	**(i)**	**(ii)**	**(iii)**	**(iv)**
(A)	(w)	(y)	(x)	(z)
(B)	(y)	(z)	(w)	(x)

(C)	(x)	(z)	(w)	(y)
(D)	(w)	(x)	(y)	(z)

437. Match the following:

List I	**List II**
(i) Egypt	(w) Library of Ashurbanipal
(ii) Turkey	(x) Villa of Papyri
(iii) Italy	(y) Library of Pergamum
(iv) Iraq	(z) Royal Library of Alexandria

Codes:	**(i)**	**(ii)**	**(iii)**	**(iv)**
(A)	(z)	(x)	(y)	(w)
(B)	(z)	(y)	(x)	(w)
(C)	(w)	(y)	(z)	(x)
(D)	(y)	(x)	(w)	(z)

438. Match the following:

List I	**List II**
(i) Daniel J. Boorstin	(w) National Library, India
(ii) Joseph Van Praet	(x) British Library
(iii) Y. M. Mulay	(y) Library of Congress
(iv) Antonio Panizzi	(z) Bibliotheque Nationale

Codes:	**(i)**	**(ii)**	**(iii)**	**(iv)**
(A)	(w)	(y)	(x)	(z)
(B)	(y)	(z)	(w)	(x)
(C)	(x)	(z)	(w)	(y)
(D)	(w)	(x)	(y)	(z)

439. Match the President of IFLA with his/her tenure:

List I	**List II**
(i) Ingrid Parent	(w) 2007-2009
(ii) Claudia Lux	(x) 2009-2011
(iii) Sinikka Sipila	(y) 2011-2013
(iv) Ellen Tise	(z) 2013-2015

Codes:	**(i)**	**(ii)**	**(iii)**	**(iv)**
(A)	(z)	(x)	(y)	(w)
(B)	(y)	(w)	(z)	(x)
(C)	(x)	(y)	(w)	(z)
(D)	(w)	(z)	(y)	(x)

440. Match the following :

List – I	**List – II**
(A) Obligation of the State	(i) First Law
(B) Shelf Arrangement & Catalogue	(ii) Second Law
(C) Open Access & Shelf Arrangement	(iii) Third Law
(D) Library location/hours	(iv) Fourth Law

Codes:	**(a)**	**(b)**	**(c)**	**(d)**
(A)	(ii)	(iv)	(iii)	(i)
(B)	(iv)	(iii)	(ii)	(i)
(C)	(i)	(iii)	(iv)	(ii)
(D)	(iii)	(ii)	(i)	(iv)

441. Match the following:

List – I	**List – II**
(A) RRRLF	(i) Delhi
(B) Connemara Public Library	(ii) Patna
(C) NISCAIR	(iii) Kolkata
(D) Khuda Baksh Oriental Public Library	(iv) Chennai

Codes:	**(a)**	**(b)**	**(c)**	**(d)**
(A)	(iv)	(iii)	(ii)	(i)
(B)	(ii)	(iii)	(iv)	(i)
(C)	(iii)	(iv)	(i)	(ii)
(D)	(iv)	(i)	(ii)	(iii)

442. Match the following:

List – I	**List – II**
(A) Right man at right library	(i) Annual financial statement
(B) Budget	(ii) Deployment
(C) Journal	(iii) TQM
(D) Identifying user's views and expectations	(iv) ISSN

Codes:	**(a)**	**(b)**	**(c)**	**(d)**
(A)	(iii)	(i)	(ii)	(iv)
(B)	(ii)	(i)	(iv)	(iii)
(C)	(iv)	(ii)	(iii)	(i)
(D)	(i)	(iii)	(iv)	(ii)

443. Match the following:

List-I	List-II
(A) Konnemara Public Library	(i) Patna
(B) Khudabaksha Oriental Public Library	(ii) Kolkata
(C) Asiatic Society Library	(iii) Chennai
(D) National Library (India)	(iv) Mumbai

Codes:	**(a)**	**(b)**	**(c)**	**(d)**
(A)	iii	i	iv	ii
(B)	iv	i	ii	iii
(C)	ii	iii	ii	iv
(D)	ii	iv	i	iii

444. Match the following :

List –I	List-II
a. 1st law of Library Science	i) Real time access
b. 2nd Law of Library Science	ii) Search engine & subject gateways
c. 3rd Law of Library Science	iii) Web access to resources
d. 4th Law of Library Science	iv) Open access initiatives

Codes:	**(a)**	**(b)**	**(c)**	**(d)**
(A)	iii	iv	ii	i
(B)	iv	i	ii	iii
(C)	ii	iii	ii	iv
(D)	ii	iv	i	iii

445. Match the following :

List – I	List – II
a. Sinha Committee	i. Library staff strength
b. Dr. S.R. Ranganathan Committee	ii. Central Medical Library
c. Report of Dr. Shaw and Dr. D. B. Krishna Rao	iii. Libraries at Panchayat, Block, District and State level

d. Dr. J. Bhore Committee	iv. National Agricultural System of Agriculture Libraries

Codes:	**(a)**	**(b)**	**(c)**	**(d)**
(A)	iii	i	ii	iv
(B)	iv	iii	ii	i
(C)	iii	i	iv	ii
(D)	i	iii	ii	iv

446. Match the following:

List – I	**List – II**
a. Public Library Extension	i. KD Metcalf
b. Academic Library Management	ii. M A Gelfand
c. University Libraries for Developing Countries	iii. L R McColvin
d. Planning Academic and Research Library Buildings	iv. M B Line

Codes:	**(a)**	**(b)**	**(c)**	**(d)**
(A)	iii	iv	ii	i
(B)	iv	ii	i	iii
(C)	iii	i	iv	ii
(D)	ii	iii	i	iv

447. Match the following :

List – I	**List – II**
a. Indian Cultural Heritage	i. TKDL
b. Race & Brittle	ii. IGNCA
c. Traditional Knowledge	iii. C-DAC
d. Mobile Digital Library	iv. National Library

Codes:	**(a)**	**(b)**	**(c)**	**(d)**
(A)	i	iv	iii	ii
(B)	iv	iii	ii	i
(C)	ii	iv	i	iii
(D)	iii	ii	iv	i

448. Match the following :

List – I	List – II
a. Special library	i. Provides bibliographical services
b. Public library	ii. Conservation of knowledge
c. National library	iii. Popularisation of Govt. information
d. Academic library	iv. Critical compilation

Codes:	(a)	(b)	(c)	(d)
(A)	i	iii	iv	ii
(B)	ii	iv	i	iii
(C)	iii	iv	i	ii
(D)	iv	iii	i	ii

449. Match the following language and their function:

List – I	List – II
a. National Library of the World	i. Wilfred Ashworth
b. Special Libraries	ii. L.J. Strauss
c. Scientific and Technical Libraries	iii. A. Esdaile
d. Handbook of Special Libraries	iv. C.M. Lewis

Codes:	(a)	(b)	(c)	(d)
(A)	i	iv	iii	ii
(B)	ii	iii	iv	i
(C)	iii	iv	ii	i
(D)	iv	ii	iii	i

450. Match the following:

List – I	List – II
a. CILIP	i. 1972
b. ASLIB	ii. 2002
c. ALA	iii. 1876
d. COMLA	iv. 1924

Codes:	(a)	(b)	(c)	(d)
(A)	ii	iv	iii	i
(B)	iv	iii	ii	i
(C)	iii	iv	i	ii
(D)	ii	iii	iv	i

451. Match the following :

List – I	List – II
a. Books are for use.	i. Adopting to future needs
b. Every reader his/ her book.	ii. Long operating hours
c. Every book its reader.	iii. Freedom of access to information & knowledge
d. Library is a growing organism.	iv. Reference Desk

Codes:	(a)	(b)	(c)	(d)
(A)	ii	iii	iv	i
(B)	iv	i	ii	iii
(C)	i	ii	iii	iv
(D)	iii	iv	i	ii

452. Match the following:

List – I	List – II
a. Information Literacy Competency Standards for Higher Education	i. IFLA
b. Seven Pillars of Information literacy	ii. CAUL
c. Guidelines on Information Literacy for Life Long Learning	iii. ACRL
d. Information Literacy Working Group	iv. SCONUL

Codes:	(a)	(b)	(c)	(d)
(A)	iii	iv	i	ii
(B)	iv	ii	iii	i
(C)	iii	i	ii	iv
(D)	ii	iii	i	iv

453. Match the following implications with the respective laws of library science:

List – I	List – II
a. Location of the library	i. Second Law
b. Obligation of the State	ii. Third Law
c. Publicity	iii. Fifth Law
d. Strength of Library Staff	iv. First Law

Codes:	**(a)**	**(b)**	**(c)**	**(d)**
(A)	iv	ii	i	iii
(B)	iv	i	ii	iii
(C)	ii	i	iii	iv
(D)	ii	iii	iv	i

454. Match the following :

List – I	**List – II**
a. ALA	i. 1909
b. CILIP	ii. 1933
c. SLA	iii. 1876
d. ILA	iv. 2002

Codes:	**(a)**	**(b)**	**(c)**	**(d)**
(A)	iv	ii	iii	i
(B)	iii	iv	i	ii
(C)	i	ii	iv	iii
(D)	iii	iv	ii	i

455. Match the following :

List – I	**List – II**
a. Sayaji Rao Gayakwad	i. Revision of salary scale
b. D.P. Chattopadyay	ii. Library building
c. K.D. Metcalf	iii. Public libraries
d. B.S. Kesavan	iv. Librarian of national library

Codes:	**(a)**	**(b)**	**(c)**	**(d)**
(A)	ii	i	iii	iv
(B)	i	ii	iii	iv
(C)	iii	i	ii	iv
(D)	iv	iii	i	ii

456. **Assertion (A) :** Provision of services outside the library regular service centre or outlet is essential to reach more and more patrons.

Reason (R) : Library extension services help libraries to cover larger population of patrons.

(A) (i) is true but (R) is false.

(B) (i) is false but (R) is true.

(C) Both (i) and (R) are true.

(D) Both (i) and (R) are false.

457. **Assertion (A) :** Open Access Publication Model involves Zero cost.

Reason (R) : Open Access increases the visibility of publication as they are available for users for free.

Codes :

(A) Both (i) and (R) true

(B) (i) is true but (R) is false

(C) (i) is false but (R) is true.

(D) Both (i) and (R) are false.

458. **Assertion (A) :** According to the fifth Law of Library Science, Library is a growing organization.

Reason (R) : All resources of library are supposed to grow.

Codes :

(A) (i) is true, but (R) is false.

(B) (i) is false, but (R) is true.

(C) Both (i) and (R) are false.

(D) Both (i) and (R) are true.

459. **Assertion (A) :** A Library legislation provides proper governance and management.

Reason (R) : It ensures free public library service to all irrespective of caste, creed and sex.

Codes :

(A) Both (i) and (R) are true.

(B) Both (i) and (R) are false.

(C) (i) is true, but (R) is false.

(D) (i) is false, but (R) is true.

460. **Assertion (A) :** Library cooperation is the prime need of the day.

Reason (R) : It is impossible for an individual library to meet all the requirements of its users.

Codes :

(A) Both A and R are true and R is the correct explanation

(B) Both A and R are true and R is not the correct explanation

(C) A is true but R is false

(D) A is false but R is true

461. **Assertion (A) :** A special library serves a specialist clientele.

Reason (R) : The collection of special library is relatively narrow in scope

Codes:

(A) Both A and R are true and R is the correct explanation

(B) A and R are true and R is not the correct explanation

(C) A is true but R is false

(D) A is false but R is true

462. **Assertion (A):** Computerization of Public Libraries in India is slow.

Reason (R): Non-availability of resources

Codes:

(A) (i) is true but (R) is false

(B) (R) is true but (i) is false

(C) Both (i) and (R) are true

(D) Both (i) and (R) are false

463. **Assertion (A) :** Libraries have no scope for the growth and development in future.

Reason (R) : E-resources can be used anywhere anytime.

Codes:

(A) Both (A) and (R) are true

(B) Both (A) and (R) are false

(C) (A) is false but (R) is true

(D) (A) is true but (R) is false

464. **Assertion (A) :** The Product of relative frequency of occurance of a word and its rank is equal to a constant.

Reason (R) : The above statement is known as Bradford's Law of scattering

Codes :

(A) (A) is false but (R) is true

(B) (A) is true but (R) is false

(C) Both (A) and (R) are true

(D) Both (A) and (R) are false

465. **Assertion (A) :** In fifth law, the word used in 'organism' not 'organisation'.

Reason R) : Libraries grow in collection size, human resources, physical facilities and services from time to time.

(A) Both (A) and (R) are true and (R) is the correct explanation of (A).

(B) Both (A) and (R) are true but (R) is not the correct explanation of (A).

(C) (A) is true but (R) is false.

(D) (A) is false but (R) is true.

466. **Assertion (A) :** Majority of academic libraries in India are lagging behind in switching over as technology-oriented service institutions.

Reason (R) : The apex academic bodies and library Associations have not taken the lead role to devise standards and policies.

Codes:

(A) (A) is true, (R) is false.

(B) (A) is false, (R) is true.

(C) Both (A) and (R) is true.

(D) Both (A) and (R) are false.

467. **Assertion (A) :** Library legislation is not a pre-requisite for providing free library service.

Reason (R) : There are states/union territories that are advanced in public library services without library legislation.

Codes :

(A) (A) is true, but (R) is false.

(B) (A) is false, but (R) is true.

(C) Both (A) and (R) are true.

(D) Both (A) and (R) are false.

468. **Assertion (A) :** An electronic library may have both born digital and converted digital documents.

Reason (R) : A document stored in Unicode is same as storing the scanned image of the document.

Codes :

(A) (A) is false, but (R) is true.

(B) (A) is true, but (R) is false.

(C) Both (A) and (R) are true.

(D) Both (A) and (R) are false.

469. **Assertion (A) :** UGC has devised performance indicators for the promotion of faculty and librarians.

Reason (R) : Performancc Λppraisal is an important tool for merit rating.

Codes:

(A) (A) is true, but (R) is false.

(B) (A) is false, but (R) is true.

(C) Both (A) and (R) are true.

(D) Both (A) and (R) are false.

470. **Assertion (A) :** According to National Knowledge Commission, 'the library and information services sector in India has not kept pace with the paradigmatic changes taking place in society'.

Reason (R) : There is no proportionate growth in library resources.

Codes :

(A) Both (A) and (R) are true.

(B) (A) is true, but (R) is false.

(C) Both (A) and (R) are false.

(D) (A) is false, but (R) is true.

471. **Assertion (A) :** Libraries are changing in the wake of emerging ICT environment.

Reason (R) : Libraries are adopting new competencies to operate services in the environment of information super highways.

Codes :

(A) Both (i) and (R) are true.

(B) (i) is true but (R) is false.

(C) (i) is false but (R) is true.

(D) Both (i) and (R) are false.

472. **Assertion (A) :** Provision of services outside the library regular service centre or outlet is essential to reach more and more patrons.

Reason (R) : Library extension services help libraries to cover larger population of patrons.

(A) (i) is true but (R) is false.

(B) (i) is false but (R) is true.

(C) Both (i) and (R) are true.

(D) Both (i) and (R) are false.

473. **Assertion (A) :** Provision of services inside the library helps in reaching out to the large number of users

Reason (R) : Library extension services do not cover the internal users of a library.

Codes :

(A) (A) is true, but (R) is false

(B) (A) is false, but (R) is true

(C) Both (A) and (R) are true

(D) Both (A) and (R) are false

474. **Assertion (A) :** Distance education for LIS courses is gaining ground in India.

Reason (R) : Majority of people prefer it as an alternative channel of education.

Codes :

(A) (A) is true but (R) is false.

(B) (A) is false but (R) is true.

(C) Both (A) and (R) are correct.

(D) Both (A) and (R) are wrong.

475. **Assertion (A) :** LIS profession is not considered at par with medical and legal professions.

Reason (R) : There is no constitutional body for LIS profession like Medical Council of India (MCI) and Bar Council of India (BCI).

Codes :

(A) Both (A) and (R) are true.

(B) Both (A) and (R) are false.

(C) (A) is true but (R) is false.

(D) (A) is false but (R) is true.

476. **Assertion (A) :** Dr. S.R. Ranganathan has been called 'Father of Library and Information Science' in India.

Reason (R) : Library Science education in India was started by Dr. S.R. Ranganathan.

Codes :

(A) (A) is false but (R) is true.

(B) (A) is true but (R) is false.

(C) Both (A) and (R) are true.

(D) Both (A) and (R) are false.

477. **Assertion (A) :** There is need for Library Legislation in all States of India.

Reason (R) : To make Public Library System independent and without political influence.

Codes :

(A) Both (A) and (R) are true.

(B) (A) is true, but (R) is false.

(C) Both (A) and (R) are false.

(D) (A) is false, but (R) is true.

478. **Assertion (A) :** In spite of political, economic and technological support, the growth of Public Library System is lopsided.

Reason (R) : The public libraries are totally depending on cess/tax amounts.

Codes:

(A) Both (A) and (R) are true

(B) Both (A) and (R) are false

(C) (A) is true, but (R) is false

(D) (A) is false, but (R) is true

479. **Assertion (A) :** RFID technology is still not widely installed in Indian Library Environment.

Reason (R) : the standardization, application and innovation are constantly changing.

Codes:

(A) Both (A) & (R) true and (R) is the correct explanation of (A).

(B) Both (A) & (R) are true, but (R) is not the correct explanation of (A).

(C) (A) is true, but (R) is false.

(D) (A) is false, but (R) is true.

480. **Assertion (A) :** All the states in India have enacted library legislation.

Reason (R) : NKC recommends for the enactment of library legislation in all the states.

Codes :

(A) Both (A) and (R) are true.

(B) Both (A) and (R) are false.

(C) (A) is true, but (R) is false.

(D) (A) is false, but (R) is true.

481. **Assertion (A) :** Proliferation of LIS schools in India produced mediocre professionals.

Reason (R) : Curriculum and teaching techniques have not been upgraded at university level.

Codes :

(A) Both (A) and (R) are partially true.

(B) Both (A) and (R) are false.

(C) (A) is true and (R) is false.

(D) (A) is false and (R) is true.

482. **Assertion (A) :** Several Library Science departments in India have shifted to integrated MLIS program.

Reason (R) : MLIS Program (integrated) is a right solution to knowledge explosion in the field.

Codes :

(A) Both (A) and (R) are false.

(B) (A) is true and (R) is false.

(C) Both (A) and (R) are true.

(D) (A) is false and (R) is true.

483. **Assertion (A) :** UGC is financially supporting all academic libraries.

Reason (R) : UGC is primarily responsible for the overall development of libraries of higher education in India.

Codes :

(A) (A) is false and (R) is true.

(B) (A) is true and (P.) is false.

(C) Both (A) and (R) are true.

(D) Both (A) and (R) are false.

484. **Assertion (A) :** Library Associations in India striving hard for the enactment of Library Acts.

Reason (R) : Library Acts help in systematic development of libraries.

Codes :

(A) Both (A) and (R) are true.

(B) Both (A) and (R) are false.

(C) (A) is true, (R) is false.

(D) (A) is false, (R) is true.

485. **Assertion (A) :** IFLA's UBC programme encourages the use and exchange of standardised bibliographic description.

Reason (R) : Use of standard enables to bring uniformity in bibliographic description and interchange of bibliographic data.

Code :

(A) Both (i) and (R) are false

(B) Both (A) and (R) are true

(C) (R) is true but (A) is false

(D) (A) is true but (R) is false

486. **Assertion (A) :** UNESCO championed the cause of public library movement.

Reason (R) : UNESCO's concern for public library movement is reflected in its 'Public Library Manifesto'.

Code :

(A) (A) is true but (R) is false

(B) (A) is false but (R) is true

(C) Both (A) and (R) are false

(D) Both (A) and (R) are true

ANSWERS

1. (B)	2. (B)	3. (C)	4. (D)
5. (A)	6. (B)	7. (D)	8. (B)
9. (B)	10. (A)	11. (D)	12. (B)
13. (D)	14. (D)	15. (B)	16. (A)
17. (B)	18. (A)	19. (C)	20. (B)
21. (C)	22. (B)	23. (B)	24. (C)
25. (B)	26. (D)	27. (D)	28. (C)
29. (A)	30. (C)	31. (C)	32. (B)
33. (B)	34. (D)	35. (C)	36. (D)
37. (C)	38. (C)	39. (A)	40. (C)
41. (A)	42. (A)	43. (C)	44. (B)
45. (B)	46. (A)	47. (D)	48. (C)
49. (B)	50. (A)	51. (D)	52. (B)
53. (D)	54. (C)	55. (B)	56. (B)
57. (B)	58. (D)	59. (D)	60. (B)
61. (B)	62. (B)	63. (C)	64. (D)
65. (A)	66. (D)	67. (B)	68. (A)
69. (B)	70. (B)	71. (B)	72. (D)
73. (D)	74. (B)	75. (D)	76. (C)
77. (B)	78. (C)	79. (A)	80. (C)
81. (D)	82. (D)	83. (C)	84. (A)
85. (C)	86. (C)	87. (B)	88. (B)
89. (C)	90. (C)	91. (B)	92. (C)
93. (B)	94. (B)	95. (A)	96. (A)
97. (A)	98. (A)	99. (C)	100. (D)
101. (B)	102. (B)	103. (D)	104. (C)
105. (C)	106. (D)	107. (C)	108. (C)
109. (A)	110. (D)	111. (D)	112. (C)
113. (A)	114. (C)	115. (C)	116. (B)
117. (A)	118. (A)	119. (A)	120. (B)
121. (B)	122. (B)	123. (B)	124. (B)
125. (D)	126. (A)	127. (D)	128. (C)
129. (D)	130. (C)	131. (A)	132. (D)
133. (A)	134. (A)	135. (D)	136. (A)
137. (C)	138. (A)	139. (A)	140. (A)
141. (B)	142. (A)	143. (C)	144. (B)
145. (A)	146. (A)	147. (B)	148. (A)
149. (A)	150. (B)	151. (D)	152. (C)
153. (D)	154. (B)	155. (C)	156. (A)
157. (A)	158. (D)	159. (C)	160. (A)
161. (A)	162. (C)	163. (B)	164. (D)
165. (D)	166. (A)	167. (A)	168. (B)

169. (C)	170. (D)	171. (B)	172. (A)
173. (A)	174. (C)	175. (C)	176. (C)
177. (D)	178. (B)	179. (B)	180. (A)
181. (C)	182. (A)	183. (B)	184. (B)
185. (C)	186. (D)	187. (A)	188. (A)
189. (D)	190. (C)	191. (D)	192. (D)
193. (D)	194. (D)	195. (C)	196. (A)
197. (B)	198. (B)	199. (B)	200. (A)
201. (D)	202. (A)	203. (A)	204. (D)
205. (C)	206. (D)	207. (A)	208. (C)
209. (B)	210. (B)	211. (A)	212. (B)
213. (A)	214. (B)	215. (B)	216. (D)
217. (D)	218. (A)	219. (A)	220. (C)
221. (D)	222. (D)	223. (D)	224. (B)
225. (D)	226. (C)	227. (D)	228. (D)
229. (C)	230. (D)	231. (B)	232. (D)
233. (B)	234. (D)	235. (D)	236. (B)
237. (D)	238. (C)	239. (D)	240. (C)
241. (D)	242. (C)	243. (D)	244. (B)
245. (D)	246. (D)	247. (D)	248. (C)
249. (B)	250. (C)	251. (C)	252. (D)
253. (C)	254. (C)	255. (D)	256. (D)
257. (C)	258. (D)	259. (D)	260. (C)
261. (B)	262. (B)	263. (A)	264. (B)
265. (C)	266. (D)	267. (A)	268. (C)
269. (B)	270. (D)	271. (B)	272. (D)
273. (C)	274. (B)	275. (B)	276. (A)
277. (B)	278. (A)	279. (B)	280. (C)
281. (C)	282. (A)	283. (B)	284. (A)
285. (C)	286. (A)	287. (B)	288. (C)
289. (B)	290. (C)	291. (A)	292. (B)
293. (D)	294. (C)	295. (D)	296. (C)
297. (C)	298. (B)	299. (B)	300. (B)
301. (C)	302. (B)	303. (B)	304. (C)
305. (C)	306. (B)	307. (A)	308. (B)
309. (A)	310. (C)	311. (B)	312. (D)
313. (B)	314. (D)	315. (D)	316. (B)
317. (D)	318. (C)	319. (D)	320. (A)
321. (A)	322. (C)	323. (A)	324. (B)
325. (A)	326. (B)	327. (B)	328. (A)
329. (C)	330. (B)	331. (A)	332. (B)
333. (B)	334. (D)	335. (B)	336. (D)
337. (A)	338. (A)	339. (C)	340. (C)

341. (A)	342. (D)	343. (A)	344. (A)
345. (B)	346. (C)	347. (B)	348. (B)
349. (C)	350. (D)	351. (C)	352. (B)
353. (C)	354. (B)	355. (C)	356. (B)
357. (C)	358. (A)	359. (B)	360. (A)
361. (A)	362. (C)	363. (D)	364. (C)
365. (B)	366. (A)	367. (A)	368. (C)
369. (A)	370. (A)	371. (D)	372. (B)
373. (A)	374. (B)	375. (A) & C	376. (C)
377. (A)	378. (D)	379. (B)	380. (D)
381. (A)	382. (B)	383. (D)	384. (D)
385. (A)	386. (C)	387. (A)	388. (C)
389. (A)	390. (C)	391. (B)	392. (D)
393. (A)	394. (A)	395. (B)	396. (D)
397. (C)	398. (B)	399. (A)	400. (D)
401. (A)	402. (B)	403. (C)	404. (D)
405. (A)	406. (C)	407. (B)	408. (A)
409. (A)	410. (C)	411. (A)	412. (A)
413. (B)	414. (B)	415. (C)	416. (D)
417. (C)	418. (B)	419. (B)	420. (A)
421. (C)	422. (D)	423. (C)	424. (D)
425. (B)	426. (C)	427. (D)	428. (D)
429. (A)	430. (C)	431. (C)	432. (B)
433. (A)	434. (A)	435. (B)	436. (B)
437. (B)	438. (B)	439. (C)	440. (A)
441. (C)	442. (B)	443. (A)	444. (A)
445. (C)	446. (A)	447. (C)	448. (D)
449. (C)	450. (A)	451. (A)	452. (A)
453. (B)	454. (B)	455. (C)	456. (C)
457. (C)	458. (D)	459. (A)	460. (A)
461. (A)	462. (C)	463. (C)	464. (B)
465. (A)	466. (C)	467. (D)	468. (C)
469. (C)	470. (A)	471. (A)	472. (C)
473. (C)	474. (C)	475. (C)	476. (B)
477. (A)	478. (C)	479. (B)	480. (B)
481. (A)	482. (A)	483. (A)	484. (A)
485. (A)	486. (B)		

3

Library Management

1. ISO 9000 standard denotes the
   (A) consistence confirmance of a product or service to a given set of standard or expectations
   (B) Total customer satisfaction
   (C) Representation of stakeholders issues.
   (D) Detailed list of measuring techniques
2. The central concept of TQM is
   (A) SWAT analysis (B) Johare's window
   (C) ISO-9002 (D) Quality circles
3. Theory X and theory Y is developed by
   (A) Peter Drucker (B) Douglas McGregor
   (C) Abraham Maslow (D) Luther Gullick
4. Who among the following persons is considered as father of modern management ?
   (A) Henry Fayol (B) Henry L. Gantt
   (C) F.W. Taylor (D) Frederick Herzberg
5. System analysis involves
   (A) Analysis and design
   (B) Analysis
   (C) Analysis, evaluation and decision
   (D) Design

6. Laws of Library Science are nothing but
   (A) advices to run libraries
   (B) instructions to library workers
   (C) guidelines to manage different types of libraries
   (D) some philosophical foundations for Library Management and Administration
7. The book entitled "Powershift" is authored by-
   (A) J.D. Bernal (B) D. Solla Price
   (C) Alvin Toffler (D) H.E. Bliss
8. Classical school of management thought was introduced by
   (A) A. Maslow (B) F. W. Taylor
   (C) H. Fayol (D) W. Frederick
9. Who should undertake system analysis study in a university library?
   (A) The Chief Librarian
   (B) The Systems Analyst
   (C) The Librarian & the System Analyst
   (D) The data entry operator
10. Who propagated the demand and supply theory of book
   (A) SR Ranganathan (B) Melvil Dewey
   (C) Adamsmith (D) Mc Colvin
11. In the acronym 'POSDCORB', 'CO' stands for
   (A) Co-ordination (B) Co-operation
   (C) Co-relation (D) Co-existence
12. 'Accession Number' means
   (A) Call Number of a book
   (B) Unique Number given to a book by a library
   (C) Book Number
   (D) Class Number
13. Financial estimation is made on the basis of
   (A) Ledger Method (B) Marginal Cost Method
   (C) Per-Capita Method (D) Cost-based Method
14. What leads to job description
   (A) Job satisfaction (B) Job analysis
   (C) Work Description (D) Job evaluation

15. Arrange the stock maintenance work in a library in proper order

(i) Stock verification (ii) Stock shelving

(iii) Stock Rectification (iv) Reshelving

Codes:

(A) iv, iii, i, ii (B) ii, iv, i, iii

(C) ii, iv, iii, i (D) iv, ii, i, iii

16. Herzberg's "two factor theory" deals with :

(A) Staff recruitment (B) Leadership

(C) Decision Making (D) Motivation

17. The function of shelf list becomes very fuzzy when :

(A) The library also has an author catalogue

(B) The library also has a title catalogue

(C) e-books are added to a catalogue

(D) Library also acquires print serials

18. CPM is an effective :

(A) Method of Knowledge Organization

(B) Project Management Technique

(C) Budgeting Technique

(D) Data Collection Technique

19. Now-a-days what is called to staff of the libraries?

(A) Staffing (B) Human workers

(C) Staff (D) Human resources

20. What is called the process of separating cover from text and removing old threads, tapes and glue etc?

(A) Pulling (B) Binding

(C) Heding (D) Re-winding

21. The title How to Build a Digital Library is jointly authored by Ian Witten and

(A) David Worthington (B) David Rosenthal

(C) David Bainbridge (D) David Hawking

22. A. B. Maslow is related to

(A) Theory X and Theory Y

(B) Hierarchy of human needs

(C) 14 principles

(D) Hygienic factors.

23. Management by Objectives (MBO) is introduced by
    (A) H. W. Wilson (B) S. R. Ranganathan
    (C) F. W. Taylor (D) Peter Drucker.
24. The term 'Exponential growth' refers to
    (A) Linear growth
    (B) Normal mode of distribution
    (C) Geometric Progression
    (D) Arithmetic Progression
25. Theory X and Theory Y relate to
    (A) Planning (B) Motivation
    (C) Innovation (D) None of the above
26. ASK (Approach, Skill, Knowledge) principle is related to
    (A) classification (B) management
    (C) ICT (D) standards.
27. Who coined the term POSDCORB ?
    (A) Henri Fayol (B) Max Weber
    (C) Gulick and Urwick (D) Wilson and Tauber
28. When Peter F. Drucker defined M.B.O. (Management by Objectives) ?
    (A) 1950 (B) 1960
    (C) 1954 (D) 1964
29. Henry Gnat introduced the chart to record what about the staff members?
    (A) Income (B) Progress
    (C) Level (D) Productivity
30. Herzberg's theory deals with
    (A) Staffing (B) Directing
    (C) Motivation (D) Planning
31. "To provide the best books to the maximum readers at the least cost" said by
    (A) Dr. S. R. Ranganathan
    (B) P. N. Kaula
    (C) E.Mayo
    (D) Melvil Dewey

32. Who is the father of Scientific Management
    (A) F.W. Taylor (B) Harold Koontz
    (C) Peter F. Drucker (D) Luther Gulick
33. CPM (Critical Path Method) is developed by
    (A) Dupoint Company (B) Aircraft Corporation
    (C) IIM (D) IBM
34. When Zero Base Budgeting system was first prepared
    (A) 1950 (B) 1960
    (C) 1970 (D) 1980
35. Posting the right person at the right place is called -
    (A) Recruitment (B) Coaching
    (C) Deployment (D) Induction
36. Zero Base Budgeting system was propounded by
    (A) Peter F. Drucker (B) P.N. Kaula
    (C) E.Mayo (D) Pter Phyrr
37. TQM is a system of continuous improvement employing participative management and centered on needs of the-
    (A) Customers (B) Staff
    (C) Organization (D) Government
38. Principle of maximum aggregate benefit is concerned with__
    (A) Growth of library (B) Library use
    (C) Library service (D) Library fee
39. Which of the following takes items of expenditure for libraries as the working data for allocation of funds?
    (A) Method of details (B) Per capita method
    (C) Principle of economy (D) Library budget
40. A budget which mainly covers items of current revenue and expenditure is called __.
    (A) Programme budget (B) Welfare economics
    (C) Current budgeting (D) Capital budgeting
41. Financial support given to libraries are of two types - Recurring and-
    (A) Ad-hoc (B) Endowments
    (C) Annual (D) Non-recurring

42. Scrutiny of financial transactions is called-
(A) Budgeting (B) Programming
(C) Accounting (D) Auditing

43. The library budget of a university is passed by the ?
(A) Senate (B) Executive Council
(C) Academic Council (D) Research Council

44. Which fund can not be used for other purposes in fund accounting ?
(A) Recurring (B) Non-recurring
(C) Restricted (D) Encumbering

45. What are the two parts of the annual report of the library?
(A) Primary and Secondary
(B) Analytical and Systematic
(C) Upper and Lower
(D) Descriptive and Statistical

46. Who is the pioneer of open access system in British libraries?
(A) Nine e.Brown (B) James Duff Brown
(C) John cotton dana (D) S. R. Ranganathan

47. Who started Newyork Charging system?
(A) Peter Drucker (B) Elton Mayo
(C) John Cotton Dana (D) Francis Bacon

48. When did electrically operated book charging system introduced first?
(A) 1926 (B) 1905
(C) 1933 (D) 1932

49. When was Browne charging system started?
(A) 1895 (B) 1896
(C) 1899 (D) 1875

50. How many columns are there in the accession register?
(A) 10 (B) 12
(C) 14 (D) 16

51. When was PERT developed?
(A) 1958 (B) 1968
(C) 1955 (D) 1948

52. Zero based budget is concerned with-
    (A) Present (B) Past
    (C) Future (D) Remote future
53. Which one is the strongest leather material being used in binding ?
    (A) Roan (B) Imitation
    (C) Pig skin (D) Sheep skin
54. Another term of PERT is
    (A) CPM (B) POSDCORB
    (C) MBO (D) HRM
55. PPBS relates to
    (A) Book selection (B) Journal selection
    (C) Budgeting (D) Library records
56. Payments for the books purchased can be made only after
    (A) accessioning
    (B) classification
    (C) Cataloguing
    (D) arrangement in the shelve
57. Who is the father of Classical School
    (A) Lyndall Urwick (B) Gulick
    (C) Cutter (D) Henri Fayol
58. POSDCORB is related to
    (A) Library cataloguing
    (B) Library reference service
    (C) Library administration
    (D) Library automation
59. Who introduced Three card system?
    (A) Krishan Kumar (B) C. K. Sharma
    (C) Cutter (D) S. R. Ranganathan
60. A good library building is an outcome of librarian and-
    (A) Registrar (B) Building Corporation
    (C) Finance Officer (D) Architect
61. Which are the storage areas for the various types of documents kept in a library?

(A) Tasks (B) Racks
(C) Stacks (D) Desks

62. Why staff manual is needed in the libraries?
(A) To present the number of staff
(B) To analyses various posts of the staff.
(C) To acquaint with objectives, duties and responsibilities fo the staff.
(D) To acquaint with salaries of the staff

63. What are the standard size of the Accession Register is
(A) 16" * 12" (B) 16" * 13"
(C) 16" * 11" (D) 16" * 18"

64. Getting books back from the users and releasing the borrower's ticket is known as
(A) charging (B) holding
(C) reserving (D) discharging

65. The Cost data is related to a specific process is known as
(A) Process Costing (B) Need Costing
(C) Job Costing (D) Change Costing

66. All part and pages of a volume are correctly sequenced in the first stage of binding process known as?
(A) sewing (B) guard
(C) pulling (D) collation

67. The three card system introduced by Ranganathan are
(A) KARDEX (B) LINDEX
(C) Ledger Card (D) Classified Index Card

68. While entering the library, the personal belongings of a reader is kept in.
(A) Cloak room (B) Property counter
(C) Gate counter (D) Store room

69. Books misplaced on the shelves by readers are restored. This work is referred to as .
(A) Shelving (B) Stock verification
(C) Shelf rectification (D) Shifting

70. What is the objective of library binding of library material?

(A) Proper organisation (B) accessibility.
(C) durability (D) humidity control

71. Sheets before and after the text of a book are called.
(A) End papers (B) Attach cover
(C) Head bands (D) Gilding

72. Which of the follwing is a process of helping employees in an organization to acquire new skills and competence on a continuing basis?
(A) Total Quality Management
(B) Management Information System
(C) Financial Resources Development
(D) Human Resources Development.

73. A skillful method of providing means mechanism and structural elements to streamline organizational work is known as
(A) Strategic planning (B) Role analysis
(C) Work culture (D) Autonomous planning

74. "A library is a public institution or establishment charged with the care of collection of books, the duty of making them accessible to those who require the use of them and the task of converting every person in its neighborhood into a habitual library goers and reader of books."Quoted by whom?
(A) Dr S R Ranganathan (B) K.N.Raj
(C) C.A.Cutter (D) W.C.Sayers

75. "Special libraries serve a specialist clientele, located within a single establishment or group and all engaged in working towards one common purpose." Who said this
(A) R.Astall (B) UNESCO
(C) J.D.Brown (D) E.C.Richardson

76. Who developed the Contingency Model of leader ?
(A) Fiddler (B) Robert House
(C) Linkert (D) Alexender

77. "It is a library with little or no physical presence of books, periodicals, reading spaceor support staff, but are that disseminate disseminate selective information

directly to distribute library customers, usually electronically". Said by whom?

(A) Kay Gapen (B) Powell
(C) Sherwell (D) H. G. Wells

78. The PERT approach is a device developed to
(A) Better utilize of time in a series of activities
(B) Allow studies to be made between people and machine
(C) Analyse a workflow to facilitate decision-making
(D) Establish quality control

79. The basic theory regarding human motivation is propounded by
(A) Taylor (B) Maslow
(C) Mayo (D) Likert

80. GOC helps libraries in determining
(A) foreign exchange rates
(B) names of foreign agents and vendors
(C) books available in the market
(D) which books to buy

81. An organizational structure is determined by
a. span of control b. hierarchy
c. space and location

Code :
(A) (a) and (b) (B) (b) and (c)
(C) (a) and (c) (D) All the factors

82. When the term performance evaluation was first started ?
(A) 1945 (B) 1950
(C) 1960 (D) 1970

83. The method of budgeting, which is not concerned with what happened previously but is more concerned with the requirements of the future is known as
(A) Line Budget (B) Programme Budget
(C) Formula Budget (D) Zero Based Budget

84. Which record is the hub of the stack in a library ?

(A) Accession register (B) Shelf list register
(C) Book catalogue (D) Staff manual.

85. A. B. Maslow is related to
(A) Theory X and Theory Y
(B) Hierarchy of human needs
(C) 14 principles
(D) Hygienic factors.

86. Who said 'some books are to be tasted, others to be swallowed and some few to be chewed and digested'?
(A) John Milton (B) William Jones
(C) Francis Bacon (D) Benjamin Franklin

87. The book 'Library Administration' was brought out by Ranganathan in
(A) 1925 (B) 1933
(C) 1931 (D) 1935

88. Organizational charts show the structure of an organization in the way
(A) horizontal (B) vertical
(C) horizontal and vertical (D) diagonal.

89. The methods of estimating funds for libraries are propotional method of details and
(A) per member
(B) per capita
(C) total users
(D) total users and estimated non- users.

90. 'Staff manual' is a record which gives information about
(A) periodicals
(B) abstracting
(C) indexing
(D) modifications introduced in classification and cataloguing procedures.

91. The number of principles of management identified by H. Fayol was
(A) sixteen (B) fifteen
(C) fourteen (D) thirteen

92. PERT is a technique for
    (A) collection of data (B) job analysis
    (C) system analysis (D) job description
93. Who developed the Path-Goal theory of leadership ?
    (A) Lincert (B) Robert House
    (C) Fedler (D) Alexender
94. Preparation of library budget without considering previous year's budget is known as
    (A) master budget (B) zero base budget
    (C) cash budget (D) financial budget
95. Authority file is used in
    (A) periodical division
    (B) classification and cataloguing division
    (C) technicaldivision
    (D) referral service division.
96. Cost benefit analysis means
    (A) performance evaluation based on cost
    (B) performance evaluation based on benefit
    (C) performance evaluation based on opening cost
    (D) performance evaluation based on closing cost.
97. For acquisition of 6000 books in a library in a year, Dr. S. R. Ranganathan in his staff formula has recommended
    (A) two professional staff
    (B) three professional staff
    (C) four professional staff
    (D) one professional staff.
98. The description of relation between work and time by using the charts is known as
    (A) organization chart (B) flow chart
    (C) Gantt chart (D) bar chart.
99. What is called the work of a leader ?
    (A) Leadership (B) Librarianship
    (C) Taskship (D) Ship

100. The process of analysing a given job into different distinct items is known as

(A) job chart (B) job analysis

(C) job allotment (D) job enrichment.

101. Span of control refers to

(A) the number of subordinates to be supervised

(B) exercise the strict control over the staff

(C) duration over which the control is to be exercised

(D) the area which is to be controlled.

102. Organization structure is the

(A) blue print of structure of an organization

(B) blue print of structure of management

(C) blue print of structure of co-ordination

(D) blue print of structure of control.

103. The fastest charging system is

(A) Newark system (B) Brown system

(C) ledger system (D) dummy system.

104. Zero base budgeting means

(A) There will be no increase in expenses or income

(B) There will be no budget

(C) The difference between income and expenditure is zero

(D) All proposals for income and expenditure will need to be justified

105. The management approach which holds that the group co-ordination and effective behaviour automatically emerge around a group natural leader is known as

(A) scientific approach (B) spontaneity approach

(C) casual approach (D) modern approach.

106. 'Living with Books' deals with library

(A) book accessioning (B) book cataloguing

(C) book classification (D) book selection.

107. If a new library wants to provide for 10000 books how many catalogue trays should it plan for?

(A) 10 (B) 40

(C) 80 (D) 100.

108. Shelf list cards
   (A) replicate the arrangement of the shelves
   (B) are used in stock verification
   (C) represent each volume on the staff.
   (D) Accession Register
109. Who developed PPBS Technique of budgeting?
   (A) Rand Corporation
   (B) Defence Department of USA
   (C) World Bank
   (D) Internation Monetary Fund.
110. "Remainders" are
   (A) funds left over after purchasing books
   (B) books which are not bought last year
   (C) the space is divided into equal units
   (D) different units are built for different functions.
111. The standard width of a library rack is
   (A) $2^{1/2}$ '
   (B) 3 '
   (C) $3^{1/2}$ '
   (D) 4 '<935 mm=935/25.399=36"=3'>
112. The Brown charging system will not show
   (A) when a particular book is to be returned
   (B) which book had been borrowed earlier by a member
   (C) the number of books over due
   (D) the number of books issued in a subject.
113. Which person in the following is not associated with theories of motivation?
   (A) Maslow (B) Herzberg
   (C) McGregor (D) Hawthorne.
114. The method of budgeting which is not concerned with what happened previously but is more concerned with the requirements of the future, is known as
   (A) Line budget (B) Programme budget
   (C) Formula budget (D) Zero base budget.
115. A library has the following sections: Children's section, Periodical section, Audio-Visual section and Braille

section, which of the following criteria have been used for departmentalisation?

(A) Function and Customer
(B) Customer and Product
(C) Function and Product
(D) Function, Product and Customer.

116. GOC stands for

(A) Government Office Control
(B) General Office Control
(C) Good Offices Committee
(D) Good Office Conduct.

117. If a new library wants to provide for 10,000 books how many double sided standard size racks are needs

(A) 20 (B) 100
(C) 10 (D) 50.

118. Functional element of management is known as

(A) PSODCORB (B) POSDCORB
(C) POSBCORB (D) POSDCROB.

119. "The library will subscribe two journals through an agent". This is a statement of

(A) objective (B) policy
(C) procedure (D) mission.

120. Modular planning of library building means

(A) the library is built in stages
(B) models are built before the final building
(C) the space is divided into equal units
(D) different units are built for different functions.

121. Kardex system is adopted in libraries for

(A) maintenance of news clipping
(B) maintenance of records of periodicals subscription
(C) filling of microforms
(D) cataloguing of books.

122. System approach enriches what to achieve a common goal?

(A) attitude of the staff (B) work environment
(C) financial position (D) management functions.

123. Staffing is concerned with providing and maintaining
   (A) financial resources (B) human resources
   (C) technical resources (D) physical resources.
124. Which function involves analysing the entire activities of an organization into homogeneous types of works and jobs?
   (A) Reporting (B) Organising
   (C) planning (D) Centralisation.
125. "Right book to the right reader at the right time" should be the principle of book selection enunciated by
   (A) Drury (B) Melvil Dewey
   (C) McColvin (D) john Otlet.
126. Acquisition work in a library comprises three distinct functions selection, procurement and
   (A) computerisation (B) accessioning
   (C) issue (D) return.
127. Modern management is characterised by a
   (A) logistic approach
   (B) scientific approach
   (C) hypothetical approach
   (D) psychological approach.
128. "Unity is Strength" is the principle of management advocated by
   (A) Barnard (B) Fayol
   (C) Taylor (D) S. R. Rangathan.
129. Which function improves the planning and control of operations by providing better information for decision making?
   (A) System Analysis
   (B) Operation Management
   (C) Management Information System
   (D) Monitoring Technique.
130. Government documents are generally divided into two categories such as
   (A) published and unpublished
   (B) parliamentary and non-parliamentary

(C) conventional and neo-conventional

(D) primary and secondary.

131. What is the central character in Drury's principle of book selection?

(A) staff (B) reader

(C) library collection (D) building.

132. Book selection committee comes under the category of

(A) Statutory Committee (B) Standing Committee

(C) Adhoc Committee (D) Working Committee.

133. MBO stands for

(A) Management By Objectives

(B) Maintenance By Objectives

(C) Management Based objectives

(D) Managed By Objectives.

134. Conversation rates create problems while buying

(A) foreign periodicals

(B) govt. documents

(C) conference proceedings

(D) reference collection.

135. Micro images printed on a sheet or film is called

(A) microfilm (B) opaque card

(C) microfiche (D) patent.

136. A page chosen and uniformly used in all documents for writing accession number is know as

(A) recto (B) clue page

(C) secret page (D) verso.

137. Which is better than cure?

(A) Preservation (B) Conservation

(C) Reservation (D) Prevention.

138. Newly acquired books are entered in

(A) Stock Register

(B) Log Book Register

(C) Accession Register

(D) Circulation Sheet Register.

139. What percentage of trade discount is usually admissible on books?

(A) 25% (B) 30%
(C) 20% (D) 10%.

140. Requesting a borrower to return the book before its due date is called
(A) holds (B) reserve
(C) recall (D) lending.

141. Procurement of foreign periodicals are done through Direct Subscription and
(A) Personal Correspondence
(B) Government
(C) Embassy
(D) Agency Method

142. Which document shows the decisions taken on practices of the library relating to classification and cataloguing?
(A) Authority File (B) Work Diary
(C) Shelf List (D) Catalogue Cards.

143. Back issues of periodicals and magazines require
(A) leather binding
(B) half leather binding
(C) full leather binding
(D) cloth binding.

144. A user who seeks extension of time for borrowed books is known as
(A) issue (B) reminder
(C) renewal (D) lending.

145. Which Commission recommended 6.5% of the total budget of a university for its library ?
(A) Kothari Commission
(B) Radhakrishnan Commission.
(C) Ranganathan Committee
(D) Sinha Committee

146. Which institution decides conversion rates of foreign currencies and discount applicable to Indian libraries while purchasing books and periodicals?
(A) NIC (B) GILA
(C) ILA (D) GOC.

147. According to ALA standards for class A binding, which board is a medium quality board as well as it is compact and hard wearing?
    (A) grey (B) split
    (C) mill (D) straw.
148. Human Resources Development is a process which aims at improving of the employees of an organization in respect of
    (A) personality (B) skills and competence
    (C) social obligation (D) technological skills.
149. Who can make or manage the institution?
    (A) authority (B) finance
    (C) personnel (D) politics.
150. Which technique allows its employees, individuals or groups to take part in decision making?
    (A) Operation Management
    (B) Personnel Management
    (C) Leadership
    (D) Participative Management.
151. Which approach gives emphasis on customers needs or expectations?
    (A) MIS (B) TQM
    (C) DSS (D) CPM.
152. One of the guiding principles of financial management is
    (A) adequate spending
    (B) irregularity in spending
    (C) rigidity in expenditure
    (D) effective control.
153. Which method takes into account the actual amount of expenditure spent on each item?
    (A) Proportional Method (B) Method of Details
    (C) Percapita Method (D) Programme Method.
154. Which budgeting does not take into account of what happened in the past but places emphasis on the current activities?

(A) Programme budgeting
(B) Performance budgeting
(C) Zero-base budgeting
(D) Centralised budgeting.

155. Systematic maintenance of the income and expenditure flow on records called as
(A) Auditing (B) Accounting
(C) Budgeting (D) Reporting.

156. The process of breaking up a specific job into the various tasks involved is
(A) Job description (B) Job analysis
(C) Job evaluation (D) Job synthesis

157. The main purpose of library accounting is to keep expenditures within the
(A) budget (B) cash book
(C) plan expenditure (D) non-plan expenditure.

158. The process of introducing new entrants into the organization is called
(A) selection (B) induction
(C) deployment (D) orientation.

159. The daily income and expenditure of an institution is entered in
(A) Ledger (B) Cash Book
(C) Bill Register (D) Book of Drawl.

160. Who among the following is considered as the father of modern management
(A) Henry Fayol (B) Henry L.Gantt
(C) Fredrick W. Taylor (D) Fredrick Herzberg

161. If there is a difference in the title of a book as shown on the title page, half title page, spine, the catalogue should render the title
(A) as on title page
(B) as on the title page, but in square brackets
(C) as on the spine
(D) as on the half title page

162. The PERT approach is a device developed to
    (A) better utilize of time in a series of activities
    (B) allow studies to be made between people and machine
    (C) Analyse a workflow to facilitate decision making
    (D) Establish quality control
163. The method of budgeting, which is not concerned with the requirements of the future is known as
    (A) Line Budget (B) Programme Budget
    (C) Formula Budget (D) Zero Based Budget
164. Among the different Boolean operators 'AND' is used
    (A) To widen the search (B) to narrow the search
    (C) to begin the search (D) to end the search
165. Which of the following is not a secondary source of information
    (A) An encyclopedia
    (B) A text book
    (C) A biographical dictionary
    (D) Patents
166. In a library which of the following positions are line positions
    (i) Junior library assistant
    (ii) Subject specialist
    (iii) Deputy Librarian
    (iv) Systems librarians
    Code :
    (A) (i) and (ii) (B) (i) and (iii)
    (C) (i) and (iv) (D) (ii) and (iv)
167. An organisational structure is determined by
    (i) Span of control (ii) Hierarchy
    (iii) Space and location
    Code :
    (A) (i) and (ii) (B) (ii) and (iii)
    (C) (i) and (iii) (D) All the factors
168. The concept of scientific management was introduced by

(A) Henry fayol (B) C.I.Bernard
(C) Peter Drucker (D) F.W.Taylor

169. The library budget prepared without considering the previous years budget is:
(A) Zerobased Budget (B) Performance Budget
(C) Line item Budget (D) Lumpsum Budget

170. On which item, the most of the money of the budget is spent ?
(A) On Books
(B) On Books and Periodicals
(C) On building
(D) On salaries of the staff.

171. Span of control refers to:
(A) The numbers of subordinates to be supervised
(B) Exercise strict control staff
(C) Duration over which the control is to be exercised
(D) The area which is to be controlled

172. Arrange the contributors in management in the proper chronological order:
(i) Peter Drucker (ii) Henry Gantt
(iii) Ishikawa (iv) Juran

Code :
(A) Peter Drucker, Henry Gantt,Juran, Ishikawa
(B) Henry Gantt, Peter Drucker,Juran, Ishikawa
(C) Henry Gantt, Juran, Ishikawa, Peter Drucker
(D) Ishikawa, Henry Gantt, Juran, Peter Drucker

173. "God has chosen me as an instrument, the honour done to me should act as an incentive to the younger generation to devote their lives whole heartedly to library science and service". Whose quotation is this?
(A) B.S.Kesavan (B) Melvil Dewey
(C) S.R.Ranganathan (D) W.C.B.Sayers

174. What are the on-line products and services of information in the libraries and information centres?

(A) Books, periodicals and bibliograpohies etc.
(B) CD-ROM, DVD, Diskettes etc.
(C) LAN, OPACS, INTERNET, E-Mail et.
(D) All of the above.

175. Which one is not the enunciator of formulating principles regarding library building ?
(A) Saules (B) Henry Falkner.
(C) A. Thamson (D) Ralp Shaw.

176. Arrange the following according to the work flow:
(A) Dissemination, Selection, Processing, Acquisition
(B) Selection, Processing, Acquisition, Dissemination
(C) Selection, Acquisition, Processing, Dissemination
(D) Processing, Acquisition, Dissemination, Selection

177. System school of management is based on the contribution of:
(A) Taylor (B) Gilberts
(C) Fayol (D) Urwick

178. "The high purpose of Book Selection is to provide the right reader at the right time". Whose quotation is this?
(A) Francis Drury (B) H.E.Bliss
(C) Melvil Dewey (D) C.A.Cutter

179. Arrange the following management developments chronologically:
(i) Synthesis Period (ii) Scientific Period
(iii) Human Relation (iv) Pre-Scientific Period

Codes:
(A) (iii), (i), (ii), (iv) (B) (iv), (ii), (iii), (i)
(C) (i), (iv), (ii), (iii) (D) (ii), (i), (iv), (iii)

180. Which of the following is not correct?
(A) Maslow's need analysis is useful for understanding motivation of employees.
(B) Theory Z is the contribution of Japanese style of Management.
(C) Money is the most powerful motivating agent.
(D) Mission of an organization is essentially abstract.

181. Opaque paper is a:
   (A) Ultra-white paper (B) Ultra-white thin paper
   (C) Transparent paper (D) Non-Transparent paper
182. 'Best is the enemy of the Good' is said by:
   (A) Drury (B) Urquart
   (C) Foskett (D) Shera
183. TQM was promulgated by
   (A) Deming and Juran (B) Maslow
   (C) Drucker (D) Taylor
184. Cost benefit analysis means
   (A) Value for money
   (B) Performance evaluation based on cost
   (C) Finding out unit cost
   (D) Performance evaluation based on inputs
185. Which design should be applicable to make Library building and furniture ?
   (A) Economic (B) Functional
   (C) Comfortable (D) L-Shaped
186. While planning and designing in library building there should be adequate provision of expansion both horizontally and .
   (A) height (B) vertically
   (C) width (C) length
187. Which is one of the indirect methods of knowing the user's needs?
   (A) Citatioin analysis (B) Interviews
   (C) Field Survey (D) Using Statics
188. Motivating the potential users to use information resources is known as-
   (A) Bibliographic instruction
   (B) User's Profile
   (C) User Education
   (D) User Orientation
189. Which part of new encyclopedia Britannica is useful for ready references?

(A) Macropaedia (B) Propaedia
(C) Micropaedia (D) Premedia

190. The person who provides reference service is called
(A) Chief librarian (B) Grade One Librarian
(C) Deputy Librarian (D) Reference Librarian

191. "To provide the best books to the maximum readers at the least cost" said by?
(A) Dr. S. R. Ranganathan
(B) P. N. Kaula
(C) E.Mayo
(D) Melvil Dewey

192. Who put his good views regarding planning of library building ?
(A) Ranganathan (B) John Perking
(C) P.N. Kaula (D) Adam Smith

193. When the word Quality was originated ?
(A) In 1950s (B) In 1960s
(C) In 1970s (D) In 1975s

194. Depth of the pigeon hole type periodicals display rack is –
(A) 40 cm (B) 20 cm
(C) 50 cm (D) 30 cm

195. Which is the strongest leather being used as one of the binding materials ?
(A) Roan (B) Imitation
(C) Pig skin (D) Sheep skin

196. What is the meaning of the term Quality ?
(A) It means a good service.
(B) It means a good product.
(C) It means a good product or good service.
(D) None of the above.

197. A skillful method of providing means mechanism and structural elements to streamline organizational work is known as?
(A) Strategic planning (B) Role analysis
(C) Work culture (D) Autonomous planning

198. A good library building is an outcome of librarian and?
   (A) Registrar (B) Building Corporation
   (C) Finance Officer (D) Architect
199. Which one of the following is not a the element of planning ?
   (A) Aims (B) Policies
   (C) Activities (D) Results
200. When the tem Quality Management was first started to use in western countries ?
   (A) In 1960s (B) In 1970s
   (C) In 1980s (D) In 1990s
201. What is the main base of the library?
   (A) Catalogue (B) Good collection
   (C) Staff (D) Building of the library.
202. Now-a-days which types of material have been entered in the main stream of collection development in the libraries?
   (A) Print materisl (B) Periodicals
   (C) Pamphlets (D) Non-print materials.
203. What are the norms prescribed by UNESCO for a book as a document in the library?
   (A) A book has at least 49 pages.
   (B) The length of the book should be 22 to 32 cms.
   (C) The thickness should be 15 to 4 cm.
   (D) All of the above
204. Main use of Shelf list is?
   (A) Cataloging (B) Circulation
   (C) Stock Verification (D) Book Selection
205. ISBN stands for?
   (A) Integrated Services Bibliographic Network
   (B) Indian Standard Book Number
   (C) International Standard Book Number
   (D) International Standard for Book and Non- book
206. What is called the service in which books are allowed to circulate among readers ?

(A) Lending (B) Borrowing
(C) Circulation (D) Providing

207. Principle of maximum aggregate benefit is concerned with
(A) Growth of library (B) Library use
(C) Library service (D) Library fee

208. What takes items of expenditure for libraries as the working data for allocation of funds?
(A) Method of details (B) Per capita method
(C) Principle of economy (D) Library budget

209. A budget which mainly covers items of current revenue and expenditure is called?
(A) Programme budget (B) Welfare economics
(C) Current budgeting (D) Capital budgeting

210. The library budget of a university is passed by the?
(A) Senate (B) Executive Council
(C) Academic Council (D) Research Council

211. Which fund can not be used for other purposes in fund accounting?
(A) Recurring (B) Non-recurring
(C) Restricted (D) Encumbering

212. Scrutiny of financial transactions is called?
(A) Budgeting (B) Programming
(C) Accounting (D) Auditing

213. What are the two parts of the annual report of the library?
(A) Primary and Secondary
(B) Analytical and Systematic
(C) Upper and Lower
(D) Descriptive and Statistical

214. Who is the pioneer of open access system in British libraries?
(A) Nine e.Brown (B) James Duff Brown
(C) John cotton dana (D) S. R. Ranganathan

215. What is very essential to build a good collection of document in the library?

(A) Policy (B) Good policy
(C) Collection policy (D) None of these

216. Who started New york Charging system?
(A) Peter Drucker (B) Elton Mayo
(C) John Cotton Dana (D) Francis Bacon

217. When did electrically operated book charging system introduced first?
(A) 1926 (B) 1905
(C) 1933 (D) 1932

218. Dummies are made of which metal in Dumeny system oif circulation ?
(A) Iron (B) Paper
(C) Wood (D) Steel

219. One of the book selection principles states that "the best reading for the largest number at th
(A) maximum (B) medium
(C) least (D) zero

220. Management involves both acquision and application of -
(A) Power (B) Knowledge
(C) Information (D) Organisation

221. Trade discount admissible on books is
(A) 15% (B) 20%
(C) 25% (D) 10%

222. Tower stacks are arranged along the
(A) Walls (B) Racks
(C) Floor (D) Stacks

223. A periodical evaluation of an employee is done through
(A) Job rotation (B) Performance appraisal
(C) Refresher course (D) Work guide

224. Which are documents that contain descriptions of the technical requirements of a product.
(A) Specifications (B) Parents
(C) Standards (D) Reports.

225. Match the following :

List – I	**List – II**
(A) Henry Fayol	(i) Hierarchy Needs
(B) F.W. Taylor	(ii) Theory X and Theory Y
(C) Abraham Maslow	(iii) Classical Theory
(D) Douglas McGregor	(iv) Scientific Management

Codes:	**(a)**	**(b)**	**(c)**	**(d)**
(A)	(iii)	(iv)	(A)	(ii)
(B)	(A)	(ii)	(iii)	(iv)
(C)	(iv)	(iii)	(ii)	(A)
(D)	(A)	(iv)	(iii)	(ii)

226. Match the following:

List-I (Writing materials)	**List-II (Place of origin)**
V. Clay Tablet	a. Algeria/Babylonia
VI. Palm Leaves	b. Egypt
VII. Paper	c. Ninveh
VIII. Papyrus	d. China
	e. India

Codes:

(E) I-c, II-b, III-a, IV-d (F) I-d, II-e, III-a, IV-c

(G) I-c, II-e, III-d, IV-b (H) I-c, II-b, III-a, IV-d

227. Match the following:

List-I	**List-II**
(a) Scientific Management	(i) Esprit de crops
(b) Unity of Command	(ii) Peter Drucker
(c) Management by Objectives	(iii) Factor of Planning
(d) Forecasting	(iv) Efficiency and Waste Prevention

Codes:	**(a)**	**(b)**	**(c)**	**(d)**
(A)	(iv)	(i)	(ii)	(iii)
(B)	(i)	(ii)	(iii)	(iv)
(C)	(ii)	(iii)	(i)	(iv)
(D)	(iii)	(i)	(iv)	(ii)

228. Match the following:

List-I	**List-II**
(a) Pre-Scientific Period	(i) Pre 1927
(b) Scientific Period	(ii) Pre 1880
(c) Human Relations	(iii) 1880-1927
(d) Synthesis	(iv) 1927-1950
	(v) 1950-2007

Codes:	**(a)**	**(b)**	**(c)**	**(d)**
(A)	(i)	(ii)	(iv)	(v)
(B)	(ii)	(iii)	(iv)	(v)
(C)	(iii)	(iv)	(v)	(ii)
(D)	(ii)	(iii)	(v)	(iv)

229. Match the following:

List-I	**List-II**
(a) Blake	(i) Chart technique
(b) Gantt	(ii) Leadership Style
(c) Maslow	(iii)Maturity/Immaturity theory
(d) McGregor	(iv) Motivation Theory
	(v) Theory X and Y

Codes:	**(a)**	**(b)**	**(c)**	**(d)**
(A)	(ii)	(iii)	(v)	(iv)
(B)	(ii)	(i)	(iv)	(v)
(C)	(iii)	(iv)	(ii)	(i)
(D)	(i)	(iv)	(iii)	(ii)

230. Match the following:

List-I	**List-II**
(a) Taylor	(i) Theory of Motivation
(b) Maslow	(ii) X and Y Theory
(c) McGregor	(iii) Scientific Management
(d) Argyris	(iv) Immaturity/Maturity Theory
	(v) Leadership Style

Codes:	**(a)**	**(b)**	**(c)**	**(d)**
(A)	(iii)	(iv)	(ii)	(i)
(B)	(iv)	(i)	(v)	(iii)
(C)	(iii)	(i)	(ii)	(iv)
(D)	(v)	(iv)	(iii)	(i)

231. Match the following:

List-I	List-II
(a) Theory of X & Y	(i) Frederic Taylor
(b) Scientific Management	(ii) Ouchi
(c) Need hierarchy	(iii) A.Maslow
(d) Theory Z	(iv) D.Mcgregor

Codes:	**(a)**	**(b)**	**(c)**	**(d)**
(A)	(iii)	(ii)	(i)	(iv)
(B)	(iv)	(iii)	(ii)	(i)
(C)	(ii)	(i)	(iv)	(iii)
(D)	(iv)	(i)	(iii)	(ii)

232. Match the following:

List-I	List-II
(a) Planning	(i) Delegation of authority
(b) Staffing	(ii) Audit
(c) Control	(iii) Promotion
(d) Organising	(iv) Resource management

Codes:	**(a)**	**(b)**	**(c)**	**(d)**
(A)	(i)	(ii)	(iii)	(iv)
(B)	(ii)	(iv)	(i)	(iii)
(C)	(iii)	(i)	(ii)	(iv)
(D)	(iv)	(iii)	(ii)	(i)

233. Match the following:

List-I	List-II
(a) Theory of Knowledge	(i) Farmington Plan
(b) IS: 1553-1960	(ii) Metadata Format
(c) Resource Sharing	(iii) Library Building
(d) TEI	(iv) Epistomology

Codes:	**(a)**	**(b)**	**(c)**	**(d)**
(A)	(i)	(iii)	(ii)	(iv)
(B)	(ii)	(iii)	(i)	(iv)
(C)	(iv)	(iii)	(i)	(ii)
(D)	(iii)	(i)	(ii)	(iv)

234. Match the following:

List-I	**List-II**
(a) Father of Scientific Management	(i) Henry Fayol
(b) Father of Administration	(ii) Elton Mayo
(c) Father of Human Relations School	(iii) F.Hertzberg
(d) Father of Corporate Strategy	(iv) F.W.Taylor

Codes:	**(a)**	**(b)**	**(c)**	**(d)**
(A)	(iv)	(ii)	(i)	(iii)
(B)	(iv)	(i)	(ii)	(iii)
(C)	(iii)	(iv)	(ii)	(i)
(D)	(ii)	(iii)	(iv)	(i)

235. Match the following:

List-I	**List-II**
(a) Fumigation	(i) Acquisition
(b) Building library collection	(ii) Preservation
(c) Kardex	(iii) Reference service
(d) Information desk	(iv) Registration of Periodicals

Codes:	**(a)**	**(b)**	**(c)**	**(d)**
(A)	(ii)	(iii)	(i)	(iv)
(B)	(ii)	(iii)	(iv)	(i)
(C)	(iii)	(ii)	(i)	(iv)
(D)	(ii)	(i)	(iv)	(iii)

236. Match the following :

A	**B**
(1) S.R. Ranganathan	(a) Zero Based Budgeting
(2) L.R. McColvin	(b) Critical Path Method
(3) Peter Phyor	(c) Three Card System
(4) Du Pont	(d) Demand Theory

Codes :	**1**	**2**	**3**	**4**
(A)	(d)	(c)	(a)	(b)
(B)	(c)	(d)	(a)	(b)
(C)	(a)	(b)	(c)	(d)
(D)	(b)	(c)	(d)	(a)

237. Match the following:

List-I	**List-II**
a) Henry Fayol	i) POSDCORB
b) F. W. Taylor	ii) Theory of Motivation
c) Luther Gullick	iii) Administrative Management Principles
d) Abraham Maslow	iv) Scientific Management

Codes:	**(a)**	**(b)**	**(c)**	**(d)**
(A)	iv	iii	i	ii
(B)	iii	iv	i	ii
(C)	i	ii	iv	iii
(D)	ii	iv	iii	i

238. Match the following:

List-I	**List-II**
a) Shelf List	i) Bibliographic references
b) Display rack	ii) Stock verification
c) New arrivals list	iii) Promote use of Books
d) Style Manual	iv) Technical Section

Codes:	**(a)**	**(b)**	**(c)**	**(d)**
(A)	iii	ii	i	iv
(B)	iv	iii	ii	i
(C)	ii	iii	iv	i
(D)	iv	iii	ii	i

239. Match the following:

List – I	**List – II**
a. Theory of Motivation	i. Factor of planning
b. Unity of Command	ii. Efficiency and waste prevention
c. MBO	iii. Maslow
d. Forecasting	iv. Peter Drucker

Codes:	**(a)**	**(b)**	**(c)**	**(d)**
(A)	i	ii	iii	iv
(B)	iv	i	ii	iii
(C)	ii	iii	iv	i
(D)	iii	i	iv	ii

240. Match the following:

List – I	List – II
(A) Right man at right library	(i) Annual financial statement
(B) Budget	(ii) Deployment
(C) Journal	(iii) TQM
(D) Identifying user's views and expectations	(iv) ISSN

Codes:	(a)	(b)	(c)	(d)
(A)	(iii)	(i)	(ii)	(iv)
(B)	(ii)	(i)	(iv)	(iii)
(C)	(iv)	(ii)	(iii)	(i)
(D)				

241. Match the following:

List – I (Budgetary technique)	List – II (Limitation of budgetary technique)
a. Line	i. Detailed information required
b. Formula	ii. Time consuming
c. PPBS	iii. Do not permit variation
d. Zerobased	iv. Do not suggest future

Codes:	(a)	(b)	(c)	(d)
(A)	ii	i	iv	iii
(B)	iii	ii	i	iv
(C)	iv	iii	i	ii
(D)	i	iv	ii	iii

242. Match the following:

List-I	List-II
(A) Budget prepared using previous period budget	(i) Formula Budget
(B) Budget based on norms and standards	(ii) Zero-based budget
(C) Budget planned integrating number of techniques	(iii) Incremental Budget

(D) Budget prepared identifying current tasks independent of previous year — (iv) Planning programming budgeting system

Codes:	**(a)**	**(b)**	**(c)**	**(d)**
(A)	(iii)	(i)	(iv)	(ii)
(B)	(i)	(iii)	(iv)	(ii)
(C)	(iii)	(ii)	(i)	(iv)
(D)	(i)	(ii)	(iii)	(iv)

243. Match the following:

List-I	**List-II**
(A) Classical School	(i) John cotton Danna
(B) X & Y Theory	(ii) Henry Fayol
(C) Newark Charging System	(iii) Peter Drucker
(D) MBO	(iv) Douglas McGregor

Codes:	**(a)**	**(b)**	**(c)**	**(d)**
(A)	(i)	(iii)	(iv)	(ii)
(B)	(iii)	(iv)	(i)	(ii)
(C)	(ii)	(iv)	(i)	(iii)
(D)	(iii)	(ii)	(iv)	(i)

244. Match the following :

List – I	**List – II**
(A) Scientific Management	(i) Peter Drucker
(B) Theory of Motivation	(ii) Maslow
(C) Theory of X and Y	(iii) F.W. Taylor
(D) MBO	(iv) McGregor

Codes:	**(a)**	**(b)**	**(c)**	**(d)**
(A)	(iii)	(ii)	(iv)	(i)
(B)	(ii)	(i)	(iii)	(iv)
(C)	(iv)	(ii)	(i)	(iii)
(D)	(i)	(iv)	(iii)	(ii)

245. **Assertion (A) :** A Library legislation provides proper governancc and management.

Reason (R) : It ensures free public library service to all irrespective of caste, creed and sex.

Codes :

(A) Both (A) and (R) are true.

(B) Both (A) and (R) are false.

(C) (A) is true, but (R) is false.

(D) (A) is false, but (R) is true.

246. **Assertion (A) :** Systems analysis identifies the flow of work.

Reason (R) : Systems analysis is not necessary if the library is to be automated.

(A) Both (A) and (R) are correct

(B) Both (A) and (R) are false

(C) (A) is true and (R) is false

(D) (R) is true and (A) is false

247. **Assertion (A) :** Collection development should be judiciously done.

Reason (R) : Almost all libraries have limited resources

Codes:

(A) Both (A) and (R) are true and (R) is the correct explanation

(B) Both (A) and (R) are true but (R) is not the right explanation

(C) (A) is true but (R) is false

(D) (A) is false but (R) is true

248. **Assertion (A) :** No single library connect all the demands of the users

Reason (R) : Resource sharing is the need of the day.

Codes :

(A) Both (A) and (R) are false

(B) Both (A) and (R) are correct

(C) (A) is false but (R) is true

(D) (R) is false but (A) is true

249. **Assertion (A) :** Book selection must be done judicioulsy.

Reason (R) : Resource sharing is the need of the day.

Codes :

(A) Both (A) and (R) are True and (R) is the correct explanation of (A).

(B) Both (A) and (R) are false

(C) Both (A) and (R) are True and (R) is not the correct explanation of (A).

(D) (A) is false but (R) is true.

250. **Assertion (A) :** Stock verification is essential in the collection development for libraries.

Reason (R) : It is a time consuming process.

Codes :

(A) (A) is true but (R) is false

(B) Both (A) and (R) are true but (R) is not the right explanation of (A).

(C) Both (Λ) and (R) are true and (R) is the right explanation of (A).

(D) Both (A) and (R) are false

251. **Assertion (A) :** Organization chart can be a useful management tool.

Reason (R) : It gives clear picture of the formal lines of communication within the library.

Codes:

(A) (A) is true but (R) is false

(B) (A) is false but (R) is true

(C) Both (i) and (R) are true

(D) Both (A) and (R) are false

252. **Assertion (A) :** ISO 9000 is a quality framework which calls for documentation to adopt TQM in a Library.

Reason (R) : ISO 9000 is a valuable component of TQM

Codes :

(A) (A) is true and (R) is false

(B) (R) is true but (A) is false

(C) Both (A) and (R) are false

(D) Both (A) and (R) are true

253. **Assertion (A) :** Para-professional staff support the professional staff in Library routines.

Reason (R) : Para-professional staff acquire skill by experience

Codes:

(A) (A) is false but (R) is true

(B) (A) is true but (R) is false

(C) Both (A) and (R) are false

(D) Both (A) and (R) are true

254. **Assertion (A) :** Demand is the only governing factor in Book selection.

Reason (R) : Patrons' requirements govern building library collections.

Codes:

(A) (A) is true and (R) is false

(B) (A) is false and (R) is true

(C) (A) and (R) both are true

(D) (A) and (R) both are false

255. **Assertion (A) :** Deacidification is a measure to preserve documents in any medium.

Reason (R) : Digital preservation needs a different preservation care.

Codes:

(A) (A) is false, but (R) is true

(B) (A) is true but (R) is false

(C) Both (A) and (R) are true

(D) Both (A) and (R) are false

256. **Assertion (A) :** Database is a collection of interrelated data stored together

Reason (R) : It is an organised, integrated collection of data

Codes:

(A) Both (A) and (R) are false

(B) (A) is false but (R) is true

(C) Both (i) and (R) are true

(D) (A) is true but (R) is false

257. **Assertion (A) :** Performance measurement is necessary to support decision making in libraries and information centres.

Reason (R) : Right decision at a right time helps libraries and information centres to achieve goals.

Codes :

(A) Both (A) and (R) are true and (R) is the correct explanation of (A).

(B) Both (A) and (R) are false.

(C) Both (A) and (R) are true, but (R) is not a correct explanation of (A).

(D) (A) is false, but (R) is true.

258. **Assertion (A) :** Informative abstracts provide a concise summary of the subject content of an article.

Reason (R) : These are title-oriented than finding-oriented.

Codes :

(A) Both (A) and (R) are true.

(B) (A) is true but (R) is false.

(C) (A) is false but (R) is true.

(D) Both (A) and (R) are false.

259. **Assertion (A) :** Cost and price are one and the same.

Reason (R) : Cost is what it costs to do something, whereas price is a matter of strategic decision.

Codes:

(A) (A) is false, (R) is true

(B) (A) is true, (R) is false

(C) Both (A) and (R) are true

(D) Both (A) and (R) are false

260. **Assertion (A) :** If changes cannot be adopted to its framework, the organisational equilibrium will be imbalanced.

Reason (R) : Organisation works in an environment which is marked by dynamic characteristics.

Codes :

(A) (A) is true, but (R) is false

(B) (A) is false, but (R) is true

(C) Both (A) and (R) are true

(D) Both (A) and (R) are false

261. **Assertion (A) :** There is need to continuous evaluation and appreciation of value of libraries.

Reason (R) : There is economic pressure on public budget.

Codes :

(A) Both (A) and (R) are true

(B) Both (A) and (R) are false

(C) (A) is true, but (R) is false

(D) (A) is false, but (R) is true

262. **Assertion (A) :** "Name Authority File" should be used in a library.

Reason (R) : All works of an author should be collocated.

Codes :

(A) (A) is true, but (R) is false

(B) Both (A) and (R) true and (R) is the correct explanation of (A).

(C) (A) is false, but (R) is true

(D) Both (A) and (R) are false

263. **Assertion (A) :** Book selection should be done judiciously.

Reason (R) : A library should acquire important and lates book selection tools.

Codes :

(A) (A) is true, but (R) is false

(B) (A) is false, but (R) is true

(C) Both (A) and (R) are true , but (R) is not the correct explanation of (A).

(D) Both (A) and (R) are true and (R) is the correct explanation of (A).

264. **Assertion (A) :** Training methods through brain storming stimulate idea generation.

Reason (R) : Training methods do not provide opportunity to unskilled to become skilled.

Codes :

(A) (A) is false but (R) is true.

(B) Both (A) and (R) are false.

(C) Both (A) and (R) are true.

(D) (A) is true but (R) is false.

265. **Assertion (A) :** The array of classes 11, 12, 13 and the array of classes 31, 32, 33 are said to be collateral arrays

Reason (R) : They are derived from the original universe 'O'.

Codes :

(A) (A) is false, (R) is true.

(B) (A) is true, (R) is false.

(C) Both (A) & (R) are true.

(D) Both (A) & (R) are false.

266. **Assertion (A) :** RDF supports the use and exchange of metadata on the web.

Reason (R) : Bibliographic standards are the means to create and disseminate secondary information.

Codes :

(A) (A) is true, (R) is false.

(B) (A) is false, (R) is true.

(C) Both (A) & (R) are correct.

(D) Both (A) & (R) are false.

267. **Assertion (A) :** Introduction of TQM in libraries is not possible.

Reason (R) : It requires open, cooperative culture and employees responsiveness for customer satisfaction.

Codes :

(A) Both (A) and (R) are true.

(B) (A) is true, but (R) is false.

(C) (A) is false, but (R) is true.

(D) Both (A) and (R) are false.

268. **Assertion (A) :** Qualitative measures must be made quantifiable in order to be convincing.

Reason (R) : Qualitative measures are a necessary complement to quantitative measures.

Codes :

(A) (A) is true, (R) is false.

(B) (A) is false, (R) is true.

(C) Both (A) & (R) are true.

(D) Both (A) & (R) are false.

269. **Assertion (A) :** E-publications have added enormous quantity of literature but adversely affected the quality of literature.

Reason (R) : Present decade has accepted E-publication as channels of fast communication.

Codes :

(A) (A) is true (R) is false.

(B) (A) is false, but (R) is correct.

(C) Both (A) & (R) are false.

(D) Both (A) & (R) are true.

270. **Assertion (A) :** TQM promotes the way in which a library is organised and perform its ICT functions.

Reason (R) : TQM is seen as a hindrance to library and information services.

Codes :

(A) Both (A) and (R) are true.

(B) Both (A) and (R) are false.

(C) (A) is false and (R) is true.

(D) (A) is true and (R) is false.

ANSWERS

1. (A)	2. (D)	3. (B)	4. (A)
5. (C)	6. (D)	7. (C)	8. (C)
9. (C)	10. (D)	11. (A)	12. (B)
13. (C)	14. (B)	15. (C)	16. (D)
17. (C)	18. (B)	19. (D)	20. (A)
21. (C)	22. (D)	23. (D)	24. (D)
25. (B)	26. (B)	27. (C)	28. (C)
29. (D)	30. (C)	31. (D)	32. (A)
33. (A)	34. (C)	35. (A)	36. (D)
37. (A)	38. (A)	39. (D)	40. (D)
41. (D)	42. (D)	43. (B)	44. (A)

45. (D)	46. (B)	47. (C)	48. (D)
49. (A)	50. (C)	51. (A)	52. (C)
53. (D)	54. (A)	55. (C)	56. (A)
57. (D)	58. (C)	59. (D)	60. (D)
61. (C)	62. (C)	63. (B)	64. (D)
65. (C)	66. (D)	67. (D)	68. (B)
69. (C)	70. (B)	71. (A)	72. (D)
73. (A)	74. (A)	75. (A)	76. (C)
77. (B)	78. (A)	79. (B)	80. (A)
81. (A)	82. (B)	83. (D)	84. (B)
85. (D)	86. (C)	87. (D)	88. (C)
89. (B)	90. (D)	91. (C)	92. (C)
93. (B)	94. (B)	95. (C)	96. (A)
97. (D)	98. (C)	99. (A)	100. (B)
101. (A)	102. (A)	103. (B)	104. (D)
105. (B)	106. (D)	107. (A)	108. (A)
109. (A)	110. (B)	111. (B)	112. (B)
113. (D)	114. (D)	115. (D)	116. (C)
117. (A)	118. (B)	119. (C)	120. (C)
121. (B)	122. (D)	123. (B)	124. (B)
125. (A)	126. (B)	127. (B)	128. (B)
129. (C)	130. (A)	131. (B)	132. (D)
133. (A)	134. (A)	135. (A)	136. (D)
137. (D)	138. (C)	139. (D)	140. (C)
141. (D)	142. (A)	143. (B)	144. (C)
145. (B)	146. (D)	147. (A)	148. (B)
149. (A)	150. (D)	151. (B)	152. (D)
153. (A)	154. (C)	155. (C)	156. (A)
157. (A)	158. (D)	159. (B)	160. (C)
161. (A)	162. (A)	163. (D)	164. (A)
165. (D)	166. (B)	167. (A)	168. (D)
169. (A)	170. (D)	171. (A)	172. (B)
173. (C)	174. (D)	175. (D)	176. (C)
177. (D)	178. (A)	179. (B)	180. (B)
181. (D)	182. (B)	183. (A)	184. (B)
185. (D)	186. (B)	187. (D)	188. (D)
189. (B)	190. (D)	191. (D)	192. (B)
193. (C)	194. (D)	195. (D)	196. (C)
197. (A)	198. (D)	199. (D)	200. (C)
201. (B)	202. (D)	203. (D)	204. (C)
205. (C)	206. (C)	207. (C)	208. (D)
209. (D)	210. (B)	211. (C)	212. (D)
213. (D)	214. (B)	215. (C)	216. (C)

217. (D)	218. (C)	219. (C)	220. (B)
221. (D)	222. (A)	223. (B)	224. (A)
225. (A)	226. (B)	227. (A)	228. (B)
229. (B)	230. (C)	231. (D)	232. (D)
233. (C)	234. (B)	235. (D)	236. (B)
237. (B)	238. (C)	239. (D)	240. (B)
241. (C)	242. (A)	243. (C)	244. (A)
245. (A)	246. (C)	247. (B)	248. (B)
249. (C)	250. (C)	251. (C)	252. (A)
253. (D)	254. (C)	255. (A)	256. (C)
257. (A)	258. (B)	259. (A)	260. (C)
261. (A)	262. (B)	263. (C)	264. (D)
265. (B)	266. (C)	267. (C)	268. (C)
269. (D)	270. (D)		

4

Classification

1. An 'Aray' is a set of
   (A) Coordinate classes (B) Subordinate classes
   (C) Main classes (D) Basic classes
2. The symbol (=) equals within parenthesis in UDC is used for
   (A) Language Common Isolate
   (B) Racial and Ethnic Groups
   (C) Common Auxiliaries of Form
   (D) Common Auxiliaries of Time
3. What is the purpose of preparing Analytical entries ?
   (A) Analyse the subject content of a book
   (B) Include subject analysis in descriptive catalogue
   (C) Provide access for part of an item
   (D) Provide access to index
4. What is the latest edition of DDC ?
   (A) 23 (B) 22
   (C) 24 (D) 20
5. Who proposed Postulational approach to library classification ?
   (A) S. R. Ranganathan (B) D. J. Foskett
   (C) Melvil Dewey (D) J. Mills
6. Identify the correct sequence of the classification schemes according to their origin.

(A) UDC, Expansive Classification, DDC, CC
(B) Expansive Classification, UDC, CC, DDC
(C) DDC, CC, Expansive Classification, UDC
(D) DDC, Expansive Classification, UDC, CC

7. What are the two types of bibliographic record formats?.
(A) Internal and External (B) Local and National
(C) Exchange and Mixed (D) Internal and Exchange

8. Which one of the following is "Broad system of ordering"?
(A) Modified classificatory system
(B) Method of acquisition
(C) An information system
(D) Cataloguing principle

9. Mark the "odd one out" :
(A) Sought Link (B) Unsought Link
(C) Key Link (D) False Link

10. Which are classes represent phonix schedule in DDC?
(A) Slightly modified (B) Completely modified
(C) Yet to be modified (D) Discontinued

11. Which of the following organization was responsible for the development of UDC ?
(A) Library of Congress (B) The British Library
(C) UNESCO (D) FID

12. Canon of Characteristics is a part of
(A) Verbal plane (B) Notational plane
(C) Idea plane (D) Structural plane

13. Arrange the following according to the year of their publication
(i) Colon Classification
(ii) Prolegomena to Library Classification
(iii) Five Laws of Library Science
(iv) Classified Catalogue Code

Codes:
(A) (iii), (iv), (i), (ii) (B) (iv), (ii), (i), (iii)
(C) (iii), (i), (iv), (ii) (D) (i), (ii), (iv), (iii)

14. Who did publish the journal entitled "International Classification"?
    (A) University of Texas
    (B) ISKO
    (C) FID
    (D) American Library Association
15. Sector Device is an extension of
    (A) Gap Device (B) Empty Device
    (C) Octave Device (D) Group Notation Device
16. Which of the following is an isolate
    (A) Botany (B) Medicine
    (C) Geography (D) France
17. Following are the works of Paul Otlet
    (i) UDC
    (ii) Traile de Documentation
    (iii) Something about bibliography
    (iv) Something about documentation

    Codes:
    (A) (i) and (iv) are correct
    (B) (iii) and (iv) are correct
    (C) (ii) and (iv) are correct
    (D) (i), (ii) and (iii) are correct
18. First Library Science School in the world was started
    (i) By Melvil Dewey
    (ii) At Colombia University, NY
    (iii) By WC B Sayers
    (iv) At London University, London

    Codes:
    (A) (i) and (ii) are correct
    (B) (i) and (iv) are correct
    (C) (iii) and (ii) are correct
    (D) (iii) and (iv) are correct
19. The achievement of US in 1876 was
    (i) Enunciation of DDC scheme
    (ii) Formation of American Library Association

(iii) Publication of first journal of librarianship

(iv) Publication of DDC

Codes:

(A) (i) and (ii) are correct

(B) (i), (ii) and (iii) are correct

(C) (i), (ii) (iii) and (iv) are correct

(D) Only (i) is correct

20. Which of the following research method is useful in a study of scattering of periodicals.

(i) Citation analysis study

(ii) Webometric study

(iii) Bibliometrics study

(iv) Scientrometic study

Codes:

(A) (i) and (iii) are correct

(B) (iv), (iii) and (i) are correct

(C) (i) is correct

(D) (i) and (ii) are correct

21. Principles of Facet sequence includes

(i) Whole –organ principle

(ii) Principle of osmosis

(iii) Cow-Calf principle

(iv) Principle of Parsimony

Codes:

(A) (i) and (iv) are correct

(B) (i) and (iii) are correct

(C) (ii) and (iv) are correct

(D) (i) and (ii) and (iii) are correct

22. Arrange the following schemes of classification according to the year of their publication.

(i) Expansive classification

(ii) Subject classification

(iii) Bibliograhic classification

(iv) Library of Congress Classification

Codes:

(A) i, iv, ii, iii (B) i, iv, iii, ii

(C) iii, iv, i, ii (D) ii, iii, i, iv

23. Identify the MARC tag that is used for variable fields containing data related to subject access to the document :

(A) 7XX (B) 6XX

(C) 5XX (D) 2XX

24. In the context of the structure, the second component of the MARC record is :

(A) Variable fields (B) Fixed fields

(C) Directory (D) Leader

25. We cannot use the characteristics 'date of first publication' and 'the date of first edition' one after the other to decide a universe of books.

Identify the canon that directs us to this guideline :

(A) Canon of Differentiation

(B) Canon of Concomitance

(C) Canon of Ascertainability

(D) Canon of Permanence

26. Which of the following is not the use of devices in classification schemes ?

(A) To avoid enumeration

(B) To provide autonomy to a classifier

(C) To satisfy the library users

(D) To satisfy the canon of helpful sequence

27. Who looks after DDC ?

(A) UNESCO (B) IFLA

(C) OCLC (D) CILIP

28. Which of the following is the correct evolutionary sequence of classification schemes ?

(A) UDC, BC, EC, DDC, CC

(B) DDC, EC, UDC, CC, BC

(C) DDC, UDC, EC, BC, CC

(D) UDC, EC, DDC, CC, BC

29. The Principle of Later-in-Time is one of the principles of
    (A) Fundamental Categories
    (B) Helpful Sequence
    (C) Facet Sequence
    (D) None of the above
30. Who had referred to notation as a shorthand sign?
    (A) P. N. Kaula (B) H.E. Bliss
    (C) E. C. Richardson (D) E. W. Hulme
31. Who has written the book "Grammar of Classification"?
    (A) W. C. B. Sayers (B) J. D. Brown
    (C) Palmer and Wells (D) S. R. Ranganathan
32. Which of the following is the publisher of Dewey Decimal Classification 23rd edition
    (A) Library of Congress
    (B) Forest Press
    (C) OCLC
    (D) British Standards Institute
33. Arrange the following categories of controlled vocabularies in increasing order of flexibility for postcoordination
    (i) classification schemes
    (ii) ontologies
    (iii) subject heading lists
    (iv) thesauri
    Codes:
    (A) (i), (ii), (iii), (iv) (B) (iv), (iii), (ii), (i)
    (C) (iii), (ii), (i), (iv) (D) (i), (iii), (iv), (ii)
34. From which edition the concept of Phoenix schedule was introduced in DDC?
    (A) DDC 8th ed. (B) DDC 13th ed.
    (C) DDC 16th ed. (D) DDC 19th ed.
35. 'A digit with ordinal value but without semantic value' is known as

(A) an empty digit
(B) an emptying digit
(C) an empty-emptying digit
(D) none of the above

36. In Colon Classification 6th edition, which of the following symbols is used to represent phase relation?
(A) λ (B) &
(C) 0 (D) Δ

37. Principles of Osmosis is concerned with
(A) Stock taking (B) Classification
(C) Reclassification (D) Preservation

38. The Cow-Calf Principle as enunciated by Dr. S. R. Ranganathan is useful to determine
(A) the sequence of isolates in an array
(B) the sequence of isolates in a chain
(C) the facet sequence
(D) none of the above

39. The latest revised ANSI/NISO standard forming the basis of MARC 21 is
(A) Z 39.2—1994 (R 2009)
(B) Z 39.19—2005 (R 2010)
(C) Z 39.84—2005 (R 2010)
(D) Z 39.50—2003 (R 2009)

40. A category-based systematic scheme of hierarchical classification incorporating hierarchical relationships among the terms, control of synonyms, quasi-synonyms and antonyms in extended sense is known as
(A) Thesaurus (B) Thesaurofacet
(C) Classaurus (D) None of the above

41. Ranganathan's modified rules of chain procedure for deriving subject headings of specific subject entry was modified by M M Job, who suggested to include
(A) Space isolate as a sought link term
(B) Time isolate as a sought link term
(C) ACI as a sought link term
(D) None of the above

42. Division into two is called :
    (A) Dichotomy (B) Decachotomy
    (C) Polychotomy (D) Monochotomy

43. The order of significance of "Thing, Material and Action" among various components of a compound subject was expanded by
    (A) J. Kaiser (B) E. J. Coates
    (C) J. R. Sharp (D) J. E. L. Farradane

44. Which principles are corollary to Wallpicture principle?
    (i) Cow-calf principle
    (ii) Principle of later-in-time
    (iii) Whole – organ principle
    (iv) All of the above

    Codes :

    (A) (i) and (ii) are correct
    (B) (ii) and (iii) are correct
    (C) (i) and (iii) are correct
    (D) (i) and (iv) are correct

45. Arrange the following according to their year of origin:
    (i) Broad System of Ordering
    (ii) Classification in Online Systems
    (iii) Automated Keyword Classification
    (iv) Classification Research Group

    Codes :

    (A) (iv), (iii), (i), (ii) (B) (i), (ii), (iv), (iii)
    (C) (iii), (i), (ii), (iv) (D) (ii), (iv), (iii), (ii)

46. "Prevention of Cholera in India" generates following index terms according to modified 'Chain Indexing', arrange them in correct order
    (i) India (ii) Cholera
    (iii) Disease (iv) Treatment
    (v) Medicine

    Codes :

    (A) (iii), (iv), (i), (ii), (v) (B) (ii), (i), (iii), (iv), (v)
    (C) (iv), (iii), (ii), (v), (i) (D) (i), (iii), (iv), (v), (ii)

47. Arrange the following according to their year of first publication :
    (i) Bliss Classification
    (ii) Dewey Decimal Classification
    (iii) Library of Congress Classification
    (iv) Universal Decimal Classification.

    Codes :

    (A) (i), (ii), (iii), (iv) (B) (i), (iii), (ii), (iv)
    (C) (iii), (i), (iv), (ii) (D) (ii), (iv), (i), (iii)

48. 'CODEN' is connected with
    (A) Books (B) Serials
    (C) Reports (D) Gray Literature

49. Association of College and Research Libraries (ACRL) (USA) is a
    (A) Division of American Library Association
    (B) Independent Association for Academic & Research Libraries
    (C) Division of Special Libraries Association (USA)
    (D) Division of IFLA

50. The distinct characteristic(s) of digital objects are
    (A) Physical Medium
    (B) Logical process
    (C) Conceptual recognition and transaction
    (D) All the above

51. "Control, Disease, Malaria, Brain" indicates that it is
    (A) Raw Title (B) Expressive Title
    (C) Kernel Title (D) Transformed Title

52. Arrange the following according to year of publication:
    i. Colon Classification
    ii. Prolegomena to Classification
    iii. Five Laws of Library Science
    iv. Classified Catalogue Code

    Codes :

(A)	iii	iv	i	ii
(B)	iv	ii	i	iii
(C)	iii	i	iv	ii
(D)	i	ii	iv	iii

53. In C.C. the title 'Medical Jurisprudence' can be classified and sharpened with the help of

(A) Subject Device (B) Alphabetical Device

(C) Classic Device (D) Enumerative Device

54. Give the following in sequence according to the year of their first publication:

(i) Bibliographic Classification

(ii) Universal Decimal Classification

(iii) Library of Congress Classification

(iv) Colon Classification

Codes :

(A) ii iii i iv (B) iv ii iii i

(C) i iii ii iv (D) iii ii iv i

55. The process of establishing headings and providing 'Cross references' is called

(A) Access points (B) Headings

(C) Authority control (D) Bibliographic Records

56. The primary difference between knowledge classification and library classification are

(i) Knowledge classification arranges knowledge itself.

(ii) Library classification arranges the expression of knowledge in the form of documents.

(iii) Knowledge classification is the basis of Library Classification.

(iv) Knowledge classification follows system of numbers, called notation.

Codes :

(A) (i) and (ii) are correct

(B) (i) and (iii) are correct

(C) (i), (ii) and (iv) are correct

(D) (i), (ii) and (iii) are correct

57. In which scheme of classification, special auxiliaries denote locally recurrent characteristics?

(A) Dewey Decimal Classification

(B) Universal Decimal Classification

(C) Bibliographic Classification

(D) Colon Classification

58. Which of the following makes a network insecured?
    (A) Encryption
    (B) Network Interface Card (NIC)
    (C) Password Capture
    (D) Static Keys

59. The notation used to increase the capacity of an array are:
    (i) Empty digit (ii) Emptying digit
    (iii) Indicator digit (iv) Speciator
    Codes:
    (A) (i) and (ii) are correct.
    (B) (iii) and (iv) are correct.
    (C) (i), (ii) and (iii) are correct.
    (D) (i), (ii) and (iv) are correct.

60. A cross reference that gives an indexer complete control over the cross references of an index is known as
    (A) see also cross reference
    (B) check also cross reference
    (C) see cross reference
    (D) inverted cross reference

61. Which of the following format represent UK MARC format ?
    (A) Single, unitary format
    (B) Designed to accommodate all types of materials
    (C) Also with some material of specific fields.
    (D) All of the above.

62. The class index entries which are derived from the class number of a document are based upon :
    (A) Unsought links (B) Missing links
    (C) False links (D) Sought links

63. Which of the following does not belong to the set of canons for the characteristics ?
    (A) Canon of Differentiation
    (B) Canon of Ascertainability
    (C) Canon of Currency
    (D) Canon of Relevance

64. Arrange the following in correct classified order as per C.C.

i. A | ii. 2:5
iii. 2a | iv. 234

Codes :

(A) iii, i, iv, ii | (B) i, iii, ii, iv
(C) iii, ii, iv, i | (D) ii, i, iii, iv

65. Arrange the sequence of the following steps followed in classifying a document according to colon classification :

i. Title with standard facet terms
ii. Analyzed title
iii. Kernel title
iv. Transformed title

Codes :

(A) ii, iv, i, iii | (B) i, ii, iii, iv
(C) iii, ii, iv, i | (D) iv, iii, ii, i

66. Tagging in web 2.0 application is called :

(A) Taxonomy | (B) Folksonomy
(C) Syndication | (D) Directory

67. What is Ontology ?

(A) An Indexing Method
(B) Classification of Internet based documents
(C) Cataloguing of Internet based documents
(D) Documentation service

68. What are the various kinds of subject indexing models?

(A) Authority lists based
(B) Pre and Post coordinate.
(C) Keyword based
(D) All of the above..

69. DDC 22nd edition is published by

(A) Forest Press | (B) OCLC
(C) IFLA | (D) UNESCO.

70. Who suggested for Book Order Vigilance Pad (BOVP)?

(A) C. A. Cutter | (B) Melvil Dewey
(C) Michael Gorman | (D) S. R. Ranganathan.

71. The subject of Research Methodology is the outcome of the mode of formation of subject, known as
   (A) Loose Assemblage (B) Fission
   (C) Distillation (D) Cluster.
72. BSO in classification stands for
   (A) Basic Subject of Organisation
   (B) Broad Subject Ordering
   (C) Bibliography of Subject Ordering
   (D) Bibliographic Subject Organisation.
73. Three great achievements in U.S.A. were noticed i.e. enunciation of DDC classification scheme, formation of Amcrican Library Association and the publication of 1 st Journal of the librarianship in the year
   (A) 1857 (B) 1859
   (C) 1876 (D) 1901.
74. Which one is not a Canon (as given by Ranganthan) ?
   (A) Canon of Comprehensiveness
   (B) Canon of Consistence
   (C) Canon of Context
   (D) Canon of Currency
75. Arrange the following subjects in ascending order according to their DDC numbers :
   (i) Horticulture (ii) Public Administration
   (iii) Metaphysics (iv) Botany
   Codes :
   (A) (i), (iv), (iii), (ii) (B) (iii), (ii), (iv), (i)
   (C) (ii), (iii), (i), (iv) (D) (iv), (ii), (i), (iii)
76. What will be the correct sequence of books on the shelves bearing the following class numbers ?
   (i) 2:51 (ii) 232
   (iii) 2;46 (iv) 2'N65
   Codes :
   (A) (i), (ii), (iii), (iv) (B) (ii), (i), (iii), (iv)
   (C) (iv), (i), (iii), (ii) (D) (iii), (iv), (ii), (i)
77. A.Sokteo is called as Dewey of Japan B.Benjamin A Custor was the editor of AARC II

(A) A only Correct (B) B only correct
(C) A&B are correct (D) None is correct

78. Who enunciated the five fundamental categories
(A) Benjamin A. Custer
(B) Paul Otlet
(C) Dr. S. R. Ranganathan
(D) W. C. Sayers

79. Who enunciated the subject Classification
(A) J. D. Brown (B) W. C. Sayers
(C) Benjamin A.Custer (D) Frist DonkerDuyvis

80. How many Auxiliary tables are there in DDC 23rd Edition
(A) 16 (B) 6
(C) 7 (D) 8

81. Colon classification was first published in
(A) 1905 (B) 1931
(C) 1933 (D) 1944

82. Phoenix schedules are part of which classification
(A) CC (B) DDC
(C) UDC (D) LCC

83. In which year DDC 23rd edition was published
(A) 2000 (B) 2011
(C) 2003 (D) 2010

84. The word classification comes from the Latin word
(A) Classis (B) Classes
(C) Clauses (D) Fiction

85. The first edition of DDC published in
(A) 1875 (B) 1876
(C) 1874 (D) 1896

86. The first edition of UDC published in
(A) 1904 (B) 1901
(C) 1905 (D) 1894

87. Who is the publishers of Sear's list of subject headings
(A) Dr. S. R. Ranganathan
(B) Brown

(C) H. W. Wilson
(D) C. A. Cutter

88. The First edition of DDC Consisted of
(A) 144 pages (B) Four volume
(C) 44 pages (D) 124 pages

89. Who is the Editor in Chief of 23rd Edition of DDC
(A) Benjamin A. Custer (B) John P. Comaromi
(C) Winton E. Matthews (D) John S. Mitchell

90. When was the different typological study towards mode of formation of subjects done?
(A) 1950 (B) 1960
(C) 1970 (D) 1975

91. In which edition "Auxiliary table for area" was first introduced?
(A) DDC 14 (B) DDC 15
(C) DDC 16 (D) DDC 17

92. What does LED stands for in CC?
(A) Latest Energy Developments
(B) Latest Effective Decade
(C) Large Energy Distribution
(D) Lowest Effective Decade

93. The Dewey Decimal Classification divides human knowledge into
(A) 10 basic categories.
(B) 100 basic categories.
(C) 1000 basic categories.
(D) 10000 basic categories.

94. Who devised Dewey Decimal Classification (DDC) System?
(A) Melville Dewey (B) Dr. S. R. Ranganathan
(C) Tim Berners-Lee (D) Vint Cerf

95. Call Number of a Book Means
(A) Book Number
(B) Class Number
(C) Both (A) and (B) are true
(D) None of the above

96. Accession Number means
    (A) Call Number of a book
    (B) Unique Number for a book inside a particular library.
    (C) Book Number
    (D) Class number
97. Who is the Editor in Chief of 19th Edition of DDC
    (A) Benjamin A. Custer (B) John P. Comaromi
    (C) Winton E. Matthews (D) John S. Mitchell
98. Who is the Editor in Chief of 20th Edition of DDC
    (A) Benjamin A. Custer (B) John P. Comaromi
    (C) Winton E. Matthews (D) John S. Mitchell
99. Who is the Editor in Chief of 21st Edition of DDC
    (A) Benjamin A. Custer (B) John P. Comaromi
    (C) Winton E. Matthews (D) John S. Mitchell
100. Who is the Editor in Chief of 22nd Edition of DDC
    (A) Benjamin A. Custer (B) John P. Comaromi
    (C) Winton E. Matthews (D) John S. Mitchell
101. Technical section performs mainly two functions namely classification and-
    (A) accessioning (B) bills payment
    (C) cataloguing (D) shelving
102. "It is a library with little or no physical presence of books, periodicals, reading space or support staff, but are that disseminate disseminate selective information directly to distribute library customers, usually electronically". Said by whom?
    (A) Kay Gapen (B) Powell
    (C) Sherwell (D) H. G. Wells
103. In Sears, List of Subject Headings preferred headings are indicated by
    (A) Marking them as preferred headings
    (B) Printing them in bold type
    (C) Underlining them
    (D) Italicising them
104. Paul Otlet used the term 'Documentation' for the first

time in a lecture at the International Congress at Brussels in

(A) 1905 (B) 1920

(C) 1931 (D) 1948

105. The real name of 'Mark Twain' is

(A) Milton

(B) Keats

(C) Samuel Longhorne Clemens

(D) William Wordsworth

106. What is number of chasrecters of fixed field of Record Lcvcl of UK MARC format ?

(A) 20 (B) 22

(C) 24 (D) 26

107. In CC, the principle that helps in the identification of personality category is

(A) Cow-calf principle (B) Whole-organ principle

(C) Neti-neti principle (D) Later-in-time principle

108. A document description is not found in a

(A) Catalogue entry (B) Citation

(C) Bibliographic entry (D) Class number

109. In UDC the inter-relationship between the two subjects is denoted by

(A) Ampersand followed by Roman Smalls

(B) A Colon

(C) Double Colon

(D) Hyphen

110. Which is the oldest classification scheme in the following

(A) UDC (B) DDC

(C) EC (E) CCC

111. Sear's List of Subject Headings (SLSH) is mainly useful for

(A) Small and medium libraries

(B) Special libraries

(C) Academic libraries

(D) College libraries

112. Which table deals with 'Standard Subdivisions' in DDC?
    (A) Table 1 (B) Table 3
    (C) Table 5 (D) Table 7

113. As per CC 'm' refers to
    (A) Anteriorising Common Isolate
    (B) Posteriorizing Common Isolate
    (C) Time Isolate
    (D) Useful Arts

114. The "Principle of Literary Warrant"was propounded by:
    (A) S.R. Ranganathan (B) W. Hulme
    (C) Melvil Dewey (D) Derek De Solla Price

115. Colon Classification (Ed.7) is
    (A) an enumerative scheme
    (B) an almost faceted scheme
    (C) a rigidly faceted scheme
    (D) a freely faceted scheme.

116. Table 3 in DDC I9th ed. stands for
    (A) standard subdivision (B) language divisions
    (C) group of persons (D) literature subdivision.

117. The concept of 'Emptying Digit' facilitates
    (A) hospitality in chain
    (B) interpolation in array
    (C) extrapolation in array
    (D) interpolation in chain.

118. In the class no.22;46:51.44 the digits 46 represent
    (A) personality (B) energy
    (C) matter (D) space.

119. The Index given in the DDC is called
    (A) an analytical index (B) relative index
    (C) subject index (D) co-ordinateindex.

120. Complex subjects are formed by
    (A) Fission (B) Lamination
    (C) Loose Assemblage (D) Distillation.

121. 20th edition of DDC is in
    (A) 1 volumc (B) 2 volumes

(C) 3 volumes (D) 4 volumes.

122. Melvil Dewey was the propounder of
   (A) dichotomy (B) decachotomy
   (C) polychotomy (D) none of these.

123. Library of Congress Classification was devised by
   (A) S. R. Ranganathan (B) C. A. Cutter
   (C) H. E. Bliss (D) a corporate body.

124. DDC is a
   (A) freely faceted schedule
   (B) almost faceted schedule
   (C) rigidly facetedschedule
   (D) phoenix schedule.

125. Bibliographic classification scheme was devised by
   (A) W.C. B. Sayers (B) E. C. Richardson
   (C) F. W. Lancaster (D) H. E. Bliss.

126. In UDC, to combine the facets, the facet indicators used are
   (A) colon
   (B) double colon
   (C) square bracket
   (D) colon, double colon, squarebracket.

127. Soil Science is a subject formed by
   (A) Agglomeration (B) Cluster
   (C) Distillation (D) Fusion

128. An example of distilled primary basic subject kind 1 is
   (A) Management (B) Statistical Calculus
   (C) Cybernetics (D) Welding

129. Peace research is a subject constructed from
   (A) Distillation (B) Cluster
   (C) Fusion (D) Fission

130. The main influencer of Library of Congress Classification (1901) is
   (A) Francis Bacon (B) Thomas Jefferson
   (C) J.C.M.Hanson (D) Melvil Dewey

131. In ACR 2 the indicator symbol for accompanying material is

(A) Plus (B) Hyphen
(C) Slash (D) Semi colon.

132. 'Statistical method' is formed with
(A) loose assemblage mode
(B) cluster mode
(C) distillation mode
(D) fissionmode.

133. 'Tree of Porphyry' is a schematic representation of
(A) decachotomy (B) dichotomy
(C) polychotomy (D) anatomy.

134. Mnemonics means
(A) division (B) subdivision
(C) standard subdivision (D) aid to memory.

135. Enumerative classification means
(A) classification scheme providing class number of necessary facets
(B) classification scheme providing class number of broad subjects
(C) classification scheme providing class number of complex subjects
(D) classification scheme providing readymade class numbers for all subjectsof past, present and anticipatable future.

136. Mode of formation of subject 'oceanography' is
(A) fission (B) fusion
(C) lamination (D) cluster.

137. P-notes are used for revision of
(A) DDC (B) UDC
(C) CC (D) BC.

138. DDC 19th edition is an
(A) freely faceted scheme
(B) rigidly faceted scheme
(C) fully enumeratedscheme
(D) almost enumerative scheme.

139. The Classification Research Group has its headquarters at

(A) India (B) New York
(C) Netherlands (D) London.

140. Principle of Osmosis is concerned with
(A) cataloguing (B) classification
(C) re-classification (D) re-cataloguing.

141. Colon Classification provides schedule for
(A) ACI (B) PCI
(C) NCI (D) FCI.

142. In Colon Classification the class number for a system is devised by
(A) input devices (B) output devices
(C) technical devices (D) chronologicaldevices.

143. The common isolates in UDC are called
(A) main tables (B) sub tables
(C) standard tables (D) auxiliary tables.

144. In the notational system of a classification scheme an 'empty digit' denotes thathas
(A) no real value (B) no semantic value
(C) no syntactical value (D) none of these.

145. In classification, the sequence of two isolate ideas in an array is determined bythe
(A) principle of filiatory sequence
(B) principle of array
(C) principle of chain
(D) principle of facet sequence.

146. Universal Decimal Classification system was tested in the
(A) Hawthorn experiment
(B) IFLA experiment
(C) IASLIC experiment
(D) ASLIB-Cranfield experiment.

147. The fundamental category 'time' is considered as
(A) most concrete element
(B) least concrete element
(C) most abstract element
(D) least abstract element.

148. Wall – picture principle helps in deciding
    (A) isolate sequence
    (B) complex subject sequence
    (C) compound subjectsequence
    (D) facet sequence.
149. The author of 'Prolegomena of Library Classification' is
    (A) W. C. B. Sayers (B) E. C. Richardson
    (C) H. E. Bliss (D) S. R. Ranganathan.
150. In chain procedure Class Index Entry is derived from
    (A) book number (B) call number
    (C) class number (D) index number.
151. According to S. R. Ranganathan's principles and postulates, the sequence ofcomponent ideas in the subject 'the effects of radiation treatment of lungcancer' is
    (A) lung, cancer, treatment, medicine, radiation, effects
    (B) medicine, lung,cancer, treatment, radiation, effects
    (C) lung, cancer, medicine, treatment,radiation, effects
    (D) medicine, treatment, lung, cancer, radiation, effects.
152. The process by which a library can identify 'active' collection for reprocessing is
    (A) principle of later in evolution
    (B) principle of earlier in evolution
    (C) principleofosmosis
    (D) principle of oasis.
153. Not a principles for facet sequence is
    (A) principle of later in evolution
    (B) whole organ principle
    (C) Cow-Calf Principle
    (D) Actand-Action-Actor-Tool Principle
154. Intra facet phase relation is used for representing relationship between

(A) two isolates belonging to the same facet
(B) two isolates belonging to the different facets
(C) three isolates belonging to the same facets
(D) three isolatesbelonging to the different facets.

155. The mode of formation involved in the subject 'Indology' is
(A) fission (B) fusion
(C) distillation (D) cluster.

156. CC 6 is a
(A) rigidly faceted classification scheme
(B) almost faceted classification scheme
(C) enumerative classification scheme
(D) freely faceted classification scheme.

157. According to CC the title 'Psychology for Doctors' is an example of
(A) intra array phase relation
(B) intra facet phase relation
(C) inter subject phaserelation
(D) intra subject phase relation.

158. Subject formed with a basic subject and one or more isolate idea defined as
(A) basic subject (B) complex subject
(C) compound subject (D) none of these.

159. Hospitality in chain can be secured by
(A) mnemonic devices
(B) gap devices
(C) gap and fractional devices
(D) inputdevices.

160. The sign used to indicate all types of phase and facet relation in UDC is
(A) double colon (B) colon
(C) square bracket (D) double inverted comma.

161. The concept of common isolates was formulated by
(A) W. C. B. Sayers (B) C. A. Cutter
(C) S. R. Ranganathan (D) H. E. Bliss.

162. The subject 'Biochemistry' is the result of
    (A) loose assemblage mode of formation
    (B) lamination mode of formation
    (C) fission mode of formation
    (D) fusion mode of formation.

163. 'Biotechnology' is an example of how knowledge grows by
    (A) Fusion (B) Lamination
    (C) Fission (D) Loose Assemblage.

164. In a classification scheme the groups Special Libraries, Medical Libraries,Hospital Libraries represent
    (A) A Facet (B) An Array
    (C) A Chain (D) A Characteristics.

165. Emptying digit device is used in CC to provide for
    (A) Hospitality in Array
    (B) Hospitality in Chain
    (C) Alternative Arrangement
    (D) Flexibility.

166. What is the edition of CC in which the fundamental categories were introduced for the first time?
    (A) 2nd (B) 3rd
    (C) 5th (D) 6th

167. In a classification scheme for persons, the following groups are created on thebasis of age: Infants, Children, Adolescents& Adults. Age represents
    (A) an array (B) a facet
    (C) a chain (D) none of these.

168. Statement 'A': All faceted scheme of classification need not be analytic synthetic.
    Statement B : All analytico-synthetic schemes are facet.
    (A) both statements are correct
    (B) only statement A is correct
    (C) only statementB is correct
    (D) both statements are incorrect.

169. Phase relation may have to be shown at the

(A) subject level (B) facet level
(C) array level (D) all of the above.

170. The topic "statistical methods for the social sciences" is an example of
(A) lamination (B) loose assemblage
(C) fission (D) fusion.

171. A system of terms used to denote the classes or ranked isolates in a scheme for classification is called as
(A) Thesaurus (B) terminology
(C) concepts (D) vocabulary.

172. The terminology of library classification is a/an
(A) interactive terminology
(B) ordinary terminology
(C) intrinsic terminology
(D) basic terminology.

173. Which terms define the basic concepts germane to the very nature ofclassification process?
(A) Normative term (B) Fundamental terms
(C) Associative terms (D) Assumedterms.

174. Classification in Sense 2 is
(A) Division (B) Assortment
(C) Entity (D) Universe.

175. Any property or quantitative measure or quality possessed by or inherent in anentity is defined as
(A) Attribute (B) Characteristic
(C) Universe (D) Class.

176. Detailed Classification required for Micro documents is known as
(A) library classification (B) book classification
(C) broad classification (D) depthclassification.

177. The subject of the document whose extension and intension are equal to thethought content of the document is defined as
(A) specific subject (B) basic subject
(C) broad subject (D) depth subject.

178. A traditional subdivision of an old main class is known as a
    (A) traditional class (B) canonical class
    (C) system main class (D) special mainclass.
179. The process of analysing a complex subject into its constituent phases isknown as a
    (A) Facet Analysis (B) Array Analysis
    (C) Phase Analysis (D) Isolate Analysis.
180. On the basis of common characteristics isolates are grouped in
    (A) sequence (B) array
    (C) category (D) facet.
181. Broader groups in an array are arranged in
    (A) evolutionary sequence
    (B) parallel sequence
    (C) filiatory sequence
    (D) helpfulsequence.
182. The Classification in which all classes and their corresponding symbols arelisted is defined as
    (A) Enumerative Classification
    (B) Faceted Classification
    (C) Freely FacetedClassification
    (D) Rigidly Faceted Classification.
183. The total number of species of digits used in the notational system of CC is
    (A) six (B) ten
    (C) three (D) fourteen.
184. In CC (7^{th}edn.) the digits asterisk, plus, double inverted comma and backwardarrow have
    (A) positive value (B) anteriorising value
    (C) posteriorising value (D) negativevalue.
185. Any number in a notational system is denoted as
    (A) symbol (B) notation
    (C) digit (D) array.
186. Placing closely related subjects in close proximity in a scheme of classification is called

(A) filiatory sequence (B) parallel sequence
(C) collocation (D) helpful sequence.

187. How many stages are in the development of the general theory of libraryclassification?
(A) two (B) three
(C) four (D) seven.

188. Who evolved a Dynamic Theory of Classification?
(A) Hulme and his associates
(B) Richardson and his associates
(C) Brown andhis associates
(D) Ranganathan and his associates.

189. Which Classification Schcmc spring from some definite source?
(A) Subject Classification
(B) International Classification
(C) DecimalClassification
(D) Bibliographic Classification.

190. Who is regarded as the first classificationist to have made a systematicattempt to set down a theory of library classification?
(A) Hulme (B) Brown
(C) Richardson (D) Sayers.

191. Who said that all classifications could be arranged into two groups, i.e.,Mechanical and Physical?
(A) Sayers (B) Hulme
(C) Ranganathan (D) Brown.

192. Which means a subject in a classification scheme is given two alternativeplaces?
(A) Alternative Location (B) Parallel Location
(C) Collocation (D) Literary Warrant.

193. Arranging subjects in the order of decreasing extension in a scheme ofclassification is called
(A) subordination (B) co-extensiveness
(C) coordinate classes (D) division.

194. Ranganathan's Colon Classification is an excellent example of

(A) Enumerative Classification
(B) Facet Classification
(C) Fully FacetedClassification
(D) Freely Faceted Analytico Synthetic Classification.

195. Rider's International Classification is
(A) Faceted Classification
(B) Freely Faceted Classification
(C) EnumerativeClassification
(D) Almost Enumerative Classification.

196. In 1978 FID was published Third Edition of
(A) BC (B) BSO
(C) LC (D) UDC.

197. Which classification systems are detailed classification meant to classify microliterature?
(A) Special Classification
(B) Broad Classification
(C) Book Classification
(D) Bibliographic Classification.

198. In India the Special Schedules for classification have been designed by
(A) DESIDOC (B) INSDOC
(C) DRTC (D) NASSDOC.

199. Universe of Subjects is ever growing and, therefore,
(A) translation is ever growing
(B) documentation is ever growing
(C) libraryscience is ever growing
(D) library service s ever growing.

200. Which mode is assembling together of two or more of a) subjects b) isolateideas?
(A) Lamination (B) Loose Assemblage
(C) Fission (D) Fusion.

201. Area Study, Generalia Person Study and Study of Entity or Phenomena aresome of the examples of
(A) Lamination (B) Fusion
(C) Fission (D) Clustering.

202. Ranganathan's approach to the structuring of subjects is based on
(A) postulational approach
(B) mnemonic approach
(C) theoretical approach
(D) practical approach.

203. Expressive title which is also called
(A) Raw title (B) Full title
(C) Kernel title (D) Analysed title.

204. Isolates such as variance, intensity, wave length, height, weight, volume, etc. are regarded as manifestation of
(A) Personality (B) Matter
(C) Energy (D) Time and Space.

205. Which is the central part of the whole subject, encompassing a range ofrelated ideas?
(A) Space (B) Time
(C) Energy (D) Personality.

206. Which is an aspect of a subject?
(A) Facet (B) Isolate
(C) Category (D) Postulate.

207. Different levels of the same fundamental category within a round of facets in acompound subject should be kept together comes under the Postulate of
(A) level (B) level cluster
(C) concreteness (D) first facet.

208. Subject is formed by a combination of two or more subjects called as
(A) Basic subject (B) Compound subject
(C) Complex subject (D) Specific subject.

209. In the influence phase relation the subject that is influenced is the
(A) first phase by the subject that influences
(B) second phase by the subjectthat influences
(C) primary phase by the subject that influences
(D) secondaryphase by the subject that influences.

210. Statistics for Engineers, and Mathematics for Economics are the examples of
   (A) general phase relation
   (B) influence phase relation
   (C) bias phase relation
   (D) comparison phase relation.
211. In UDC, Common Isolates are called
   (A) auxiliary subdivisions
   (B) common subdivisions
   (C) special subdivisions
   (D) form subdivisions.
212. In CC, Bibliography, Concordance, Tale, Atlas are some of the ACI which areapplicable before
   (A) time facet in the class number
   (B) space facet in the class number
   (C) energyfacet in the class number
   (D) personality facet in the class number.
213. In DDC 19th edition a complete list of Standard Subdivisions appear in volume1 as Table
   (A) 1 (B) 2
   (C) 3 (D) 3A.
214. In UDC the common auxiliaries of form are put in parentheses with aconnecting symbol
   (A) double inverted comma
   (B) ampersand
   (C) nought
   (D) comma.
215. The electronic version of DDC 21 (1996), named
   (A) Computerised Dewey (B) Electronic Dewey
   (C) Dewey on CD (D) Dewey forWindows.
216. The responsibility for the maintenance and updating of UDC lies with
   (A) ALA (B) LA
   (C) IFLA (D) FID.
217. In 1951, S. R. Ranganathan was founded

(A) CRG (B) LRC
(C) FID/CA (D) ISKO.

218. Add to device is one of the synthetic devices in
(A) CC (B) LC
(C) BC (D) DDC.

219. A mark borne by a book that denotes its exact or fixed position on a shelf is called
(A) Interfile (B) Shelf mark
(C) Book mark (D) Class mark.

220. Geopolitics formed by the mode of
(A) fission (B) fusion
(C) cluster (D) loose assemblage.

221. Who was the first grammarian of library classification?
(A) E.C.Richardson (B) W.C.B.Sayers
(C) S.R.Ranganathan (D) C.A.Cutter.

222. Who adopted the 'One Place' theory?
(A) James Duff Brown (B) S.R.Ranganathan
(C) E.W.Hulme (D) F.W.Lancaster.

223. Who wrote 'Principles of Book Classification'?
(A) E.W.Hulme (B) W.C.B.Sayers
(C) S.R.Ranganathan (D) Thomas Childers.

224. Who used first the word 'canon'?
(A) W.C.B.Sayers (B) James Duff Brown
(C) E.W.Hulme (D) C.A.Cutter.

225. Sayer's canon of classification appeared in which year?
(A) 1910 (B) 1915
(C) 1916 (D) 1918.

226. In which year Sayer's 'Introduction to library classification' was published?
(A) 1908 (B) 1911
(C) 1917 (D) 1918.

227. In which year Sayer's 'Manual of Classification' was published?
(A) 1916 (B) 1918
(C) 1925 (D) 1926.

228. Who defined 'A notation is a symbol of marks...things'?
(A) H.E.Bliss (B) S.R.Ranganathan
(C) W.C.B.Sayers (D) C.A.Cutter.

229. Who defined 'A number forming a member of notational system'?
(A) S.R.Ranganathan (B) H.E.Bliss
(C) E.W.Hulme (D) C.A.Cutter.

230. In which year 'Prolegomena to library classification' was published?
(A) 1949 (B) 1948
(C) 1937 (D) 1946.

231. Who wrote the book 'Classification, theoretical and practical'?
(A) E.C.Richardson (B) E.W.Hulme
(C) S.R.Ranganathan (D) W.C.B.Sayers.

232. In which year the book 'Classification, theoretical and practical' was published?
(A) 1901 (B) 1902
(C) 1903 (D) 1904.

233. In which year UDC abridged edition was published?
(A) 1962 (B) 1963
(C) 1961 (D) 1964.

234. In which year UDC International Medium edition (BS1000M) was published?
(A) 1985 (B) 1986
(C) 1987 (D) 1988.

235. Who wrote the book 'Organization of knowledge in library science and thesubject approach to books'?
(A) D.J.Fosket (B) E.W.Hulme
(C) H.E.Bliss (D) E.C.Richardson.

236. Who wrote 'Nayakosa'?
(A) A.C.Foskett (B) H.E.Bliss
(C) D.J.Foskett (D) S.R.Ranganathan.

237. Who wrote the book 'Manual of library classification and self arrangement'?

(A) J.D.Brown (B) E.C.Richardson
(C) E.W.Hulme (D) S.R.Ranganathan.

238. What are the two parts of UDC abridged edition?
(A) main tables and index
(B) main tables and relative index
(C) syntagmatictables and relative index
(D) syntagmatic tables and index.

239. Who wrote the book 'Essentials of library classification'?
(A) S.R.Ranganathan (B) E.W.Hulme
(C) C.A.Cutter (D) A.C.Foskett.

240. In which place and year 1st International study Conference on ClassificatiionResearch held?
(A) Dorking (1957) (B) Elsinore (1964)
(C) Mumbai (1975) (D) Augsberg (1982).

241. How many entries belong to DDC18?
(A) 26141 (B) 26142
(C) 26143 (D) 26144.

242. Who wrote the book 'Manual of Classification for librarians andbibliographers'?
(A) W.C.B.Sayers (B) E.C. Richardson
(C) E.W.Hulme (D) S.R.Ranganathan.

243. Who wrote 'Introduction to cataloguing and classification of books'?
(A) Margaret Mann (B) C.A.Cutter
(C) A.C.Foskett (D) D.J.Foskett.

244. In which year BSO concept took place?
(A) 1969 (B) 1970
(C) 1971 (D) 1972

245. Who is/are the inventor(s) of BSO concept?
(A) UNESCO/ICSU (B) IFLA
(C) ALA (D) LA.

246. In which year BSO 1st edition published by whom?
(A) 1978 (B) 1979
(C) 1980 (D) 1981.

247. In which year BSO manual published?

(A) 1978 (B) 1979
(C) 1980 (D) 1981.

248. Who was the propounder of 'Dichotomy'?
(A) Melvil Dewey (B) Immanuel Kant
(C) A.C.Foskett (D) C.A.Cutter.

249. Who was the propounder of 'Polychotomy'?
(A) C.A.Cutter (B) D.J.Foskett
(C) Tom Childers (D) Derek Austin.

250. In a classification of persons,the groups – infants, children, adolescents and adults are known as
(A) A facet (B) A chain
(C) An array (D) A characteristic

251. One of the main methods of number building using different subject schedule in the DDC is by the
(A) Relative index (B) Table of auxiliaries
(C) Add notes (D) None of the above

252. Identify the pair of names responsible for the origin of UDC
(A) Paul Otlet and DonkerDuyvis
(B) Paul Otlet and Henri La Fontain
(C) S.C.Bradford and Paul Otlet
(D) S.C.Bradford and DonkerDuyvis

253. Among the canons of verbal plane, which canon restrains the use of critical phrases in classification systems
(A) Canon of currency (B) Canon of context
(B) Canon of reticence (D) Canon of relevance

254. In CC, the principle that helps in the identification of personality category is
(A) cow-calf principle (B) whole-organ principle
(C) Net-neti principle (D) later-in-time

255. In DDC Phoenix schedules represent
(A) classes which are slightly modified
(B) classes which are completely changed
(C) classes to be modified in the future
(D) classes not to be modified

256. In UDC, the inter-relationship between two subjects denoted by
   (A) Ampersand followed by Roman smalls
   (B) A colon
   (C) Double colon
   (D) Hyphen
257. An entry that is made for the subject of a chapter in a book is referred to as
   (A) Cross Reference Entry
   (B) Cross Reference Index Entry
   (C) Class Index Entry
   (D) Book Index Entry
258. In Sears List of Subject Headings preferred headings are indicated by
   (A) Making them as preferred heading
   (B) Printing them in bold type
   (C) Underlining them
   (D) Italicising them
259. In which field of discipline, citation indexing was first developed ?
   (A) Science (B) Mathematics
   (C) Social Science (D) Law
260. 'Book Number' helps in:
   (A) Individualising the book within the same class number
   (B) Individualising the book among the books with same authors
   (C) Individualising among the books with same year of publication
   (D) Knowing the subject of the book.
261. The study of Epistomology deals with:
   (I) Modes of formation of subjects
   (II) Classification of knowledge
   (III) Cataloguing of composite books
   (IV) Origin, source and nature of knowledge

In the type of items, there may be more than one answer. Identify the correct combination:

(A) I and II are correct

(B) II and III are correct

(C) I, II and III are correct

(D) II and IV are correct

262. Arrange the following classification schemes according to the year of publication use the code below:

I. Colon Classification (1933)

II. Dewey Decimal Classification (1876)

III. Bibliographic Classification (1935)

IV. Sibject Classification (1905)

Codes:

(A) II, IV, I, III (B) III, II, I, IV

(C) I, IV, III, II (D) IV, II, III, I

263. Which is the correct sequence of the following in the chronological order of publication

(A) 14th edition of DDC, 1st edition of CC, Rider's International Classification, Broad System of Ordering

(B) 1st edition of CC, 14th edition of DDC, Broad System of Ordering, Rider's International Classification

(C) Rider's International Classification, 1st edition of CC, 14th edition of DDC, Broad System of Ordering

(D) 1st edition of CC(1934), Rider's International Classification, 14th edition of DDC (1942), Broad System of Ordering (1978)

264. Select the right sequence of contribution of classificationists in the chronological order

(A) Francis Bacon (17th century), W.T.Harris (1870), Melvil Dewey (1876), J.D.Brown (1905)

(B) W.T.Harris, Francis Bacon, Melvil Dewey, J.D.Brown

(C) Francis Bacon, Melvil Dewey, J.D.Brown, W.T.Harris

(D) Francis Bacon, J.D.Brown, W.T.Harris, Melvil Dewey

265. Arrange the contributors in management in the proper chronological order:

(i) Peter Drucker (ii) Henry Gantt

(iii) Ishikawa (iv) Juran

Codes:

(E) Peter Drucker, Henry Gantt, Juran, Ishikawa

(F) Henry Gantt, Peter DruckerJuran, Ishikawa

(G) Henry Gantt, Juran, Ishikawa, Peter Drucker

(H) Ishikawa, Henry Gantt, Juran, Peter Drucker

266. Arrange the following according to the work flow:

(E) Dissemination, Selection, Processing, Acquisition

(F) Selection, Processing, Acquisition, Dissemination

(G) Selection, Acquisition, Processing, Dissemination

(H) Processing, Acquisition, Dissemination, Selection

267. Arrange the following according to the preferred order of sources for information

(i) Colophon (ii) Outside the issue

(iii) Title Page (iv) Preface

Codes:

(A) (i)(ii)(iv)(iii) (B) (ii)(iii)(iv)(i)

(C) (iii)(i)(iv)(ii) (D) (i)(iii)(iv)(ii)

268. Arrange the following classification schemes in the order of year of origin

(A) UDC, Expansive classification, DDC, CC

(B) Expansive classification, UDC, CC, DDC

(C) DDC, CC, Expansive classification, UDC

(D) DDC, Expansive classification, UDC, CC

269. The provision of phase relations in DDC was made available from

(A) 14th edition (B) 2nd edition

(C) 7th edition (D) 11th edition

270. Arrange the following schemes of classification according to their year of origin:

(i) Colon Classification

(ii) Expansive Classification

(iii) Universal Decimal Classification

(iv) Dewey Decimal Classification

Codes:

(A) (ii)(iii)(iv)(i) (B) (iii)(iv)(i)(ii)

(C) (iv)(ii)(iii)(i) (D) (i)(ii)(iv)(iii)

271. Arrange the following schemes of classification according to their year of publication :

(i) CC (ii) DDC

(iii) LC (iv) UDC

Codes :

(A) (ii), (i), (iii), (iv) (B) (ii), (iii), (iv), (i)

(C) (i), (ii), (iv), (iii) (D) (iv), (iii), (ii), (i)

272. The process of supplying the relevant documents on a specific topic to the user is known as .

(A) Bibliographic Service.

(B) Current Awareness service

(C) Document Delivery Service

(D) Reprographic serive

273. How many Auxiliary tables are there in DDC 23rd Edition

(A) 16 (B) 6

(C) 7 (D) 8

274. Who said search strategy is the mirror in the dark ?

(A) Brown (B) Katz

(C) Calvin Moores (D) Ranganathan

275. The word classification comes from the Latin word

(A) Classis (B) Classes

(C) Clauses (D) Fiction

276. Which is one of the records of circulation section?

(A) Accession Register (B) Day book

(C) Catalogue Card (D) AACR-2 (R)

277. In which year DDC 23rd edition was published?

(A) 2000 (B) 2011

(C) 2003 (D) 2010

278. What is called the process of searching proper answer of an information or a question ?

(A) Data Part (B) File
(C) Model (D) Compiler

279. Handbook on International Standards governing international transfer (1977) was brought?
(A) ISO (B) RSI
(C) FID (D) UNO

280. When was the different typological study towards mode of formation of subjects done?
(A) 1950 (B) 1960
(C) 1970 (D) 1975

281. In which edition "Auxiliary table for area" was first introduced?
(A) DDC 14 (B) DDC 15
(C) DDC 16 (D) DDC 17

282. Who enunciated the subject Classification?
(A) J. D. Brown (B) W. C. Sayers
(C) Benjamin A.Custer (D) Frist DonkerDuyvis

283. Colon classification was first published in?
(A) 1905 (B) 1931
(C) 1933 (D) 1944

284. Phoenix schedules are part of which classification?
(A) CC (B) DDC
(C) UDC (D) LCC

285. Desirableness of personal contact between reader and library material is stressed by
(A) H.P.Luhn (B) Derek Austin
(C) Samuel H.Green (D) S.C.Bradford

286. Arrange the following books in order of their publication:
(i) Classified Catalogue Code (1934)
(ii) Prolegomena to Library Classification (1937)
(iii) Five Laws of Library Science (1931)
(iv) Colon Classification (1933)

Codes:
(A) (i)(iv)(iii)(ii) (B) (iii)(ii)(iv)(i)
(C) (iii)(iv)(i)(ii) (D) (iv)(i)(ii)(iii)

287. **Assertion (A) :** Loose Assemblage is the process of linking together different classes.

Reason (R) : This mode was formerly known as subject bundle.

(A) (A) is false but (R) is true.

(B) (A) is true but (R) is false.

(C) Both (A) and (R) are true.

(D) Both (A) and (R) are false.

288. **Asertion (A) :** Arrangement of documents by subject will satisfy more users.

Reason (R) : Many users search for documents by title.

Codes :

(A) Both A and R are true and R is the correct explanation

(B) Both A and R are true and R is not the correct explanation

(C) A is true but R is false

(D) A is false but R is true

289. **Assertion (A) :** Classification as a tool for organisation of knowledge will continue to persist

Reason (R) : In the age of e-documents classification is redundant.

Codes:

(A) Both (A) and (R) are true

(B) (A) is correct and (R) is false

(C) (R) is correct and (A) is false

(D) Both (A) and (R) are false

290. **Assertion (A) :** Dewey Decmal Classification is popularly used in libraries with large collections.

Reason (R) : It is being regularly updated.

Codes:

(A) (A) is True but (R) is False

(B) (A) is False but (R) is True

(C) Both (A) and (R) are False

(D) Both (A) and (R) are True

291. **Assertion (A) :** Metadata hold much promise for information retrieval and access in the digital age.

Reason (R) : Metadata can save a number of function inclusing description, resource discovery and management of resource..

Code:

(A) (A) is true and (R) is false

(B) (R) is true and (A) is false

(C) Both (A) and (R) are true

(D) Both (A) and (R) are false

292. **Assertion (A):** Any change in the environment of the subject can not affect the state of the subject

Reason (R): A subject can be viewed as a system consisting of a set of interacting component ideas.

Code:

(A) (A) is true and (R) is false

(B) (R) is true and (A) is false

(C) Both (A) and (R) are true

(D) Both (A) and (R) are false

293. **Assertion (A) :** Classification and indexing have always been of central intellectual interest in IR

Reason (R) : Conceptual analysis of the content of the queries and documents are essential input to an IR system.

Code:

(A) (A) is true and (R) is false

(B) (R) is true and (A) is false

(C) Both (A) and (R) are true

(D) (A) and (R) both are partially true

294. **Assertion (A) :** Dewey Decimal is an enumerative scheme of classification.

Reason (R) : The scheme has developed several devices and is no more an enumerative scheme of classification.

Codes :

(A) (A) is true, but (R) is false.

(B) (A) is not true, but (R) is true.

(C) Both (A) and (R) are true.

(D) Both (A) and (R) are false.

295. **Assertion (A) :** Classification plays a significant role in online retrieval.

Reason (R) : Classification played an important role in manual system.

Codes :

(A) (A) is true, but (R) is false

(B) Both (A) and (R) are false

(C) Both (A) and (R) are true

(D) (A) is false, but (R) is true

296. **Assertion (A) :** The array of classes 11, 12, 13 and the array of classes 31, 32, 33 are said to be collateral arrays.

Reason (R) : They are derived from the original universe 'O'.

Codes :

(A) (A) is false, (R) is true.

(B) (A) is true, (R) is false.

(C) Both (A) & (R) are true.

(D) Both (A) & (R) are false.

297. **Assertion (A) :** Library Science profession in India enjoys the status at par with medical, legal and management professions.

Reason (R) : S.R. Ranganathan's contributions and teachings for Indian librarianship secured a status to the profession.

Codes:

(A) (A) is true, but (R) is false.

(B) (A) is false, but (R) is true.

(C) Both (A) and (R) are true.

(D) Both (A) and (R) are false.

298. **Assertion (A) :** In conducting research, Social Sciences are not considered at par with natural sciences.

Reason (R) : Research in Social Sciences can't be performed so rigorously as can be in Natural Sciences.

Codes:

(A) Both (A) and (R) are true.

(B) Both (A) and (R) are false.

(C) (A) is true, but (R) is false.

(D) (A) is false, but (R) is true.

299. **Assertion (A) :** It would be logical to replace catalogue with metadata.

Reason (R) : Metadata is useful for organising and managing information resources.

Codes:

(A) (A) is false and (R) is true.

(B) (A) and (R) are true.

(C) (A) is true and (R) is false.

(D) (A) and (R) are false.

300. **Assertion (A):** The use of the symbol 'double colon' (: :) in UDC allows fixed order of component numbers in a compound subject.

Reason (R) : The fixed order facilitates easy access in computer based information retrieval.

Codes:

(A) (A) is true and (R) is false.

(B) (A) is false and (R) is true.

(C) Both (A) and (R) are true.

(D) Both (A) and (R) are false.

301. **Assertion (A) :** Colon classification is popular in online catalogues.

Reason (R) : Traditional classification systems are used in online searching advantageously.

Codes :

(A) (A) is true, but (R) is false.

(B) Both (A) & (R) true, but (R) is not the correct explanation of (A).

(C) (A) is false, but (R) is true.

(D) Both (A) & (R) are true.

302. **Assertion (A) :** Gap device is a nonscientific solution to the problem of growing universe.

Reason (R) : A classificationist cannot forcast the areas/subjects wherein some new ones may emerge.

Codes:

(A) (A) and (R) is false.

(B) (A) is true and (R) is false.

(C) (A) is false and (R) is true.

(D) (A) and (R) are false.

303. **Assertion (A) :** Colon classification is the most successful classification schemes in India.

Reason (R) : The most important factor behind the success of any classification scheme is the revision and publication of different editions at regular intervals.

Codes :

(A) Both (A) and (R) are true.

(B) (A) is true but (R) is false.

(C) (A) is false but (R) is true.

(D) Both (A) and (R) are false.

304. **Assertion (A) :** Proliferation of LIS schools in India produced mediocre professionals.

Reason (R) : Curriculum and teaching techniques have not been upgraded at university level.

Codes :

(A) Both (A) and (R) are partially true.

(B) Both (A) and (R) are false.

(C) (A) is true and (R) is false.

(D) (A) is false and (R) is true.

305. **Assertion (A) :** Several Library Science departments in India have shifted to integrated MLIS program.

Reason (R) : MLIS Program (integrated) is a right solution to knowledge explosion in the field.

Codes :

(A) Both (A) and (R) are false.

(B) (A) is true and (R) is false.

(C) Both (A) and (R) are true.

(D) (A) is false and (R) is true.

306. **Assertion (A) :** UGC is financially supporting all academic libraries.

Reason (R) : UGC is primarily responsible for the overall development of libraries of higher education in India.

Codes :

(A) (A) is false and (R) is true.

(B) (A) is true and (R) is false.

(C) Both (A) and (R) are true.

(D) Both (A) and (R) are false.

307. **Assertion (A) :** The entire scholarly publishing system is in danger of eroding due to increasing influence of predatory publishing.

Reason (R) : Many prey on Junior researchers and graduate students with personalized messages praising their earlier work and inviting them to submit a new manuscript.

Codes :

(A) (A) is true but (R) is false.

(B) (A) is false but (R) is true.

(C) Both (A) and (R) are false.

(D) Both (A) and (R) are true.

308. **Assertion (A) :** Metrics based evaluation is not suitable for assessing research performance of individual.

Reason (R) : Construction of citation profiles depend upon the databases used.

Codes :

(A) Both (A) and (R) are true.

(B) Both (A) and (R) are false.

(C) (A) is true, but (R) is false.

(D) (A) is false, but (R) is true.

309. **Assertion (A) :** Effective methods of communicating in H.R. Management of libraries still remains elusive.

Reason (R) : The management do not have the needed direction of approach, precision of thoughts and their expression and empathy.

Codes :

(A) (A) is true, (R) is false.

(B) Both (A) and (R) are false.

(C) (A) is true, (R) is partially true.

(D) (A) is false, (R) is true.

310. **Assertion (A) :** UDC is used in subject gateways for resource discovery with high recall.

Reason (R) : In online environment, a faceted scheme has a distinct advantage over an enumerative one.

Codes :

(A) (A) is true but (R) is false.

(B) (A) is true, (R) is partially true.

(C) (A) is false, (R) is true.

(D) (A) is partially true, (R) is true.

311. **Assertion (A) :** MARC should never be used outside the context of the cataloguing rules.

Reason (R) : MARC is simply a coding scheme for entering bibliographic information into computer records.

Codes :

(A) Both (A) and (R) are true.

(B) (A) is true but (R) is false.

(C) (A) is false but (R) is true.

(D) Both (A) and (R) are false.

312. **Assertion (A) :** Library Associations in India striving hard for the enactment of Library Acts.

Reason (R) : Library Acts help in systematic development of libraries.

Codes :

(A) Both (A) and (R) are true.

(B) Both (A) and (R) are false.

(C) (A) is true, (R) is false.

(D) (A) is false, (R) is true.

313. **Assertion (A) :** It is a time to separate the copyright issues for scholarly works from entertainment works.

Reason (R) : The scholarly works are public funded fact based, collaborative and intellectual heritage of the institution.

Codes :

(A) (A) is false and (R) is true.

(B) Both (A) and (R) are true but (R) is not the correct explanation of (A).

(C) Both (A) and (R) are false.

(D) (A) is true but (R) is false.

314. **Assertion (A) :** With quick and comprehensive availability of informative through internet resources, need for reference service with a human touch is decreasing.

Reason (R) : Internet resources can satisfy all types of information needs of information seekers.

Codes :

(A) (A) is true and (R) is false.

(B) Both (A) and (R) are false.

(C) (A) is false and (R) is true.

(D) (A) and (R) are true.

315. **Assertion (A) :** Scholar frequency to visit academic libraries has decreased tremendously over the period of last two decades.www.netugc.in

Reason (R) : E-scholarly resources are easily accessible to cvcryonc from anywhere anytime.

Codes :

(A) Both (A) and (R) are true.

(B) Both (A) and (R) are false.

(C) (A) is true, but (R) is false.

(D) (A) is false, but (R) is true.

316. **Assertion (A) :** H-index lacks sensitivity to performance changes.

Reason (R) : It can never decrease and is insensitive to number of citations received.

Codes :

(A) Both (A) and (R) are false.

(B) Both (A) and (R) are true.

(C) (A) is true but (R) is false.

(D) (A) is false, but (R) is true.

317. **Assertion (A) :** Z 39.50 standard protocol enables communication among networked computers through a single search interface.

Reason (R) : Z 39.50 application in library consortia environment can enhance resource sharing.

Codes :

(A) Both (A) and (R) are true.

(B) Both (A) and (R) are false.

(C) (A) is true and (R) is false.

(D) (A) is false and (R) is true.

318. **Assertion (A) :** The principle of canonical sequence states when subjects in a array of subjects are traditionally referred to in a specific sequence, it

Reasons (R) : In classification scheme, the principle of canonical sequence is mainly followed to arrange the array of subject.

Codes:

(A) Both (A) and (R) are true

(B) (A) is false, but (R) is true

(C) (A) is true, but (R) is false.

(D) Both (A) and (R) are false

319. **Assertion (A) :** Colan classification is an enumerative classification scheme.

Reason (R) : Colan classification has adopted analytico-synthetic approach for the construction of class number

Codes :

(A) (A) is false, but (R) is true.

(B) (A) is true, but (R) is false.

(C) Both (A) and (R) are true.

(D) Both (A) and (R) are false.

320. **Assertion (A) :** The objective of "Cross Ref" is to improve access to published scholarly works through collaborative technologies.

Reason (R) : "Cross Ref" is a non-profit membership association founded and directed by publishers.

Codes :

(A) Both (A) and (R) are true.

(B) Both (A) and (R) are true, but (R) is not the correct explanation.

(C) (A) is true, but (R) is false.

(D) (A) is false, but (R) is true.

321. **Assertion (A) :** All classification schemes adopt 'phase relations'.

Reason (R) : Subject formation by loose assemblage leads to complex subjects and isolates.

Codes:

(A) (A) is true, but (R) is false.

(B) Both (A) and (R) are true.

(C) Both (A) and (R) are false.

(D) (A) is false, but (R) is true.

322. **Assertion (A) :** In Colon Classification, 2 represents mother country and 44 represents India. A given library in India can use 2 or 44 for India.

Reason (R) : The above is in conformity with Canon of Homonym.

Codes :

(A) Both (A) and (R) are true and(R) is the correct explanation of (A).

(B) Both (A) and (R) are true but(R) is not the correct explanation of (A).

(C) (A) is true, but (R) is false.

(D) (A) is false, but (R) is true.

323. **Assertion (A) :** To increase the specificity, we need to accept long notations.

Reason (R) : An important quality of notation is brevity.

Codes :

(A) Both (A) and (R) are true and (R) is the correct explanation of (A).

(B) (A) is false, but (R) is true.

(C) (A) is true, but (R) is false.

(D) Both (A) and (R) are true, but (R) is not the correct explanation of (A).

324. **Assertion (A) :** DDC is an enumerative classification scheme.

Reason (R) : DDC has adapted analytic-synthetic approach for the enumeration of classes.

(A) (A) is true, but (R) is false

(B) (A) is false, but (R) is true

(C) Both (A) and (R) are true

(D) Both (A) and (R) are false

325. **Assertion (A) :** In library classification, an empty digit helps in interpolation between two consecutive ordinal numbers.

Reason (R) : An empty digit is a digit with ordinal value but no semantic value.

Codes :

(A) Both (A) and (R) are true and(R) is the correct explanation of (A).

(B) Both (A) and (R) are true, but(R) is not a correct explanation of (A).

(C) (A) is true, but (R) is false.

(D) (A) is false, but (R) is true.

326. Match the following:

List-I	**List-II**
(a) Management Service	(i) Fission
(b) Biophysics	(ii) Distillation
(c) Gandhiana	(iii) Agglomeration
(d) Life Sciences	(iv) Clustering
	(v) Fusion

Codes:	**(a)**	**(b)**	**(c)**	**(d)**
(A)	(ii)	(v)	(iv)	(iii)
(B)	(ii)	(iv)	(i)	(iii)
(C)	(iv)	(v)	(ii)	(i)
(D)	(iii)	(v)	(i)	(ii)

327. Match the following:

List-I (Work)	**List-II (Author)**
(a) Subject Classification	(i) J.Atchinson
(b) Thesaurofacet	(ii) C.A.Cutter
(c) Classified Catalogue Code	(iii) J.D.Brown
(d) Rules for Dictionary Catalogue	(iv) S. R. Ranganathan

Codes:	**(a)**	**(b)**	**(c)**	**(d)**
(A)	(iii)	(i)	(iv)	(ii)
(B)	(ii)	(iii)	(i)	(iv)
(C)	(iv)	(ii)	(iii)	(i)
(D)	(i)	(ii)	(iii)	(iv)

328. Match the following:

List-I	**List-II**
(a) UDC	(i) H.E.Bliss
(b) DDC	(ii) C.A.Cutter
(c) Expansive classification	(iii) Otlet and La Fontain
(d) Bibliographic classification	(iv) M.Dewey

Codes:	**(a)**	**(b)**	**(c)**	**(d)**
(A)	(iii)	(i)	(ii)	(iv)
(B)	(iii)	(iv)	(ii)	(i)
(C)	(iii)	(ii)	(iv)	(i)
(D)	(i)	(ii)	(iii)	(iv)

329. Match the following items given in List – I and List – II

List-I	**List-II**
(a) Nascent micro thought	(i) Colon classification
(b) Acess points	(ii) Motivation
(c) Physiological needs	(iii) Documentation
(d) Analytico –synthetic classification	(iv) AACR II

Codes:	**(a)**	**(b)**	**(c)**	**(d)**
(A)	(iii)	(iv)	(ii)	(i)
(B)	(iii)	(ii)	(i)	(iv)
(C)	(ii)	(i)	(iv)	(iii)
(D)	(i)	(ii)	(iii)	(iv)

330. Match the following:

List-I	**List-II**
(a) Melvil Dewey	(i) Belgium
(b) Berwick Sayers	(ii) USA
(c) B.S.Kesavan	(iii) Britain
(d) Paul Otlet	(iv) India

Codes:	**(a)**	**(b)**	**(c)**	**(d)**
(A)	(ii)	(iv)	(i)	(iii)
(B)	(iv)	(iii)	(i)	(ii)
(C)	(ii)	(iii)	(iv)	(i)
(D)	(ii)	(i)	(iii)	(iv)

331. Match the following:

List-I (Subjects)	**List-II (Modes of Formation)**
(a) India	(i) Agglomeration
(b) Agriculture of Wheat	(ii) Lamination
(c) Biochemistry	(iii) Fusion
(d) Biological Sciences	(iv) Denudation

Codes:	**(a)**	**(b)**	**(c)**	**(d)**
(A)	(iv)	(ii)	(iii)	(i)
(B)	(i)	(iii)	(ii)	(iv)
(C)	(iv)	(iii)	(i)	(ii)
(D)	(ii)	(iv)	(iii)	(i)

332. Match the following:

List-I	**List-II**
(a) Elements of Library Classification	(i) D.J.DeSolla Price
(b) Little Science big Science	(ii) S.R.Ranganathan
(c) Documentation	(iii) D.J.Fosket
(d) Subjcct Approach	(iv) S.C.Bradford

to Information

Codes:	**(a)**	**(b)**	**(c)**	**(d)**
(A)	(ii)	(i)	(iv)	(iii)
(B)	(iii)	(ii)	(i)	(iv)
(C)	(iv)	(ii)	(iii)	(i)
(D)	(i)	(ii)	(iii)	(iv)

333. Match the following:

List-I	**List-II**
I. DDC	a. J.D.Brown
II. Expansive Classification	b. H.E.Bliss
III. Subject Classification	c. Melvil Dewey
IV. Bibliographic classification	d. C.A.Cutter

Codes:

(A) I-b, II-d, III-c, IV-a

(B) (B) I-c, II-b, III-a, IV-d

(C) (C) I-a, II-b, III-d, IV-c

(D) (D) I-c, II-d, III-a, IV-b

334. Match the following:

List-I	**List-II**
i. Mysticism	a. Y7
ii. Useful Arts	b. Y
iii. Sociology	c. Δ
iv. Anthropology	d. M

Codes:

(A) I-c, II-d, III-b, IV-a

(B) I-d, II-b, III-c, IV-a

(C) I-b, II-c, III-d, IV-a

(D) I-a, II-d, III-c, IV-b

335. Match the following :

List – I	**List – II**
(A) C.A. Cutter	(i) Bibliographic Classification
(B) J.D. Brown	(ii) Expansive Classification
(C) S.R.Ranganathan	(iii) Subject Classification
(D) H.E. Bliss	(iv) Colon Classification

Codes:

(A) (ii) (iii) (iv) (i)   (B) (i) (ii) (iii) (iv)

(C) (iv) (i) (ii) (iii)   (D) (iii) (ii) (iv) (i)

336. Match the following :

List – I	**List – II**
(A) C.A. Cutter	(i) Bibliographic classification
(B) H.E. Bliss	(ii) Expansive classification
(C) J.D. Brown	(iii) Universal classification
(D) Paul Otlet& Henry LaFontaine	(iv) Subject classification

Codes:	**(a)**	**(b)**	**(c)**	**(d)**
(A)	(ii)	(i)	(iv)	(iii)
(B)	(ii)	(iii)	(iv)	(i)
(C)	(i)	(iii)	(iv)	(ii)
(D)	(iii)	(iv)	(ii)	(i)

337. Match the following items given in List – I and List – II

List-I	**List-II**
(a) DDC 19th edition	(i) John Camaroni
(b) DDC 20th edition	(ii) Melvil Dewey
(c) DDC 21st edition	(iii) John Mitchell
(d) DDC 22nd edition	(iv) Benjamin Custer

Codes:	**(a)**	**(b)**	**(c)**	**(d)**
(A)	(ii)	(iv)	(iii)	(i)
(B)	(ii)	(i)	(iv)	(iii)
(C)	(ii)	(iv)	(i)	(iii)
(D)	(iv)	(iii)	(ii)	(i)

338. Match the following:

List-I	**List- II**
a) Subject Classification	i) J. Atchinson
b) Thesauro-facet	ii) C. A. Cutter
c) Classified Catalogue Code	iii) J. D. Brown
d) Rules of Dictionary Catalogue	iv) S. R. Ranganathan

Codes:	**(a)**	**(b)**	**(c)**	**(d)**
(A)	iii	i	iv	ii
(B)	ii	iii	i	iv
(C)	iv	ii	iii	i
(D)	i	iii	ii	iv

339. Match the following:

List-I	**List-II**
a) C. A. Cutter	i) Indexing
b) Berwick Sayers	ii) Cataloguing
c) Derek Austin	iii) Computers
d) Charles Babbage	iv) Classification

Codes:	**(a)**	**(b)**	**(c)**	**(d)**
(A)	i	iii	iv	ii
(B)	ii	iv	i	iii
(C)	iii	ii	i	iv
(D)	iv	ii	iii	i

340. Match the following:

List I	**List II**
(i) DDC	(w) 15th ed.
(ii) SLSH	(x) 34th ed.
(iii) DDC, Abridged	(y) 23rd ed.
(iv) LCSH	(z) 20th ed.

Codes:	**(i)**	**(ii)**	**(iii)**	**(iv)**
(A)	(y)	(x)	(z)	(w)
(B)	(y)	(z)	(x)	(w)
(C)	(w)	(y)	(z)	(x)
(D)	(y)	(z)	(w)	(x)

341. Match the following :

List – I	**List – II**
(A) Law of Parsimony	(i) Classification
(B) Principle of Osmosis	(ii) F. W. Lancaster
(C) Paperless Society	(iii) Overall economy
(D) APUPA pattern	(iv) Reclassification

Codes:	**(a)**	**(b)**	**(c)**	**(d)**
(A)	(ii)	(i)	(iv)	(iii)
(B)	(iv)	(ii)	(i)	(iii)
(C)	(iii)	(iv)	(ii)	(i)
(D)	(i)	(iii)	(ii)	(iv)

342. Match the following:

List – I	**List – II**
a. Classification	i. LISA
b. Cataloguing	ii. UDC
c. Subject Heading	iii. AACR
d. Library Science Abstracts	iv. LCSH

Codes:	**(a)**	**(b)**	**(c)**	**(d)**
(A)	ii	i	iv	iii
(B)	ii	iii	iv	i
(C)	iv	iii	i	ii
(D)	ii	iv	i	iii

343. Match the following:

List – I	**List – II**
a. Collateral classes	i. Class comprising two or more entities
b. Multiple classes	ii. Classes of the same order but not belonging to one in the same order
c. Chain of classes	iii. A subject fixed with others in the universal of subject
d. Co-ordinate classes	iv. A sequence of classes made up of any given class and its universe

Codes:	**(a)**	**(b)**	**(c)**	**(d)**
(A)	ii	iv	i	iii
(B)	i	iii	ii	iv
(C)	ii	i	iv	iii
(D)	i	iv	ii	iii

344. Match the following :

List – I	List – II
a. Henri La Fontaine	i. Expansive Classification
b. H.E. Bliss	ii. Bibliographic Classification
c. C.A. Cutter	iii. LC
d. J.C.M Hansar	iv. UDC

Codes:	(a)	(b)	(c)	(d)
(A)	iv	ii	i	iii
(B)	iii	ii	iv	i
(C)	ii	iv	i	iii
(D)	i	iii	ii	iv

345. Match the following:

List – I	List – II
a. Algorith	i. Instruction to the computer
b. Flow charts	ii. Debugging
c. Program code	iii. Pictorially represented direction lines
d. Program test	iv. Set of explicit and finite steps

Codes:	(a)	(b)	(c)	(d)
(A)	ii	iii	iv	i
(B)	iii	i	iv	ii
(C)	iv	iii	i	ii
(D)	i	ii	iv	iii

346. Match the following language and their function:

List – I	List – II
a. Procedural	i. Scan arbitrary files and extra information
b. Special purpose	ii. Manipulate data and change memory
c. Practical extraction report	iii. Create documents to view with web server
d. Hyper textmark up	iv. Data base queries

Codes:	(a)	(b)	(c)	(d)
(A)	ii	iv	i	iii
(B)	i	iii	ii	iv
(C)	iii	iv	i	ii
(D)	ii	iii	iv	i

347. Match the following :

List – I		**List – II**	
a.	Intra-Facet Relation	i.	S : 5210t3
b.	Intra-Array Phase Relation	ii.	Q 20 m4
c.	Intra-Facet Phase Relation	iii.	SO b2
d.	Inter-Subject Phase Relation	iv.	X.440j56

Codes:	**(a)**	**(b)**	**(c)**	**(d)**
(A)	iv	i	ii	iii
(B)	iv	ii	iii	i
(C)	ii	iii	i	iv
(D)	i	iv	iii	ii

348. Match the following :

List – I		**List – II**	
a.	Organisational chart	i.	Identification of responsibility for specific tasks
b.	Flow charts	ii.	Examine specific detailed procedure
c.	Activity charts	iii.	Division of responsibility & functions
d.	Decision table	iv.	Diagrams composed of symbols and directional lines

Codes:	**(a)**	**(b)**	**(c)**	**(d)**
(A)	i	iv	ii	iii
(B)	ii	iii	iv	i
(C)	iii	iv	i	ii
(D)	iv	ii	iii	i

349. Match the following :

List – I		**List – II**	
a.	Information should be as accurate as possible	i.	Broadus
b.	Get the best title on any subject but add midiocres that are well read	ii.	Haines
c.	Know the community's character and interest	iii.	McColvin

d. Consider the duration as well as intensity of the demand — iv. Drury

Codes:	(a)	(b)	(c)	(d)
(A)	iii	iv	ii	i
(B)	ii	iii	i	iv
(C)	i	ii	iv	iii
(D)	iv	i	iii	ii

350. Match the following:

List – I	List – II
a. National Library of the World	i. Wilfred Ashworth
b. Special Libraries	ii. L.J. Strauss
c. Scientific and Technical Libraries	iii. A. Esdaile
d. Handbook of Special Libraries	iv. C.M. Lewis

Codes:	(a)	(b)	(c)	(d)
(A)	i	iv	iii	ii
(B)	ii	iii	iv	i
(C)	iii	iv	ii	i
(D)	iv	ii	iii	i

351. Match the following :

List – I	List – II
a. Halftone	i. Translate instructions from original software to new platforms
b. Threshold	ii. Imaging with varying densities
c. Emulation	iii. Transfer of digital materials
d. Migration	iv. Minimum level to detect a signal

Codes:	(a)	(b)	(c)	(d)
(A)	i	iii	iv	ii
(B)	iii	ii	iv	i
(C)	ii	iv	i	iii
(D)	ii	i	iii	iv

ANSWERS

1. (A)	2. (B)	3. (C)	4. (A)
5. (A)	6. (B)	7. (D)	8. (A)
9. (C)	10. (B)	11. (D)	12. (C)
13. (C)	14. (B)	15. (C)	16. (D)
17. (A)	18. (D)	19. (A)	20. (B)
21. (B)	22. (A)	23. (B)	24. (C)
25. (B)	26. (C)	27. (C)	28. (B)
29. (B)	30. (C)	31. (A)	32. (C)
33. (D)	34. (C)	35. (C)	36. (C)
37. (C)	38. (C)	39. (A)	40. (C)
41. (B)	42. (A)	43. (B)	44. (C)
45. (A)	46. (C)	47. (A)	48. (B)
49. (A)	50. (D)	51. (C)	52. (C)
53. (A)	54. (D)	55. (C)	56. (D)
57. (B)	58. (C)	59. (A)	60. (D)
61. (D)	62. (D)	63. (A)	64. (C)
65. (C)	66. (A)	67. (B)	68. (D)
69. (B)	70. (D)	71. (D)	72. (B)
73. (C)	74. (D)	75. (C)	76. (D)
77. (A)	78. (C)	79. (A)	80. (B)
81. (C)	82. (B)	83. (B)	84. (A)
85. (B)	86. (C)	87. (C)	88. (C)
89. (D)	90. (A)	91. (D)	92. (B)
93. (A)	94. (A)	95. (C)	96. (B)
97. (A)	98. (B)	99. (C)	100. (D)
101. (C)	102. (B)	103. (B)	104. (C)
105. (C)	106. (C)	107. (B)	108. (D)
109. (B)	110. (B)	111. (A)	112. (A)
113. (D)	114. (B)	115. (D)	116. (D)
117. (B)	118. (C)	119. (B)	120. (C)
121. (D)	122. (B)	123. (D)	124. (D)
125. (D)	126. (D)	127. (B)	128. (A)
129. (B)	130. (C)	131. (A)	132. (C)
133. (B)	134. (D)	135. (D)	136. (D)
137. (B)	138. (D)	139. (B)	140. (C)
141. (B)	142. (D)	143. (D)	144. (B)
145. (D)	146. (D)	147. (B)	148. (D)
149. (D)	150. (C)	151. (B)	152. (C)
153. (A)	154. (A)	155. (D)	156. (D)
157. (C)	158. (C)	159. (C)	160. (B)
161. (C)	162. (D)	163. (A)	164. (C)
165. (A)	166. (B)	167. (A)	168. (A)
169. (D)	170. (B)	171. (B)	172. (A)
173. (B)	174. (B)	175. (A)	176. (D)

177. (A)	178. (B)	179. (C)	180. (D)
181. (C)	182. (A)	183. (A)	184. (B)
185. (D)	186. (A)	187. (A)	188. (D)
189. (A)	190. (C)	191. (B)	192. (A)
193. (A)	194. (D)	195. (C)	196. (B)
197. (A)	198. (C)	199. (D)	200. (B)
201. (D)	202. (A)	203. (B)	204. (B)
205. (D)	206. (A)	207. (B)	208. (C)
209. (A)	210. (C)	211. (A)	212. (B)
213. (A)	214. (A)	215. (D)	216. (D)
217. (B)	218. (D)	219. (C)	220. (B)
221. (B)	222. (A)	223. (A)	224. (A)
225. (B)	226. (D)	227. (D)	228. (A)
229. (A)	230. (C)	231. (A)	232. (A)
233. (C)	234. (A)	235. (C)	236. (D)
237. (A)	238. (D)	239. (A)	240. (A)
241. (A)	242. (A)	243. (A)	244. (C)
245. (A)	246. (A)	247. (B)	248. (B)
249. (A)	250. (C)	251. (A)	252. (B)
253. (C)	254. (D)	255. (B)	256. (B)
257. (A)	258. (B)	259. (A)	260. (A)
261. (D)	262. (A)	263. (D)	264. (A)
265. (D)	266. (C)	267. (C)	268. (D)
269. (A)	270. (C)	271. (B)	272. (A)
273. (B)	274. (B)	275. (A)	276. (B)
277. (B)	278. (B)	279. (A)	280. (A)
281. (D)	282. (A)	283. (C)	284. (B)
285. (A)	286. (C)	287. (C)	288. (B)
289. (B)	290. (B)	291. (C)	292. (B)
293. (C)	294. (A)	295. (D)	296. (B)
297. (B)	298. (A)	299. (A)	300. (A)
301. (C)	302. (A)	303. (C)	304. (A)
305. (B)	306. (A)	307. (D)	308. (A)
309. (C)	310. (A)	311. (A)	312. (D)
313. (B)	314. (A)	315. (C)	316. (B)
317. (A)	318. (A)	319. (A)	320. (B)
321. (D)	322. (A)	323. (D)	324. (A)
325. (A)	326. (A)	327. (A)	328. (B)
329. (B)	330. (C)	331. (A)	332. (A)
333. (D)	334. (A)	335. (D)	336. (B)
337. (B)	338. (A)	339. (B)	340. (D)
341. (C)	342. (B)	343. (C)	344. (A)
345. (C)	346. (A)	347. (A)	348. (C)
349. (A)	350. (C)	351. (C)	

5
Cataloguing

1. FRBR is developed by
   (A) LC (B) UNESCO
   (C) IFLA (D) FID
2. Which one is not correct about the database ?
   (A) It exists only inside a computer system in digital format
   (B) It is created using an appropriate authoring tool.
   (C) It is stored in the memory system of the computer
   (D) It is displayed not using audiovisual tool.
3. In cataloguing, the square brackets [ ] are used
   (A) to enclose information taken from outside
   (B) to enclose the details of printed / manufacturer
   (C) to enclose series statements
   (D) to enclose statement of accompanying material
4. Which Section of AACR – II (R) deals with serial publications ?
   (A) Part – A, Section – 3 (B) Part – B, Section – 3
   (C) Part – A, Section – 12 (D) Part – B, Section – 12
5. When two or more basic subjects having same relational approach form a specific subject, the relation is termed as
   (A) Speciater relation (B) Co-ordinate relation
   (C) Phase relation (D) Hierarchical relation

6. As specified by AACR-II (R), the source of information for machine readable data file is
   (A) Internal user label (B) Title page
   (C) Colophone (D) Title frame
7. Who used the phrase 'control-access directional type sources'?
   (A) R.E. Bopp (B) B.C. Wynar
   (C) W.A. Katz (D) R. Balay
8. The distinct characteristic(s) of digital objects are
   (A) Physical Medium
   (B) Logical process
   (C) Conceptual recognition and transaction
   (D) All the above
9. METS stands for
   (A) Machine Encoded Transmission System
   (B) Metadata Encoded for Textual Sources
   (C) Machine Encoded Textual Standard
   (D) Metadata Encoding Transmission Standard
10. Which of the following principles are associated with library building planning?
   (i) Principle of Uniformity
   (ii) Principle of Comfort ability
   (iii) Principle of Simplicity
   (iv) Principle of Continuity

   Codes:
   (A) (i), (ii) and (iii) are correct
   (B) (ii), (iii) and (iv) are correct
   (C) (i), (ii) and (iv) are correct
   (D) (iii), (iv) and (i) are correct
11. How do we render the name 'Bernardo Augustine De Voto'?
   (A) Voto, Bernardo, Augustine De
   (B) De Voto, Augustine, Bernardo
   (C) Bernardo Augustine, De Voto
   (D) De Voto, Bernardo Augustine

12. The first printed works are called

(A) Impensis (B) Incunabula

(C) Impression (D) Imprimatur

13. What are the four entities of FRBR model?

(A) Personality, Matter, Energy, Space

(B) Books, Form, Availability, Type

(C) Work, Expression, Manifestation, Item

(D) Discipline, Entity, Action, Personality

14. Which of the following is/ are part(s) of classified catalogue?

(A) An author-title file

(B) Subject file arranged by library classification

(C) An alphabetical index to the subject file

(D) All of the above

15. MARC records contain

(i) Description of library materials

(ii) Searchable headings

(iii) Elements to organize collection

(iv) List of index terms

Codes :

(A) (i), (ii), (iii) are correct.

(B) (ii), (iii), (iv) are correct.

(C) (iii), (iv), (i) are correct.

(D) (iv), (i), (ii) are correct.

16. Arrange the following MARC formats in order of year of their emergence :

(i) CAN MARC (ii) US MARC

(iii) LC MARC (iv) MARC 21

Codes :

(A) i ii iii iv (B) ii iii iv i

(C) iii i ii iv (D) iv ii iii i

17. The primary distinction between RDA and AACR is

(A) Structural (B) Relational

(C) Non-structural (D) Combinational

18. Arrange the following ISBDs according to their year of formulation:

(i) ISBD (PM) (ii) ISBD (CF)

(iii) ISBD (M) (iv) ISBD (S)

Codes:

(A) (iii), (ii), (i), (iv) (B) (iii), (iv), (i), (ii)

(C) (iv), (i), (iii), (ii) (D) (iv), (ii), (iii), (i)

19. DMAIC is the acronym for :

(A) Define, Measure, Access, Improve and Control

(B) Define, Measure, Analyse, Improve and Control

(C) Describe, Measure, Analyse, Improve and Control

(D) Define, Measure, Access, Instruct and Control

20. What is meant by the term database ?

(A) It is a record keeping instrument.

(B) It is a computer based record keeping system.

(C) It is a computer based system

(D) It is computer based accessing system.

21. Semouv Lubutzsky and Mary Piggot are associated with which of the following ?

(A) Classification (B) Cataloguing

(C) Indexing (D) Management

22. Arrange the following according to their publication year :

i. Sears' list of subject headings

ii. Panizzi code

iii. AACR-I

iv. CCC

Codes :

(A) iv, ii, iii, i (B) i, iii, ii, iv

(C) ii, i, iv, iii (D) iii, iv, i, ii

23. The 'Rules of Dictionary Catalogue' were developed by

(A) C. A. Cutter (B) C. A. Babbage

(C) J. D. Brown (D) Anthony Panizzi

24. Arrange the following catalogue codes in chorological order of its development.

(i) AACR-I
(ii) Rules for Dictionary Catalogue
(iii) CCC
(iv) ALA Code

Codes:

(A) (iii) (ii) (iv) (i) (B) (i) (ii) (iv) (iii)
(C) (iv) (i) (iii) (ii) (D) (iii) (iv) (ii) (i)

25. Arrange the following physical forms of catalogues in order of development.

(i) Sheaf (ii) Register
(iii) OPAC (iv) Card

Codes:

(A) (iv) (i) (ii) (iii) (B) (ii) (i) (iv) (iii)
(C) (i) (iv) (ii) (iii) (D) (i) (ii) (iii) (iv)

26. The complete catalogue record of a document is known as

(A) Title Entry (B) Added Entry
(C) Analytical Entry (D) Main Entry

27. The paper entitled "The crisis in Cataloging" published in Library Quarterly (Vol. 11, Oct. 1941) was authored by

(A) Seymour Lubetzky (B) Michael Gorman
(C) Andrew Osborn (D) David J. Haykin

28. Who initiated shared cataloguing

(A) Library of Congress
(B) Imperial Library
(C) British Museum
(D) National Library of Australia

29. 'Charles Ammi Cutter' is well known for

(A) Classified Catalogue
(B) Alphabetico- classified catalogue
(C) Mixed catalogue
(D) Dictionary catalogue

30. Arrange the names of the persons in the order of their contribution to cataloguing in ascending order.

(i) Anthony Panizzi (ii) SymursLubetzky

(iii) Charles Ammi Cutter (iv) S.R. Ranganathan

Codes:

(A) i, iii, ii, iv (B) ii, iii, iv, i

(C) iii, iv, i, ii (D) iv, i, ii, iii

31. As per rules laid down in AACR-II, the entry element "Ministry of Finance, Government of India" will be rendered as :

(A) India. Ministry of Finance

(B) Finance, India, Ministry of ....

(C) Ministry of Finance, India

(D) India, Ministry of Finance

32. The generic tasks for which users use a database described in the FRBR model are :

(A) 'to find', 'to identify', 'to select' and 'to acquire or obtain'

(B) 'to browse', 'to identify', 'to select' and 'to acquire or obtain'

(C) 'to find', 'to select', 'to acquire' and 'to read'

(D) 'to discover', 'to categorize', 'to select' and 'to acquire'

33. Arrange the following according to their year of origin:

(i) Rules for Dictionary Catalogue

(ii) ALA Code

(iii) FRBR

(iv) AACR-I

Codes:

(A) (i), (ii), (iii), (iv) (B) (iv), (i), (ii), (iii)

(C) (i), (ii), (iv), (iii) (D) (i), (iv), (ii), (iii)

34. Second group of entities in FRBR consist of :

(A) Author and Conference proceedings

(B) Person and Corporate body

(C) Publisher and Corporate body

(D) Author and Publisher

35. According to AACR-II, the statement of responsibility in case of sound recordings "Texas country by Willie Nelson and others" will be rendered as :
    (A) Texas Country/Willie Nelson and others
    (B) Texas Country/Willie Nelson .... [et al.]
    (C) Texas Country/Willie Nelson (et al.)
    (D) Texas Country/Willie Nelson .... (et al.)
36. Ranganathan's modified rules of chain procedure for deriving subject headings of specific subject entry was modified by M M Job, who suggested to include
    (A) Space isolate as a sought link term
    (B) Time isolate as a sought link term
    (C) ACI as a sought link term
    (D) None of the above
37. According to IFLA's FRBR, the objectives of an information system can be expressed by the following tasks:
    (A) locate, select, obtain and collocate
    (B) find, select, obtain and navigate
    (C) identify, find, obtain and collocate
    (D) find, identify, select and obtain
38. What is the new name of ISBD (S)?
    (A) ISBD (JR)　　(B) ISBD (CR)
    (C) ISBD (ER)　　(D) None of the above
39. What is the relationship between ISBD and cataloguing codes ?
    (A) They are not related at all
    (B) Cataloguing codes will include bibliographic description
    (C) ISBD includes cataloguing rules
    (D) ISBD can replace cataloguing rules
40. UNIMARC was developed under the umbrella of
    (A) OCLC　　(B) IFLA
    (C) UNESCO　　(D) None of the above
41. WorldCat is maintained by

(A) Library of Congress
(B) Online Computer Library Center
(C) American Library Association
(D) None of the above

42. 260 tag in MARC format marks
(A) The edition
(B) The publication information
(C) The physical description
(D) A topical subject heading

43. Arrange the following according to their development:
(I) CCC (II) ISBD
(III) CCF (IV) MARC II
Codes :
(A) (I), (IV), (II), (III) (B) (I), (II), (IV), (III)
(C) (I), (IV), (III), (II) (D) (IV), (II), (III), (I)

44. 'Union List' is the record of
(A) Library members living in a Union Territory
(B) Periodicals available in a group of libraries
(C) Library unions located in a Union Territory
(D) List of members of a library union.

45. Who is the author of "Subject Catalogue" ?
(A) E. J. Coates (B) J. Kaiser
(C) C. A. Cutter (D) J. W. Metcalfe

46. Arrange the following in chronological order :
(i) ISBD
(ii) MARC
(iii) CCF
(iv) Resource Description and Access (RDA)
Codes :
(A) (ii), (i), (iii), (iv) (B) (i), (iv), (iii), (ii)
(C) (iii), (iv), (i), (ii) (D) (ii), (iv), (i), (iii)

47. CCF stands for
(A) Common Communication Format
(B) Centre for Communication Format
(C) Committee for Communication Format
(D) Common Curriculum Format

48. Real Time Access refers to
    (A) Access in advance
    (B) Access after some time
    (C) Access when searched for
    (D) None of the above
49. In AACR –II, the total number of volumes of a serial publication available in a library is mentioned under section.:
    (A) Tracing (B) Note
    (C) Collation (D) None of the above
50. Who Invented the Dictionary Catalogue?
    (A) Dr. S. R. Ranganathan
    (B) C. A. Cutter
    (C) D. B. Krishna Rao
    (D) K. N. Raj
51. What is the another name of Added entries?
    (A) Main entry (B) Cross reference entry
    (C) Secondary entries (D) Subject entry
52. When was SLSH published?
    (A) 1903 (B) 1897
    (C) 1923 (D) 1933
53. When was MARC project completed?
    (A) 1987 (B) 1967
    (C) 1947 (D) 1968
54. The term prenatal cataloguing first used by
    (A) Michael Gorman (B) Dr. S.R.Ranganathan
    (C) E.B.Ross (D) Melvin Dewey
55. Mention the name of Library catalogue cards that are filed in specially designed drawers
    (A) Charging tray (B) Catalogue cabinet
    (C) Display rack (D) Filling equipment
56. What is the second function of Technical section among two functions that performs along with classification?
    (A) accessioning (B) bills payment
    (C) cataloguing (D) shelving

57. Virtual accommodates Different version of the MARC Standard?
    (A) USMARC (B) UKMARC
    (C) CANMARC (D) SWEMARC/All of above
58. Which library first introduced the printed catalog
    (A) British Museum (B) Library of Congress
    (C) Lelin State (D) Imperial Library
59. In AACR-II the indicator symbol for statement of responsibility is
    (A) Dot (B) Semicolon
    (C) Slash (D) Colon
60. The CCF was developed by
    (A) LC (B) UNESCO
    (C) IFLA (D) FID
61. According to CCC, the heading for work with three authors is
    (A) The first author (B) The title
    (C) The principal author (D) All the three authors
62. Which of the following areas is not a part of the description prescribed by AACR-II?
    (A) Title and statement of responsibility area
    (B) Edition
    (C) Publication and distribution
    (D) Address and location
63. Which one of the following is not a part of the MARC record structure?
    (A) Leader (B) Directory
    (C) Record terminator (D) Check digit
64. A document description is not found in a
    (A) Catalogue entry (B) Citation
    (C) Bibliographic entry (D) Class number
65. According to AACR-II, the heading of the main entry for conference proceeding edited by an individual is prepared under
    (A) name of editor (B) place of conference
    (C) title of the volume (D) name of the conference

66. The subject headings "Money" and "Inflation" are both used in a retrieval system
    (A) be linked by a "see also" reference
    (B) be linked by a "see" reference
    (C) be linked by both "see" and "see also" references
    (D) not be linked
67. In AACR-II, the indicator symbol for accompanying material is:
    (A) Plus (B) Hyphen
    (C) Slash (D) Semicolon
68. MARC was started in the year
    (A) 1962 (B) 1975
    (C) 1966 (D) 1985
69. What is a collection of terms or records in MARC called?
    (A) System (B) Network
    (C) Website (D) Database
70. According to CCC, the heading for work with three authors is
    (A) The first author (B) The title
    (C) The principal author (D) All the three authors
71. Which of the following areas is not a part of the description prescribed by AACR-II?
    (A) Title and statement of responsibility area
    (B) Edition
    (C) Publication and distribution
    (D) Address and location
72. The Principle of Later-in- is one of the principles of:
    (A) Fundemantal Categories
    (B) Helpful Sequence
    (C) Facet Sequence
    (D) None of the above
73. The GMD in a catalogue entry according to AACR-II revised edition is given :
    (A) After the title proper (B) Before the title
    (C) After the statement of responsibility
    (D) Before the statement of responsibility

74. Arrange the physical forms of catalogue in the chronological sequence :
    (A) Register, Sheaf Catalogue, Card Catalogue, OPAC
    (B) Sheaf Catalogue, Register, Card Catalogue, OPAC
    (C) Card Catalogue, Sheaf Catalogue, Register, OPAC
    (D) Sheaf Catalogue, Card Catalogue, Register, OPAC
75. 'Canons of Cataloguing' were first formulated by
    (A) Seymour Lubetzky (B) C. A. Cutter i
    (C) S. R. Ranganathan (D) A. Panizzi.
76. According to CCC (Ed. 5) Ministry of Education, Government of West Bengal will be rendered a
    (A) West Bengal, Ministry of Education
    (B) West Bengal, Education (Ministry of ...)
    (C) WEST BENGAL, EDUCATION (Ministry of.)
    (D) Ministry of Education (West Bengal).
77. Which of the following is a pseudonymous name?
    (A) SuryakantaTripathi 'Nirala'
    (B) George Orwell
    (C) Prem Chand
    (D) MahadeviVerma.
78. ISBN consists of
    (A) 8 digits (B) 14 digits
    (C) 10 digits (D) 13 digits
79. British Museum catalogue code was formulated by
    (A) S. Lubetzky (B) C. A. Cutter
    (C) A. Panizzi (D) C. C. Jewett.
80. Cataloguing in Publication stands for
    (A) co-operative cataloguing
    (B) prenatal cataloguing
    (C) selective cataloguing
    (D) descriptive cataloguing.
81. MARC was first launched by
    (A) The British Library, London
    (B) Library of Congress
    (C) INSDOC
    (D) DESIDOC.

82. OPAC stands for
    (A) Online Public Access Catalogue
    (B) Online Processing of Automated Catalogue
    (C) Online Programmers of Analogue Computer
    (D) Online Programmeming and Control.
83. 'Three cards system' is used for
    (A) cataloguing of books
    (B) acquisition and control of periodicals
    (C) shelf list
    (D) circulation of books.
84. Canon of modulation is concerned with
    (A) canon of array
    (B) canon of chain
    (C) canon of ascertainibility
    (D) canon of recall value.
85. According to S. R. Ranganathan the two canons for chain are
    (A) canon of ascertainibility and recall value
    (B) canon of array and filiatory sequence
    (C) canon of decreasing extension and modulation
    (D) none of these.
86. Analytical entry is known in CCC as
    (A) CRIE (B) CRE
    (C) BIE (D) CIE.
87. The latest canon of cataloguing enunciated by S. R. Ranganathan
    (A) canon of ascertainability
    (B) canon of modulation
    (C) canon of decreasing extension
    (D) canon of recall value.
88. ISBD was first introduced in
    (A) AACRI, 1967 (B) AACRII, 1978
    (C) AACRII-R, 1988 (D) AACRII-R, 1993
89. Analytical entry is prepared for
    (A) composite books (B) periodicals
    (C) yearbooks (D) part of a document.

90. Rules for description are not given in
    (A) ALA Code (B) Jewett's Code
    (C) AA Code (D) AACR Code.
91. Dr. S. R. Ranganathan undertook a comparative study of five cataloguing codes in the works of
    (A) Definition of Cataloguing
    (B) Objectives of Cataloguing
    (C) Principles of Cataloguing
    (D) Headings and Canons.
92. In AACRII, size of a document 20.5 cm. 32 cm can be written as
    (A) 20 cm. 32 cm (B) 20.5 cm. 32 cm
    (C) 21 cm. 32 cm (D) none of these.
93. The concept of Principle Author recognises by
    (A) AA Code
    (B) ALA Code
    (C) British Museum Code
    (D) AACRI & II Code.
94. AA Code was devised by ALA & LA in the year of
    (A) 1907 (B) 1908
    (C) 1909 (D) 1910.
95. Vatican code was published in
    (A) 1930 (B) 1931
    (C) 1932 (D) 1933
96. MARC was launched in the year of
    (A) 1965 (B) 1966
    (C) 1967 (D) 1968.
97. ISBN is given in the main entry of
    (A) AACRI (B) CCC
    (C) AACRII (D) AACRII-R.
98. Title that does not disclose the subject of the work is called
    (A) sub-title (B) parallel title
    (C) fanciful title (D) none of these.
99. The author of 'Cataloging : a text book few use in Libraries' is:

(A) B. Sengupta (B) C.G. Viswananthan
(C) Henry A. Sharp (D) J.J. Ball

100. The particular canon of cataloguing prescribes that the information found on title and overflow pages should be used for preparing main entry is
(A) canon of parsimony
(B) canon of recall value
(C) canon of ascertanibility
(D) none of these.

101. The main reason for using uniform titles as headings for certain works in a library catalogue is
(A) because users generally look under the particular title
(B) because users generally look under the single titlc
(C) because users generally look underthe uniform title
(D) none of these.

102. According to CCC the best way to make the choice of heading is to depend on the
(A) canon of symmetry
(B) canon of individualisation
(C) canon of ascertainibility
(D) none of these.

103. The purpose of a 'see also' reference in a library catalogue is to direct a user from a
(A) standard term to the non standard term
(B) semi standard term to the standard term
(C) semi standard term to the non standard term
(D) non standard term to the standard term.

104. A book with two or more independent contributions is called
(A) simple book (B) complex book
(C) compound book (D) composite book.

105. In CCC, if the name of the author is taken from outside it will be put within
(A) square brackets (B) round brackets
(C) second brackets (D) none of these.

106. The code based on ICCP is

(A) CCC (B) AACRII

(C) AACRII-R (D) AACRI.

107. The institution not associated with the preparation AACRI

(A) ALA (B) LC

(C) LA (D) ILA.

108. According to AACRII when the title page gives the name of only editor, the main entry will be made

(A) under the title of the book

(B) under the editor of the book

(C) under thecompiler of the book

(D) under the translator of the book.

109. 'Cataloguing in Publication' programme was introduced by

(A) ALA (B) LC

(C) LA (D) British Library.

110. ICCP was held in Paris in the year

(A) 1960 (B) 1961

(C) 1962 (D) 1963

111. The code does not allow to find out information from outside the title andoverflow pages in determining the choice of heading

(A) British Museum code

(B) Jewett's code

(C) Cutter's Dictionary Cataloguecode

(D) Vatican code.

112. According to AACRII when there are four authors and no one is principal authorand one editor, the entry will be prepared under the

(A) author (B) editor

(C) title (D) subject.

113. To carry out a search on 'Poverty in Gujrat and Rajasthan' a search statement would need to be framed as

(A) Poverty AND (Gujrat AND Rajasthan)
(B) Poverty AND (Gujrat ORRajasthan)
(C) Poverty OR (Gujrat AND Rajasthan)
(D) Poverty OR (Gujrat OR Rajasthan)

114. According to AACRII, if a book has been edited by four persons, the main entryshould be under
(A) the first editor (B) all editors
(C) title (D) the first three editors.

115. A list of books and other reading materials available in a particular library iscalled as
(A) Union Catalogue (B) Library Catalogue
(C) Bibliography (D) DictionaryCatalogue.

116. If a catalogue represents the collection of two or more libraries, it is known as
(A) Accession List (B) Bibliography
(C) Union Catalogue (D) Trade Catalogue.

117. The first edition of Ranganathan's classified catalogue code appeared in
(A) 1930 (B) 1934
(C) 1964 (D) 1945.

118 Sheaf form of library catalogue is also referred to as
(A) card (B) ledger
(C) printed (D) loose-leaf.

119. Which consists of strips mounted on a frame or cards held flat, hinged andwith edge of each card protruding so as to make the heading visible?
(A) Microform card (B) Three card system
(C) Catalogue (D) Visible index card.

120. The microform catalogues are being used extensively since
(A) 1960's (B) 1970's
(C) 1980's (D) 1990's.

121. The arrangement of catalogue entries in a logical and systematic order to fall into a helpful sequence for strong and retrieval is referred to as
(A) Card form (B) Alphabetical form
(C) Classified form (D) Inner form.

122. Which catalogue is a variation and extension of an author catalogue?
    (A) Classified catalogue
    (B) Name catalogue
    (C) Alphabetical catalogue
    (D) Author catalogue.
123. The British Museum Cataloguing Rules is also known as
    (A) Baber's Rules (B) Panizzi's Rules
    (C) Vatican Rules (D) Jewett's Rules.
124. AACRII was published in
    (A) 1967 (B) 1974
    (C) 1978 (D) 1988.
125. To direct the user of a catalogue from a form of the name of a person or acorporate body or the title of a work that might reasonably be sought to theform that has been chosen as a name heading or a uniform title is the functionof a
    (A) See reference (B) See also reference
    (C) Cross reference (D) Directreference.
126. A record of all additional entries is known as
    (A) Unit Card (B) Book Index Entry
    (C) Tracing (D) Added Entry.
127. In CCC, Class Index Entry consists of successively the following sections a)heading section b) second section, and c)
    (A) call number (B) index number
    (C) class number (D) book number.
128. ALA filing Rules was first published in
    (A) 1968 (B) 1942
    (C) 1961 (D) 1956.
129. Which section in the CCC is that section which records authorship or itssubstitute element?
    (A) Heading section (B) Leading section
    (C) Title section (D) Author section

130. Which Filing Rules has their origins in the report of a Working Party onComputer Filing set up by the Library Association Cataloguing and IndexingGroup?
    (A) BLAISE (B) LC
    (C) ALA (D) Berghoeffer.

131. The structure of the main entry according to AACR-2R consists of
    (A) four parts (B) five parts
    (C) six parts (D) eight parts.

132. According to the needs of a document and needs of a particular Library,AACR, prescribed
    (A) one level of description
    (B) two levels of description
    (C) three levels ofdescription
    (D) four levels of description.

133. In Bibliographic data formats, codes used to identify different data elements inthe record viz., author, title, scale of map, starting dates of journals etc. isknown as
    (A) Record label (B) Directory
    (C) Data fields (D) Content designator.

134. Each CCF record begins with a fixed length label of
    (A) 4 characters (B) 20 characters
    (C) 24 characters (D) 16 characters.

135. GMD in AACR-2R stands for
    (A) General Material Description
    (B) General Material Designation
    (C) Geographical Material Description
    (D) General Monographic Designation.

136. The internationally agreed upon number given to a book is known as
    (A) ISSN (B) ISBD
    (C) ISBN (D) ISCN.

137. Cutter Number or Cutter Mark is used for
    (A) Call number (B) Book number
    (C) Class number (D) Collection number.

138. In AACR-2R, the courts are entered under their
   (A) Jurisdiction
   (B) Name directly
   (C) Name of thegovernment.
   (D) Under the country name
139. In CCC, Conferences and Congresses are entered under the
   (A) name of the sponsor
   (B) name of the place where it is held
   (C) name bywhich they are known
   (D) under the country name.
140. In AACR-2R the anonymous works of personal authors are to be enteredunder
   (A) Title (B) Editor
   (C) Subject (D) Collaborator.
141. Which lists within its frame all bibliographic elements, which are required todescribe and identify all types of materials, which are likely to appear in library collection?
   (A) MARC lists (B) CCF lists
   (C) UNIMARC lists (D) ISBD (G) lists.
142. According to AACR-2R, chief source of information for microforms is
   (A) title page (B) container box
   (C) title frame (D) container and label.
143. Three types of analytical entries in CCC are author analytical, title analyticaland
   (A) series analytical (B) subject analytical
   (C) name analytical (D) editionanalytical.
144. According to AACR-2R, collections of treaties between two parties are to beentered under
   (A) Title (B) Uniform title
   (C) country name (D) Signing parties.
145. Containing more than one unit concept in them and a number of terms may be used to fully describe these concepts is called as

(A) Multi work concept (B) Complex subject
(C) compound subject (D) Metasubject.

146. How many rules for treatment of pseudonyms in CCC?
(A) 5 (B) 10
(C) 15 (D) 20.

147. Subject headings lists and thesauri are two types of
(A) natural indexing language
(B) free indexing language
(C) controlled indexinglanguage
(D) uncontrolled indexing language.

148. Which system contain tools which will automatically create classified listing ofthe resource and a search mechanism for Internet resources?
(A) Prompt cat (B) First Search
(C) ROADS (D) World Cat.

149. Computer Aided Subject System (COMPASS) was introduced in 1991 for
(A) INB (B) ABPR
(C) Books in Print (D) BNB.

150. AACR-II includes rules for
(A) Bibliographic description and choice of subject heading
(B) Choice of main entry and subject heading
(C) Choice of analytical entry and subject heading
(D) bibliographic description and choice of main and added entries

151. As per AACR-II, in case of translated works, the translator gets
(A) Main entry (B) Added entry
(C) A Cross reference (D) Analytical entry

152. If there is a difference in the title of a book as shown on the title page, half title page, spine, the catalogue should render the title
(A) as on title page
(B) as on the title page, but in square brackets
(C) as on the spine
(D) as on thc half title page

153. Which are of the following is not a part of the MARC record structure?
(A) leader (B) directory
(C) record terminator (D) check digit

154. In a thesaurus under a item "internal migration" – which of the following lines would you expect to find
(A) BT Migration
(B) NT Rural to Urban Migration
(C) RT International Migration
(D) All the above

155. The following is not an example of repackaging of information
(A) Trend report (B) Catalogue
(C) Summary (D) Digest

156. According to AACR-II, the heading of the main entry for conference proceeding edited by an individual is prepared under
(A) Name of editor (B) Place of conference
(C) Title of the volume (D) Name of the conference

157. In Sears List of Subject Headings preferred headings are indicated by
(E) Making them as preferred heading
(F) Printing them in bold type
(G) Underlining them
(H) Italicising them

158. The component of an ISO-2709 meant primarily machine processing of the record is
(A) the Label (B) the Directory
(C) the Datafields (D) the record Separator

159. According to CCC, the heading for work with three authors is
(A) The first author (B) The title
(C) The principal author (D) All the three authors

160. Which of the following area is not a part of the description prescribed by AACR-II?

(A) Title and statement of responsibility area
(B) Edition
(C) Publication and distribution
(D) address and location

161. Principles of later-in-time is one of the
(A) Five Laws of Library Science
(B) Cataloguing Principles
(C) Principles of Helpful Sequence
(D) Circulation Rules

162. The decision to make or not to make an entry under a subject term is governed by the
(A) Canon of Ascertainability
(B) Canon of Prepotence
(C) Canon of Sought Heading
(D) Canon of Context

163. The catalogue codes were developed in the order as:
(A) Anglo American Code (Joint Code), Rules for Dictionary Catalogue, ALA rules for author and title entries, AACRI
(B) Rules for Dictionary Catalogue, ALA rules for author and title entries, AACRI, Anglo American Code (Joint Code),
(C) Rules for Dictionary Catalogue, Anglo American Code (Joint Code), ALA rules for author and title entries, AACRI
(D) ALA rules for author and title entries, AACRI Rules for Dictionary Catalogue, Anglo American Code (Joint Code)

164. Arrange the following in the chronological sequence:
(i) CCF (ii) Metadata
(iii) ISBD (iv) MARC

Codes:
(A) (iv) (iii) (i) (ii) (B) (iii) (iv) (i) (ii)
(C) (i) (iii) (iv) (ii) (D) (iii) (i) (iv) (ii)

165. Pre-natal Cataloguing means:

(A) Simplified Cataloguing
(B) Pre-Publication Cataloguing
(C) Selective Cataloguing
(D) Shared Cataloguing

166. An entry in an Abstracting journal consist of
(A) Bibliographic citation
(B) An abstract and bibliographic citation
(C) Annotation
(D) Bibliographic citation, an abstract and initials of the abstractor

167. OCLC project, MARC Project are the examples of .
(A) Co-operative storage of materials.
(B) Co-operative acquisition of materials.
(C) Co-operative processing of materials.
(D) Co-operative sharing of materials.

168. Identify the chronological order of the following Cataloguing Codes:
(i) AACR II (ii) CCC
(iii) AA Code (iv) ALA code

Codes :
(A) (iii), (iv), (i), (ii) (B) (ii), (iv), (iii), (i)
(C) (iii), (ii), (iv), (i) (D) (iv), (i), (ii), (iii)

169. Arrange different codes according to year of origin:
(A) Anthony Pannizi code, Cutter's rules for dictionary catalogue, classified catalogue code, Anglo American cataloguing rules-II.
(B) Anthony Pannizi code, classified catalogue code, Cutter's rules for dictionary catalogue, Anglo American cataloguing rules-II.
(C) Anthony Pannizi code, Anglo American cataloguing rules-II, classified catalogue code, Cutter's rules for dictionary catalogue,.
(D) Anthony Pannizi code, Cutter's rules for dictionary catalogue, Anglo American cataloguing rules-II, classified catalogue code.

170. Arrange the following Standards according to the year of their introduction.
    (A) ISBN, ICCP, CCF, ISDS
    (B) CCF, ICCP, ISBN, ISDS
    (C) ICCP, ISBN, ISDS, CCF.
    (D) ISDS, ISBN, ICCP, CCF.
171. RDA stands for
    (A) Resource Description Agency
    (B) Reference Description and Access.
    (C) Reference Description Agency
    (D) Resource Description and Access.
172. 260 tag in MARC format marks:
    (A) The edition
    (B) The publication information
    (C) The physical description
    (D) A topical subject heading.
173. Arrange the following according to their development:
    (I) CCC (II) ISBD
    (III) CCF (IV) MARC II

    Codes:

    (A) (I), (IV), (II), (III) (B) (I), (II), (IV), (III)
    (C) (I), (IV), (III), (II) (D) (IV), (II), (III), (I)
174. The code which recognised the concept of 'Principal Author' is:
    (A) DDC (B) CCC
    (C) AACR-I (D) Vatican Code.
175. Who is the publisher of Sear's List of subject headings
    (A) Dr. S.R. Ranganathan (B) Brown
    (C) H.W. Wilson (D) C.A. Cutter.
176. Sheets before and after the text of a book are called?
    (A) End Papers (B) Attach cover
    (C) Head bands (D) Gilding
177. On which of the following technologies semantic web is not based?
    (A) RDF (B) Ontologies
    (C) Cloud seeding (D) URI

178. Match the following :

List – I	**List – II**
(A) AACR-1	(i) 1978
(B) AACR-2	(ii) 1967
(C) ALA code	(iii) 1934
(D) CCC	(iv) 1949

Codes:	**(a)**	**(b)**	**(c)**	**(d)**
(A)	(iv)	(ii)	(iii)	(i)
(B)	(ii)	(i)	(iii)	(iv)
(C)	(i)	(iii)	(iv)	(ii)
(D)	(ii)	(i)	(iv)	(iii)

179. Match the following :

List – I	**List – II**
(A) International Conference on Cataloguing Principles	(i) 1969
(B) International Meeting of Cataloguing Experts	(ii) 1961
(C) International Symposium of Bibliographic Exchange format	(iii) 1990
(D) First CCF Users meeting	(iv) 1978

Codes:	**(a)**	**(b)**	**(c)**	**(d)**
(A)	(ii)	(i)	(iv)	(iii)
(B)	(iii)	(ii)	(iv)	(i)
(C)	(iv)	(iii)	(i)	(ii)
(D)	(iii)	(i)	(iv)	(ii)

180. Match the following:

List-I	**List-II**
(a) CCF	(i) OCLC
(b) UNIMARC	(ii) American Library Association
(c) DUBLIN CORE	(iii) Library of Congress
(d) USMARC	(iv) Unesco
	(v) IFLA

Codes:	**(a)**	**(b)**	**(c)**	**(d)**
(A)	(v)	(iv)	(i)	(iii)
(B)	(iv)	(v)	(i)	(ii)
(C)	(iii)	(v)	(iv)	(ii)
(D)	(ii)	(iv)	(v)	(i)

181. Match the following:

List-I	**List-II**
(a) Pre-natal Cataloguing	(i) Shared Cataloguing Programme
(b) NPAC	(ii) Library of Congress
(c) CIP	(iii) NUCSSI
(d) Union Catalogue	(iv) S.R.Ranganthan

Codes:	**(a)**	**(b)**	**(c)**	**(d)**
(A)	(iii)	(ii)	(i)	(iv)
(B)	(iv)	(i)	(ii)	(iii)
(C)	(i)	(iv)	(iii)	(ii)
(D)	(ii)	(iii)	(i)	(iv)

182. Match the following items given in List – I and List – II

List-I	**List-II**
(a) Principles of librarianship	(i) Berwick Sayers
(b) Practical guidelines for classification	(ii) S.R.Ranganathan
(c) Rules for Dictionary cataloguing	(iii) D.J.Urquart
(d) Five Laws of library science	(iv) C.A.Cutter

Codes:	**(a)**	**(b)**	**(c)**	**(d)**
(A)	(iii)	(i)	(iv)	(ii)
(B)	(i)	(ii)	(iii)	(iv)
(C)	(iii)	(ii)	(iv)	(i)
(D)	(i)	(iii)	(iv)	(ii)

183. Match the following items given in List – I and List – II

List-I | **List-II**

(a) Nascent micro thought — (i) Colon classification
(b) Acess points — (ii) Motivation
(c) Physiological needs — (iii) Documentation
(d) Analytico–synthetic classification — (iv) AACR II

Codes:	**(a)**	**(b)**	**(c)**	**(d)**
(E)	(iii)	(iv)	(ii)	(i)
(F)	(iii)	(ii)	(i)	(iv)
(G)	(ii)	(i)	(iv)	(iii)
(H)	(i)	(ii)	(iii)	(iv)

184. Match the following:

List-I	**List-II**
(a) UBC	(i) FID
(b) UDC	(ii) IFLA
(c) MARC	(iii) ASTINFO
(d) Document Supply System	(iv) Library of Congress

Codes:	**(a)**	**(b)**	**(c)**	**(d)**
(A)	(ii)	(iv)	(i)	(iii)
(B)	(ii)	(i)	(iv)	(iii)
(C)	(i)	(ii)	(iii)	(iv)
(D)	(iii)	(ii)	(iv)	(i)

185. Match the following:

List – I	**List – II**
a. DCMES	i. Defined Functional Requirements of Records
b. MARC	ii. Rules for Bibliographic Records
c. RDA	iii. Retrieval and Data Exchange
d. FRBR	iv. Coding Scheme for computerized Bibliographic Records

Codes:	**(a)**	**(b)**	**(c)**	**(d)**
(A)	iii	iv	ii	i
(B)	iv	ii	iii	i
(C)	i	ii	iii	iv
(D)	ii	iv	i	iii

186. Match the following :

List – I	List – II
a. Carol Kuhlthau	i. 8 stages
b. David Ellis	ii. ISB is a 6 stage process
c. M.J. Belkin	iii. ISB is of 8 key activities
d. Marchionnini	iv. ISB is 4 dimension characteristic

Codes:	(a)	(b)	(c)	(d)
(A)	ii	iii	iv	i
(B)	ii	iii	i	iv
(C)	iii	i	iv	ii
(D)	iv	ii	i	iii

187. Match the following:

List – I	List – II
a. Union Catalogue	i. Primary sources
b. Pamphlets & Brochures	ii. Unpublished sources
c. Indexing & Abstracting Sources	iii. Tertiary sources
d. Memoirs of diaries	iv. Secondary sources

Codes:	(a)	(b)	(c)	(d)
(A)	iv	iii	ii	i
(B)	ii	iv	iii	i
(C)	iii	i	iv	ii
(D)	i	ii	iv	iii

188. Match the following:

List – I	List – II
a. Principle of Osmosis	i. Security
b. Theory of Literary Warrants	ii. Sinha Committee
c. Public Libraries are stagnating pools of books	iii. Reclassification
d. Firewall	iv. Dr. S.R. Ranganathan

Codes:	(a)	(b)	(c)	(d)
(A)	iv	ii	iii	i
(B)	iii	iv	ii	i
(C)	iv	iii	i	ii
(D)	i	ii	iv	iii

189. Match the following MARC 21 tags with respective fields:

List – I	List – II
a. 020	i. Publication and Distribution
b. 100	ii. Series Statement
c. 260	iii. ISBN
d. 440	iv. Personal name

Codes:	(a)	(b)	(c)	(d)
(A)	i	ii	iii	iv
(B)	ii	iv	iii	i
(C)	iii	ii	iv	i
(D)	iii	iv	i	ii

190. Match the following:

List-I	List-II
(A) Anthony Penezzi	(i) C.C.C.
(B) C. A. Cutter	(ii) ALA code
(C) S. R. Ranganathan	(iii) British Museum
(D) Seymour Lubetzky	(iv) Rules for Dictionary Catalogue

Codes:	(a)	(b)	(c)	(d)
(A)	(ii)	(iii)	(i)	(iv)
(B)	(iii)	(iv)	(i)	(ii)
(C)	(i)	(ii)	(iii)	(iv)
(D)	(iv)	(i)	(ii)	(iii)

191. Match the following:

List-I	List-II
(a) C. A. Cutter	(i) Indexing
(b) Berwick Sayers	(ii) Cataloguing
(c) Derek Austin	(iii) Computers
(d) Charles Babbage	(iv) Classification

Codes:	**(a)**	**(b)**	**(c)**	**(d)**
(A)	i	iii	iv	ii
(B)	ii	iv	i	iii
(C)	iii	ii	i	iv
(D)	iv	ii	iii	i

192. **Assertion (A) :** RDF supports the use and exchange of metadata on the web.

    Reason (R) : Bibliographic standards are the means to create and disseminate secondary information.

    Codes :

    (A) (A) is true, (R) is false.
    (B) (A) is false, (R) is true.
    (C) Both (A) & (R) are correct.
    (D) Both (A) & (R) are false.

193. **Assertion (A) :** There is a dismal scene relating to the development of public libraries especially rural libraries in India.

    Reason (R) : Majority of the states do not have library legislation.

    Codes :

    (A) Both (A) and (R) are true.
    (B) Both (A) and (R) are false.
    (C) (A) is true but (R) is false.
    (D) (A) is false but (R) is true.

194. **Assertion (A) :** It would be logical to replace catalogue with metadata.

    Reason (R) : Metadata is useful for organising and managing information resources.

    Codes :

    (A) (A) is false and (R) is true.
    (B) (A) and (R) are true.
    (C) (A) is true and (R) is false.
    (D) (A) and (R) are false.

195. **Assertion (A) :** Colon classification is popular in online catalogues.

Reason (R) : Traditional classification systems are used in online searching advantageously.

Codes :

(A) (A) is true, but (R) is false.

(B) Both (A) & (R) true, but (R) is not the correct explanation of (A).

(C) (A) is false, but (R) is true.

(D) Both (A) & (R) are true.

196. **Assertion (A) :** MARC should never be used outside the context of the cataloguing rules.

Reason (R) : MARC is simply a coding scheme for entering bibliographic information into computer records.

Codes :

(A) Both (A) and (R) are true.

(B) (A) is true but (R) is false.

(C) (A) is false but (R) is true.

(D) Both (A) and (R) are false.

197. **Assertion (A) :** UGC has devised performance indicators for the promotion of faculty and librarians.

Reason (R) : Performance Appraisal is an important tool for merit rating.

Codes :

(A) (A) is true, but (R) is false.

(B) (A) is false, but (R) is true.

(C) Both (A) and (R) are true.

(D) Both (A) and (R) are false.

198. **Assertion(A) :** An ISO 2709 : 2008 record structure and review format has 'Record Label', 'Directory', 'Data fields' and 'Record Separator'.

Reason (R) : ISO 2709 is a subset of MARC.

Codes :

(A) (A) is true, but (R) is false.

(B) (A) is false, but (R) is true.

(C) Both (A) and (R) are true.

(D) Both (A) and (R) are false.

199. **Assertion (A) :** Cataloguing in Publication Program (CIP) is initiated by Library of Congress.

Reason (R) : It helps individual libraries in copying down the data.

Codes:

(A) (A) is false and (R) is true

(B) (A) is true and (R) is false

(C) Both (A) and (R) are true

(D) Both (A) and (R) are false

200. **Assertion (A) :** ISBDs were devised by UNESCO.

Reason (R) : They are the standards for all types of bibliographic activities.

(A) (A) is false but (R) is true.

(B) (A) is true but (R) is false.

(C) Both (A) and (R) are true.

(D) Both (A) and (R) are false.

201. **Assertion (A) :** Use of microfilming is becoming obsolete day by day.

Reason (R) : ICT has developed digital technologies, which are quick, cheap and easy to handle.

(A) Both (A) and (R) are true but (R) is not a correct explanation.

(B) Both (A) and (R) are false.

(C) (A) is true but (R) is false.

(D) Both (A) and (R) are true and (R) is the correct explanation of (A).

202. **Assertion (A) :** Web-OPAC is a computerized library catalogue available to the patrons on line

Reason (R) : It can be search by the users with in the four walls of the library only

(A) (A) is true, but (R) is false

(B) (A) is false, but (R) is true

(C) Both (A) and (R) are true

(D) Both (A) and (R) are false

203. **Assertion (A) :** Library catalogues meet most of the approaches of the users.

Reason (R) : Catalogues include all the details of the document

Codes:

(A) Both (A) and (R) are true

(B) (A) is true but (R) are false

(C) Both are partially true

(D) (R) is true and (A) is false

204. **Assertion (A) :** ISBD (S) is concerned with the serial publications.

Reason (R) : It is not used for the serials which have ceased their publication.

Codes:

(A) (A) is true but (R) is false

(B) (A) is false but (R) is true

(C) Both (A) and (R) are true

(D) Both (A) and (R) are false

205. **Assertion (A) :** AACR2 like CCC can satisfy all approaches of the users.

Reason (R) : Both AACR2 and CCCare comprehensive cataloguing codes.

Codes:

(A) (A) is true and (R) is false

(B) (R) is true but (A) is false

(C) Both (A) and (R) are true

(D) Both (A) and (R) are false

206. **Assertion (A) :** Any change in the environment of the subject can not affect the state of the subject

Reason (R) : A subject can be viewed as a system consisting of a set of interacting component ideas.

Code:

(A) (A) is true and (R) is false

(B) (R) is true and (A) is false

(C) Both (A) and (R) are true

(D) Both (A) and (R) are false

207. **Assertion (A) :** Use of microfilming is becoming obsolete day by day.

Reason (R) : ICT has developed digital technologies, which are quick, cheap and easy to handle.

(A) Both (A) and (R) are true but (R) is not a correct explanation.

(B) Both (A) and (R) are false.

(C) (A) is true but (R) is false

(D) Both (A) and (R) are true and (R) is the correct explanation of (A).

ANSWERS

1. (C)	2. (D)	3. (A)	4. (C)
5. (C)	6. (A)	7. (C)	8. (D)
9. (D)	10. (B)	11. (D)	12. (B)
13. (C)	14. (D)	15. (B)	16. (C)
17. (A)	18. (B)	19. (B)	20. (B)
21. (B)	22. (C)	23. (A)	24. (A)
25. (B)	26. (D)	27. (C)	28. (A)
29. (D)	30. (A)	31. (A)	32. (A)
33. (C)	34. (B)	35. (B)	36. (B)
37. (D)	38. (B)	39. (B)	40. (B)
41. (A)	42. (B)	43. (B)	44. (B)
45. (A)	46. (A)	47. (A)	48. (C)
49. (C)	50. (B)	51. (C)	52. (C)
53. (B)	54. (B)	55. (B)	56. (C)
57. (D)	58. (A)	59. (C)	60. (B)
61. (A)	62. (D)	63. (C)	64. (D)
65. (A)	66. (D)	67. (A)	68. (A)
69. (D)	70. (B)	71. (D)	72. (B)
73. (A)	74. (A)	75. (C)	76. (C)
77. (C)	78. (D)	79. (C)	80. (B)
81. (B)	82. (A)	83. (B)	84. (B)
85. (C)	86. (B)	87. (D)	88. (B)
89. (D)	90. (C)	91. (D)	92. (C)
93. (D)	94. (B)	95. (B)	96. (B)
97. (C)	98. (C)	99. (C)	100. (C)
101. (C)	102. (C)	103. (D)	104. (D)
105. (A)	106. (D)	107. (D)	108. (A)
109. (B)	110. (B)	111. (D)	112. (C)
113. (A)	114. (C)	115. (B)	116. (C)
117. (B)	118. (D)	119. (D)	120. (A)

121. (C)	122. (B)	123. (B)	124. (C)
125. (A)	126. (D)	127. (B)	128. (B)
129. (A)	130. (A)	131. (D)	132. (C)
133. (D)	134. (C)	135. (B)	136. (C)
137. (B)	138. (A)	139. (C)	140. (A)
141. (D)	142. (C)	143. (B)	144. (B)
145. (A)	146. (A)	147. (C)	148. (C)
149. (D)	150. (D)	151. (B)	152. (A)
153. (D)	154. (D)	155. (B)	156. (D)
157. (B)	158. (B)	159. (C)	160. (D)
161. (C)	162. (A)	163. (C)	164. (A)
165. (B)	166. (B)	167. (C)	168. (C)
169. (A)	170. (C)	171. (D)	172. (C)
173. (A)	174. (C)	175. (C)	176. (A)
177. (C)	178. (D)	179. (A)	180. (B)
181. (B)	182. (A)	183. (B)	184. (B)
185. (A)	186. (A)	187. (C)	188. (B)
189. (D)	190. (B)	191. (B)	192. (C)
193. (C)	194. (A)	195. (C)	196. (A)
197. (C)	198. (A)	199. (C)	200. (C)
201. (D)	202. (A)	203. (A)	204. (A)
205. (C)	206. (B)	207. (D)	

6

Computer Application

1. The factors that influence computer file organisation are

   (i) Speed of access (ii) Storage space

   (iii) Fixed length fields (iv) File volatility

   Codes :

   (A) (i), (ii) and (iii) are correct

   (B) (i), (ii) and (iv) are correct

   (C) (ii), (iii) and (iv) are correct

   (D) (i), (iii) and (iv) are correct

2. Major problems of 'Information Communication Technology' are

   (i) Information overload

   (ii) Information insecurity

   (iii) Lack of innovative technologies

   (iv) Lack of control over communication

   Codes :

   (A) (ii) and (iv) are correct

   (B) (i) and (iv) are correct

   (C) (i), (ii) and (iv) are correct

   (D) (i), (ii) and (iii) are correct

3. Which of the following are 'Open Source Content Management Systems'?

(i) Drupal (ii) Atex
(iii) Joomla (iv) OpenCms

Codes :

(A) (i), (ii) and (iv) are correct
(B) (i), (ii) and (iii) are correct
(C) (ii), (iii) and (iv) are correct
(D) (i), (iii) and (iv) are correct

4. Which one of the following is not a switching system?
(A) Packet (B) Circuit
(C) Router (D) Message

5. Which of the following are library networks ?
(i) Internet (ii) DELNET
(iii) NICNET (iv) OCLC

Codes :

(A) (i) and (ii) are correct.
(B) (ii) and (iv) are correct.
(C) (i) and (iii) are correct.
(D) (i) and (iv) are correct.

6. The general image file formats are:
(i) TIFF (ii) JPEG
(iii) MPEG (iv) PNG

Codes :

(A) (i), (ii) and (iii) are correct.
(B) (i), (iii) and (iv) are correct.
(C) (i), (ii) and (iv) are correct.
(D) (ii), (iii) and (iv) are correct.

7. Which of the following are common types of protocols ?
(i) HTTP (ii) FTP
(iii) Telnet (iv) Gopher

Codes :

(A) (i) and (ii) are correct.
(B) (i), (ii) and (iv) are correct.
(C) (iii) and (iv) are correct.
(D) (i), (ii) and (iii) are correct.

8. Which of the following are not the elements of DOI system ?

(i) Policies | (ii) Subject
(iii) Description | (iv) Resolution

Codes :

(A) (i), (ii) and (iii) are correct.
(B) (i), (iii) and (iv) are correct.
(C) (i), (ii) and (iv) are correct.
(D) (ii), (iii) and (iv) are correct.

9. METS stands for

(A) Machine Encoded Transmission System
(B) Metadata Encoded for Textual Sources
(C) Machine Encoded Textual Standard
(D) Metadata Encoding Transmission Standard

10. Arrange the following according to their year of origin:

(i) UNICODE | (ii) XML
(iii) HTML | (iv) SGML

Codes :

(A) (iv), (iii), (i), (ii) | (B) (iii), (iv), (ii), (i)
(C) (ii), (iv), (i), (iii) | (D) (i), (ii), (iii), (iv)

11. The information network that connects Universities and Colleges in United Kingdom :

(A) JANET | (B) SERCNET
(C) OCLC | (D) BONET

12. Internet filtering is

(A) A form of censorship
(B) Acceptable user policy
(C) Access to inappropriate material
(D) Blocking internet facility

13. Which one of the following is a Bulletin Board Service on Internet?

(A) Picaso | (B) Google talk
(C) Blog | (D) Oovoo

14. Virus is a software which can

(A) Manipulate data | (B) Replicate itself
(C) Damage computer | (D) All the above

15. Which one of the following protocol is used in file transfer over internet ?
    (A) FTP (B) SMTP
    (C) POP (D) TCP/IP
16. BIOS contain:
    (i) Operating System Program
    (ii) Bootstrap Program
    (iii) Application System Program
    (iv) Convert Character to Code Program
    Codes :
    (A) (i) and (ii) are correct
    (B) (ii) and (iii) are correct
    (C) (iii) and (iv) are correct
    (D) (ii) and (iv) are correct
17. Science Citation Index is published by
    (A) Thomson Reuters (B) H.W. Wilson
    (C) Whitaker (D) R.R. Bowker
18. Which one of the following is not a virtual library?
    (A) Without walls.
    (B) With distributed physical locations.
    (C) Providing integrated and unified remote access to geographically distributed collections.
    (D) Which does not exist in reality.
19. In 1974, Zurkowski used for the first time, which of the following term ?
    (A) Digital Literacy (B) Media Literacy
    (C) Computer Literacy (D) Information Literacy
20. Which of the factor is not helping in limiting the external validity ?
    (A) Reactive effect
    (B) Ecological validity
    (C) Interaction between selection bias of experimental variables
    (D) Ecological effect

21. Semantic differential scale is concerned with
    (A) Pool of items
    (B) Selection from two opposite positions
    (C) Five point scale
    (D) Selection from a check list
22. E-Journal articles can be identified with the help of
    (A) Digital Journal Identifier
    (B) Journal Source Identifier
    (C) Journal Article Identifier
    (D) Digital Object Identifier
23. The national convention regularly organized by DELNET is known as
    (A) CALIBER (B) ICDL
    (C) NACLIN (D) DELNETCON
24. Digital library function incorporate:
    (i) Creating and capturing
    (ii) Storage and management
    (iii) Search and access
    (iv) Abstracting and reviewing

    Codes :
    (A) (i), (ii) and (iii) are correct.
    (B) (i), (iii) and (iv) are correct.
    (C) (ii), (iii) and (iv) are correct.
    (D) (i), (ii) and (iv) are correct.
25. Which topology of computer network provides faster server access ?
    (i) BUS Network Topology
    (ii) RING Network Topology
    (iii) MULTIPLE RING Network Topology
    (iv) STAR Network Topology

    Codes :
    (A) (i) and (ii) are correct.
    (B) (i) and (iii) are correct.
    (C) (ii) and (iii) are correct.
    (D) (ii) and (iv) are correct.

26. Which of the following are ISDN services ?

(i) RSS (ii) Teletext

(iii) Voice mail (iv) Video conference

Codes :

(A) (i), (iii) and (iv) are correct.

(B) (i), (ii) and (iv) are correct.

(C) (ii), (iii) and (iv) are correct.

(D) (i), (ii) and (iii) are correct.

27. Planting the virus 'Trojan Horse' in computer network is

(i) Hacking (ii) Tampering

(iii) Decryption (iv) Intrusion

Codes :

(A) (i), (iii) and (iv) are correct

(B) (ii), (iii) and (iv) are correct

(C) (i), (ii) and (iii) are correct

(D) (i), (ii) and (iv) are correct

28. Identify the correct order as per increasing data storage capacity :

(A) CDROM, DVD, Cartridge, BlueRay Disc

(B) DVD, Cartridge, BlueRay Disc, CDROM

(C) Cartridge, CDROM, DVD, BlueRay Disc

(D) BlueRay Disc, DVD, Cartridge, CDROM

29. The distinct characteristic(s) of digital objects are

(A) Physical Medium

(B) Logical process

(C) Conceptual recognition and transaction

(D) All the above

30. ERIC is sponsored by

(A) US National Health Institute

(B) Health and Rehabilitation Services Division, A LA

(C) Department of Health Education & Welfare, Government of US A

(D) Institute of Education Sciences of the United States Department of Education

31. A technique displaying graphic information on screen, pixel by pixel with bits held in main memory is
    (A) Bit handling (B) Bit mapping
    (C) Bit pattern (D) Bit matrix
32. A network in which the host computer controls different nodes which further control other nodes, is known as
    (A) Star Network (B) Ring Network
    (C) Hierarchical Network (D) Multipoint Network
33. Template is a
    (A) Structured specification
    (B) Recursive routine
    (C) Assembler program
    (D) I/O measure
34. 'Open Journal Access System' in India is mainly managed by
    (A) NIC (B) CSIR
    (C) ICSSR (D) INFLIBNET
35. In the world wide web, name the acronym that describes the internet address of a file
    (A) ULA (B) RELUR
    (C) URI (D) URL
36. TKDL is developed and managed by
    (A) National Library and RRRLF
    (B) CSIR and RRRLF
    (C) CSIR and AYUSH
    (D) AYUSH and National Library
37. Web impact factor is developed by
    (A) P. Ingwersen (B) L. Bornebora
    (C) M. Thelwall (D) R. Rousseau
38. Which of the following is/are related to open access initiatives ?
    (i) Creative Commons (ii) DOAJ
    (iii) FOSS (iv) GNU

Codes :

(A) (i), (iii) and (iv) are correct.

(B) (i), (ii) and (iii) are correct.

(C) (ii) and (iii) are correct.

(D) (i) and (ii) are correct.

39. User-friendly interface caters to

(i) Human-computer Interaction

(ii) Individual users with customisation

(iii) Simplify execution of operations

(iv) Basis for computer-computer interface

Codes :

(A) (i), (ii) and (iv) are correct.

(B) (i) and (iii) are correct.

(C) (ii) and (iii) are correct.

(D) (i), (iii) and (iv) are correct.

40. Arrange the following in chronological order of their establishment:

(i) ARPANET

(ii) DARPA

(iii) SPUTNIK

(iv) ICCB (Internet Configuration Control Board)

Codes :

(A) iv i iii ii (B) iii ii i iv

(C) ii iii iv i (D) i ii iv iii

41. Which is known as malicious software.

(A) Malware (B) Shareware

(C) Firmware (D) None of this.

42. LAMP stands for

(A) Library Archives Management Programme

(B) Laser Analysis and Multimedia Performance

(C) Linux Apache. MySQL Perl

(D) Library Automation Management protocol

43. Name the storage medium (compatible with speed of CPU) for storing instructions or data temporarily during processing

(A) RAM (B) ROM
(C) Cache (D) EPROM

44. Which set of rules is applicable for exchange of files over Internet?
(A) FTP/IP (B) HTTP
(C) HTML (D) HYPERLINK

45. An Application Program Interface (API) language is used for
(A) Network Management
(B) Graphical user Interface
(C) Relational Interface in Data Base Management
(D) Database Management System

46. The following is a collaborative network of Reference Librarians
(A) Worldcat (B) INDEST
(C) Question point (D) Global scholar

47. Which of the following is not a synchronous virtual reference service ?
(A) Chat (B) E-mail
(C) Video-conferencing (D) Voice over IP

48. What does encrypting a file mean ?
(A) Set the read only property
(B) Hiding the file
(C) Set a password
(D) Scrambling the contents

49. The owner of Internet is:
(A) American Mathematical Society
(B) Department of Science and Technology, Govt. of India
(C) British Standard Institute
(D) None of the above

50. Which of the following identifies user by a login permission to a licensed site.
(A) Authorization (B) Authentication
(C) Digital signature (D) All of the above

51. Which of the following is not the component of a search engine ?
    (A) Spider
    (B) Index
    (C) Search of retrieval mechanism
    (D) Natural language technique
52. 'Communities' is a component of following digital library software
    (A) GSDL (B) D space
    (C) Fedora (D) i-core
53. Which one of the following is not an operation involved in quality circles ?
    (A) Problem identification
    (B) Problem selection
    (C) Solution recommendation
    (D) Problem shifting
54. Which of the following web address is acts as permanent identifier ?
    (A) URL (B) DOI
    (C) PURL (D) UDI
55. Arrange in sequence, the steps in programming:
    (i) Program code
    (ii) Program Documentation
    (iii) Program test
    (iv) Program design

    Codes :
    (A) iii ii i iv (B) iv i iii ii
    (C) iv iii ii i (D) ii iv i iii
56. Which of the following is/are the major activities/ services of a library and networks in India ?
    (i) Consortium purchase
    (ii) Indexing of Internet resources
    (iii) Document delivery
    (iv) Staff training

Codes :

(A) (i), (iii), (iv) are correct.

(B) (ii), (iii), (iv) are correct.

(C) (i), (ii), (iii) are correct.

(D) (i), (ii), (iii), (iv) are correct.

57. Which of the following makes a network insecured?

(A) Encryption

(B) Network Interface Card (NIC)

(C) Password Capture

(D) Static Keys

58. Which of the following three types of basic languages are used in computer programming?

(A) Procedural, Non-procedural and Unconditional

(B) Zero, Low and High levels

(C) Machine, Assembly and High level languages

(D) COBOL, BASIC and C

59. Which of the following are Web-zine?

(i) Email Magazine (ii) E-Conference

(iii) Online Bulletin (iv) Electronic News Letter

Codes:

(A) (i), (iii) and (iv) (B) (i), (ii) and (iii)

(C) (ii), (iii) and (iv) (D) (i), (ii) and (iv)

60. Rich Text Format (RTF) is concerned with

(i) Formatting features like Font type, size, etc.

(ii) Transporting text documents across different computers.

(iii) Multimedia formatting.

(iv) Formatting based on binary concept.

Codes:

(A) (ii) and (iii) are correct.

(B) (iii) and (iv) are correct.

(C) (i) and (ii) are correct.

(D) (i) and (iv) are correct.

61. DMAIC is the acronym for :
    (A) Define, Measure, Access, Improve and Control
    (B) Define, Measure, Analyse, Improve and Control
    (C) Describe, Measure, Analyse, Improve and Control
    (D) Define, Measure, Access, Instruct and Control
62. A template is a
    (A) Structured specification
    (B) Recursive routine
    (C) Assembler program
    (D) I/O measure
63. The mode of displaying graphic informationpixel by pixel with bits in main memory is
    (A) Bit handling (B) Bit mapping
    (C) Bit pattern (D) Bit matrix
64. An alerting service in the digital environment is offered through :
    (i) RSS feeds (ii) E-mail
    (iii) Blogs (iv) Bulletin Board
    Codes :
    (A) (i), (iii) are correct.
    (B) (ii), (iii), (iv) are correct.
    (C) (i), (ii), (iii) are correct.
    (D) (i), (ii), (iv) are correct.
65. Identify open source softwares for library management.
    (i) New Genlib (ii) SOUL
    (iii) LIBSYS (iv) KOHA
    Codes :
    (A) (i) and (ii) are correct.
    (B) (ii) and (iii) are correct.
    (C) (iii) and (iv) are correct.
    (D) (i) and (iv) are correct.
66. Arrange the following web browsers in chronological order :
    (i) Safari (ii) Chrome
    (iii) Netscape Navigator (iv) Firefox

Codes :

(A) (iv) (i) (ii) (iii) (B) (i) (ii) (iii) (iv)

(C) (ii) (i) (iv) (iii) (D) (iii) (i) (iv) (ii)

67. Which one is E-Bibliographic database?

(A) Nature (B) Blackwell

(C) ISID (D) Springer

68. Which one of the following protocols is used in transferring file over internet?

(A) POP (B) FTP

(C) SMTP (D) TCP/IP

69. In CDS/ISIS 'delimiters' means

(A) Field address (B) Field repeatability

(C) Field format (D) Subfield indicators

70. A situation where a digital resource is no longer readable is called

(A) Digital Divide (B) Digital Representation

(C) Digital Rendering (D) Digital Obsolescence

71. Which of the following are not the features of ISDN?

i. Simultaneous Digital Transmission

ii. Set of communication standards

iii. Creates and combines packets

iv. Program to visit web pages

Codes:

(A) i& ii are correct. (B) ii& iii are correct.

(C) iii& iv are correct. (D) i& iv are correct.

72. Which of the following facilitate formal communication on the web?

i. Wikis ii. Chat

iii. RSS feeds iv. Split screens

Codes:

(A) i& ii are correct. (B) ii&iii are correct.

(C) i& iii are correct. (D) iii& iv are correct.

73. Semantic Web is based on which of the following:

i. RDF ii. Ontologies

iii. URL iv. Cloud seeding

Codes:

(A) i, ii & iii are correct.

(B) ii, iii & iv are correct.

(C) i, iii & iv are correct.

(D) i, ii & iv are correct.

74. Which of the following are not web 2.0 Tools?

i. Ontologies ii. Facebook

iii. Intelligent Web iv. RSS Feeds

Codes:

(A) i& ii are correct. (B) i& iii are correct.

(C) ii& iii are correct. (D) iii& iv are correct.

75. Which of the following are plagiarism detection software?

(i) Turnitin (ii) Ithenticate

(iii) Tulips (iv) Veri Guide

Codes:

(A) (i) and (ii) (B) (i), (ii) and (iii)

(C) (i), (ii) and (iv) (D) (ii) and (iii)

76. Which of the following are statistical programming software?

i. GAUSS ii. SAS

iii. SPSS iv. SLIM

Codes:

(A) i, iii and iv (B) i, ii and iii

(C) i, ii and iv (D) ii, iii and iv

77. Arrange the following according to their year of emergence:

i. ERNET ii. NICNET

iii. C-DOT iv. C-DAC

Codes:

(A) ii, iii, i, iv (B) iii, ii, iv, i

(C) iv, ii, iii, i (D) i, iv, iii, ii

78. Arrange the following in the order of development:

i. GML ii. Hypermedia

iii. SGML iv. Memex

Codes:

(A) i, ii, iii, iv (B) iv, ii, i, iii

(C) ii, iii, iv, i (D) iii, ii, i, iv

79. KOHA is written in which of the following language ?

(A) C, C++ (B) Java

(C) Karel++ (D) Pearl

80. Which of the following is an example of URN ?

(A) URL (B) URI

(C) DOI (D) ISBN

81. Identify the founders of Wikipedia from the following :

i. Michael E Davis ii. Jimmy Wales

iii. Richard Stallman iv. Larry Sanger

Codes :

(A) ii and iii are correct. (B) i and ii are correct.

(C) i and iii are correct. (D) ii and iv are correct.

82. Identify the assistive softwares :

i. Cybrarian ii. Dragon

iii. Jaws iv. Librarian

Codes :

(A) i and ii are correct. (B) i and iii are correct.

(C) ii and iii are correct. (D) iii and iv are correct.

83. Which of the following are features of 'Open Journal System' ?

i. License to access content

ii. Access restricted to limited group

iii. Online submission

iv. Subscription module with delayed open access options

Codes :

(A) i and ii are correct. (B) ii and iii are correct.

(C) iii and iv are correct. (D) ii and iv are correct.

84. Identify the types of OCR technology

i. Matrix matching ii. Instructional analysis

iii. Feature extraction iv. Structural analysis

Codes :

(A) i, ii, iv are true. (B) i, ii, iii are true.

(C) ii, iii, iv are true. (D) i, iii, iv are true.

85. Which of the following are features of flash memory ?

i. Erasable & Programmable Read Only Memory

ii. Non-volatile memory

iii. Temporary storage unit

iv. Dynamic RAM

Codes :

(A) i, ii, iii are correct. (B) i, ii, iv are correct.

(C) i, ii are correct. (D) ii, iv are correct.

86. SQL is based on which of the following ?

i. Query string

ii. Relational algebra

iii. Relational calculus

iv. Web search queries

Codes :

(A) i, ii are correct. (B) ii, iii are correct.

(C) iii, iv are correct. (D) ii, iv are correct.

87. What are the approaches to plagiarism check of academic publications ?

i. String matching ii. Bag of words analysis

iii. Citation analysis iv. Parse trees

Codes :

(A) ii, iv are correct. (B) i, ii, iii are correct.

(C) i,iv are correct. (D) i, iii, iv are correct.

88. Identify the technology of digitization.

i. Bit-depth ii. Resolution

iii. Manipulation iv. Image enhancement

Codes :

(A) ii, iii, iv are correct. (B) i, iii, iv are correct.

(C) i, ii, iv are correct. (D) i, ii, iii are correct.

89. Which of the following are the types of validity of measurement ?

i. Construct ii. Current
iii. Content iv. Predictive

Codes :

(A) i, ii, iii are true. (B) ii, iii, iv are true.
(C) i, iii, iv are true. (D) i, ii, iv are true.

90. Which are not open source library softwares ?

i. Bibliosys ii. Evergreen
iii. New Genlib iv. Virtua

Codes :

(A) i and ii are correct. (B) i and iii are correct.
(C) i and iv are correct. (D) ii and iv are correct.

91. Identify the compression protocols :

i. TIFF ii. JPEG
iii. ZIFF iv. LZW

Codes :

(A) i, iii, iv are correct. (B) i, ii, iv are correct.
(C) ii, iii, iv are correct. (D) i, ii, iii are correct.

92. "Internet Public Library" is being maintained by

(A) MIT, Massachusettes
(B) University of Michigan
(C) University of Arizona
(D) Drexal University

93. The main component of Third Generation Computer is

(A) Transistor (B) Vacuum Tube
(C) Microchip (D) Integrated circuits

94. A protocol that manages data transfer on the internet is

(A) HTTP (B) FTP/OP
(C) FTP/IP (D) TCP/IP

95. The acronym 'DOI' stands for

(A) Digital Object Items
(B) Digital Object Identifier
(C) Digital Object Isolates
(D) Digital Object Information

96. The convention of INFLIBNET organized to discuss the progress of library automation and library service is known as

    (A) DELNET (B) NACLIN
    (C) UGC-INFONET (D) CALIBER

97. HTML is related to

    (A) HTTP (B) TCP/IP
    (C) SGML (D) XML

98. The logical operators AND, OR and NOT are devised by

    (A) F. W. Laucaster (B) David Boole
    (C) Charles Babbage (D) George Boole

99. URL stands for

    (A) Universal Research Locator
    (B) Universal Resource Locator
    (C) Uniform Resource Locator
    (D) Uniform Resource Log.in

100. Multiplexer is a data communication

    (A) Software (B) Equipment
    (C) Process (D) Network

101. Arrange the following networks according to their year of establishment.

    (i) BONET (ii) DELNET
    (iii) INFLIBNET (iv) CALIBNET

    Codes :

    (A) (i) (ii) (iv) (iii) (B) (ii) (i) (iv) (iii)
    (C) (ii) (iv) (iii) (i) (D) (iv) (ii) (iii) (i)

102. Arrange the following work components of WINISIS according to the order of sequence of operation.

    (i) FST (ii) FDT
    (iii) Print format (iv) Workshet

    Codes :

    (A) (iv) (i) (ii) (iii) (B) (i) (iv) (ii) (iii)
    (C) (ii) (iv) (iii) (i) (D) (ii) (i) (iv) (iii)

103. Which of the following is associated with Mortimer Taube ?

(A) PERT/CPM (B) Cataloguing
(C) Classification (D) Indexing

104. In which of the following network topologies, all the computers are directly connected to a Central Computer?
(A) Ring topology (B) Bus topology
(C) Peer to Peer topology (D) Star topology

105. Which of the following database programs is used in DSpace?
(A) PostgreSQL (B) MSSQL
(C) MySQL (D) None of the above

106. Which one of the following is not a Web 2.0 enable product?
(A) Wiki (B) Blog
(C) Facebook (D) None of the above

107. What is LYCOS ?
(A) Database (B) Browser
(C) Web Portal (D) e-Book

108. Which one of the following is called a volatile memory?
(A) Random Access Memory (RAM)
(B) Read Only Memory (ROM)
(C) Erasable Programable ROM (EPROM)
(D) None of the above

109. Which one of the following search devices will lead to an increase in the Recall output?
(A) Boolean 'AND' (B) Boolean 'NOT'
(C) Proximity operators (D) Truncation

110. CDS/ISIS was introduced first by
(A) DRTC (B) IBM
(C) CSIR (D) UNESCO

111. 'Google earth' is
(A) Web Image (B) Search Engine
(C) Virtual Globe (D) Webmap Search

112. In computer terminology, the term 'bug' stands for

(A) Error in Programming
(B) Computer Virus
(C) Error in Humanware Selection
(D) Error in Software Selection

113. Following one is not a web 2.0 Tool

(A) Blog (B) Facebook
(C) UGC-Infonet (D) RSS-feeds

114. NICNET and INDONET are the networks of which category

(A) LAN (B) MAN
(C) WAN (D) NIC

115. Arrange the following networks chronologically according to their year of establishment

(i) INFLIBNET (ii) DELNET
(iii) BLAISE (iv) JANET

Codes:

(A) ii, iv, iii, i (B) iii, iv, ii, i
(C) I, iii, iv, i (D) iii, iv, i, ii

116. Arrange the following according to the year of their development

(i) Java 1.0 (ii) COBOL
(iii) Visual Basic (iv) C++

Codes:

(A) iv, iii, i, ii (B) ii, iii, iv, i
(C) i, ii, iv, iii (D) ii, iv, iii, i

117. Arrange the stages in the 'Technology transfer model' in a proper order

(i) Awareness (ii) Adoption
(iii) Trail (iv) Introduction

Codes:

(A) iv, i, iii, ii (B) iii, iv, i, ii
(C) iv, ii, iii, i (D) iii, i, ii, iv

118. In Binary Number System digit 4 is represented by :

(A) 10 (B) 11
(C) 100 (D) 101

119. Open System Interconnection was an effort to :
   (A) Standardise networking
   (B) Provide Internet Connectivity
   (C) Provide e-mails
   (D) Standardise bibliographic description

120. What is not true about spamming ?
   (A) It is the abuse of electronic messaging system
   (B) The most widely recognized form of spam is e-mail spam
   (C) Spamming is expensive to advertise
   (D) Spamming costs huge in terms of loss of productivity

121. What is used to present text and static graphics in Hypertext ?
   (A) Hyperline (B) Infoline
   (C) Hyperlinks (D) Dataline

122. A router :
   (A) Receives a signal and retransmit it at a higher level
   (B) Helps to interface with another network
   (C) Essentially translates protocols
   (D) Forwards data packets between telecommunication networks

123. Which of the following.is not an open source library software.
   (A) Greenstone (B) NewGenLib
   (C) Drupal (D) Libsuit

124. POP stands for :
   (A) Print Office Protocol (B) Post Offer Protocol
   (C) Pre Office Protocol (D) Post Office Protocol

125. Which of the following key combinations when pressed, restarts the computer ?
   (A) Ctrl+Alt+V (B) Ctrl+Alt+Z
   (C) Ctrl+Alt+Del (D) Ctrl+Alt+C

126. "Information is piecemeal, fragmented and particular." Who said ?

(A) Daniel Bell (B) Fritz Machlup
(C) Brookers (D) Belkin

127. WordNetis :
(A) A Thesaurus
(B) A Classification Scheme
(C) A Library Network
(D) An Ontology

128. Which of the following is not a bibliographic network ?
(A) OCLC (B) ISO
(C) CAS (D) A-G Canada

129. The edition statement is given in parenthesis immediately after the title of the documents in :
(A) Chicago Manual of Style
(B) Modern Language Associate
(C) American Psychological Association
(D) Scientific Style and Format

130. In web 2.0 tagging is called :
(A) Economy (B) Taxonomy
(C) Synonymy (D) Folksonomy

131. The word 'hyper' in hypertext means
(A) extension into broader dimensions
(B) extension into similar dimensions
(C) extension into other dimensions
(D) extension into narrower dimensions

132. Who has coined the term 'blog'?
(A) John Berger (B) Peter Merholz
(C) MichealZeinne (D) David Weiner

133. Which digital library software was developed at Cornell University?
(A) FEDORA (B) EPrints
(C) GSDL (D) DSpace

134. When DSpace was first released under the terms of the BSD open source license?
(A) 2000 (B) 2002
(C) 2004 (D) 1998

135. Arrange the following technologies according to the year of their inventions in descending order:
    (i) Internet
    (ii) Satellite Communication
    (iii) Telephone
    (iv) Television
    Codes:
    (A) (i), (ii), (iv), (iii) (B) (ii), (iii), (i), (iv)
    (C) (iii), (iv), (ii), (i) (D) none of the above
136. The indexing techniques (0-3) as used in WINISIS will produce
    (A) post coordinate index (B) pre coordinate index
    (C) both (A) and (B) (D) none of the above
137. Identify the correct order of the evolution of the following storage devices in descending order:
    (A) DVD, Magnetic tape, Floppy, CD
    (B) Magnetic tape, DVD, CD, Floppy
    (C) DVD, CD, Floppy, Magnetic tape
    (D) DVD, Floppy, Magnetic tape, CD
138. One of the following search engine is exclusively meant for scientific information :
    (A) Google (B) Yahoo
    (C) SCIRUS (D) Altavista
139. GUI stands for :
    (A) Graphic User Interface
    (B) Graphic User Interaction
    (C) Graphic Utility Interface
    (D) Great Union of India
140. Who enunciated the term 'hypertext' ?
    (A) E. Garfield (B) Bill Gates
    (C) Ted Nelson (D) Raj Reddy
141. Mozilla is.-.
    (A) An operating system (B) Library software
    (C) A web browser (D) A search engine

142. High Level Language is-
    (A) Disk space dependent
    (B) O. S. dependent
    (C) Machine independent
    (D) Machine dependent

143. Protocol means-
    (A) Interchange of data between two devices
    (B) Interchange of data between two computers
    (C) Linkage between two computers
    (D) Linkage between two devices

144. What is not open source software for library management ?
    (A) KOHA (B) AVANT1
    (C) php my Library (D) 2.39-50.

145. Which one of the following protocols is used in transferring file over internet ?
    (A) POP (B) FTP
    (C) SMTP (D) TCP/IP

146. Transistors were used in which generation of computers ?
    (A) First generation (B) Second generation
    (C) Third generation (D) None of the above

147. Linux is an example of
    (A) Application software (B) System software
    (C) Library software (D) All of the above

148. How different nodes in a network are connected and how they communicate are determined ?
    (A) By Network Connectivity
    (B) By Network Topology
    (C) By Network Compatibility
    (D) None of the above

149. WorldCat is maintained by
    (A) Library of Congress
    (B) Online Computer Library Center
    (C) American Library Association
    (D) None of the above

150. World Wide Web was first designed by
    (A) Charles Babbage (B) F.W. Lancaster
    (C) Ted Nelson (D) Tim Berner's Lee
151. A computer that connects one network to another for the purpose of file transfer is known as ...
    (a) Highway (b) Search Engine
    (c) Gateway (d) Super way
152. INIS is an example of
    (A) distributed input and centralised output
    (B) centralised input and output
    (C) centralised input and distributed output
    (D) distributed input and output.
153. Which of the following network is not primarily for academic purposes?
    (A) ERNET (B) JANET
    (C) NICNET (D) INFLIBNET.
154. Transboarder data flow means
    (A) exchange of documents between countries
    (B) free flow of books between countries
    (C) exchange of electronic information between countries
    (D) none of these.
155. INFLIBNET is a programme sponsored by
    (A) NISSAT
    (B) Planning Commission
    (C) Ministry of Electronics
    (D) UGC.
156. The World Cat Service is provided by
    (A) RLIN (B) OCLC
    (C) LC (D) WLN.
157. Which is the World's largest and most comprehensive bibliographic database?
    (A) First search (B) OCLC Access Service
    (C) World Cat (D) Prompt Cat.
158. CD-ROM is a

(A) computer language (B) storage device
(C) application software (D) operating system.

159. PC falls in the category of
(A) super computer (B) mainframe computer
(C) mini computer (D) micro computer.

160. LAN stands for
(A) Library Automation Network
(B) Library and Network
(C) Library Area Network
(D) Local Area Network.

161. VDUs in computers are used for
(A) input (B) output
(C) control (D) storage.

162. The IT used for simulation of the human thought is known as
(A) thinking simulation
(B) third generation computers
(C) thought process mechanism
(D) artificial intelligence.

163. RAM stands for
(A) Read Access Memory
(B) Read and Memory
(C) Read Active Memory
(D) Random Access Memory.

164. The example of programmeming language is
(A) CPU (B) VDU
(C) Hard Drive (D) Pascal.

165. Arithmetic and Logical Unit in the context of computer denotes
(A) software (B) hardware
(C) programmeming unit (D) printing unit.

166. Modem is a
(A) software device (B) scanner
(C) CD drive
(D) hardware device that converts from one form to another.

167. The example of a high level language is
   (A) adobe photo shop (B) Auto CAD
   (C) macromedia flash (D) ForTran.
168. CD-ROM stands for
   (A) Compact Disk Read Output Memory
   (B) Compact disk Read On Memory
   (C) Compact Disk Read Over Memory
   (D) Compact Disk Read Only Memory.
169. The memory part of computer's CPU is also known as
   (A) external storage unit (B) internal storage unit
   (C) data storage unit (D) language storage unit.
170. Basic is a
   (A) hardware item
   (B) part of Internet communication
   (C) programmeming language
   (D) none of these.
171. Valves and tubes were used as main processors in
   (A) 1st generation computers
   (B) 2nd generation computers
   (C) 3rd generation computers
   (D) 4th generation computers.
172. MINISIS requires for its operation
   (A) Pentium1 computer system
   (B) Pentium2 computer system
   (C) 486 computer system
   (D) HP3000 computer system.
173. Volatile memory is referred to as
   (A) ROM (B) EPROM
   (C) RAM (D) none of these.
174. In the context of computers 'BIT' stands for
   (A) Binary Information Technology
   (B) Booting Information Technology
   (C) Binary Input Technology
   (D) Binary Digit.

175. Computerised library house keeping is done with
(A) system software (B) application software
(C) CPU (D) VDU.
176. DBase is a
(A) application software (B) system software
(C) internal storage (D) external storage.
177. In WordStar for opening a file the option given is
(A) A (B) B
(C) C (D) D.
178. In computer terminology 'C' refers to
(A) programmeming language
(B) cabinet
(C) cache memory
(D) COBOL.
179. CDS/ISIS is operated through
(A) Unix (B) Linux
(C) DOS (D) Windows.
180. In CDS/ISIS for creating a new record the option given is
(A) L (B) M
(C) N (D) P.
181. IBM stands for
(A) International Binary Machines
(B) International Booting Machines
(C) International Business Machines, Inc.
(D) none of these.
182. Byte refers to
(A) a string of five binary digits
(B) a sting of six binary digits
(C) a string of seven binary digits
(D) a string of eight binary digits.
183. The following are the useful input devices
(A) Keyboard, RAM and CD-ROMs
(B) OCR, Light Pens and Keyboards
(C) CD-ROM, OCR and Floppy Disks
(D) Hard Disks, Magnetic Tapes and Light Pens.

184. Which of the following is not a computer programmeming language?
(A) FORTRAN (B) Basic
(C) COBOL (D) ASCII.

185. In the binary system of numbers 100 represents the decimal number
(A) 100 (B) 1
(C) 4 (D) 3.

186. In relation to computer Basic is
(A) core memory (B) hardware
(C) model (D) language.

187. Arrange the following storage devices according to increasing capacity
(a) magnetic tapes (b) CD-ROMs
(c) Floppy disks (d) Magnetic disks.

Code :
(A) (c), (a), (d), (b) (B) (a), (b), (c), (d)
(C) (d), (c), (a), (b) (D) (d), (a), (b), (c).

188. The following software is a typical example of an operating system
(A) DOS (B) WordStar
(C) dBase III+ (D) Lotus 1-2-3.

189. Computers are used for handling large mass of
(A) information and its quick retrieval
(B) books and its quick retrieval
(C) news and its quick retrieval
(D) libraries and its quick retrieval.

190. OCR stands for
(A) Online Computer Retrieval
(B) Optical Character Recognition
(C) Online Centre for Reprographics
(D) Optical Computer Recorder

191. A plotter is a
(A) An input device (B) A memory device
(C) An output device (D) None of the above

192. The device that coverts analog signal to digital and vice versa is
   (A) MODEM (B) Analog computer
   (C) Digital computer (D) Digicom
193. Among the different Boolean operators 'AND' is used
   (E) to widen the search (F) to narrow the search
   (G) to begin the search (H) to end the search
194. Which of the following types of memory is volatile
   (A) ROM (B) PROM
   (C) WORM (D) RAM
195. Which of the following is not a programming language?
   (A) FORTRAN (B) BΛSIC
   (C) COBOL (D) ASCII
196. When you creat a worksheet in CDS/ISIS you are defining
   (A) the external user view
   (B) the internal file structure
   (C) the conceptual frame
   (D) all of the above
197. Which of the following networks does not have its own telecommunication infrastructure
   (A) NICNET (B) ERNET
   (C) INIS (D) EURONET
198. OPAC stands for
   (A) Online Public Access Catalogue
   (B) Online Periodicals Access Centre
   (C) Online Patents Access
   (D) None of the above
199. Windows NT is the name of
   (A) Cable TV
   (B) Network
   (C) A Computer Operating System
   (D) an online database
200. Boolean Logic was propounded by:
   (A) B.C.Vickery (B) S.C.Bradford
   (C) J.Buckland (D) George Boole

201. The abbreviation MB to state the storage capacity refers to:

(A) Mega bytes (B) Million Bits
(C) Million bytes (D) mega bits

202. The concept of Micro photography was developed by:

(A) Johan Gutenberg
(B) Chester cardson
(C) John Benjamin Dancer (1839)
(D) Ohi Battle

203. Which among the following is a digital library software used in the creation of an inhouse digital library

(A) LIBSYS (B) Greenstone
(C) Alice for Windows (D) Micro CDS/ISIS

204. The Compact Disk is conceptually referred to as:

(I) Magnetic storage (II) Compact storage
(III) Optical storage (IV) All the above

In the type of items, there may be more than one answer. Identify the correct combination:

(A) I, II and III are correct
(B) II and III are correct
(C) I and III are correct
(D) (II) and (IV) are correct

205. Arrange the following units of storage capacity in increasing order of magnitude. Use the code given below:

I. Gigabyte II. Kilobyte
III. Terabyte IV. Megabyte

Codes :

(A) IV, II, III, I (B) I, III, II, IV
(C) III, IV, I, II (D) II, IV, I, III

206. Arrange the following components in order in which they were used in computers. Use the code given below:

I. Transistors (2nd gen.)
II. Vacuum Tubes (1st gen.)
III. Large Scale Integrated Circuit (3rd gen.)
IV. Very Large Scale Integrated Circuit (4th gen.)

Codes:

(A) I, III, II, IV (B) II, I, III, IV

(C) II, III, IV, I (D) IV, I, III, II

207. URL stands for:

(A) Uniform Resource Locator

(B) Universal Resource Locator

(C) Unified Resource Locator

(D) Uniform Reference Locator

208. A series of interconnected documents stored on the Internet is called:

(A) Websites (B) Domain Name

(C) Home Page (D) Web Page

209. The term 'Bandwidth' refers to:

(A) The amount of data that can be sent through communication media

(B) The amount of data in a multimedia file

(C) The speed of transmission of data

(D) Number of bands available in a computer

210. OCLC is:

(i) Online Computer Library Center

(ii) At Dublin (Ohio)

(iii) At New York

(iv) Ohio College Library Center

Code :

(A) (i) and (ii) are correct

(B) (i) and (iii) are correct

(C) (iii) and (iv) are correct

(D) (ii) and (iv) are correct

211. Use of integrated circuits was made in

(A) First Generation Computers

(B) Second Generation Computers

(C) Third Generation Computer

(D) Fourth Generation Computers

212. The Network Topology in which nodes are connected to a central hub is known as

(A) Ring Topology (B) Bus Topology
(C) Star Topology (D) Mesh Topology

213. Computer Memory is measured in
(A) Bytes (B) Kilobytes
(C) Megabytes (D) All of the above

214. DELNET stands for
(A) Developing Library Network
(B) Department of Electronics Library Network
(C) Distance Education Library Network
(D) Delhi Library Network

215. Arrange the following chronologically according to their use in computers :
(i) Vacuum tube (ii) Microchip
(iii) Integrated circuits (iv) Transistors
Codes :
(A) (i), (iii), (ii), (iv) (B) (i), (ii), (iii), (iv)
(C) (i), (iv), (iii), (ii) (D) (ii), (iv), (iii), (i)

216. Who is the Father of a computer
(A) Steve Jobs (B) Vint Cerf
(C) Tim Berners-Lee (D) Charles Babbage

217. World Wide Web (WWW) was first designed by whom?
(A) Charles Babbage (B) F. W. Lancaster
(C) Ted Nelson (D) Tim Berner's Lee

218. Which generation computers uses integrated circuits(ICs)?
(A) First (B) Second
(C) Third (D) Fourth

219. The generatation of Computer denotes the concept of Artificial Intelligence (AI) is
(A) Second Generation Computers
(B) Third Generation Computers
(C) Fourth Generation Computers
(D) Fifth Generation Computers

220. The unit that measures computer memory is ;
(A) Bytes (B) Kilobytes
(C) Megabytes (D) All of the above

221. Who was first used the term "Cyberspace" ?
(A) Andrew Pollock (B) William Gibson
(C) John Postal (D) Joe Flower
222. When CD-ROM was prepared and made?
(A) 1985 (B) 1982
(C) 1980 (D) 1977
223. In how many ways switching system can be established?
(A) Two (B) Three
(C) Five (D) Seven
224. Which type of switching system is telephone network?
(A) Circuit switching (B) Packet switching
(C) Message switching (D) None of the above
225. NICNET and INDONET are the networks of which category?
(A) LAN (B) MAN
(C) WAN (D) IN
226. Who designed analytical engine?
(A) Charles Babbage (B) Pascal
(C) James watt (D) Boyl
227. Calculating machine is developed by
(A) Charles Babbage (B) Pascal
(C) Shakuntala Devi (D) Boyl
228. What is a bug?
(A) Computer Virus
(B) Error in Computer Configuration
(C) Error in a Programme
(D) None of these
229. Which is not a programming language?
(A) FORTRAN (B) BASIC
(C) COBOL (D) ASCII
230. ENIAC stands for?
(A) Electronic Numerical Integrator and Calculator
(B) Electrified Numerical Integration and Calculator
(C) Electronic Number Integrator and Calculator
(D) Electrical Numerical Integrator and Calculator

231. ISO-9960 is related with?
    (A) Standard for encoding data on CD-ROM
    (B) Standard for Computer Hardware
    (C) Standard for Information Processing
    (D) Standard for Networking
232. ASCII has how many codes?
    (A) 256 (B) 526
    (C) 265 (D) 254
233. INTERNET was initially developed by US Department of
    (A) Commerce (B) Defense
    (C) Interior (D) State
234. Information retrieval is fastest from
    (A) Floppy Disk (B) Magnetic Tape
    (C) Hard Disk (D) None of the above
235. An University providing Open Access to Sanskrit dissertations through Internet
    (A) Jawaharlal Nehru University
    (B) Delhi University
    (C) Mahatma Gandhi University
    (D) University of Madras
236. In which of the following the term "Truncation" is used
    (A) Budgeting (B) Search Formulation
    (C) Coordination (D) Classified bibliography
237. UNIX is a
    (A) Single user operating system
    (B) Double user operating system
    (C) Triple user operating system
    (D) Multi user operating system
238. The CD alphabets in CDS/ISIS stands for
    (A) Computerized Documentation
    (B) Condensed Disk
    (C) Confirmed Disc
    (D) Compact Disc
239. Electronic telecommunications system joining millions of computers together.

(A) E-mail (B) Internet
(C) US Mail (D) UPS

240. Following is not a social bookmarking site:
(A) Digg (B) Delicious
(C) Sqidoo (D) Facebook

241. Following is not a network protocol:
(A) HTTP (B) SMTP
(C) TCP/IP (D) Z39.50

242. LOCKOSS (Software) is an international community initiative by:
(A) MIT Libraries
(B) Stanford University
(C) University of Waikato
(D) University of Southampton

243. Identify the odd one from the following:
(A) Koha (B) VTLS
(C) SLIM++ (D) SOUL

244. Following is not a Web 2.0 tool:
(A) Blog (B) Facebook
(C) UGC-INFONET 2.0 (D) RSS feeds

245. PDA stands for:
(A) Personal Digital Assistance
(B) Personal Document Archive
(C) Personal Digital Archive
(D) Program Download Accessories

246. PLONE is a:
(A) Content Mnagement System
(B) Digital Library Software
(C) ILMS
(D) Federated Search Engine

247. Pi is the e-book reading device by:
(A) Amazon (B) Sony
(C) Infibeam (D) Nokia

248. Following is an example of microblogging:
(A) Wordpress (B) Blogspot
(C) Livejournal (D) Twitter

249. Who invented OSI Model in 1982
  (A) BSO
  (B) ISI
  (C) Indian standerdorgganisation
  (D) International standard organization
250. Where ISDN was first started in 1990
  (A) USA (B) UK
  (C) India (D) Singapore
251. Now-a-days how many tipes of Protocol are used ?
  (A) 5 (B) 4
  (C) 3 (D) 2
252. Which type of protocol is used by interface for public data network(PDN) ?
  (A) X.25 (B) X.12
  (C) X.13 (D) X.20
253. In Which five year plan the INFLIBNET was established
  (A) Fourth five year plan (B) Fifth five year plan
  (C) sixth five year plan (D) seventh five year plan
254. INFLIBNET headquarters is located at
  (A) Ahmedabad (B) New Delhi
  (C) Bangalore (D) Chennai
255. What is the full form of ERNET?
  (A) Engineering Network
  (B) Eastern Regional Network
  (C) Electronic Research Network
  (D) Education and Research Network
256. Which network in India provided the first e-mail service in the country?
  (A) NICNET (B) DELNET
  (C) ERNET (D) INFLIBNET
257. What is full text e-Resource ?
  (A) JCCC
  (B) ISID
  (C) Science finder scholar
  (D) ACS

258. What is file extension of erlang.?
(A) .NET (B) .ERL
(C) .HRL (D) .SML

259. Which of the following is the Electronic Library ?
(A) A Magazine (B) A Journal Name
(C) A Library (D) An Encyclopedia

260. What is e-prints ?
(A) A catalogue (B) A journal
(C) A repository Software (D) An encyclopedia

261. What two is a Library Management Software for small libraries?
(A) Library Solution and Follet
(B) Follet and MSN
(C) MSN and Tar
(D) LYCOS and Live Search

262. What is APS ?
(A) A Search Engine?
(B) A Full-text e-resource
(C) Bibliographic database
(D) Library Management Software

263. "Shodhganga" is a national level repository of:
(A) E-Books (B) E-Journals
(C) E-Theses (D) Journal Articles
(E) None of the above

264. One of the following is not an open source software :
(A) D'space (B) Windows
(C) Green-stone (D) Linux

265. Who provides the ISBN?
(A) Niscair (B) Nissat
(C) Insdoc (D) RRRLF

266. RRRLF provides the?
(A) ISSN (B) ISBN
(C) CCF (D) MARC

267. Windows NT is the name of

(A) Cable TV
(B) Network
(C) A Computer Operating Sytem
(D) An On-line database

268. Among the different Boolean operators "AND" is used
(A) to widen the search
(B) to narrow the search
(C) to begin the search
(D) to end the search

269. Which of the following types of memory is volatile
(A) ROM (B) PROM
(C) WORM (D) RAM

270. Who mainly provides internet service in India
(A) Department of Electronics
(B) NIC
(C) CMC
(D) VSNL

271. Which of the following networks does not have its own tele-communicationinfrastructure
(A) NICNET (B) ERNET
(C) INIS (D) EURONET

272. OPAC stands for
(A) Online Public Access Catalogue
(B) Online Periodicals Access Centre
(C) Online Patents Access Centre
(D) None of the above

273. Which of the following cannot be regarded as 'multimedia'
(A) A tape-slide programme
(B) A CD-ROM with text and visuals
(C) Microfilm
(D) A web page

274. Which of the following is a process of Information ?
(A) Books (B) CD-ROM
(C) Computers (D) None of the above

275. What is the full form of ERNET?
   (A) Engineering Network
   (B) Eastern Regional Network
   (C) Electronic Research Network
   (D) Education and Research Network
276. Which network in India provided the first e-mail service in the country?
   (A) NICNET (B) DELNET
   (C) ERNET (D) INFLIBNET
277. Microchip was invented by ...
   (A) Microsoft (B) IBM
   (C) DELL (D) Intel
278. Which are the facets relating to INFLIBNET ?
   (A) CALIBER (B) PLANNER
   (C) UGC-INFONET (D) SOUL
   Of these :
   (A) (a), (c) and (d) (C) (a), (b) and (c)
   (B) (c), (b) and (a) (D) all of these.
279. What is not open source software for library management ?
   (A) KOHA (B) AVANT1
   (C) php my Library (D) 2.39-50.
280. Which of the following is not correctly matched ?
   (A) DELNET - Telecommunication Network
   (B) Digital Library - Print Material
   (C) Thesaurus - List of Descriptors
   (D) ISBN - Serial Number
281. In which of the following network topologies, all the computers are connected to a central computer :
   (A) Ring (B) Star
   (C) Bus (D) Peer to Peer
282. If the size of the study population is very small, the following sampling method will give better results :
   (A) Purposive (B) Stratified
   (C) Random (D) Census

283. Which of the following search devices will lead to an increase in the Recall output ?
    (A) Boolean 'And' (B) Boolean 'Not'
    (C) Proximity Operators (D) Truncation
284. DELNET is a
    (A) wide area network (B) local area network
    (C) national network (D) regional network.
285. British Library Automated Information Services (BLAISE) is useful in the field of
    (A) Biochemistry (B) Biomedicine
    (C) Biophysics (D) Biology.
286. NICNET is a project sponsored by
    (A) Government of India (B) UGC
    (C) INFLIBNET (D) NISSAT.
287. AGRIS is mainly sponsored by
    (A) ICAR (B) IFLA
    (C) UNISIST & FAO (D) UNESCO.
288. INFLIBNET stands for
    (A) Informing Library Network
    (B) Information and Librarians Network
    (C) Information and Library Network
    (D) Indian National Frontier Library Network.
289. The library network mainly for university libraries in India is known as
    (A) CALIBNET (B) MALIBNET
    (C) INFLIBNET (D) DELNET.
290. National Information Centre on Chemistry and Chemical Technology (NICCHEM) is located at
    (A) Pune (B) Lucknow
    (C) Hyderabad (D) Bangalore.
291. NICDAP stands for
    (A) National Information Centre for Data Access Programmeming
    (B) National Information Centre for Document Access Programmeming

(C) National Information Centre for Development and Programmeming

(D) National Information Centre for Drug and Pharmaceutical.

292. ERIC databases in USA covers the information regarding

(A) education (B) energy

(C) environment (D) mathematics.

293. NISSAT's sectoral information centre on drug is located at

(A) Pune (B) Lucknow

(C) New Delhi (D) Chennai.

294. The Library and Information Division of ICAR is the national centre for all

(A) INIS activities (B) AGRIS activities

(C) FAO activities (D) UNISIST activities.

295. NISSAT is responsible for rendering of information services in the field of

(A) research and development

(B) science and technology

(C) agriculture

(D) medicine.

296. INIS stands for

(A) Indian Naval Information System

(B) Indian Narcotics Information Service

(C) International Nuclear Information System

(D) Indian National Information System.

297. BLAISE is operating in

(A) Canada (B) U. K.

(C) U. S. A. (D) India.

298. The library and information and information services division of BARC is the national centre for

(A) all UNISIST activities in India

(B) all FAO activities in India

(C) all INIS activities in India

(D) all IFLA activities in India.

299. The currently used full form of OCLC is
    (A) Ohio College Library Center
    (B) Online Computer Library Center
    (C) Online Catalogue of Library of Congress
    (D) none of these.
300. Identify the development in following library software in correct chronological sequence
    (A) Sanjaya, LibSys SLIM, SOUL
    (B) SLIM, LibSys, SOUL, Sanjaya
    (C) Libsys, Sanjaya, SOUL, SLIM
    (D) Sanjaya, SOUL, SLIM, LibSys
301. In which of the following network topologies, all the computers are connected to a central computers are connected to a central computer:
    (A) Ring (B) Star
    (C) Bus (D) Peer to Peer
302. Formatting a document in computer means:
    (A) Editing the content
    (B) Changing the appearance
    (C) Adding new content
    (D) Changing the font size only
303. Which of the following search devices will lead to an increase in the Recall output?
    (A) Boolean 'And' (B) Boolean 'Not'
    (C) Proximity Operators (D) Truncation
304. The chronological sequence of the technology is:
    (A) Telephone, Television, Satellite Communication, INTERNET
    (B) Telephone, Satellite Communication, Television, INTERNET
    (C) Telephone, Television, INTERNET, Satellite Communication
    (D) Telephone, INTERNET, Television, Satellite Communication
305. Identify the correct order of evolution of computers:

(A) PC-XT, PC-AT, Main frame, Micro
(B) PC-AT, PC-XT, Main frame, Micro
(C) Micro, PC-AT, PC-XT, Main frame
(D) Main frame, Micro, PC-AT, PC-XT

306. Identify the correct order of evolution of the following storage order
(A) Paper, Micro card, Magnetic tape, Clay tablet
(B) Clay tablet, Paper, Micro card, Magnetic tape
(C) Micro card, Magnetic tape, Clay tablet, Paper
(D) Magnetic tape, Clay tablet, Paper, Micro card

307. Which one of the sequences is in ascending order?
(A) Bytes, Gigabytes, Megabytes, Terrabytes
(B) Bytes (8 bits), Megabytes (2^{10}bytes/10^3 bytes), Gigabytes (2^{20} bytes/10^6 bytes), Terrabytes (2^{40} bytes/10^{12} bytes)
(C) Bytes, Terrabytes, Megabytes, Gigabytes
(D) Megabytes, Bytes, Terrabytes, Gigabytes

308. OCLC Project, MARC Project are the examples of:
(A) Co-operative storage of materials
(B) Co-operative acquisition of materials
(C) Co-operative processing of materials
(D) Co-operative stharing of materials

309. The unit of measuring the speed of the transmission of the data is called:
(A) Band (B) Protocol
(C) HTTP (D) RAM

310. The following is the search engine for scientific information only:
(A) Google (B) SCIRUS
(C) Yahoo (D) Alta Vista

311. OAI stands for:
(A) Open Access Initiatives
(B) Open Archives Initiatives
(C) On-line Archives Initiatives
(D) On-line Access Initiatives

312. Arrange the following in the chronological sequence of their development.
    (i) Pascal (1970) (ii) Cobol (1959)
    (iii) Fortran (1957) (iv) Basic (1979)
    Codes:
    (A) (i) (ii) (iv) (iii) (B) (iii) (ii) (i) (iv)
    (C) (ii) (iv) (iii) (i) (D) (iii) (iv) (ii) (i)
313. The first page of Website is known as:
    (A) Cover Page (B) Home Page
    (C) Title Page (D) Half Title Page
314. Blog is a:
    (A) Off-line Journal (B) Internet Journal
    (C) Web Directory (D) Search Engine
315. The owner of Internet is:
    (E) American Mathematical Society
    (F) Department of Science and Technology, Govt. of India
    (G) British Standard Institute
    (H) None of the above
316. Which of the following is not an Open Source Software?
    (A) Green Stone (B) D-Space
    (C) Plone (D) Delmark
317. NACLIN is sponsored by:
    (A) INFLIBNET (B) DELNET
    (C) AGRINET (D) CALIBNET
318. One of the following is not an open source software:
    (A) DSpace (B) Windows
    (C) Green Stone (D) Linux
319. DESIDOC is documentation centre for:
    (A) Indigenous Knowledge
    (B) Defence Science
    (C) Rural Development
    (D) Khadi& Village Industries
320. Arrange the following in the order of computer generations:

(i) Integrated circuit (ii) Transistor
(iii) Vacuum Tube (iv) Chip

Codes:

(A) (iv) (ii) (iii) (i) (B) (iii) (ii) (iv) (i)
(C) (i) (ii) (iii) (iv) (D) (iii) (iv) (ii) (i)

Actual order is (iii) (ii) (i) (iv).

321. Appropriate communication media for CD-Net is
(A) Twisted wires (B) Optical fibre
(C) Co-axial cables (D) Ethernet cables

322. An E-book which does not require an internet connection to access its contents is
(A) Web book (B) Palm book
(C) Electronic Ink e-book (D) Digital book

323. The input centre for INIS in India is
(A) DRDO (B) DSIR
(C) TFIR (D) BARC

324. The term 'Cyberspace' was first used by
(A) Andrew Pollock (B) William Gibson
(C) John Postal (D) Joe Flower

325. RFID Technology is used in
(A) Acquisition (B) Serial Control
(C) Circulation Control (D) OPAC

326. The Boolean operator 'AND' is related to
(A) Productive (B) Additive
(C) Logical Difference (D) None of the above

327. The process of configuring the disks into tracks and sectors is called
(A) Booting (B) Formatting
(C) Labelling (D) All the above

328. Arrange in chronological order the following persons who were associated with computing history:
(i) J.PresperEckart (ii) John W. Mauchly
(iii) August Ada (iv) Charles Babbage

Codes:

(A) (iii) (ii) (i) (iv) (B) (ii) (i) (iii) (iv)
(C) (i) (iv) (iii) (ii) (D) (iv) (iii) (ii) (i)

329. Arrange the following layers of OSI model in the sequence in which they function:

(i) Network Layer
(ii) Physical Layer
(iii) Transport Layer
(iv) Data Link Layer

Codes:

(A) (iii) (iv) (ii) (i)
(B) (iv) (ii) (i) (iii)
(C) (ii) (iv) (i) (iii)
(D) (i) (ii) (iii) (iv)

330. Use of integrated circuits was made in

(A) First Generation Computers
(B) Secord Generation Computers
(C) Third Generation Computers
(D) Fourth Generation Computers

331. The Network Topology in which nodes are connected to a central hub is known as

(A) Ring Topology
(B) Bus Topology
(C) Star Topology
(D) Mesh Topology

332. Computer Memory is measured in

(A) Bytes
(B) Kilobytes
(C) Megabytes
(D) All of the above

333. Transistors were used in which generation of computers?

(A) First generation
(B) Second generation
(C) Third generation
(D) None of the above

334. How different nodes in a network are connected and how they communicate are determined?

(A) By Network Connectivity
(B) By Network Topology
(C) By Network Compatibility
(D) None of the above

335. JSTOR is an online system for archiving and accessing academic journals. It is located in

(A) Germany
(B) UK
(C) USA
(D) Budapest

336. Arrange the following softwares according to their development:

I. E-Print II. DSpace
III. Greenstone IV. Koha

Codes:

(A) (IV), (III), (II), (I) (B) (III), (II), (I), (IV)
(C) (I), (II), (III), (IV) (D) (II), (III), (IV), (I)

337. Arrange the following chronologically according to their development:
(I) Punched Card
(II) Floppy Disc (1.44 MB)
(III) Magnetic Disc (20-1000 MB)
(IV) Optical Disc (700 MB-4.7 GB)

Codes:

(A) (II), (III), (I), (IV) (B) (I), (III), (II), (IV)
(C) (I), (II), (III), (IV) (D) (IV), (I), (II), (III)

338. What is the meaning of E-Documents?
(A) All Documents other than printed
(B) Non-Paper documents
(C) Inelectronic form such as Cassettes, CD-ROMs, etc.
(D) Audio visual tools

339. What two is a Library Management Software for small libraries?
(A) Library Solution and Follet
(B) Follct and MSN
(C) MSN and Tar
(D) LYCOS and Live Search

340. Which generation computers uses integrated circuits(ICs)?
(A) First (B) Second
(C) Third (D) Fourth

341. The concept of Artificial Intelligence (AI) belongs to?
(A) Second Generation Computers
(B) Third Generation Computers
(C) Fourth Generation Computers
(D) Fifth Generation Computers

342. Which is not a programming language?
(A) FORTRAN (B) BASIC
(C) COBOL (D) ASCII

343. ISO-9960 is related with?
(A) Standard for encoding data on CD-ROM
(B) Standard for Computer Hardware
(C) Standard for Information Processing
(D) Standard for Networking

344. What is the full form of ERNET?
(A) Engineering Network
(B) Eastern Regional Network
(C) Electronic Research Network
(D) Education and Research Network

345. Match the following electronic applications of information society with relevant service :

List – I	**List – II**
a. E-Commerce	i. Saakshat
b. E-Governance	ii. Living progress
c. E-Education	iii. G2C initiatives
d. E-Health	iv. SnapDeal

Codes:	**(a)**	**(b)**	**(c)**	**(d)**
(A)	iii	iv	i	ii
(B)	ii	iii	iv	i
(C)	iv	iii	i	ii
(D)	iv	ii	i	iii

346. Match the following :

List – I	**List – II**
a. Internet	i. Knowledge navigation
b. Computing	ii. Collection of E-resources
c. WWW	iii. Tools and Techniques for accessing
d. Digital Library	iv. Delivery Mechanism

Codes:	**(a)**	**(b)**	**(c)**	**(d)**
(A)	iv	i	iii	ii
(B)	iv	iii	i	ii
(C)	ii	i	iii	iv
(D)	iii	iv	ii	i

347. Match the following :

List-I	**List-II**
(A) E-Mail	(i) Bulletin Board
(B) FTP	(ii) Remote Log In
(C) TELNET	(iii) Library Network
(D) USENET	(iv) Moving/Downloading Files
	(v) Exchanging Message

Codes:	**(a)**	**(b)**	**(c)**	**(d)**
(A)	(iv)	(iii)	(v)	(i)
(B)	(v)	(iv)	(ii)	(i)
(C)	(ii)	(iv)	(i)	(iii)
(D)	(v)	(i)	(iv)	(iii)

348. Match the following :

List-I	**List-II**
(A) MS-DOS	(i) Multi-User Operating System
(B) UNIX	(ii) DTP Software
(C) Excel	(iii) DBMS
(D) Pagemaker	(iv) Single User Operating System
	(v) Spreadsheet Software

Codes:	**(a)**	**(b)**	**(c)**	**(d)**
(A)	(iv)	(v)	(i)	(ii)
(B)	(v)	(i)	(ii)	(iii)
(C)	(iii)	(i)	(ii)	(v)
(D)	(iv)	(i)	(v)	(ii)

349. Match the following:

List-I	**List-II**
(a) SOUL	(i) DESIDOC
(b) WINISIS	(ii) ALGORITHM
(c) SANJAY	(iii) Informatics (India)
(d) SLIM	(iv) INFLIBNET
	(v) UNESCO

Codes:	**(a)**	**(b)**	**(c)**	**(d)**
(A)	(iv)	(v)	(i)	(ii)
(B)	(v)	(iii)	(iv)	(i)
(C)	(iv)	(v)	(ii)	(iii)
(D)	(v)	(iv)	(i)	(ii)

350. Match the following:

List-I (Medium/Connectivity)	**List-II (Type)**
(a) Fax	(i) Optical Storage
(b) CD-ROM	(ii) Magnetic Storage
(c) Floppy Disk	(iii) Switching System
(d) Circuit	(iv) Image transmission

Codes:	**(a)**	**(b)**	**(c)**	**(d)**
(A)	(iv)	(i)	(ii)	(iii)
(B)	(ii)	(iii)	(i)	(iv)
(C)	(i)	(ii)	(iii)	(iv)
(D)	(iii)	(ii)	(i)	(iv)

351. Match the following:

List-I	**List-II**
(a) Search Engine	(i) Internet Explorer
(b) Subject Gateway	(ii) Dogpile
(c) Net Browser	(iii) FTP
(d) Meta Search Engine	(iv) SOSIG
	(v) Altavista

Codes:	**(a)**	**(b)**	**(c)**	**(d)**
(A)	(iv)	(iii)	(ii)	(i)
(B)	(v)	(iv)	(i)	(ii)
(C)	(v)	(i)	(ii)	(iii)
(D)	(v)	(i)	(iv)	(ii)

352. Match the following:

List-I	**List-II**
(a) ERNET	(i) Japan
(b) JANET	(ii) Global
(c) RLIN	(iii) India
(d) OCLC	(iv) United Kingdom
	(v) USA

Codes:	**(a)**	**(b)**	**(c)**	**(d)**
(A)	(v)	(iv)	(i)	(iii)
(B)	(iv)	(v)	(i)	(ii)
(C)	(iii)	(iv)	(v)	(ii)
(D)	(iii)	(ii)	(iv)	(v)

353. Match the following:

List-I	**List-II**
(a) E-Mail	(i) Bulletin Board
(b) FTP	(ii) Remote Log In
(c) TELNET	(iii) Library Network
(d) USENET	(iv) Moving/Downloading Files
	(v) Exchanging Message

Codes:	**(a)**	**(b)**	**(c)**	**(d)**
(A)	(iv)	(iii)	(v)	(i)
(B)	(v)	(iv)	(ii)	(i)
(C)	(ii)	(iv)	(i)	(iii)
(D)	(v)	(i)	(iv)	(iii)

354. Match the following:

List-I	**List-II**
(a) MS-DOS	(i) Multi-User Operating System
(b) UNIX	(ii) DTP Software
(c) Excel	(iii) DBMS
(d) pagemaker	(iv) Single User Operating System
	(v) Spreadsheet Software

Codes:	**(a)**	**(b)**	**(c)**	**(d)**
(A)	(iv)	(v)	(i)	(ii)
(B)	(v)	(i)	(ii)	(iii)
(C)	(iii)	(i)	(ii)	(v)
(D)	(iv)	(i)	(v)	(ii)

355. Match the following:

List-I	**List-II**
(a) Search Engine	(i) PASCAL
(b) Browser	(ii) UNIX
(c) Operating System	(iii)Yahoo
(d) Programming Language	(iv) Netscape
	(v) HTTP

Codes:	**(a)**	**(b)**	**(c)**	**(d)**
(A)	(i)	(iv)	(v)	(ii)
(B)	(iv)	(iii)	(ii)	(i)
(C)	(iii)	(iv)	(ii)	(i)
(D)	(iv)	(ii)	(i)	(v)

356. Match the following:

List-I	**List-II**
(a) Simplex	(i) Communication channel is used in both the directions but only in one direction at a time
(b) Half Duplex	(ii) Communication channel is used in one direction
(c) Full Duplex	(iii) Bits of information are transmitted continuously
(d) Asynchronous transmission	(iv) Information is sent at random intervals with start and stop bits for each batch of information

Codes:	**(a)**	**(b)**	**(c)**	**(d)**
(A)	(ii)	(i)	(iv)	(iii)
(B)	(i)	(iv)	(iii)	(ii)
(C)	(iv)	(ii)	(i)	(iii)
(D)	(iv)	(i)	(iii)	(ii)

357. Match the following:

List-I	**List-II**
(a) SOUL	(i) INFOTEK
(b) LIBSYS	(ii) ALGORITHM
(c) SLIM	(iii) UNESCO
(d) WINISIS	(iv) INFLIBNET
	(v) DESIDOC

Codes:	**(a)**	**(b)**	**(c)**	**(d)**
(A)	(iii)	(v)	(iv)	(i)
(B)	(iv)	(i)	(ii)	(iii)
(C)	(v)	(iv)	(i)	(iii)
(D)	(i)	(iii)	(v)	(ii)

358. Match the following:

List-I	**List-II**
(a) Protocol	(i) Java
(b) Language	(ii) Internet Explorer
(c) Browser	(iii) Altavista

(d) Search Engine (iv) DOS

(v) HTTP

Codes:	**(a)**	**(b)**	**(c)**	**(d)**
(A)	(iv)	(v)	(i)	(iii)
(B)	(v)	(i)	(ii)	(iii)
(C)	(ii)	(iv)	(v)	(i)
(D)	(i)	(v)	(iv)	(ii)

359. Matching the following:

List-I	**List-II**
(a) Windows	(i) A revolving disc on which data is stored
(b) Microprocessor	(ii) It is used for processing of text
(c) Wordprocessor	(iii) Collection of programmes forcomputer system
(d) Software	(iv) A graphical user interface working as DOS

Codes:	**(a)**	**(b)**	**(c)**	**(d)**
(A)	(iv)	(i)	(ii)	(iii)
(B)	(iii)	(ii)	(i)	(iv)
(C)	(ii)	(iii)	(iv)	(i)
(D)	(i)	(ii)	(iii)	(iv)

360. Match the following:

List-I	**List-II**
(a) Software	(i) Key board
(b) Hardware	(ii) CD
(c) Storage Device	(iii) SOUL
(d) I/O Device	(iv) CPU

Codes:	**(a)**	**(b)**	**(c)**	**(d)**
(A)	(ii)	(iv)	(iii)	(i)
(B)	(ii)	(iii)	(iv)	(i)
(C)	(iii)	(ii)	(iv)	(i)
(D)	(iii)	(iv)	(ii)	(i)

361. Match the following:

List-I	List-II
(a) SHE	(i) Nuclear Energy
(b) MESH	(ii) Education
(c) ERIC	(iii) Medicine
(d) INIS	Iv) Engineering

Codes:	**(a)**	**(b)**	**(c)**	**(d)**
(A)	(i)	(iii)	(ii)	(iv)
(B)	(iv)	(iii)	(ii)	(i)
(C)	(ii)	(iii)	(i)	(iv)
(D)	(i)	(ii)	(iii)	(iv)

362. Match the following:

List-I	List-II
(a) Mission Oriented	(i) Patent Information System
(b) Social Science Oriented	(ii) DESIDOC
(c) ERIC	(iii) NISSAT
(d) INIS	(iv) NASSDOC

Codes:	**(a)**	**(b)**	**(c)**	**(d)**
(A)	(iii)	(iv)	(ii)	(i)
(B)	(iv)	(iii)	(ii)	(i)
(C)	(i)	(ii)	(iii)	(iv)
(D)	(ii)	(iii)	(iv)	(i)

363. Match the following:

List-I	List-II
(a) Web Navigation Element	(i) Telecommunication
(b) Shift+Tab	(ii) SQL
(c) ANSI Standard	(iii) Hyperlink
(d) TELNET	(iv) Select the previous link

Codes:	**(a)**	**(b)**	**(c)**	**(d)**
(A)	(i)	(ii)	(iii)	(iv)
(B)	(iv)	(iii)	(ii)	(i)
(C)	(iii)	(iv)	(ii)	(i)
(D)	(ii)	(iii)	(i)	(iv)

364. Match the following:

List-I	**List-II**
(a) Macfee	(i) DOAJ
(b) Directory	(ii) Antivirus
(c) Personal Web pages	(iii) Vendor on Internet
(d) Amazon.com	(iv) Blogs

Codes:	**(a)**	**(b)**	**(c)**	**(d)**
(A)	(ii)	(i)	(iv)	(iii)
(B)	(i)	(iv)	(iii)	(ii)
(C)	(ii)	(iii)	(iv)	(i)
(D)	(iv)	(iii)	(ii)	(i)

365. Match the following:

List-I	**List-II**
(a) Theory of Knowledge	(i) Farmington Plan
(b) IS: 1553-1960	(ii) Metadata Format
(c) Resource Sharing	(iii) Library Building
(d) TEI	(iv) Epistomology

Codes:	**(a)**	**(b)**	**(c)**	**(d)**
(A)	(i)	(iii)	(ii)	(iv)
(B)	(ii)	(iii)	(i)	(iv)
(C)	(iv)	(iii)	(i)	(ii)
(D)	(iii)	(i)	(ii)	(iv)

366. Match the following:

List – I	**List – II**
(A) Textual representation	(i) Pascal
(B) Computer language	(ii) Gopher
(C) Network tool	(iii) Boolean operators
(D) Searching technique	(iv) ASCI

Codes:	**(a)**	**(b)**	**(c)**	**(d)**
(A)	(iv)	(i)	(ii)	(iii)
(B)	(i)	(iv)	(iii)	(ii)
(C)	(iii)	(ii)	(iv)	(i)
(D)	(ii)	(iv)	(iii)	(i)

367. Match the following:

List – I	**List – II**
(A) Hubs	(i) A physical layer device used to interconnect the media segments of an extended network
(B) Repeater	(ii) A physical layer device that connects multiple computers each via a dedicated cable
(C) Bus Topology	(iii) Multiple bridges known for transfer of data between different parts
(D) Switches	(iv) A straight line data highway that carries network information from one network station to another

Codes:	**(a)**	**(b)**	**(c)**	**(d)**
(A)	(iii)	(iv)	(ii)	(i)
(B)	(ii)	(i)	(iv)	(iii)
(C)	(iv)	(i)	(iii)	(ii)
(D)	(i)	(iii)	(ii)	(iv)

368. Match the following:

List – I	**List – II**
a. File transfer protocol	i. Data transmission capacity
b. Multimedia	ii. Integration of text, colour sound and animation
c. Bandwidth	iii. Bulletin Board
d. Electronic Notice Board	iv. Internet

Codes:	**(a)**	**(b)**	**(c)**	**(d)**
(A)	iv	ii	i	iii
(B)	i	iii	ii	iv
(C)	ii	i	iv	iii
(D)	i	iv	ii	iii

369. Match the following:

List – I	List – II
a. ISDN	i. Web page
b. URL	ii. Video Conferencing
c. Firewall	iii. Internet Standard for Information Transmission
d. HTTP	iv. Protecting unauthorized access internet

Codes:	(a)	(b)	(c)	(d)
(A)	iii	iv	i	ii
(B)	iv	i	iii	ii
(C)	ii	i	iv	iii
(D)	i	iii	ii	iv

370. Match the following:

List – I	List – II
a. OCLC	i. Bio-Med
b. INFLIBNET	ii. Web-Dewey
c. IISC	iii. N-List
d. NLM	iv. Digital Library of India

Codes:	(a)	(b)	(c)	(d)
(A)	ii	iii	iv	i
(B)	iii	i	ii	iv
(C)	iv	ii	iii	i
(D)	i	iii	iv	ii

371. Match the following:

List-I	List-II
(A) HTML File	(i) Text Format
(B) PDF File	(ii) Film Format
(C) JPG File	(iii) Web Format
(D) AVI File	(iv) Image Format

Codes:	(a)	(b)	(c)	(d)
(A)	(i)	(ii)	(iv)	(iii)
(B)	(iii)	(i)	(iv)	(ii)
(C)	(i)	(iv)	(ii)	(iii)
(D)	(iv)	(iii)	(i)	(ii)

372. Match the following:

List-I	**List-II**
(A) DRUPAL	(i) Integrated Library Management Software
(B) Moodle	(ii) Digital Library Software
(C) D space	(iii) Content Management Software
(D) New Gen Lib	(iv) Learning Management Software

Codes:	**(a)**	**(b)**	**(c)**	**(d)**
(A)	(iv)	(iii)	(ii)	(i)
(B)	(ii)	(i)	(iv)	(iii)
(C)	(iii)	(iv)	(ii)	(i)
(D)	(i)	(ii)	(iii)	(iv)

373. Match the following:

List-I	**List-II**
(A) Face Book	(i) Video Networking site
(B) Research Gate	(ii) Social Networking site
(C) Oovoo	(iii) Academic Networking site
(D) Flicker	(iv) Photo Networking site

Codes:	**(a)**	**(b)**	**(c)**	**(d)**
(A)	(i)	(iii)	(ii)	(iv)
(B)	(iv)	(i)	(ii)	(iii)
(C)	(ii)	(iii)	(i)	(iv)
(D)	(iii)	(iv)	(i)	(ii)

374. Match the following:

List – I	**List – II**
a. Altavista	i. Subject search engine
b. Lycos	ii. Meta search engine
c. Geoindex	iii. Regional search engine
d. Savvysearch	iv. General search engine

Codes:	**(a)**	**(b)**	**(c)**	**(d)**
(A)	iii	ii	i	iv
(B)	iii	iv	ii	i
(C)	iv	iii	i	ii
(D)	iv	i	ii	iii

375. Match the following:

List – I	**List – II**
a. Pen drive	i. Communication device
b. i-Pad	ii. Web server device
c. Wifi Modem	iii. Storage device
d. Cloud computing	iv. Computing device

Codes:	**(a)**	**(b)**	**(c)**	**(d)**
(A)	i	iii	ii	iv
(B)	iii	iv	i	ii
(C)	iv	iii	ii	i
(D)	iii	ii	i	iv

376. Match the following:

List – I	**List – II**
a. Informix	i. Image software
b. Omni Page	ii. Remote login software
c. TIFF viewer	iii. DBMS software
d. Team Viewer	iv. OCR software

Codes:	**(a)**	**(b)**	**(c)**	**(d)**
(A)	ii	i	iii	iv
(B)	iii	iv	i	ii
(C)	i	ii	iii	iv
(D)	iv	iii	ii	i

377. Match the following:

List – I	**List – II**
a. Means of improving operations and services	i. Preservation
b. Preparation of to-do-list	ii. Standards
c. Performance guidelines	iii. Time management
d. Reinforce the spines of books	iv. Evaluation

Codes:	**(a)**	**(b)**	**(c)**	**(d)**
(A)	iv	iii	ii	i
(B)	iv	ii	iii	i
(C)	ii	iv	iii	i
(D)	iii	ii	i	iv

378. Match the following dialogue systems:

List – I	**List – II**
a. Menu	i. Computer recognizable dialogues
b. Icons	ii. Communicating with computers with everyday language
c. Natural language	iii. List of options available
d. Common language	iv. Pictorial representation of objects

Codes:	**(a)**	**(b)**	**(c)**	**(d)**
(A)	i	iii	iv	ii
(B)	ii	iv	iii	i
(C)	iii	iv	ii	i
(D)	iv	ii	iii	i

379. Match the following:

List – I	**List – II**
a. Remote resource sensing satellite	i. Processing data
b. Memory chips	ii. Transportation of data
c. VLSI chips	iii. Capture data
d. Optical fibre	iv. Storage data

Codes:	**(a)**	**(b)**	**(c)**	**(d)**
(A)	i	ii	iii	iv
(B)	iv	iii	ii	i
(C)	ii	iii	iv	i
(D)	iii	iv	i	ii

380. Match the following:

List-I	**List-II**
a. INFLIBNET	i) Digital Library
b. INDEST-AICTE	ii) Resource aggregator
c. DELNET	iii) E-consortia
d. e-Gyankosh	iv) Organisation

Codes:	(a)	(b)	(c)	(d)
(A)	i	ii	iii	iv
(B)	iv	iii	ii	i
(C)	iii	ii	I	iv
(D)	ii	iii	iv	i

381. Match the following :

List – I	List – II
a. Internal Files	i. WPD
b. Universal File Format	ii. OeB
c. Corel's Word Perfect	iii. HTML
d. Microsoft Reader	iv. RTF

Codes:	(a)	(b)	(c)	(d)
(A)	i	iii	ii	iv
(B)	ii	iv	iii	i
(C)	iv	ii	i	iii
(D)	iii	iv	i	ii

382. Match the following:

List – I	List – II
a. PDFA	i. High Colour depth images
b. HTML	ii. Rules for encoding documents electronically
c. TIFF	iii. File format for long term archiving
d. XML	iv. Language for web pages

Codes:	(a)	(b)	(c)	(d)
(A)	ii	iii	i	iv
(B)	iii	iv	i	ii
(C)	i	iii	ii	iv
(D)	iv	ii	iii	i

383. Match the following:

List – I	List – II
a. Introduction to Modern information Retrieval	i. H. Borko& C. Bernie (McGraw Hill)
b. Indexing Concepts and Methods (Academic Press)	ii. G. Salton & M.J. McGill

c. Thesaurus Construction: A Practical Manual (Aslib) — iii. J.E. Rowley & R. Hartley

d. Organizing Knowledge; An introduction to Managing Access to Information (Ashgate) — iv. J. Aitchison& A. Gilchrist

Codes:	**(a)**	**(b)**	**(c)**	**(d)**
(A)	i	ii	iii	iv
(B)	ii	i	iv	iii
(C)	iv	i	ii	iii
(D)	iii	i	iv	ii

384. Match the following :

List – I	**List – II**
a. Icon	i. Character strings
b. Menus	ii. Select objects on the screen
c. Dialogue Bou	iii. Bit mapped region
d. Pointing devices	iv. Obtain information from the end users

Codes:	**(a)**	**(b)**	**(c)**	**(d)**
(A)	i	ii	iii	iv
(B)	iii	iv	ii	i
(C)	ii	iii	iv	i
(D)	iii	i	iv	ii

385. Match the following :

List – I	**List – II**
a. Resource Description	i. MARC
b. Resource Discovery	ii. ISO 10160/10161
c. Resource Exchange	iii. Dublin Care
d. Interlibrary Loan	iv. Z 39.50

Codes:	**(a)**	**(b)**	**(c)**	**(d)**
(A)	ii	i	iv	iii
(B)	iv	ii	i	iii
(C)	iii	iv	ii	i
(D)	iii	iv	i	ii

386. Match the following language and their function:

List – I	List – II
a. Procedural	i. Scan arbitrary files and extra information
b. Special purpose	ii. Manipulate data and change memory
c. Practical extraction report	iii. Create documents to view with web server
d. Hyper textmark up	iv. Data base queries

Codes:	(a)	(b)	(c)	(d)
(A)	ii	iv	i	iii
(B)	i	iii	ii	iv
(C)	iii	iv	i	ii
(D)	ii	iii	iv	i

387. Match the functions performed by different layers of OSI model :

List – I	List – II
a. Delivery of Packets from source of destination	i. Application layer
b. Data transmission rate	ii. Data link layer
c. Access to network resources	iii. Network layer
d. Provide hop-topop delivery	iv. Physical layer

Codes:	(a)	(b)	(c)	(d)
(A)	i	iii	ii	iv
(B)	ii	iv	i	iii
(C)	iii	iv	i	ii
(D)	iii	i	iv	ii

388. Match the following:

List – I	List – II
a. Phenomenon	i. Physical Media for grouping of Information
b. Spectrum	ii. Facts or Occurrence
c. Modes	iii. Transfer Process
d. Diffusion	iv. A broad range of varied but related ideas

Codes:	**(a)**	**(b)**	**(c)**	**(d)**
(A)	i	iii	iv	ii
(B)	ii	iv	i	iii
(C)	ii	iii	iv	i
(D)	iv	i	iii	ii

389. Match the following :

List – I	**List – II**
a. Meta search engine	i. HotBot
b. Web directory	ii. Search Engine
c. Subject gateway	iii. Galaxy
d. Archie	iv. Library Spot

Codes:	**(a)**	**(b)**	**(c)**	**(d)**
(A)	i	iii	iv	ii
(B)	iii	ii	i	iv
(C)	ii	iv	i	iii
(D)	i	iii	ii	iv

390. Match the following:

List – I	**List – II**
a. Virtua	i. Veeru Technologies\ (KIIKM)
b. Alice	ii. Infotech Consultants Pvt. Ltd.
c. Libsys	iii. Softlink, Australia
d. New Genlib	iv. VTLS, Virginia

Codes:	**(a)**	**(b)**	**(c)**	**(d)**
(A)	i	iii	ii	iv
(B)	ii	iv	i	iii
(C)	iv	ii	iii	i
(D)	iv	iii	ii	i

391. Match the following file formats with the creators:

List – I	**List – II**
a. RTF	i. Sun Micro System
b. PDF	ii. Aldus
c. TIFF	iii. Microsoft
d. AU	iv. Adobe

Codes:	**(a)**	**(b)**	**(c)**	**(d)**
(A)	iv	iii	ii	i
(B)	iii	iv	ii	i
(C)	ii	iii	iv	i
(D)	i	ii	iv	iii

392. Match the following search techniques with their relevant example :

List – I	**List – II**
a. Truncation	i. Wom?n
b. Wild cards	ii. Comput*
c. Proximity	iii. edu AND biochemistry AND antibodics
d. Field searching	iv. "content collection"/5

Codes:	**(a)**	**(b)**	**(c)**	**(d)**
(A)	ii	iii	iv	i
(B)	iv	iii	ii	i
(C)	i	ii	iii	iv
(D)	ii	i	iv	iii

393. Match the following :

List – I	**List – II**
a. Infringement	i. Unauthorized use of I.P.
b. Enforcement	ii. Criminal penalties
c. Mis-appropriation	iii. Breach of trade secret
d. Counterfeit	iv. Intentional forgery

Codes:	**(a)**	**(b)**	**(c)**	**(d)**
(A)	ii	iii	iv	i
(B)	i	ii	iii	iv
(C)	iii	iv	i	ii
(D)	iv	i	iii	ii

394. Match the following :

List – I	**List – II**
a. Informing about best books	i. Support service
b. Guidance to use citation manual	ii. Bibliography
c. Providing prints for downloads	iii. Readers advisory
d. Providing list of URLs	iv. Users education

Codes:	**(a)**	**(b)**	**(c)**	**(d)**
(A)	ii	iii	i	iv
(B)	iii	iv	i	ii
(C)	iv	ii	iii	i
(D)	ii	iv	iii	i

395. Match the following :

List – I	**List – II**
a. HTML	i. Intrepretation by web browser
b. XML	ii. Describes data
c. UNICODE	iii. Display data
d. VB Script	iv. Platform independent

Codes:	**(a)**	**(b)**	**(c)**	**(d)**
(A)	i	iii	ii	iv
(B)	iii	iv	i	ii
(C)	ii	iv	i	iii
(D)	iii	ii	iv	i

396. Match the following national organizations with their relevant mission :

List – I	**List – II**
a. National Mission on Libraries	i. Digitization of AYUSH literature
b. National Mission for Manuscripts	ii. Nurturing of talent
c. T.K.D.L.	iii. Capacity building
d. NME-ICT	iv. Connects India's past with present

Codes:	**(a)**	**(b)**	**(c)**	**(d)**
(A)	i	ii	iii	iv
(B)	iii	iv	i	ii
(C)	iv	iii	ii	i
(D)	ii	i	iii	iv

397. Match the following:

List-I	**List-II**
(A) Pen Drive	(i) Browser
(B) Soul	(ii) Search Engine
(C) Net Scope	(iii) Output device
(D) Google	(iv) Library Software

Codes:	**(a)**	**(b)**	**(c)**	**(d)**
(A)	(iii)	(iv)	(i)	(ii)
(B)	(iv)	(iii)	(i)	(ii)
(C)	(ii)	(iii)	(i)	(iv)
(D)	(iv)	(ii)	(iii)	(i)

398. Match the following :

List-I	**List-II**
(1) Protocol	(a) Jawa
(2) Language	(b) Internet Explorer
(3) Browser	(c) Alta Vista
(4) Search Engine	(d) HTTP

Codes :	**1**	**2**	**3**	**4**
(A)	(a)	(c)	(b)	(d)
(B)	(d)	(a)	(b)	(c)
(C)	(c)	(a)	(d)	(b)
(D)	(b)	(a)	(d)	(c)

399. Match the following:

List-I	**List-II**
(a) Scopus	(i) Access to You- Tube
(b) Web of Science	(ii) Internet browser
(c) Google Account	(iii) Thomson ISI
(d) Google Chrome	(iv) Elsevier

Codes:	**(a)**	**(b)**	**(c)**	**(d)**
(A)	iii	ii	i	iv
(B)	ii	iv	i	iii
(C)	i	iii	ii	iv
(D)	iv	iii	i	ii

400. Match the following :

List I	**List II**
(A) CDS/ISIS	(i) NISCAIR
(B) Sanjay	(ii) CMC
(C) Granthalaya	(iii) UNESCO
(D) Maitrayee	(iv) DESIDOC

Codes:	**(a)**	**(b)**	**(c)**	**(d)**
(A)	(i)	(iii)	(ii)	(iv)
(B)	(ii)	(iii)	(iv)	(i)
(C)	(iv)	(i)	(ii)	(iii)
(D)	(iii)	(iv)	(i)	(ii)

401. Arrange the following softwares according to their development :

(I) E-Print (II) D-space

(III) Greenstone (IV) Koha

Codes :

(A) (IV), (III), (II), (I) (B) (III), (II), (I), (IV)

(C) (I), (II), (III), (IV) (D) (II), (III), (IV), (I)

402. Arrange the following chronologically according to their development :

(I) Punched Card (II) Floppy Disc

(III) Magnetic Disc (IV) Optical Disc

Codes :

(A) (II), (III), (I), (IV) (B) (I), (III), (II), (IV)

(C) (I), (II), (III), (IV) (D) (IV), (I), (II), (III)

403. Arrange the following according to the year of establishments :

(i) NICNET (ii) INDONET

(iii) INFLIBNET (iv) MALIBNET

Codes :

(A) (iv), (i), (iii), (ii) (B) (iv), (ii), (i), (iii)

(C) (ii), (i), (iv), (iii) (D) (i), (iii), (iv), (ii)

404. Match the following:

List-I	**List-II**
(e) OCLC	(i) City
(f) INFLIBNET	(ii) International
(g) CALIBNET	(iii) Regional
(h) ASTINFO	(iv) National

Codes:	**(a)**	**(b)**	**(c)**	**(d)**
(A)	(ii)	(i)	(iv)	(iii)
(B)	(ii)	(iv)	(i)	(iii)

(C) (iii) (ii) (iv) (i)

(D) (iii) (i) (ii) (iv)

405. **Assertion (A) :** Libraries are facing a threat and are bound to disappear soon.

Reason (R) : Internet and WWW provide access to Oceans of information Worldwide.

Codes:

(A) (A) is true but (R) is false

(B) (A) is false but (R) is true

(C) Both (A) and (R) is true

(D) Both (A) and (R) is false

406. **Assertion (A) :** Web OPAC is a computerised library catalogue available to the patrons online.

Reason (R) : It can be searched by the users within the four walls of the library only.

Codes:

(A) (A) is true but (R) is false.

(B) (A) is false but (R) is true.

(C) Both (A) and (R) are true.

(D) Both (A) and (R) are false.

407. **Assertion (A) :** Electronic access to information is becoming easy day by day.

Reason (R) : The printed materials pouring out of the world presses do not show any decline.

Codes:

(A) Both (A) and (R) are true but (R) is not a correct explanation of (A).

(B) (A) is true but (R) is false.

(C) (A) is false but (R) is true.

(D) Both (A) and (R) are false.

408. **Assertion (A) :** Use of microfilming is becoming obsolete day by day.

Reason (R) : ICT has developed digital technologies, which are quick, cheap and easy to handle.

Codes:

(A) Both (A) and (R) are true but (R) is not a correct explanation.

(B) Both (A) and (R) are false.

(C) (A) is true but (R) is false

(D) Both (A) and (R) are true and (R) is the correct explanation of (A).

409. **Assertion (A) :** Libraries are changing in the wake of emerging ICT environment.

Reason (R) : Libraries are adopting new competencies to operate services in the environment of information super highways.

Codes:

(A) Both (A) and (R) are true

(B) (A) is true but (R) is false

(C) (A) is false but (R) is true

(D) Both (A) and (R) are false

410. **Assertion (A) :** Mass media promote a culture of violence in the society.

Reason (R) : Because violence sells in the market as people themselves are violent in character.

(A) Both (A) and (R) are true and (R) is the correct explanation of (A).

(B) Both (A) and (R) are true, but (R) is not the correct explanation of (A).

(C) (A) is true, but (R) is false.

(D) Both (A) and (R) are false.

411. **Assertion (A) :** Operators using 'AND', 'OR' and 'NOT' are mostly used in online IR.

Reason (R) : User interfaces cannot transform the natural language input into Boolean search query

Codes:

(A) Both (A) and (R) are true

(B) (A) is true but (R) is false

(C) (R) is true but (A) is false

(D) Both (A) and (R) are false

412. **Assertion (A) :** Web OPAC is a computerised library catalogue available to the patrons online.

Reason (R) : It can be searched by the users within the four walls of the library only.

Codes :

(A) (A) is true but (R) is false.

(B) (A) is false but (R) is true.

(C) Both (A) and (R) are true.

(D) Both (A) and (R) are false.

413. **Assertion (A) :** Electronic access to information is becoming easy day by day.

Reason (R) : The printed materials pouring out of the world presses do not show any decline.

Codes :

(A) Both (A) and (R) are true but (R) is not a correct explanation of (A).

(B) (A) is true but (R) is false.

(C) (A) is false but (R) is true.

(D) Both (A) and (R) are false.

414. **Assertion (A) :** Use of microfilming is becoming obsolete day by day.

Reason (R) : ICT has developed digital technologies, which are quick, cheap and easy to handle.

Codes :

(A) Both (A) and (R) are true but (R) is not a correct explanation.

(B) Both (A) and (R) are false.

(C) (A) is true but (R) is false.

(D) Both (A) and (R) are true and (R) is the correct explanation of (A).

415. **Assertion (A) :** Libraries are changing in the wake of emerging ICT environment.

Reason (R) : Libraries are adopting new competencies to operate services in the environment of information super highways.

Codes :

(A) Both (A) and (R) are true.

(B) (A) is true but (R) is false.

(C) (A) is false but (R) is true.

(D) Both (A) and (R) are false.

416. **Assertion (A) :** Internet access provides information in abundance.

Reason (R) : Information available on internet always lacks authenticity.

Codes :

(A) Both (A) and (R) are true and (R) is the correct explanation of (A).

(B) (A) is false, but (R) is true.

(C) Both (A) and (R) are true, but (R) is not a correct explanation of (A).

(D) (A) is true but (R) is false.

417. **Assertion (A) :** Computerization of Public Libraries in India is slow.

Reason (R) : Non-availability of resources.

Codes :

(A) (A) is true but (R) is false

(B) (R) is true but (A) is false

(C) Both (A) and (R) are true

(D) Both (A) and (R) are false

418. **Assertion (A) :** Users can have access to large number of E-journals through consortia.

Reason (R) : Users are not aware of using web-resources.

Codes :

(A) (A) is false and (R) is true

(B) (A) is true and (R) is false

(C) Both (A) and (R) are true, but (R) is not the right explanation of (A)

(D) Both (A) and (R) are false

419. **Assertion (A) :** Arrangement of documents by subject will satisfy more users.

Reason (R) : Many users search for documents by title.

Codes :

(A) Both A and R are true and R is the correct explanation

(B) Both A and R are true and R is not the correct explanation

(C) A is true but R is false

(D) A is false but R is true

420. **Assertion (A) :** Computerization of Public Libraries in India is slow.

Reason (R) : Non-availability of resources

Codes:

(A) (A) is true but (R) is false

(B) (R) is true but (A) is false

(C) Both (A) and (R) are true

(D) Both (A) and (R) are false

421. **Assertion (A) :** Users can have access to large to large number of E-journals through consortia.

Reason (R) : Users are not aware of using web resources.

Codes:

(A) (A) is false and (R) is true

(B) (A) is true and (R) is false

(C) Both (A) and (R) are true but (R) is not the right explanation of (A)

(D) Both (A) and (R) are false

422. **Assertion (A) :** internet is an important tool for the dissemination of information.

Reason (R) : Large number of open sources are available

Codes:

(A) (A) is True but (R) is False

(B) (A) is False but (R) is True

(C) Both (A) and (R) are True

(D) Both (A) and (R) are False

423. **Assertion (A) :** Many projects and initiatives are taken to create digital libraries.

Reason (R) : Digital library improves the professional status of librarians.

Codes :

(A) Both (A) and (R) are true

(B) Both (A) and (R) are false

(C) (A) is true but (R) is the correct explanation

(D) (A) is false but (R) is true

424. **Assertion (A) :** INDEST conceived J-Gate as a customized gate for e-journals subscribed by the member libraries

Reason (R) : J-Gate provides a common access platform for all its members to search and share resources subscribed by the member libraries.

Codes :

(A) Both (A) and (R) are true and (R) is the correct explanation

(B) Both (A) and (R) are true but (R) is not the correct explanation

(C) (A) is true but (R) is false

(D) (A) is false but (R) is true

425. **Assertion (A) :** XML , just like HTML is a meta language that is capable of containing extendable elements.

Reason (R) : XML develop and deploy new specific mark up, enabling automatic authoring and processing of networked information.

Codes:

(A) Is false but (R) is true.

(B) Both (A) and (R) are true and (R) is not the correct explanation.

(C) (A) is true and (R) is false

(D) Both (A) and (R) are true.

426. **Assertion (A) :** Measuring the Internet and in particular the web is a difficult task.

Reason (R) : Web is considered as a new publishing medium with inadequate editorial process.

Codes:

(A) Both (A) and (R) are true and (R) is the correct explanation.

(B) Both (A) and (R) are true and (R) is not the correct explanation

(C) (A) is true but (R) is false.

(D) (A) is false but (R) is true

427. **Assertion (A) :** In contemporary digital environment, IPR become the focal point.

Reason (R) : Many fold increase of unfair use of I.P.

Codes:

(A) (A) and (R) are true.

(B) (A) and (R) are false.

(C) (A) is true and (R) is false.

(D) (A) is false and (R) is true.

428. **Assertion (A) :** Library automation is at a slow pace in Indian Libraries.

Reason (R) : Lack of UGC (India) support lead to this situation.

Codes:

(A) Both (A) and (R) are true.

(B) Both (A) and (R) are false.

(C) (A) is true but (R) is false.

(D) (A) is false but (R) is true.

429. **Assertion (A) :** The development of Institutional Repositories in India is at a slow pace.

Reason (R) : This can be attributed to the non-availability of open source software and lack of interest among the LIS professionals.

Codes :

(A) Both (A) and (R) are true.

(B) Both (A) and (R) are false.

(C) (A) is true but (R) is partially true.

(D) (A) is false and (R) is true

430. **Assertion (A) :** Subject gateways offer the users an alternative to 'vacuum Cleaner' type of search engines, such as Google, Infoseek, Alta Vista etc.

Reason (R) : Subject gateways hold manually created records, rich resource description containing relevant information.

Codes:

(A) Both (A) and (R) are true.

(B) Both (A) and (R) are true and (R) is not the correct explanation

(C) (A) is true but (R) is false

(D) (A) is false but (R) is true

431. **Assertion (A) :** Netiquette mandates that you do your best to act within the laws of cyberspace and society.

Reason (R) : Failing to respect other people's privacy is bad Netiquette.

Codes :

(A) Both (A) and (R) are false.

(B) Both (A) and (R) are true.

(C) (A) is true, but (R) is false.

(D) (A) is false, but (R) is true.

432. **Assertion (A) :** Modern Integrated Library Management Softwares offer user friendly Graphical User Interfaces (GUI) on the web.

Reason (R) : Almost every module of modern Integrated Library Management Software is accessible through the internet.

Codes :

(A) Both (A) and (R) are correct.

(B) (A) is correct but (R) is wrong.

(C) Both (A) and (R) are wrong.

(D) (A) is wrong but (R) is correct.

433. **Assertion (A) :** Open Systems Interconnection allows connectivity of ICT components.

Reason (R) : Network Printer goes slow if it is OSI compatible.

Codes :

(A) Both (A) and (R) are true.

(B) Both (A) and (R) are false.

(C) (A) is false, but (R) is true.

(D) (A) is true, but (R) is false.

434. **Assertion (A) :** Internet can replace libraries.

Reason (R) : Google searches will satisfy the maximum users needs.

Codes :

(A) Both (A) and (R) are true.

(B) Both (A) and (R) are false.

(C) (A) is true but (R) is false.

(D) (A) is false but (R) is true.

435. **Assertion (A) :** A combination of hypertext and Hypermedia contains text, images, sounds and other information

Reason (R) : Hypermedia information is represented in a linear fashion.

Codes :

(A) (A) is true and (R) is false.

(B) Both (A) and (R) are true.

(C) (A) is false and (R) is true.

(D) Both (A) & (R) are false.

436. **Assertion (A) :** E-publications have added enormous quantity of literature but adversely affected the quality of literature.

Reason (R) : Present decade has accepted E-publication as channels of fast communication.

Codes :

(A) (A) is true (R) is false.

(B) (A) is false, but (R) is correct.

(C) Both (A) & (R) are false.

(D) Both (A) & (R) are true.

437. **Assertion (A) :** Encyclopedias are not relevant for finding geographically information.

Reason (R) : Encyclopedias are the substitute for all categories of reference sources.

Codes :

(A) (A) is false but (R) is true.

(B) Both (A) and (R) are true.

(C) Both (A) and (R) are false.

(D) (A) is true but (R) is false.

438. **Assertion (A) :** LIS profession is not considered at par with medical and legal professions.

Reason (R) : There is no constitutional body for LIS profession like Medical Council of India (MCI) and Bar Council of India (BCI).

Codes :

(A) Both (A) and (R) are true.

(B) Both (A) and (R) are false.

(C) (A) is true but (R) is false.

(D) (A) is false but (R) is true.

439. **Assertion (A) :** With the emergence of Internet, there is no need for reference service in this technology-based era.

Reason (R) : Internet has allowed access to every one to seek his/her information from anywhere, any time.

Codes:

(A) Both (A) and (R) are true.

(B) Both (A) and (R) are false.

(C) (A) is false but (R) is partially true.

(D) (A) is true, but (R) is false.

440. **Assertion (A) :** Micrographic services have lost acceptance for preservation and dissemination of archival material.

Reason (R) : ICT has brought in cost effective alternatives and replaced micrographic services.

Codes :

(A) (A) is true and (R) is partially true.

(B) Both (A) & (R) are false.

(C) (A) is true, (R) is false.

(D) (A) is false, (R) is true.

441. **Assertion (A) :** Institutions generate information through research and development activities.

Reason (R) : All such generated information forms the grey literature.

Codes :

(A) Both (A) and (R) are true.

(B) Both (A) and (R) are false.

(C) (A) is true, (R) is partially true.

(D) (A) is false, (R) is true.

442. **Assertion (A) :** RFID technology is still not widely installed in Indian Library Environment.

Reason (R) : the standardization, application and innovation are constantly changing.

Codes:

(A) Both (A) & (R) true and (R) is the correct explanation of (A).

(B) Both (A) & (R) are true, but (R) is not the correct explanation of (A).

(C) (A) is true, but (R) is false.

(D) (A) is false, but (R) is true.

443. **Assertion (A) :** Metrics based evaluation is not suitable for assessing research performance of individual.

Reason (R) : Construction of citation profiles depend upon the databases used.

Codes :

(A) Both (A) and (R) are true.

(B) Both (A) and (R) are false.

(C) (A) is true, but (R) is false.

(D) (A) is false, but (R) is true.

444. **Assertion (A) :** With quick and comprehensive availability of informative through internet resources, need for reference service with a human touch is decreasing.

Reason (R) : Internet resources can satisfy all types of information needs of information seekers.

Codes :

(A) (A) is true and (R) is false.

(B) Both (A) and (R) are false.

(C) (A) is false and (R) is true.

(D) (A) and (R) are true.

445. **Assertion (A) :** Scholar frequency to visit academic libraries has decreased tremendously over the period of last two decades.

Reason (R) : E-scholarly resources are easily accessible to everyone from anywhere anytime.

Codes :

(A) Both (A) and (R) are true.

(B) Both (A) and (R) are false.

(C) (A) is true, but (R) is false.

(D) (A) is false, but (R) is true.

446. **Assertion (A) :** Mail survey, a data collection technique in which questionnaires are mailed to potential respondents, who in then fill and return at their convenience become obsolete.

Reason (R) : Survey-Monkey, the free online survey tool has totally replaced the traditional Mail survey.

Codes:

(A) (A) is true, but (R) is false.

(B) (A) is false, but (R) is true.

(C) Both (A) and (R) are true.

(D) Both (A) and (R) are false.

447. **Assertion (A) :** Majority of academic libraries in India are lagging behind in switching over as technology-oriented service institutions.

Reason (R) : The apex academic bodies and library Associations have not taken the lead role to devise standards and policies.

Codes :

(A) (A) is true, (R) is false.

(B) (A) is false, (R) is true.

(C) Both (A) and (R) is true.

(D) Both (A) and (R) are false.

448. **Assertion (A) :** One of the key lessons of the web 2.0 era is that users can add value.

Reason (R) : Web 2.0 serve communities of people and are created and maintained by and for the people.

Codes :

(A) Both (A) and (R) are true.

(B) Both (A) and (R) are false.

(C) (A) is true and (R) is false.

(D) (R) is true and (A) ıs false.

449. **Assertion (A) :** RSS is considered as an alternative to the current awareness service.

Reason (R) : RSS feeds enable us to syndicate data automatically.

Codes :

(A) Both (A) and (R) are true.

(B) Both (A) and (R) are false.

(C) (A) is false, but (R) is true.

(D) (A) is true, but (R) is false.

450. **Assertion (A) :** An electronic library may have both born digital and converted digital documents.

Reason (R) : A document stored in Unicode is same as storing the scanned image of the document.

Codes :

(A) (A) is false, but (R) is true.

(B) (A) is true, but (R) is false.

(C) Both (A) and (R) are true.

(D) Both (A) and (R) are false.

451. **Assertion (A) :** Social networking tools are very effective for marketing of Library products and services.

Reason (R) : They help to reach out the patrons anywhere and at any time.

Codes:

(A) Both (A) and (R) are true.

(B) Both (A) and (R) are false.

(C) (A) is true, but (R) is false.

(D) (A) is false, but (R) is true.

452. **Assertion (A) :** There is no need for libraries to invest on reference collection.

Reason (R) : Web is a treasure of all types of information that can replace reference desk.

Codes:

(A) Both (A) and (R) are true.

(B) Both (A) and (R) are false.

(C) (A) is true, but (R) is false.

(D) (A) is false, but (R) is true.

453. **Assertion (A) :** Subject gateways are suitable for all types of users for finding their information.

Reason (R) : Subject gateways are developed by subject and computer experts.

Codes:

(A) (A) is true, but (R) is false.

(B) (A) is false, but (R) is true.

(C) Both (A) & (R) are true.

(D) Both (A) & (R) are false.

454. **Assertion (A) :** PANDEX is a indexing system which sometimes allows changing the lead term to a standard form in order to provide better collocation of terms.

Reason (R) : It facilitates the first input string to be truncated after 18 characters and second after 11 characters.

Codes:

(A) Both (A) and (R) are true.

(B) Both (A) and (R) are false.

(C) (A) is false, but (R) is true.

(D) (A) is true, but (R) is false.

455. **Assertion (A) :** SGML is an international standard that describes the relationship between a document's content and its structure.

Reason (R) : Its primary purpose is to facilitate the sharing of data\ across different information systems particularly via Internet.

Codes:

(A) Both (A) and (R) are false.

(B) (A) is true, but (R) is false.

(C) Both (A) and (R) are true.

(D) (A) is false, but (R) is true.

456. **Assertion (A) :** In the digital environment, the users expect from the library the ability to connect broad range of information resources in a variety of formats with a single point access.

Reason (R) : Libraries already have much of what is required in the digital environment.

Codes:

(A) (A) is true, but (R) is false.

(B) Both (A) and (R) are true.

(C) Both (A) and (R) are false.

(D) (A) is false, but (R) is true.

457. **Assertion (A):** The diary technique enables the researcher to keep record of information activities of the users for a specified period of time.

Reason (R) : The diary technique is the most suitable technique of user studies over other techniques.

Codes:

(A) Both (A) and (R) are false.

(B) (A) is true, but (R) is false.

(C) Both (A) and (R) are true.

(D) (A) is false, but (R) is tru

458. **Assertion (A) :** Wikis have provided everybody an opportunity for authoring, editing and publishing.

Reason (R) : Web has provided very generic rules for creation, maintenance and development of Wikis.

Codes :

(A) (A) is true, but (R) is false.

(B) (A) is false, but (R) is true.

(C) Both (A) and (R) are true.

(D) Both (A) and (R) are false.

459. **Assertion (A) :** Webliographies are bibliographic tools for print and electronic documents.

Reason (R) : Webliography denotes an enumerative list of hypertext links surrounding a common subject following standard citation styles.

Codes :

(A) (A) is true, but (R) is false.

(B) (A) is false, but (R) is true.

(C) Both (A) and (R) are true.

(D) Both (A) and (R) are false.

460. **Assertion (A) :** An ISO 2709 : 2008 record structure and review format has 'Record Label', 'Directory', 'Data fields' and 'Record Separator'.

Reason (R) : ISO 2709 is a subset of MARC.

Codes :

(A) (A) is true, but (R) is false.

(B) (A) is false, but (R) is true.

(C) Both (A) and (R) are true.

(D) Both (A) and (R) are false.

461. **Assertion (A) :** Social networking tools are very effective for marketing of library products and services.

Reason (R) : It does not help to reach out the patrons any where any time.

Codes :

(A) (A) is true, but (R) is false.

(B) (A) is false, but (R) is true.

(C) Both (A) and (R) are true.

(D) Both (A) and (R) are false.

462. **Assertion (A) :** To increase accessibility to information for differently abled users we need to accept assistive technologies.

Reason (R) : Information for all.

Codes :

(A) Both (A) and (R) are true, but (R) is not.the correct explanation of (A)

(B) Both (A) and (R) are true and (R)is the correct explanation of (A).

(C) (A) is true, but (R) is false.

(D) (A) is false, but (R) is true.

463. **Assertion (A) :** The plagiarism detection software implements a generic detection approach for all types of materials.

Reason (R) : There is no difference between text and source code plagiarism.

Codes :

(A) (A) is true, but (R) is false.

(B) (A) is false, but (R) is true.

(C) Both (A) and (R) are true.

(D) Both (A) and (R) are false.

464. **Assertion (A) :** Web has become a hub for all activities of library users.

Reason (R) : Web is being used as popular publishing media.

Codes:

(A) Both (A) and (R) are true, but (A) is not correct explanation.

(B) (A) is true and (R) is false

(C) (A) is false and (R) is true

(D) Both (A) and (R) are false

465. **Assertion (A) :** Web-OPAC is a computerized library catalogue available to the patrons on-line

Reason (R) : It can be search by the users with in the four walls of the library only

(A) (A) is true, but (R) is false

(B) (A) is false, but (R) is true

(C) Both (A) and (R) are true

(D) Both (A) and (R) are false

466. **Assertion (A) :** Libraries are changing in the wake of emerging ICT cnvironment.

Reason (R) : Libraries are adopting new competencies to operate services in the environment of the information super highway

(A) (A) is true, but (R) is false
(B) (A) is false, but (R) is true
(C) Both (A) and (R) are false
(D) Both (A) and (R) are true

467. Arrange the following library management software according to their year of origin:
(i) Koha (ii) NewGenLib
(iii) SOUL (iv) CDS/ISIS
Codes:
(A) (iv), (i), (ii), (iii) (B) (i), (ii), (iii), (iv)
(C) (iv), (ii), (i), (iii) (D) (iv), (i), (iii), (ii)

468. RSS feed is a tool of :
(A) Graphic design (B) Web 1.0
(C) Web 2.0 (D) Architecture

ANSWERS

1. (B)	2. (C)	3. (D)	4. (C)
5. (B)	6. (C)	7. (D)	8. (B)
9. (D)	10. (A)	11. (A)	12. (A)
13. (C)	14. (D)	15. (A)	16. (D)
17. (A)	18. (B)	19. (D)	20. (D)
21. (B)	22. (D)	23. (C)	24. (A)
25. (D)	26. (C)	27. (B)	28. (C)
29. (D)	30. (D)	31. (B)	32. (C)
33. (A)	34. (D)	35. (D)	36. (C)
37. (A)	38. (D)	39. (B)	40. (B)
41. (A)	42. (C)	43. (C)	44. (B)
45. (B)	46. (C)	47. (B)	48. (D)
49. (D)	50. (B)	51. (D)	52. (B)
53. (D)	54. (C)	55. (B)	56. (A)
57. (C)	58. (D)	59. (A)	60. (C)
61. (D)	62. (A)	63. (B)	64. (D)
65. (D)	66. (D)	67. (D)	68. (D)
69. (D)	70. (D)	71. (C)	72. (C)
73. (A)	74. (B)	75. (C)	76. (B)
77. (A)	78. (B)	79. (D)	80. (A)
81. (D)	82. (C)	83. (C)	84. (D)
85. (C)	86. (B)	87. (B)	88. (C)
89. (C)	90. (C)	91. (B)	92. (D)
93. (D)	94. (D)	95. (B)	96. (D)
97. (D)	98. (D)	99. (C)	100. (B)

101. (D)	102. (C)	103. (D)	104. (D)
105. (A)	106. (D)	107. (C)	108. (A)
109. (D)	110. (D)	111. (C)	112. (A)
113. (C)	114. (C)	115. (B)	116. (D)
117. (A)	118. (C)	119. (A)	120. (C)
121. (C)	122. (D)	123. (D)	124. (D)
125. (C)	126. (B)	127. (D)	128. (B)
129. (C)	130. (D)	131. (C)	132. (B)
133. (A)	134. (B)	135. (A)	136. (B)
137. (C)	138. (C)	139. (A)	140. (C)
141. (C)	142. (D)	143. (B)	144. (D)
145. (D)	146. (B)	147. (B)	148. (C)
149. (A)	150. (D)	151. (C)	152. (C)
153. (C)	154. (C)	155. (D)	156. (B)
157. (C)	158. (B)	159. (D)	160. (D)
161. (B)	162. (D)	163. (D)	164. (D)
165. (B)	166. (D)	167. (D)	168. (D)
169. (B)	170. (C)	171. (A)	172. (D)
173. (C)	174. (D)	175. (B)	176. (A)
177. (D)	178. (A)	179. (C)	180. (C)
181. (C)	182. (D)	183. (B)	184. (C)
185. (A)	186. (D)	187. (A)	188. (A)
189. (A)	190. (B)	191. (C)	192. (C)
193. (A)	194. (D)	195. (D)	196. (B)
197. (C)	198. (A)	199. (C)	200. (D)
201. (A)	202. (C)	203. (B)	204. (B)
205. (D)	206. (B)	207. (A)	208. (A)
209. (C)	210. (A)	211. (C)	212. (C)
213. (D)	214. (D)	215. (C)	216. (D)
217. (C)	218. (C)	219. (D)	220. (D)
221. (B)	222. (A)	223. (B)	224. (A)
225. (C)	226. (A)	227. (B)	228. (C)
229. (D)	230. (A)	231. (A)	232. (A)
233. (B)	234. (C)	235. (B)	236. (B)
237. (D)	238. (A)	239. (B)	240. (C)
241. (D)	242. (B)	243. (A)	244. (C)
245. (A)	246. (A)	247. (C)	248. (D)
249. (D)	250. (A)	251. (A)	252. (A)
253. (D)	254. (A)	255. (D)	256. (A)
257. (D)	258. (C)	259. (B)	260. (C)
261. (A)	262. (B)	263. (C)	264. (B)
265. (D)	266. (B)	267. (C)	268. (A)
269. (D)	270. (B)	271. (D)	272. (A)

273. (A) 274. (B) 275. (D) 276. (B)
277. (D) 278. (D) 279. (D) 280. (B)
281. (B) 282. (B) 283. (A) 284. (A)
285. (B) 286. (C) 287. (C) 288. (C)
289. (C) 290. (A) 291. (D) 292. (A)
293. (B) 294. (B) 295. (B) 296. (C)
297. (B) 298. (C) 299. (B) 300. (C)
301. (B) 302. (A) 303. (D) 304. (B)
305. (D) 306. (B) 307. (B) 308. (C)
309. (A) 310. (B) 311. (A) 312. (B)
313. (B) 314. (C) 315. (D) 316. (D)
317. (B) 318. (B) 319. (B) 320. (B)
321. (B) 322. (D) 323. (D) 324. (B)
325. (C) 326. (B) 327. (A) 328. (D)
329. (C) 330. (C) 331. (C) 332. (D)
333. (B) 334. (B) 335. (B) 336. (A)
337. (C) 338. (B) 339. (A) 340. (C)
341. (D) 342. (D) 343. (A) 344. (D)
345. (C) 346. (B) 347. (B) 348. (D)
349. (A) 350. (A) 351. (B) 352. (C)
353. (B) 354. (D) 355. (C) 356. (C)
357. (B) 358. (B) 359. (A) 360. (D)
361. (B) 362. (A) 363. (C) 364. (A)
365. (C) 366. (A) 367. (B) 368. (A)
369. (C) 370. (A) 371. (B) 372. (C)
373. (C) 374. (C) 375. (B) 376. (B)
377. (A) 378. (C) 379. (D) 380. (B)
381. (D) 382. (B) 383. (D) 384. (D)
385. (D) 386. (A) 387. (C) 388. (B)
389. (A) 390. (D) 391. (B) 392. (C)
393. (A) 394. (D) 395. (A) 396. (B)
397. (A) 398. (B) 399. (D) 400. (D)
401. (A) 402. (C) 403. (D) 404. (D)
405. (B) 406. (A) 407. (B) 408. (D)
409. (A) 410. (C) 411. (A) 412. (A)
413. (A) 414. (D) 415. (A) 416. (A)
417. (C) 418. (C) 419. (B) 420. (C)
421. (C) 422. (A) 423. (A) 424. (A)
425. (B) 426. (B) 427. (A) 428. (C)
429. (A) 430. (B) 431. (B) 432. (A)
433. (D) 434. (B) 435. (A) 436. (D)
437. (B) 438. (A) 439. (C) 440. (A)
441. (C) 442. (B) 443. (A) 444. (A)

445. (C)	446. (D)	447. (C)	448. (C)
449. (A)	450. (B)	451. (A)	452. (B)
453. (B)	454. (D)	455. (B)	456. (A)
457. (B)	458. (C)	459. (B)	460. (A)
461. (A)	462. (B)	463. (D)	464. (A)
465. (A)	466. (D)	467. (D)	468. (C)

7
Research Methodology

1. The 'Central Value Distribution' is known as
   (A) Mean (B) Median
   (C) Mode (D) Measurement
2. What is Hypothesis ?.
   (A) Final solution of a problem
   (B) Tentative solution of a problem
   (C) Blueprint of research problem
   (D) Tool of data collection
3. Inductive logic proceeds from- .
   (A) Particular to general (B) General to particular
   (C) General to general (D) Particular to particular
4. System analysis involves-
   (A) Analysis and design
   (B) Analysis
   (C) Analysis, evaluation and decision
   (D) Design
5. "Law of single variable" is an essential component of ....
   (A) Experimental Research
   (B) Historical Rcsearch
   (C) Case Study
   (D) Survey Research

6. Name of the Research done to find the solution for an immediate problem ;
   (A) Conceptual Research (B) Pure Research
   (C) Applied Research (D) Qualitative Research
7. One of the following is a non-probability sampling method. Which is the one?
   (A) Purposive sampling (B) Convenience sampling
   (C) Cluster sampling (D) Snowball sampling
8. Research Scholars generally prefer
   (A) Primary sources of information
   (B) Tertiary sources of information
   (C) Secondary sources of information
   (D) Primary & Secondary sources of information
9. Arrange the following stages in research according to the sequence of their occurrence:
   (i) Theory (ii) Axiom
   (iii) Law (iv) Hypothesis

   Codes:

   (A) (i), (ii), (iii), (iv) (B) (iv), (i), (iii), (ii)
   (C) (ii), (iii), (iv), (i) (D) (iii), (i), (iv), (ii)
10. Which one of the sampling methods will give better results if the size of the study population is very small?
    (A) Purposive (B) Stratified Random
    (C) Simple Random (D) Census
11. Which one of the variable are not to be expressed quantitative terms
    (A) Martial status (B) Experience
    (C) Income (D) Age
12. Literature Review means
    (A) Future Status Research
    (B) Background study
    (C) Objectives of Research
    (D) Scope if the study
13. 'Mode' is the value of the variable having maximum
    (A) Appearance (B) Frequency
    (C) Occurrence (D) Repetition

14. In 'graph', the horizontal axis is called
    (A) W-axis (B) Y-axis
    (C) X- axis (D) Z-axis
15. Bar charts, Pie Charts and Histograms are the examples of
    (A) Graphic Representation
    (B) Line Representation
    (C) Table Representation
    (D) Statistical Representation
16. 'Hypothesis' is a
    (i) Solution of the problems
    (ii) Statements of the assumptions
    (iii) Statements to be tested
    (iv) Fact

    Codes:
    (A) (i) and (ii) are correct
    (B) (ii) and (iii) are correct
    (C) (i) and (iii) are correct
    (D) (i) and (iv) are correct
17. Which of the following cannot be measured using an ordinal scale ?
    (A) Age (B) Annual income
    (C) Grade point average (D) Religion
18. 'Cranfield Studies' are an example of :
    (A) Survey research
    (B) Experimental research
    (C) Historical research
    (D) Case study
19. The group which is manipulated by an independent variable is known as :
    (A) Experimental group (B) Informal group
    (C) Multiple group (D) Controlled group
20. People who are available, volunteer or can be easily recruited are used in the sampling method called :

(A) Simple random sampling
(B) Convenience sampling
(C) Cluster sampling
(D) Systematic sampling

21. A question that directs participants to different follow-up questions depending on their response is called
(A) Response set
(B) Probe
(C) Semantic differential
(D) Contingency question

22. Arrange the following in correct order :
(i) Deductive phase (ii) Empirical phase
(iii) Verification phase (iv) Hypothesizing phase
Codes :
(A) (i), (ii), (iv), (iii) (B) (iv), (i), (ii), (iii)
(C) (iii), (i), (iv), (ii) (D) (ii), (iv), (i), (iii)

23. Delphi technique is associated with :
(A) Statistics
(B) Budgeting
(C) Forecasting
(D) Quality control technique

24. A regression curve is :
(A) A model of a mathematical relationship between two variables
(B) A model of a direct relationship between two variables
(C) A model of an inverse relationship between two variables
(D) A model to depict central tendency

25. Which of the following is not the use of devices in classification schemes ?
(A) To avoid enumeration
(B) To provide autonomy to a classifier
(C) To satisfy the library users
(D) To satisfy the canon of helpful sequence

26. When each member of a population has an equal chance of being selected, the sampling is called :
    (A) Probability sampling
    (B) Quota sampling
    (C) Snowball sampling
    (D) Purposive sampling
27. Identify the right sequence :
    (A) Theory, Law, Hypothesis, Axiom
    (B) Axiom, Hypothesis, Law, Theory
    (C) Hypothesis, Axiom, Law, Theory
    (D) Law, Hypothesis, Theory, Axiom
28. Arrange the following steps of research according to the sequence of their occurrence
    (i) formulation of hypothesis of research
    (ii) designing of data and analysis plan
    (iii) selection of data gathering method
    (iv) report writing

    Codes:

    (A) (iii) (ii) (i) (iv) (B) (i) (iii) (ii) (iv)
    (C) (iii) (i) (iv) (ii) (D) (ii) (iv) (i) (iii)
29. A category-based systematic scheme of hierarchical classification incorporating hierarchical relationships among the terms, control of synonyms, quasi-synonyms and antonyms in extended sense is known as
    (A) Thesaurus (B) Thesaurofacet
    (C) Classaurus (D) None of the above
30. In Dublin Core Metadata Schema, which of the following elements does not have any qualifier?
    (A) Title (B) Creator
    (C) Subject (D) Descriptors
31. The chi-square technique is used to compare the observed data with that of
    (A) Collected raw data (B) Expected data
    (C) Analysed data (D) Graphical data

32. Which of the following is not related to case study approach in a research design ?
    (A) Indepth Study
    (B) Study of one/limited cases
    (C) General study
    (D) Little concern about generalisation to a large population
33. "Students' visit to Library is influenced by the availability of Internet". State "Students' visit to library" is which kind of variable?
    (A) Independent Variable
    (B) Intervening Variable
    (C) Dependent Variable
    (D) Intercept Variable
34. Idiographic hypothesis is directed towards predicting the behaviour of
    (A) An Individual
    (B) Group of People
    (C) Masses
    (D) People from same school of thought
35. In the process of reasoning when we start with a specific statement, and conclude to a general statement, it is called
    (A) Deductive Reasoning
    (B) Inductive Reasoning
    (C) Abnormal Reasoning
    (D) Transcendental Reasoning
36. Solomon Four group design is related to
    (A) Field studies
    (B) Pretest-post test control group design
    (C) Data Analysis Model
    (D) Statistical Technique
37. Research is conducted to :
    (i) Generate new knowledge
    (ii) Develop a theory
    (iii) Develop communication skills
    (iv) Re-interpret existing knowledge

Codes :

(A) (i), (iii) and (ii) are correct

(B) (iii), (ii) and (i) are correct

(C) (i), (ii) and (iv) are correct

(D) (i), (iii) and (iv) are correct

38. Which of the factor is not helping in limiting the external validity ?
(A) Reactive effect
(B) Ecological validity
(C) Interaction between selection bias of experimental variables
(D) Ecological effect

39. In spiral of scientific method, the span of Zenith to descendent is
(A) Empirical phase (B) Hypothesizing phase
(C) Deductive phase (D) Verification phase

40. Which of the following variable cannot be expressed in quantitative terms ?
(A) Socio-Economic status
(B) Marital status
(C) Numerical Aptitude
(D) Professional Attitude

41. Research in automatic classification for information retrieval of term or cluster of terms is called
(A) Evaluation theory (B) Theory of clumps
(C) Time binding theory (D) Dynamic theory

42. 'Research-in-progress' database in India is_______.
(A) Vidyanidhi
(B) Shodhganga
(C) Shodhgangotri
(D) Indian National Depository Library

43. When the population is heterogenous, which of the following methods give better results?
(A) Purposive Sampling
(B) Quota Sampling
(C) Random Sampling
(D) Stratified Random Sampling

44. The correlational coefficient is
    (A) A strength of relationship between two variables.
    (B) A typical relationship between two variables.
    (C) A linear relationship between two variables.
    (D) Non-linear relationship between two variables.

45. The normal curve in a distribution is
    (i) Symmetrical, bell shaped continuously curve
    (ii) Asymmetrical, bell shaped continuously curve
    (iii) Symmetrical, bell shaped curve which does not touch the 'X' axis
    (iv) Bell shaped curve

    Codes :
    (A) (i) and (iv) are correct.
    (B) (i) and (iii) are correct.
    (C) (ii) and (iv) are correct.
    (D) (i) is correct.

46. Books of Unknown or doubtful authorship is known as:
    (A) Apograph (B) Incunabulla
    (C) Apocryphal books (D) Blue Books

47. If we plot 'recall' and precision on 'X' and 'Y' axis to draw a graph, then we get a
    (A) Downward sloping straight line
    (B) Upward sloping straight line
    (C) '?' shaped curve
    (D) Hyperbola

48. Under which approach of Wersig-Neveling's information theory, information is seen as static relations between physical objects which may be perceived or not?
    (A) The meaning approach
    (B) The structural approach
    (C) The process approach
    (D) The knowledge approach

49. In which scheme of classification, special auxiliaries denote locally recurrent characteristics?

(A) Dewey Decimal Classification
(B) Universal Decimal Classification
(C) Bibliographic Classification
(D) Colon Classification

50. Which of the following makes a network insecured?
(A) Encryption
(B) Network Interface Card (NIC)
(C) Password Capture
(D) Static Keys

51. Whose model of communication of knowledge suggests that communication is an open system?
(A) G. Garbner (B) Juger Hebermans
(C) Shannon & Weaver (D) M. Foucault

52. Which of the following are reasons for obsolescence of information?
(i) Information is considered invalid.
(ii) Information is valid but mostly available online.
(iii) Works are extensively cited.
(iv) Information is valid but inadequate for exploration.

Codes:
(A) (i) and (ii) are correct.
(B) (ii) and (iii) are correct.
(C) (i) and (iv) are correct.
(D) (ii) and (iv) are correct.

53. Which of the following are news summaries?
(i) Data India
(ii) Times of India Index
(iii) New York Times Index
(iv) Asian Recorder

Codes:
(A) (i), (ii) and (iii) are correct.
(B) (ii) and (iii) are correct.
(C) (ii) (iii) and (iv) are correct.
(D) (i) and (iv) are correct.

54. Which of the following are Web-zine?
    (i) Email Magazine (ii) E-Conference
    (iii) Online Bulletin (iv) Electronic News Letter
    Codes:
    (A) (i), (iii) and (iv) (B) (i), (ii) and (iii)
    (C) (ii), (iii) and (iv) (D) (i), (ii) and (iv)
55. In reference service, assimilation means:
    (i) Recording the retrieved information
    (ii) Sharing reference service experience with colleagues
    (iii) Furnishing the exact information
    (iv) Acquaintance with reference material
    Codes:
    (A) (i) and (ii) are correct.
    (B) (i) and (iv) are correct.
    (C) (ii) and (iii) are correct.
    (D) (ii) and (iv) are correct.
56. Which of the following are the functions of the physical layer in OSI Model?
    (i) Defines protocol for flow control.
    (ii) Reliable sending of data packets.
    (iii) Defines electrical specifications.
    (iv) Functional and procedural means of transferring data.
    Codes:
    (A) (iii) and (iv) are correct.
    (B) (ii), (iii) and (iv) are correct.
    (C) (i) and (iv) are correct.
    (D) (i) and (iii) are correct.
57. Rich Text Format (RTF) is concerned with
    (i) Formatting features like Font type, size, etc.
    (ii) Transporting text documents across different computers.
    (iii) Multimedia formatting.
    (iv) Formatting based on binary concept.

Codes:

(A) (ii) and (iii) are correct.

(B) (iii) and (iv) are correct.

(C) (i) and (ii) are correct.

(D) (i) and (iv) are correct.

58. Which of the following are non probability sampling?

(i) Quota sampling

(ii) Judgement Sampling

(iii) Cluster Sampling

(iv) Multi-stage sampling

Codes:

(A) (i) and (iv) are correct.

(B) (ii) and (iii) are correct.

(C) (i) and (ii) are correct.

(D) (iii) and (iv) are correct.

59. Arrange the following ISBDs according to their year of formulation:

(i) ISBD (PM) (ii) ISBD (CF)

(iii) ISBD (M) (iv) ISBD (S)

Codes:

(A) (iii), (ii), (i), (iv) (B) (iii), (iv), (i), (ii)

(C) (iv), (i), (iii), (ii) (D) (iv), (ii), (iii), (i)

60. Arrange the following in the chronological order of their first year of publication:

(i) Arts and Humanities Index

(ii) Social Science Citation Index

(iii) ISI Web of Science

(iv) Science Citation Index

Codes:

(A) (iv), (ii), (i), (iii) (B) (ii), (iii), (iv), (i)

(C) (iii), (ii), (i), (iv) (D) (iv), (i), (iii), (ii)

61. Arrange the following processes of research in order:

(i) Theory Building

(ii) Reflecting and Integrating of Idea

(iii) Research Design

(iv) Review of Literature

Codes:

(A) (iv), (iii), (ii), (i) (B) (iii), (i), (iv), (ii)

(C) (ii), (iv), (iii), (i) (D) (i), (ii), (iv), (iii)

62. A cross reference that gives an indexer complete control over the cross references of an index is known as :
    (A) see also cross reference
    (B) check also cross reference
    (C) see cross reference
    (D) inverted cross reference
63. DMAIC is the acronym for :
    (A) Define, Measure, Access, Improve and Control
    (B) Define, Measure, Analyse, Improve and Control
    (C) Describe, Measure, Analyse, Improve and Control
    (D) Define, Measure, Access, Instruct and Control
64. A template is a
    (A) Structured specification
    (B) Recursive routine
    (C) Assembler program
    (D) I/O measure
65. 'Delphi Technique' was first discussed in a monograph by
    (A) O. Helmer (B) E. Nagel
    (C) D.M. Potter (D) J.H. Shera
66. The service that helps the students to acquire soft skills, writing skills and job-oriented skills is
    (A) Reader's advisory (B) Career guidance
    (C) Referral service (D) User education
67. Skill Development Programme (SDP) for public librarians in India is initiated by
    (A) Ministry of Human Resource Development, Govt. of India
    (B) Directorate of Library Services, Govt. of West Bengal
    (C) Raja Ram Mohan Roy Library Foundation
    (D) Indian Library Association

68. Which of the following concepts are associated with professional ethics ?
    (i) Accountability
    (ii) Unique training
    (iii) High quality service
    (iv) Professional independence

    Codes :
    (A) (i), (ii), (iii) are correct.
    (B) (i), (iii) are correct.
    (C) (i), (ii), (iv) are correct.
    (D) (iii), (iv) are correct.

69. Which of the following are characteristics of a review ?
    (i) Analyses research topic
    (ii) Indicates inter-relation of ideas
    (iii) Presents an integrated picture of development and program
    (iv) Provides only current information

    Codes :
    (A) (ii), (iii), (iv) are correct.
    (B) (i), (iii), (iv) are correct.
    (C) (i), (ii), (iii) are correct.
    (D) (i), (ii), (iv) are correct.

70. An alerting service in the digital environment is offered through :
    (i) RSS feeds
    (ii) E-mail
    (iii) Blogs
    (iv) Bulletin Board

    Codes :
    (A) (i), (iii) are correct.
    (B) (ii), (iii), (iv) are correct.
    (C) (i), (ii), (iii) are correct.
    (D) (i), (ii), (iv) are correct.

71. The important methods of measuring impact factor of any information retrieval system are :
    (i) Expression Rate
    (ii) Precision Rate
    (iii) Recall Rate
    (iv) Depression Rate

Codes :

(A) (i) and (iii) are correct.
(B) (ii) and (iv) are correct.
(C) (ii) and (iii) are correct.
(D) (iii) and (iv) are correct.

72. Arrange the stages in the preparation of State-of the Art Report.
(i) Consultation with subject expert
(ii) Scope determination
(iii) Appraisal of information
(iv) Identification of the collection

Codes :

(A) (ii) (iv) (iii) (i) (B) (iv) (ii) (iii) (i)
(C) (iii) (i) (iv) (ii) (D) (i) (ii) (iii) (iv)

73. Arrange the following according to their year of origin:
(i) Statistical Bibliography
(ii) Librametery
(iii) Bibliometrics
(iv) Webometrics

Codes :

(A) (ii) (iii) (i) (iv) (B) (iii) (ii) (i) (iv)
(C) (i) (ii) (iii) (iv) (D) (ii) (i) (iii) (iv)

74. Which form of reasoning is the process of drawing a specific conclusion from a set of premises?
(A) Rationalism
(B) Deductive reasoning
(C) Inductive reasoning
(D) Probabilistic

75. Which of the following are the steps in operational research process?
i. Construction of mathematical model
ii. Deriving solution from the model.
iii. Graphic representation of work on a time scale.
iv. Developing network diagram showing interrelationships.

Codes:

(A) i and ii are correct. (B) ii and iii are correct.

(C) iii and iv are correct. (D) iv and i are correct.

76. Name the characteristics of information in which the more information we have, the more we use, the more it becomes useful.
    (A) Synergetic Characteristics
    (B) Diffusive Characteristics
    (C) Compressible Characteristics
    (D) Shareable Characteristics

77. LOCKSS (Lots of Copies Keep Stuff Safe) project was launched by :
    (A) Mellon Foundation
    (B) Stanford University
    (C) University of California
    (D) OCLC

78. Identify the founders of Wikipedia from the following :

    i. Michael E Davis ii. Jimmy Wales

    iii. Richard Stallman iv. Larry Sanger

    Codes :

    (A) ii and iii are correct. (B) i and ii are correct.

    (C) i and iii are correct. (D) ii and iv are correct.

79. Alerting service is provided
    i. Before and after the publication of primary source
    ii. For specific search formulation by user
    iii. For retrieval of information
    iv For individuals as well as groups

    Codes :

    (A) i and ii are correct. (B) i and iv are correct.

    (C) ii and iii are correct. (D) iii and iv are correct.

80. Hierarchical relationship among concepts indicates
    i. Genus-species relationship
    ii. Equivalance relationship
    iii. Whole-part relationship
    iv. Associate relationship

Codes :

(A) ii and iv are correct. (B) iii and ii are correct.

(C) i and iii are correct. (D) iv and i are correct.

81. The 'Principle of Facet Sequence' includes
    - i. Cow-calf principle
    - ii. Wall-picture principle
    - iii. Whole organ principle
    - iv. Principle of osmosis

    Codes :

    (A) i, ii and iv are correct.

    (B) i, ii and iii are correct.

    (C) i, iii and iv are correct.

    (D) ii and iv are correct.

82. Which of the following are features of 'Open Journal System' ?
    - i. License to access content
    - ii. Access restricted to limited group
    - iii. Online submission
    - iv. Subscription module with delayed open access options

    Codes :

    (A) i and ii are correct. (B) ii and iii are correct.

    (C) iii and iv are correct. (D) ii and iv are correct.

83. SQL is based on which of the following ?
    - i. Query string
    - ii. Relational algebra
    - iii. Relational calculus
    - iv. Web search queries

    Codes :

    (A) i, ii are correct. (B) ii, iii are correct.

    (C) iii, iv are correct. (D) ii, iv are correct.

84. What are the approaches to plagiarism check of academic publications ?
    - i. String matching
    - ii. Bag of words analysis
    - iii. Citation analysis
    - iv. Parse trees

    Codes :

    (A) ii, iv are correct. (B) i, ii, iii are correct.

    (C) i,iv are correct. (D) i, iii, iv are correct.

85. Which of the following are the types of validity of measurement ?

i. Construct ii. Current

iii. Content iv. Predictive

Codes :

(A) i, ii, iii are true. (B) ii, iii, iv are true.

(C) i, iii, iv are true. (D) i, ii, iv are true.

86. Identify the compression protocols :

i. TIFF ii. JPEG

iii. ZIFF iv. LZW

Codes :

(A) i, iii, iv are correct. (B) i, ii, iv are correct.

(C) ii, iii, iv are correct. (D) i, ii, iii are correct.

87. Arrange the following according to the procedural steps:

i. Receipt of recommendations

ii. Preparing master card

iii. Checking titles of and bibliographical details

iv. Duplication checking from library catalogue

Codes :

(A) i, ii, iii, iv (B) i, iii, ii, iv

(C) iii, i, iv, ii (D) iv, iii, i, ii

88. Arrange the following according to their date of origin:

i. Librametry ii. Statistical bibliography

iii. Statistical analysis iv. Bibliometrics

Codes :

(A) i, iii, ii, iv (B) ii, iii, i, iv

(C) iii, i, ii, iv (D) iii, ii, i, iv

89. Arrange the following steps in the order of accessioning the book :

i. Arrange books as per bill

ii. Check books as per order placed

iii. Enter the accession number in the register

iv. Write accession number on back of title page of other relevant pages

Codes :

(A) i, ii, iii, iv (B) ii, iii, i, iv
(C) iii, i, ii, iv (D) ii, i, iii, iv

90. When the population is heterogenous, which of the following methods give better results?
(A) Purposive Sampling
(B) Quota Sampling
(C) Random Sampling
(D) Stratified Random Sampling

91. Questionnaire is a :
(A) Research method
(B) Measurement technique
(C) Tool for data collection
(D) Data analysis technique

92. "Controlled Group" is a term used in-
(A) Survey research
(B) Historical research
(C) Experimental research
(D) Descriptive research

93. Inductive logic proceeds from :
(A) General to General (B) Particular to General
(C) General to Particular (D) Particular to Particular

94. Which of the following is not a "Graphic representation"?
(A) Pie Chart (B) Bar Chart
(C) Table (D) Histogram

95. How is stochastic equation of information solved ?
(A) By statistical rules
(B) By dynamic rules
(C) By statistical and dynamic rules
(D) None of these.

96. What is Delphi method ?
(A) It is a programming language
(B) It is a method of research
(C) It is a software
(D) It is used for cost-benefit analysis.

97. Mean, Median and Mode are
    (A) Measure of Central tendency
    (B) Measure of deviation
    (C) Measure of Information System
    (D) Measure of Sampling

98. Arrange the following steps in research in the sequence of their occurrence :
    (I) Report writing (II) Research design
    (III) Collection of data (IV) Analysis of data

    Codes :
    (A) (III), (IV), (II), (I) (B) (I), (III), (IV), (II)
    (C) (II), (III), (IV), (I) (D) (IV), (II), (III), (I)

99. In "Spiral of Scientific Method", Zenith marks
    (A) Facts (B) Empirical laws
    (C) Fundamental laws (D) Deduced laws

100. Arrange the following in a logical sequence :
    (i) Formulation of a hypothesis
    (ii) Data analysis
    (iii) Selection of sample
    (iv) Report writing

    Codes :
    (A) (i), (ii), (iii), (iv) (B) (iv), (ii), (i), (iii)
    (C) (ii), (i), (iv), (iii) (D) (i), (iii), (ii), (iv)

101. Which of the following is a term used for working assumption of a solution to a problem ?
    (A) Research (B) Hypothesis
    (C) Bibliography (D) Thesis

102. Arrange the structure of the Research report in correct order :
    (i) Table of contents (ii) Appendices
    (iii) Text (iv) Title page

    Codes :
    (A) (iii), (i), (iv), (ii) (B) (i), (ii), (iii), (iv)
    (C) (ii), (iii), (iv), (i) (D) (iv), (i), (iii), (ii)

103. Study carrels are exclusive areas meant for-

(A) students (B) public
(C) women (D) researchers

104. Which of the following is the first step in starting the research process?
(A) Searching sources of information to locate problem.
(B) Survey of related literature
(C) Identification of problem
(D) Searching for solutions to the problem

105. A common test in research demands much priority on
(A) Reliability (B) Useability
(C) Objectivity (D) All of the above

106. Action research means
(A) A longitudinal research
(B) An applied research
(C) A research initiated to solve an immediate problem
(D) A research with socioeconomic objective

107. A reasoning where we start with certain particular statements and conclude with a universal statement is called
(A) Deductive Reasoning
(B) Inductive Reasoning
(C) Abnormal Reasoning
(D) Transcendental Reasoning

108. Research is conducted to
I. Generate new knowledge
II. Not to develop a theory
III. Obtain research degree
IV. Reinterpret existing knowledge
Which of the above are correct?
(A) I, III & II (B) III, II & IV
(C) II, I & III (D) I, III & IV

109. Which of the following variables cannot be expressed in quantitative terms?
(A) Socio-economic Status
(B) Marital Status

(C) Numerical Aptitude
(D) Professional Attitude

110. The essential qualities of a researcher are
(A) Spirit of free enquiry
(B) Reliance on observation and evidence
(C) Systematization or theorizing of knowledge
(D) All the above

111. In the process of conducting research 'Formulation of Hypothesis" is followed by
(A) Statement of Objectives
(B) Analysis of Data
(C) Selection of Research Tools
(D) Collection of Data

112. A research paper is a brief report of research work based on
(A) Primary Data only
(B) Secondary Data only
(C) Both Primary and Secondary Data
(D) None of the above

113. Among the different Boolean operators "AND" is used
(A) to widen the search (B) to narrow the search
(C) to begin the search (D) to end the search

114. In an empirical study on the impact of television viewing on violence, violence would be
(A) the dependent variable
(B) an independent variable
(C) an intervening variable
(D) not a variable at all

115. A big difference between the mean and median is an indication that
(A) there is a mistake in the calculation
(B) the calculation is correct
(C) there is a wide variation in the data
(D) None of the above

116. Which of the following research methods is useful in a study on measuring the active life of periodicals

(A) Survey (B) Citation Analysis
(C) Interview (D) Case study

117. The 'Five Laws of Library Science' propounded by Dr. S. R. Ranganathan, is which type of research ?
(A) Applied research (B) Pure research
(C) Basic research (D) Survey research.

118. The subject of Research Methodology is the outcome of the mode of formation of subject, known as
(A) Loose Assemblage (B) Fission
(C) Distillation (D) Cluster.

119. Inductive logic proceeds from
(A) general to specific (B) general to general
(C) specific to general (D) specific to specific.

120. Hypothesis is a
(A) law (B) postulate
(C) canon (D) tentative generalisation

121. The scientific method can be applied for research in the field of
(A) Humanities (B) Natural Sciences
(C) Social Sciences (D) all of them.

122. Research design gives the
(A) blue print of the proposed research work
(B) blue print of introduction of research
(C) blue print of conclusion of research
(D) none of these.

123. First Ph. D. awarded in Library Science by an Indian University was
(A) S. R. Ranganathan (B) B. S. Kesavan
(C) M. A. Gopinath (D) D. B. Krishna Rao.

124. Solo research is an investigation conducted by
(A) a team (B) an individual
(C) a department (D) none of these.

125. Historical method of research can be applied
(A) in History (B) in Social Science
(C) in Humanities (D) in all subjects.

126. Interview is a
   (A) method of research
   (B) method of hypothesis
   (C) method of applied research
   (D) method of pure research.

127. First exponent of scientific method was
   (A) Plato (B) Socrates
   (C) Dante (D) Aristotle.

128. Correct sequence of cardinal points in the spiral of scientific method is
   (A) Ascendant, Zenith, Descendant, Nadir, Ascendant...
   (B) Zenith, Descendant, Nadir, Ascendant, Zenith...
   (C) Descendant, Nadir, Ascendant, Zenith, Descendant...
   (D) Nadir, Ascendant, Zenith, Descendant, Nadir...

129. Research done to find a solution for an immediate problem of the society/ industry/business organization is known as
   (A) social research (B) industrial research
   (C) applied research (D) pure research.

130. Deductive logic proceeds from
   (A) general to specific (B) specific to specific
   (C) specific to general (D) general to general.

131. Nadir, Ascendant, Zenith and Descendant are the four cardinal points of spiral of
   (A) natural science method
   (B) social science method
   (C) scientific method
   (D) human science method.

132. The cardinal point which rests at 900 from Nadir on the spiral of scientific method is
   (A) ascendant (B) zenith
   (C) descendant (D) nadir.

133. In historical method of research, not a tool for collection of data is

(A) eye witness (B) inscription
(C) historical evidence (D) newspaper.

134. Research aims at immediate results is
(A) pure research (B) applied research
(C) social research (D) industrial research.

135. One of the cardinal points on the spiral of the scientific method
(A) natural science (B) social science
(C) human science (D) ascendant.

136. In research on information needs of Chartered Accountants a questionnaire is that to every fifth number of the official register of Chartered Accountants. Would this
(A) random sampling
(B) stratified sampling
(C) the whole population
(D) not a representative sample.

137. In a questionnaire 'open ended' questions are
(A) the questions are open to interpretation
(B) the answers may be incomplete
(C) answers may be filled in by respondents
(D) those where long answers are required.

138. In a study undertaken to find out how uses approach the library catalogue, all those who use the catalogue on a particular day are interviewed. Would this be considered as?
(A) a random sample
(B) a stratified sample
(C) the whole population
(D) not a representational sample.

139. In a questionnaire, close ended questions are those where:
(A) the questions and answers are close to each other
(B) the answers are given as options
(C) the questions are clear and distinct
(D) short answers are required.

140. A study aimed at finding the best method of shelving library materials
    (A) basic research (B) fundamental research
    (C) applied research (D) no research at all.
141. Formulation of hypothesis is an important component of
    (A) content analysis (B) research design
    (C) processing of data (D) report writing.
142. If you are asked to arrange the concepts "information", "knowledge" and "data" in ascending order of complexity which of the following sequence is correct?
    (A) data – information – knowledge
    (B) knowledge – information – data
    (C) information – data –knowledge
    (D) information – knowledge – data.
143. Sometimes the terms 'data' and 'knowledge' are synonymously used for
    (A) wisdom (B) intelligence
    (C) news (D) information.
144. A state with its organs of executive, legislature and judiciary, business generates vast amount of
    (A) knowledge (B) wisdom
    (C) information (D) facts.
145. When data is processed, interpreted and presented in an organised form, it becomes
    (A) news (B) facts
    (C) knowledge (D) information.
146. Growth of information beyond a manageable limit characterises the explosion of
    (A) books (B) libraries
    (C) information (D) news.
147. Data on national income presented in a tabular form may be termed as
    (A) descriptive information
    (B) statistical information
    (C) enumerative information
    (D) societal information.

148. The Metrological Department is responsible for daily collection of

(A) measurement data (B) income data
(C) atmospheric data (D) demographic data.

149. The forecast note on weather conditions, based on processed and interpreted atmospheric data is

(A) data (B) news
(C) facts (D) information.

150. The behavioural data of chemical compound under different physical conditions observed through experiment are

(A) knowledge (B) raw facts
(C) information (D) processed data.

151. The data on national income statistics when reveal the changes that have taken place over a period of time is

(A) statistical information
(B) descriptive information
(C) analytical information
(D) uninterpreted information.

152. Which are the building block of knowledge and all three are handled in libraries offering different types of services?

(A) Wisdom and information
(B) Data and information
(C) News and information
(D) Intelligence and information.

153. Just as, cotton can be loomed into yarns which can be weaved into cloth, data can be weaved into information which can be used to form an organised body of

(A) knowledge (B) information
(C) wisdom (D) facts.

154. Office of the Registrar General was established to conduct what type of censuses to collect population data?

(A) decennial censuses (B) quarterly censuses
(C) annual censuses (D) biennial censuses.

155. The progress of a nation is often judged by percentage of national income that is spent on
   (A) education (B) business
   (C) R&D (D) surveys.
156. Who enacts various laws?
   (A) Supreme Court (B) High Court
   (C) Legislatures (D) Registrar.
157. Who are both consumers and producers of information?
   (A) Teachers (B) Students
   (C) Researchers (D) Govt. officials.
158. Large scale use of information in all countries by a wide cross section of people has resulted in coining of terms like
   (A) information explosion
   (B) mass production of information
   (C) information society
   (D) information use.
159. Futurologists are specialists in
   (A) social forecasting (B) astrology
   (C) astronomy (D) weather forecasting.
160. Quantitative growth of a thing at a particular rate of growth is known as
   (A) periodic growth (B) exponential growth
   (C) statistical growth (D) qualitativegrowth.
161. In research, inductive logic proceeds from
   (i) Particular to particular
   (ii) Particular to general
   (iii) General to particular
   (iv) General to general
162. Basic research is not concerned with
   (i) Discovering casual relations between facts
   (ii) Discovering direct solutions to various practical problems
   (iii) Discovering universal laws and theories
   (iv) refuting established theories

163. Brenda Dervin and M.Kochen have researched on
   (E) Information retrieval
   (F) Information needs
   (G) Computerized library system
   (H) Classification

164. A survey to determine the reading habits of students is
   (A) a descriptive study
   (B) an experimental study
   (C) a historical study
   (D) could be any of the above

165. Information about Indian research studies on bakery and milling is input to IFIS through
   (i) The Central Rice Research Institute
   (ii) Indian Agricultural Research Institute
   (iii) National Institute of Nutrition
   (iv) Central Food Technological Research Institute

166. In an empirical study on the impact of television viewing on violence, violence would be
   (i) the dependent variable
   (ii) an independent variable
   (iii) an intervening variable
   (iv) not a variable at all

167. A big difference between the mean and median is an indication that
   (i) There is a mistake in the calculation
   (ii) The calculation is correct
   (iii) There is a wide variation in the data
   (iv) None of the above

168. Formulation of Research Hypothesis implies:
   (A) Creating a legal basis for research
   (B) Enunciation of Postulates
   (C) Enumeration of canons
   (D) Formation of tentative generalization

169. ADONIS is a:
   - (i) Bibliographic database only
   - (ii) Numerical database only
   - (iii) Full text database
   - (iv) None of the above

   Code:

   (A) (i) and (ii) are correct (B) (ii) and (iii) are correct
   (C) (iii) is correct (D) (iv) is correct

170. Fundamental facts of research are available in

   (A) Primary sources (B) Secondary sources
   (C) Tertiary sources (D) None of the above

171. Arrange the following research steps according to the sequence of their occurrence
   - (i) Formulation of hypothesis of research
   - (ii) Designing of data and analysis plan
   - (iii) Selection of data gathering method
   - (iv) Report writing

   Codes:

   (A) (iii), (ii), (i), (iv) (B) (i), (iii), (ii), (iv)
   (C) (iii), (i), (iv), (ii) (D) (ii), (iv), (i), (iii)

172. Questionnaire is a:
   - (A) Research method
   - (B) Measurement Technique
   - (C) Tool for data collection
   - (D) All the above

173. A common test in research demands much priority on

   (A) Reliability (B) Useability
   (C) Objectivity (D) All of the above

174. Which of the following is the first step in starting the research process?
   - (A) Searching sources of information to locateproblem.
   - (B) Survey of related literature
   - (C) Identification of problem
   - (D) Searching for solutions to the problem

175. If a researcher conducts a research on finding out which administrative style contributes more to institutional effectiveness ? This will be an example of

(A) Basic Research (B) Action Research

(C) Applied Research (D) None of the above

176. Normal Probability Curve should be

(A) Positively skewed (B) Negatively skewed

(C) Leptokurtic skewed (D) Zero skewed

177. Research has shown that the most frequent symptom of nervous instability among teachers is

(A) Digestive upsets (B) Explosive behaviour

(C) Fatigue (D) Worry

178. Casual relationship between variables is identified in which type of research.

(A) Historical (B) Experimental

(C) Survey (D) Casestudy

179. Now days what is a most important vital resource for societal development of a country?

(A) Books (B) Kowledge

(C) Information (D) Data

180. A research paper is a brief report of research work based on

(A) Primary Data only

(B) Secondary Data only

(C) Both Primary and Secondary Data

(D) None of the above

181. Newton gave three basic laws of motion. This research is categorized as

(A) Descriptive Research

(B) Sample Survey

(C) Fundamental Research

(D) Applied Research

182. In the process of conducting research 'Formulation of Hypothesis" is followed by

(A) Statement of Objectives

(B) Analysis of Data

(C) Selection of Research Tools
(D) Collection of Data

183. Which one of the following does not come under the methods of data classification ?
(A) Qualitative (B) Normative
(C) Spatial (D) Quantitative

184. Which one of the following is not a source of data ?
(A) Administrative records
(B) Population census
(C) GIS
(D) Sample survey

185. The essential qualities of a researcher are
(A) spirit of free enquiry
(B) reliance on observation and evidence
(C) systematization or theorizing of knowledge
(D) all the above

186. Research is conducted to
I. Generate new knowledge
II. Not to develop a theory
III. Obtain research degree
IV. Reinterpret existing knowledge
Which of the above are correct ?
(A) I, III & II (B) III, II & IV
(C) II, I & III (D) I, III & IV

187. Which of the following variables cannot be expressed in quantitative terms ?
(A) Socio-economic Status
(B) Marital Status
(C) Numerical Aptitude
(D) Professional Attitude

188. A doctor studies the relative effectiveness of two drugs of dengue fever. His research would be classified as
(A) Descriptive Survey
(B) Experimental Research
(C) Case Study
(D) Ethnography

189. The term 'phenomenology' is associated with the process of
    (A) Qualitative Research (B) Analysis of Variance
    (C) Correlational Study (D) Probability Sampling
190. The 'Sociogram' technique is used to study
    (A) Vocational Interest
    (B) Professional Competence
    (C) Human Relations
    (D) Achievement Motivation
191. Which one of the following methods serve to measure correlation between two variables ?
    (A) Scatter Diagram
    (B) Frequency Distribution
    (C) Two-way table
    (D) Coefficient of Rank Correlation
192. Which of the following phrases is not relevant to describe the meaning of research as a process ?
    (A) Systematic Activity (B) Objective Observation
    (C) Trial and Error (D) Problem Solving
193. Which of the following is not an example of a continuous variable ?
    (A) Family size (B) Intelligence
    (C) Height (D) Attitude
194. To test null hypothesis, a researcher uses :
    (A) t test (B) ANOVA
    (C) X2 (D) factorial analysis
195. A research problem is feasible only when :
    (A) it has utility and relevance
    (B) it is researchable
    (C) it is new and adds something to knowledge
    (D) all the above
196. Bibliography given in a research report :
    (A) shows vast knowledge of the researcher
    (B) helps those interested in further research
    (C) has no relevance to research
    (D) all the above

197. Fundamental research reflects the ability to :
    (A) Synthesize new ideals
    (B) Expound new principles
    (C) Evaluate the existing material concerning research
    (D) Study the existing literature regarding various topics
198. The study in which the investigators attempt to trace an effect is known as :
    (A) Survey Research
    (B) 'Ex-post Facto' Research
    (C) Historical Research
    (D) Summative Research
199. What do you consider as the main aim of inter disciplinary research?
    (A) To bring out holistic approach to research.
    (B) To reduce the emphasis of single subject in research domain.
    (C) To over simplify the problem of research.
    (D) To create a new trend in research methodology.
200. One of the aims of the scientific method in research is to :
    (A) improve data interpretation
    (B) eliminate spurious relations
    (C) confirm triangulation
    (D) introduce new variables
201. The depth of any research can be judged by :
    (A) title of the research.
    (B) objectives of the research.
    (C) total expenditure on the research.
    (D) duration of the research.
202. The basis on which assumptions are formulated :
    (A) Cultural background of the country
    (B) Universities
    (C) Specific characteristics of the castes
    (D) All of these
203. We use Factorial Analysis :
    (A) To know the relationship between two variables
    (B) To test the Hypothesis

(C) To know the difference between two variables
(D) To know the difference among the many variables

204. The experimental study is based on :
(A) The manipulation of variables
(B) Conceptual parameters
(C) Replication of research
(D) Survey of literature

205. The main characteristic of scientific research is :
(A) empirical (B) theoretical
(C) experimental (D) all of the above

206. Authenticity of a research finding is its :
(A) Originality (B) Validity
(C) Objectivity (D) All of the above

207. Which technique is generally followed when the population is finite ?
(A) Area Sampling Technique
(B) Purposive Sampling Technique
(C) Systematic Sampling Technique
(D) None of the above

208. A null hypothesis is
(A) when there is no difference between the variables
(B) the same as research hypothesis
(C) subjective in nature
(D) when there is difference between the variables

209. The research which is exploring new facts through the study of the past is called
(A) Philosophical research
(B) Historical research
(C) Mythological research
(D) Content analysis

210. The process not needed in Experimental Research is
(A) Observation (B) Manipulation
(C) Controlling (D) Content Analysis

211. Manipulation is always a part of

(A) Historical research (B) Fundamental research
(C) Descriptive research (D) Experimental research

212. Which correlation co-efficient best explains the relationship between creativity and intelligence ?
(A) 1.00 (B) 0.6
(C) 0.5 (D) 0.3

213. The research is always -
(A) verifying the old knowledge
(B) exploring new knowledge
(C) filling the gap between knowledge
(D) all of these

214. The research that applies the laws at the time of field study to draw more and more clear ideas about the problem is:
(A) Applied research
(B) Action research
(C) Experimental research
(D) None of these

215. When a research problem is related to heterogeneous population, the most suitable sampling method is:
(A) Cluster Sampling (B) Stratified Sampling
(C) Convenient Sampling (D) Lottery Method

216. The process not needed in experimental research is :
(A) Observation
(B) Manipulation and replication
(C) Controlling
(D) Reference collection

217. A research problem is not feasible only when :
(A) it is researchable
(B) it is new and adds something to knowledge
(C) it consists of independent and dependent variables
(D) it has utility and relevance

218. If a researcher conducts a research on finding out which administrative style contributes more to institutional effectiveness ? This will be an example of

(A) Basic Research (B) Action Research
(C) Applied Research (D) None of the above

219. Normal Probability Curve should be
(A) Positively skewed (B) Negatively skewed
(C) Leptokurtic skewed (D) Zero skewed

220. A hypothesis is a
(A) law (B) canon
(C) postulate (D) supposition

221. Suppose you want to investigate the working efficiency of nationalised bank in India, which one of the following would you follow ?
(A) Area Sampling (B) Multi-stage Sampling
(C) Sequential Sampling (D) Quota Sampling

222. Controlled group condition is applied in
(A) Survey Research
(B) Historical Research
(C) Experimental Research
(D) Descriptive Research

223. Which one of the following is a research tool ?
(A) Graph (B) Illustration
(C) Questionnaire (D) Diagram

224. Research is not considered ethical if it
(A) tries to prove a particular point.
(B) does not ensure privacy and anonymity of the respondent.
(C) does not investigate the data scientifically.
(D) is not of a very high standard.

225. The research that aims at immediate application is
(A) Action Research
(B) Empirical Research
(C) Conceptual Research
(D) Fundamental Research

226. When two or more successive footnotes refer to the same work which one of the following expressions is used?

(A) ibid (B) et.al

(C) op.cit : (D) loc.cit.

227. Nine year olds are taller than seven year olds. This is an example of a ıeference drawn from

(A) Vertical study (B) Cross-sectional study

(C) Time series study (D) Experimental study

228. Ex Post Facto research means

(A) The research is carried out after the incident

(B) The research is carried out prior to the incident

(C) The research is carried out along with the happening of an incident.

(D) The research is carried out keeping in mind the possibilities of an incident.

229. Research ethics do not include

(A) Honesty (B) Subjectivity

(C) Integrity (D) Objectivity

230. Which one of the following is an indication of the quality of a research journal ?

(A) Impact factor (B) h-index

(C) g-index (D) i10-index

231. Good 'research ethics' means

(A) Not disclosing the holdings of shares/stocks in a company that sponsors your research.

(B) Assigning a particular research problem to one Ph.D./research student only.

(C) Discussing with your colleagues confidential data from a research paper that you are reviewing for an academic journal.

(D) Submitting the same research manuscript for publishing in more than one journal.

232. Which of the following sampling methods is based on probability ?

(A) Convenience sampling

(B) Quota sampling

(C) Judgement sampling

(D) Stratified sampling

233. Which one of the following references is written according to American Psychological Association (APA) format?
   (A) Sharma, V. (2010). Fundamentals of Computer Science. New Delhi : Tata McGraw Hill
   (B) Sharma, V. 2010. Fundamentals of Computer Science. New Delhi : Tata McGraw Hill
   (C) Sharma.V. 2010. Fundamentals of Computer Science, New Delhi : Tata McGraw Hill
   (D) Sharma, V. (2010), Fundamentals of Computer Science, New Delhi : Tata McGraw Hill

234. Arrange the following steps of research in correct sequence :
   1. Identification of research problem
   2. Listing of research objectives
   3. Collection of data
   4. Methodology
   5. Data analysis
   6. Results and discussion

   (A) 1-2-3-4-5-6 (B) 1-2-4-3-5-6
   (C) 2-1-3-4-5-6 (D) 2-1-4-3-5-6

235. Identify the incorrect statement :
   (A) A hypothesis is made on the basis of limited evidence as a starting point for further investigations.
   (B) A hypothesis is a basis for reasoning without any assumption of its truth.
   (C) Hypothesis is a proposed explanation for a phenomenon.
   (D) Scientific hypothesis is a scientific theory.

236. A research paper
   (A) is a compilation of information on a topic.
   (B) contains original research as deemed by the author.
   (C) contains peer-reviewed original research or evaluation of research conducted by others.
   (D) can be published in more than one journal.

237. Which one of the following belongs to the category of good 'research ethics'?
   (A) Publishing the same paper in two research journals without telling the editors.
   (B) Conducting a review' of the literature that acknowledges the contributions of other people in the relevant field or relevant prior work.
   (C) Trimming outliers from a data set without discussing your reasons, in a research paper.
   (D) Including a colleague as an author on a research paper in return for a favour even though the colleague did not make a serious contribution to the paper

238. Which of the following sampling methods is not based on probability?
   (A) Simple Random Sampling
   (B) Stratified Sampling
   (C) Quota Sampling
   (D) Cluster Sampling

239. Which one of the following references is written as per Modem Language Association (MLA) format?
   (A) Hall, Donald. Fundamentals of Electronics, New Delhi : Prentice Hall of India, 2005
   (B) Hall, Donald, Fundamentals of Electronics, New Delhi : Prentice Hall of India, 2005
   (C) Hall, Donald, Fundamentals of Electronics, New Delhi, - Prentice Hall of India, 2005
   (D) Hall, Donald. Fundamentals of Electronics. New Delhi : Prentice Hall of India, 2005

240. A working hypothesis is
   (A) a proven hypothesis for an argument.
   (B) not required to be tested
   (C) a provisionally accepted hypothesis for further research
   (D) a scientific theory

241. Inductive logic proceeds from
    (A) general to specific (B) general to general
    (C) specific to general (D) specific to specific.
242. The scientific method can be applied for research in the field of
    (A) Humanities (B) Natural Sciences
    (C) Social Sciences (D) all of them.
243. Research design gives the
    (A) blue print of the proposed research work
    (B) blue print of introduction of research
    (C) blue print of conclusion of research
    (D) none of these.
244. First Ph. D. awarded in Library Science by an Indian University was
    (A) S. R. Ranganathan (B) B. S. Kesavan
    (C) M. A. Gopinath (D) D. B. Krishna Rao.
245. Solo research is an investigation conducted by
    (A) a team (B) an individual
    (C) a department (D) none of these.
246. Historical method of research can be applied
    (A) in History (B) in Social Science
    (C) in Humanities (D) in all subjects.
247. Interview is a
    (A) method of research
    (B) method of hypothesis
    (C) method of applied research
    (D) method of pure research.
248. First exponent of scientific method was
    (A) Plato (B) Socrates
    (C) Dante (D) Aristotle.
249. Correct sequence of cardinal points in the spiral of scientific method is
    (A) Ascendant, Zenith, Descendant, Nadir, Ascendan...
    (B) Zenith, Descendant, Nadir, Ascendant, Zenith...

(C) Descendant, Nadir, Ascendant, Zenith, Descendant...

(D) Nadir, Ascendant, Zenith, Descendant, Nadir...

250. Research done to find a solution for an immediate problem of the society/ industry/business organization is known as

(A) social research (B) industrial research

(C) applied research (D) pure research.

251. Deductive logic proceeds from

(A) general to specific (B) specific to specific

(C) specific to general (D) general to general

252. Nadir, Ascendant, Zenith and Descendant are the four cardinal points of spiral of

(A) natural science method

(B) social science method

(C) scientific method

(D) human science method.

253. The cardinal point which rests at 90^0 from Nadir on the spiral of scientific method is

(A) ascendant (B) zenith

(C) descendant (D) nadir.

254. In historical method of research, not a tool for collection of data is

(A) eye witness (B) inscription

(C) historical evidence (D) newspaper.

255. Research aims at immediate results is

(A) pure research (B) applied research

(C) social research (D) industrial research.

256. One of the cardinal points on the spiral of the scientific method

(A) natural science (B) social science

(C) human science (D) ascendant.

257. In research on information needs of Chartered Accountants a questionnaire is that to every fifth number of the official register of Chartered Accountants, Would this

(A) random sampling
(B) stratified sampling
(C) the whole population
(D) not a representative sample.

258. In a questionnaire 'open ended' questions are
(A) the questions are open to interpretation
(B) the answers may be incomplete
(C) answers may be filled in by respondents
(D) those where long answers are required.

259. 'Cranfield Studies' are an example of
(A) survey research (B) experimental research
(C) historical research (D) case study.

260. In a study undertaken to find out how uses approach the library catalogue, all those who use the catalogue on a particular day are interviewed. Would this be considered as?
(A) a random sample
(B) a stratified sample
(C) the whole population
(D) not a representational sample.

261. In a questionnaire, close ended questions are those where:
(A) the questions and answers are close to each other
(B) the answers are given as options
(C) the questions are clear and distinct
(D) short answers are required.

262. A study aimed at finding the best method of shelving library materials
(A) basic research (B) fundamental research
(C) applied research (D) no research at all.

263. Formulation of hypothesis is an important component of
(A) content analysis (B) research design
(C) processing of data (D) report writing.

264. If you are asked to arrange the concepts "information", "knowledge" and "data" in ascending order of

complexity which of the following sequence is correct?

(A) data – information – knowledge

(B) knowledge – information – data

(C) information – data –knowledge

(D) information – knowledge – data.

265. Sometimes the terms 'data' and 'knowledge' are synonymously used for

(A) wisdom (B) intelligence

(C) news (D) information.

266. A state with its organs of executive, legislature and judiciary, business generates vast amount of

(A) knowledge (B) wisdom

(C) information (D) facts.

267. When data is processed, interpreted and presented in an organised form, it becomes

(A) news (B) facts

(C) knowledge (D) information.

268. Growth of information beyond a manageable limit characterises the explosion of

(A) books (B) libraries

(C) information (D) news.

269. Data on national income presented in a tabular form may be termed as

(A) descriptive information

(B) statistical information

(C) enumerative information

(D) societal information.

270. The Metrological Department is responsible for daily collection of

(A) measurement data (B) income data

(C) atmospheric data (D) demographic data.

271. The forecast note on weather conditions, based on processed and interpreted atmospheric data is

(A) data (B) news

(C) facts (D) information.

272. The behavioural data of chemical compound under different physical conditions observed through experiment are
(A) knowledge (B) raw facts
(C) information (D) processed data.

273. The data on national income statistics when reveal the changes that have taken place over a period of time is
(A) statistical information
(B) descriptive information
(C) analytical information
(D) uninterpreted information.

274. Which are the building block of knowledge and all threc are handled in libraries offering different types of services?
(A) Wisdom and information
(B) Data and information
(C) News and information
(D) Intelligence and information.

275. Office of the Registrar General was established to conduct what type of censuses to collect population data?
(A) decennial censuses (B) quarterly censuses
(C) annual censuses (D) biennial censuses.

276. The progress of a nation is often judged by percentage of national income that is spent on
(A) education (B) business
(C) R&D (D) surveys.

277. Who are both consumers and producers of information?
(A) Teachers (B) Students
(C) Researchers (D) Govt. officials.

278. Large scale use of information in all countries by a wide cross section of people has resulted in coining of terms like
(A) information explosion
(B) mass production of information

(C) information society

(D) information use.

279. Quantitative growth of a thing at a particular rate of growth is known as

(A) periodic growth (B) exponential growth

(C) statistical growth (D) qualitative growth.

280. "Controlled Group" is a term used in............. .

(A) Survey research

(B) Historical research

(C) Experimental research

(D) Descriptive research

281. Inductive logic proceeds from :

(A) General to General (B) Particular to General

(C) General to Particular (D) Particular to Particular

282. Which of the following is not a "Graphic representation"?

(A) Pie Chart (B) Bar Chart

(C) Table (D) Histogram

283. The 'Five Laws of Library Science' propounded by Dr. S. R. Ranganathan, is which type of research ?

(A) Applied research (B) Pure research

(C) Basic research (D) Survey research.

284. The subject of Research Methodology is the outcome of the mode of formation of subject, known as

(A) Loose Assemblage (B) Fission

(C) Distillation (D) Cluster.

285 **Assertion (A) :** A sample is the representation of a whole.

Reason (R) : The sample is subjected to observation and analysis.

(A) (A) is false but (R) is true.

(B) (A) is true but (R) is false.

(C) Both (A) and (R) are true.

(D) Both (A) and (R) are false.

286. Arrange the following steps in research in the sequence of their occurrence :

(A) Report writing (B) Research design
(C) Collection of data (D) Analysis of data

Codes :

(A) (C), (D), (B), (A) (B) (A), (C), (D), (B)
(C) (B), (C), (D), (A) (D) (D), (B), (C), (A)

287. The spiral of scientific method involves the following steps in correct sequence :

(i) Zenith (ii) Ascendant
(iii) Nadir (iv) Descendant

Codes :

(A) (i), (iii), (ii), (iv) (B) (ii), (iii), (i), (iv)
(C) (iii), (ii), (i), (iv) (D) (i), (iv), (iii), (ii)

288. Match the following:

List – I	**List – II**
a. Mean	i. Most frequently occurring value
b. Mode	ii. Average
c. Median	iii. Measure of dispersion
d. Standard Deviation	iv. Middle Value

Codes:	**(a)**	**(b)**	**(c)**	**(d)**
(A)	iii	iv	i	ii
(B)	ii	i	iv	iii
(C)	iv	iii	i	ii
(D)	ii	iii	iv	i

289. Match the following :

List – I	**List – II**
a. Finding solution to the problem	i. Historical Research of pilferage in libraries
b. Implementation of could computing	ii. Action research services in special libraries
c. A study of mathematician turned librarian	iii. Experimental Research
d. Use of web resources in Central Universities of India	iv. Survey Research

Codes:	**(a)**	**(b)**	**(c)**	**(d)**
(A)	ii	iii	i	iv
(B)	iii	ii	iv	i
(C)	iv	i	ii	iii
(D)	i	iv	iii	ii

290. Match the following:

List – I	**List – II**
a. Every unit of population has equal chance of being selected	i. Systematic sampling
b. Every nth case is selected from the list of population	ii. Cluster sampling
c. Units are randomly selected from the subgroups	iii. Random sampling
d. Geographic area based units	iv. Stratified sampling

Codes:	**(a)**	**(b)**	**(c)**	**(d)**
(A)	i	iv	iii	ii
(B)	iv	ii	i	iii
(C)	iii	i	iv	ii
(D)	ii	iii	iv	i

291. Match the following:

List – I	**List – II**
a. Approach of measuring two opposite sets of items	i. Semantic differential scale
b. Approach of measurement yielding a single score	ii. Cumulative scale
c. Approach of measurement adopting bipolar objective rating to study a social phenomenon	iii. Sociometric scale
d. Approach to measure interaction pattern among close associates in a variety of groups	iv. Summated scale

Codes:	(a)	(b)	(c)	(d)
(A)	ii	iii	i	iv
(B)	iii	i	iv	ii
(C)	i	ii	iv	iii
(D)	iv	ii	i	iii

292. Match the following :

List I	List II
(a) $\sum\left(\frac{O-E}{F}\right)^2$	(i) df (degree of freedom)
(b) $\frac{\Sigma X}{N}$	(ii) S.D. (Standard Dcviation)
(c) (R – 1) (C – 1)	(iii) Mean
(d) $\sqrt{\frac{\Sigma X^2}{N}}$	(iv) Chi-square

Codes:	(a)	(b)	(c)	(d)
(A)	iv	i	iii	ii
(B)	iv	iii	i	ii
(C)	iii	i	ii	iv
(D)	ii	i	iii	iv

293. Match the following:

List – I	List – II
a. Algorith	i. Instruction to the computer
b. Flow charts	ii. Debugging
c. Program code	iii. Pictorially represented direction lines
d. Program test	iv. Set of explicit and finite steps

Codes:	(a)	(b)	(c)	(d)
(A)	ii	iii	iv	i
(B)	iii	i	iv	ii
(C)	iv	iii	i	ii
(D)	i	ii	iv	iii

294. Match the following:

List – I	**List – II**
a. CILIP	i. 1972
b. ASLIB	ii. 2002
c. ALA	iii. 1876
d. COMLA	iv. 1924

Codes:	**(a)**	**(b)**	**(c)**	**(d)**
(A)	ii	iv	iii	i
(B)	iv	iii	ii	i
(C)	iii	iv	i	ii
(D)	ii	iii	iv	i

295. Match the following:

List – I	**List – II**
a. Phenomenon	i. Physical Media for grouping of Information
b. Spectrum	ii. Facts or Occurrence
c. Modes	iii. Transfer Process
d. Diffusion	iv. A broad range of varied but related ideas

Codes:	**(a)**	**(b)**	**(c)**	**(d)**
(A)	i	iii	iv	ii
(B)	ii	iv	i	iii
(C)	ii	iii	iv	i
(D)	iv	i	iii	ii

296. Match the following:

List – I	**List – II**
a. Union Catalogue	i. Primary sources
b. Pamphlets & Brochures	ii. Unpublished sources
c. Indexing & Abstracting Sources	iii. Tertiary sources
d. Memoirs of diaries	iv. Secondary sources

Codes:	**(a)**	**(b)**	**(c)**	**(d)**
(A)	iv	iii	ii	i
(B)	ii	iv	iii	i
(C)	iii	i	iv	ii
(D)	i	ii	iv	iii

297. Match the following:

List – I	List – II
a. Fundamentals of Reference Service	i. A.J. Walford
b. Introduction to Reference works	ii. S.R. Ranganathan
c. Reference service	iii. F.N. Cheney and W.J. Williams
d. Guide to Reference Books	iv. William A Katz

Codes:	(a)	(b)	(c)	(d)
(A)	ii	i	iv	iii
(B)	iii	iv	i	ii
(C)	iv	ii	iii	i
(D)	iii	iv	ii	i

298. Match the following:

List – I	List – II
a. Information on important recent happenings of India	i. India – A Reference Annual
b. Total number of foreigners visited in India in 2012	ii. Keesing's Record of World Events
c. Name of Prime Minister of India	iii. Statistical Yearbook
d. Postal Address of Anna Hazare	iv. Who's Who

Codes:	(a)	(b)	(c)	(d)
(A)	iv	i	ii	iii
(B)	ii	iii	i	iv
(C)	iii	ii	i	iv
(D)	i	iv	iii	ii

299. Match the following:

List – I	**List – II**
a. Scaler Chain	i. Direct dealing with subordinates
b. Espirit de Corps	ii. Production, efficiency and prevention of waste
c. Scientific	iii. Emphasis on Team Work Management
d. Span of control	iv. Top to Bottom

Codes:	**(a)**	**(b)**	**(c)**	**(d)**
(A)	iv	iii	ii	i
(B)	iii	iv	i	ii
(C)	iv	ii	iii	i
(D)	ii	iii	i	iv

300. Match the following:

List – I	**List – II**
a. Check Card	i. Reader's Ticket
b. Kardex	ii. Three Card System
c. Newark System	iii. Periodicals
d. Browne System	iv. Borrower's Card

Codes:	**(a)**	**(b)**	**(c)**	**(d)**
(A)	ii	iii	iv	i
(B)	iii	iv	i	ii
(C)	ii	iv	iii	i
(D)	iv	i	ii	iii

301. Match the following:

List – I	**List – II**
a. Skewness	i. Numbers of frequently appearing variables
b. Modality	ii. Degree of association between two/ more variables
c. F-distribution	iii. Structure of distribution
d. Correlation	iv. Ratio of two Chi square variables

Codes:	(a)	(b)	(c)	(d)
(A)	i	iv	ii	iii
(B)	iii	i	iv	ii
(C)	iv	ii	iii	i
(D)	ii	iii	i	iv

302. Match the following electronic applications of information society with relevant service :

List – I		List – II	
a.	E-Commerce	i.	Saakshat
b.	E-Governance	ii.	Living progress
c.	E-Education	iii.	G2C initiatives
d.	E-Health	iv.	SnapDeal

Codes:	(a)	(b)	(c)	(d)
(A)	iii	iv	i	ii
(B)	ii	iii	iv	i
(C)	iv	iii	i	ii
(D)	iv	ii	i	iii

303. Match the following :

List – I		List – II	
a.	Books are for use.	i.	Adopting to future needs
b.	Every reader his/ her book	ii.	Long operating hours
c.	Every book its reader.	iii.	Freedom of access to information & knowledge
d.	Library is a growing organism.	iv.	Reference Desk

Codes:	(a)	(b)	(c)	(d)
(A)	ii	iii	iv	i
(B)	iv	i	ii	iii
(C)	i	ii	iii	iv
(D)	iii	iv	i	ii

304. Match the following :

List – I	**List – II**
a. Biographical source	i. Full text sources online
b. Encyclopaedia	ii. ODLIS
c. Directory	iii. Linkedin
d. Dictionary	iv. Liswiki

Codes:	**(a)**	**(b)**	**(c)**	**(d)**
(A)	i	ii	iii	iv
(B)	ii	iii	i	iv
(C)	iv	ii	iii	i
(D)	iii	iv	i	ii

305. Match the following :

List – I	**List – II**
a. ETC	i. UK
b. NTC	ii. India
c. BLLD	iii. USA
d. NISCAIR	iv. Netherland

Codes:	**(a)**	**(b)**	**(c)**	**(d)**
(A)	iv	iii	i	ii
(B)	ii	I	iii	iv
(C)	iii	iv	ii	i
(D)	i	ii	iv	iii

306. Match the following :

List – I	**List – II**
a. Systematic indexing	i. Derek Austin
b. PRECIS	ii. Mortimer Taube
c. Uniterm	iii. J. Kaiser
d. Chain Procedure	iv. S.R. Ranganathan

Codes:	**(a)**	**(b)**	**(c)**	**(d)**
(A)	ii	i	iv	iii
(B)	iv	iii	ii	i
(C)	i	ii	iii	iv
(D)	iii	i	ii	iv

307. Match the following :

List – I	**List – II**
a. Meta search engine	i. HotBot
b. Web directory	ii. Search Engine
c. Subject gateway	iii. Galaxy
d. Archie	iv. Library Spot

Codes:	**(a)**	**(b)**	**(c)**	**(d)**
(A)	i	iii	iv	ii
(B)	iii	ii	i	iv
(C)	ii	iv	i	iii
(D)	i	iii	ii	iv

308. Match the following :

List – I	**List – II**
a. Nominal variable	i. Temperature in centigrade
b. Interval variable	ii. Students and Faculty
c. Ordinal variable	iii. Classification of gender
d. Ratio	iv. Grades of students

Codes:	**(a)**	**(b)**	**(c)**	**(d)**
(A)	ii	iii	i	iv
(B)	iii	i	iv	ii
(C)	i	iv	iii	ii
(D)	iv	ii	iii	i

309. Match the following :

List – I	**List – II**
a. Internet	i. Knowledge navigation
b. Computing	ii. Collection of E-resources
c. WWW	iii. Tools and Techniques for accessing
d. Digital Library	iv. Delivery Mechanism

Codes:	**(a)**	**(b)**	**(c)**	**(d)**
(A)	iv	i	iii	ii
(B)	iv	iii	i	ii
(C)	ii	i	iii	iv
(D)	iii	iv	ii	i

310. Match the following:

List – I (Hypothesis)	**List – II (Characteristics)**
a. Null	i. Statement of expectations
b. Working (Directional)	ii. Relational propositions
c. Explanatory	iii. No relation between variables
d. Descriptive	iv. Existence of variables

Codes:	**(a)**	**(b)**	**(c)**	**(d)**
(A)	i	iv	ii	iii
(B)	iii	iv	ii	i
(C)	iii	ii	i	iv
(D)	iii	i	ii	iv

311. Match the following:

List – I	**List – II**
a. Behaviour Science	i. Cognitive Process of Information
b. Philosophi cal Studies	ii. Studies on Epistomology
c. Ontology	iii. Information Processing in living things
d. Biological Science	iv. Study of nature of existence

Codes:	**(a)**	**(b)**	**(c)**	**(d)**
(A)	iv	iii	i	ii
(B)	iii	ii	iv	i
(C)	ii	i	iii	iv
(D)	i	ii	iv	iii

312. Match the following:

List – I	**List – II**
a. Similar activities are grouped	i. Bureaucratic System
b. Grouping activities into divisions	ii. Functional System
c. Integration of projects into functional system	iii. Departmentalisation

d. Control and Supervision through hierarchy of positions — iv. Matrix structure

Codes:	(a)	(b)	(c)	(d)
(A)	iv	i	ii	iii
(B)	iii	ii	iv	i
(C)	i	ii	iii	iv
(D)	ii	iii	iv	i

313. Match the following search techniques with their relevant example :

List – I	List – II
a. Truncation	i. Wom?n
b. Wild cards	ii. Comput*
c. Proximity	iii. edu AND biochemistry AND antibodies
d. Field searching	iv. "content collection"/5

Codes:	(a)	(b)	(c)	(d)
(A)	ii	iii	iv	i
(B)	iv	iii	ii	i
(C)	i	ii	iii	iv
(D)	ii	i	iv	iii

314. Match the following :

List – I	List – II
a. Infringement	i. Unauthorized use of I.P.
b. Enforcement	ii. Criminal penalties
c. Mis-appropriation	iii. Breach of trade secret
d. Counterfeit	iv. Intentional forgery

Codes:	(a)	(b)	(c)	(d)
(A)	ii	iii	iv	i
(B)	i	ii	iii	iv
(C)	iii	iv	i	ii
(D)	iv	i	iii	ii

315. Match the following :

List – I	**List – II**
a. ALA	i. 1909
b. CILIP	ii. 1933
c. SLA	iii. 1876
d. ILA	iv. 2002

Codes:	**(a)**	**(b)**	**(c)**	**(d)**
(A)	iv	ii	iii	i
(B)	iii	iv	i	ii
(C)	i	ii	iv	iii
(D)	iii	iv	ii	i

316. Match the following :

List – I	**List – II**
a. Sayaji Rao Gayakwad	i. Revision of salary scale
b. D.P. Chattopadyay	ii. Library building
c. K.D. Metcalf	iii. Public libraries
d. B.S. Kesavan	iv. Librarian of national library

Codes:	**(a)**	**(b)**	**(c)**	**(d)**
(A)	ii	i	iii	iv
(B)	i	ii	iii	iv
(C)	iii	i	ii	iv
(D)	iv	iii	i	ii

317. Match the following publishers with the relevant databases :

List – I	**List – II**
a. Elsevier	i. Academic search
b. Thomson Reuters	ii. Aerospace & high technology
c. EBSCO	iii. Scopus
d. ProQuest	iv. Web of knowledge

Codes:	**(a)**	**(b)**	**(c)**	**(d)**
(A)	ii	i	iv	iii
(B)	i	iii	ii	iv
(C)	iii	iv	i	ii
(D)	iv	ii	iii	i

318. Match the following :

List – I	**List – II**
a. Informing about best books	i. Support service
b. Guidance to use citation manual	ii. Bibliography
c. Providing prints for downloads	iii. Readers advisory
d. Providing list of URLs	iv. Users education

Codes:	**(a)**	**(b)**	**(c)**	**(d)**
(A)	ii	iii	i	iv
(B)	iii	iv	i	ii
(C)	iv	ii	iii	i
(D)	ii	iv	iii	i

319. Match the following :

List – I	**List – II**
a. Market segmentation	i. User behaviour
b. Consumer analysis	ii. Market mix
c. Market positioning	iii. Category of users
d. Market program	iv. Prioritising users

Codes:	**(a)**	**(b)**	**(c)**	**(d)**
(A)	i	iii	ii	iv
(B)	iii	i	iv	ii
(C)	ii	iv	i	iii
(D)	iv	ii	iii	i

320. Match the following :

List – I	**List – II**
a. India	i. Agglomeration
b. Agriculture of wheat	ii. Fusion
c. Bio-chemistry	iii. Denudation
d. Biological sciences	iv. Lamination

Codes:	**(a)**	**(b)**	**(c)**	**(d)**
(A)	iii	iv	ii	i
(B)	iv	ii	iii	i
(C)	ii	iii	i	iv
(D)	i	ii	iv	iii

321. Match the following :

List – I	List – II
a. Standing order	i. For serial publications till cancellation
b. Blanket order	ii. Routine publications on order
c. Firm order	iii. For publications on recommendation
d. Approval order	iv. For supply of institutional publications as and when published

Codes:	(a)	(b)	(c)	(d)
(A)	iv	ii	i	iii
(B)	iii	ii	i	iv
(C)	i	iv	ii	iii
(D)	ii	iv	i	iii

322. Match the following :

List – I	List – II
a. HTML	i. Intrepretation by web browser
b. XML	ii. Describes data
c. UNICODE	iii. Display data
d. VB Script	iv. Platform independent

Codes:	(a)	(b)	(c)	(d)
(A)	i	iii	ii	iv
(B)	iii	iv	i	ii
(C)	ii	iv	i	iii
(D)	iii	ii	iv	i

323. Match the following national organizations with their relevant mission :

List – I	List – II
a. National Mission on Libraries	i. Digitization of AYUSH literature
b. National Mission for Manuscripts	ii. Nurturing of talent
c. T.K.D.L.	iii. Capacity building
d. NME-ICT	iv. Connects India's past with present

Codes:	**(a)**	**(b)**	**(c)**	**(d)**
(A)	i	ii	iii	iv
(B)	iii	iv	i	ii
(C)	iv	iii	ii	i
(D)	ii	i	iii	iv

324. Match the following :

List – I	**List – II**
a. Simple random	i. Natural order
b. Systematic random	ii. Representative
c. Stratified random	iii. Equal chance
d. Judgement	iv. Sub-groups

Codes:	**(a)**	**(b)**	**(c)**	**(d)**
(A)	ii	i	iii	iv
(B)	iii	i	iv	ii
(C)	iv	ii	i	iii
(D)	iii	ii	iv	i

325. Match the following :

List – I	**List – II**
a. Semantic differential scale	i. Graded structure
b. Thurston scale	ii. Opposition positions
c. Interval scale	iii. Group of Judgement
d. Likert scale	iv. Equal units of measurement

Codes:	**(a)**	**(b)**	**(c)**	**(d)**
(A)	iv	iii	i	ii
(B)	i	iv	iii	ii
(C)	iii	ii	i	iv
(D)	ii	iii	iv	i

326. Match the following :

List – I	**List – II**
a. Barren Hypothesis	i. Indian men marry at 26-28 years age
b. Idiographic Hypothesis	ii. Seema will top this year
c. Nomothetic Hypothesis	iii. Loss of limbs
d. Crude Hypothesis	iv. Quality of collection

Codes:	**(a)**	**(b)**	**(c)**	**(d)**
(A)	iv	iii	ii	i
(B)	iii	ii	iv	i
(C)	ii	i	iii	iv
(D)	i	iv	ii	iii

327. Match the following :

List – I	**List – II**
a. Multiple choice questions	i. Personal opinion of interviewer
b. Loaded questions	ii. No sets of answers
c. Contingency questions	iii. Alternative answers
d. Open ended questions	iv. Sub-group of respondents

Codes:	**(a)**	**(b)**	**(c)**	**(d)**
(A)	i	iv	iii	ii
(B)	iv	ii	iii	i
(C)	iii	i	iv	ii
(D)	ii	iii	i	iv

328. Match the following :

List – I	**List – II**
a. Mean	i. Σ (O–E)2 E
b. Degree of freedom (df)	ii. n + 1 2
c. Median	iii. (r – 1) (c – 1)
d. Chi-square (χ2)	iv. Σx n

Codes:	**(a)**	**(b)**	**(c)**	**(d)**
(A)	ii	iv	i	iii
(B)	iii	ii	i	iv
(C)	iv	iii	ii	i
(D)	i	ii	iv	iii

329. Match the following:

List – I	**List – II**
a. Collateral classes	i. Class comprising two or more entities
b. Multiple classes	ii. Classes of the same order but not belonging to one in the same order

c. Chain of classes — iii. A subject fixed with others in the universal of subject

d. Co-ordinate classes — iv. A sequence of classes made up of any given class and its universe

Codes:	**(a)**	**(b)**	**(c)**	**(d)**
(A)	ii	iv	i	iii
(B)	i	iii	ii	iv
(C)	ii	i	iv	iii
(D)	i	iv	ii	iii

330. Match the following :

List-I (Research Methods)	**List-II (Type)**
(A) Content Analysis	(i) Data Collection Tool
(B) Questionnaire	(ii) Qualitative Methods of Analysis
(C) Observation	(iii) Methods of Research
(D) Case Study	(iv) Direct Method

Codes:	**(a)**	**(b)**	**(c)**	**(d)**
(A)	(i)	(iv)	(iii)	(ii)
(B)	(ii)	(i)	(iv)	(iii)
(C)	(iii)	(ii)	(i)	(iv)
(D)	(iv)	(iii)	(ii)	(i)

331. Match the following:

List-I (Types of users of information)	**List-II (Purpose of use of information)**
I. Students	a. Decision making
II. Professionals	b. To impart knowledge
III. Government Officials	c. To prepare for the course programme
IV. Teachers	d. To pursue their respective vocation

Codes:

(A) I-c, II-d, III-a, IV-b (B) I-d, II-a, III-b, IV-c

(C) I-c, II-b, III-d, IV-a (D) I-b, II-b, III-c, IV-d

332. **Assertion (A) :** Formulation of hypotheses is based on assumptions.

Reason (R) : Hypotheses cannot be tested based on objectives of the study.

(A) (A) is true, but (R) is false
(B) (A) is false, but (R) is true
(C) Both (A) and (R) are false
(D) Both (A) and (R) are true

333. **Assertion (A) :** Delphi Method of research draws opinion from the panel of experts in a research area.

Reason (R) : Opinions expressed by the panel of experts is valuable in formulating inference.

(A) (A) is true, but (R) is false
(B) (A) is false, but (R) is true
(C) Both (A) and (R) are true
(D) Both (A) and (R) are false

334. **Assertion (A) :** Provision of services inside the library helps in reaching out to the large number of users

Reason (R) : Library extension services do not cover the internal users of a library.

(A) (A) is true, but (R) is false
(B) (A) is false, but (R) is true
(C) Both (A) and (R) are true
(D) Both (A) and (R) are false

335. **Assertion (A) :** Historical research has been regarded to be truly scientific by a member of experts.

Reason (R) : Historical evidences can be replicated.

Codes:

(A) Both A and R are true
(B) A is false, but R is true
(C) Both A and R are false
(D) A is partially true, but R is true

336. **Assertion (A) :** Random samples are not representative of the whole population.

Reason (R) : Random numbers are used in forming a random sample.

Codes :

(A) (A) is true, but (R) is false.
(B) (A) is false, but (R) is true.
(C) Both (A) and (R) are true.
(D) Both (A) and (R) are false.

337. **Assertion (A) :** In conducting research, Social Sciences are not considered at par with natural sciences.

Reason (R) : Research in Social Sciences can't be performed so rigorously as can be in Natural Sciences.

Codes:

(A) Both (A) and (R) are true.
(B) Both (A) and (R) are false.
(C) (A) is true, but (R) is false.
(D) (A) is false, but (R) is true.

338. **Assertion (A) :** Research starts in mind first and then in laboratories.

Reason (R) : Systematically conducted research leas to generalization.

Codes:

(A) (A) is true, but (R) is false.
(B) (A) is false, but (R) is true.
(C) Both (A) and (R) are true.
(D) Both (A) and (R) are false.

339. **Assertion (A) :** Systematic and efficient use of statistical tools in research helps in precise interpretation of research results.

Reason (R) : Statistical tools cannot give specific explanations of the data.

Codes:

(A) Both (A) and (R) are true.
(B) (A) is true and (R) is false.
(C) Both (A) and (R) are false.
(D) (A) is false and (R) is true.

340. **Assertion (A) :** All research require hypotheses to be proposed and tested.

Reason (R) : No research is complete without testing of hypotheses.

Codes:

(A) (A) is false but (R) is true.

(B) Both (A) and (R) are false.

(C) (A) is true but (R) is false.

(D) Both (A) and (R) are true.

341. **Assertion (A) :** Over the past few years, the usage of bound volume of journals in libraries has decreased considerably.

Reason (R) : Availability of electronic journals in large numbers has lead to such decrease..

Codes :

(A) Both (A) and (R) are true.

(B) (A) is false but (R) is true.

(C) Both (A) and (R) are false.

(D) (A) is partially true, but (R) is true. (NO one is correct)

342. **Assertion (A) :** Mail survey, a data collection technique in which questionnaires are mailed to potential respondents, who in then fill and return at their convenience become obsolete.

Reason (R) : Survey-Monkey, the free online survey tool has totally replaced the traditional Mail survey.

Codes:

(A) (A) is true, but (R) is false.

(B) (A) is false, but (R) is true.

(C) Both (A) and (R) are true.

(D) Both (A) and (R) are false.

343. **Assertion (A) :** Case situations are seldom comparable and as such the information gathered in case studies is often not comparable.

Reason (R) : The subject under case study are usually described in terms of the characteristics exhibited by the subject/case itself.

Codes:

(A) Both (A) and (R) are true.

(B) Both (A) and (R) are false.

(C) (A) is true, but (R) is false.

(D) (A) is false, but (R) is true.

344. **Assertion (A) :** Intellectual Property Rights facilitate free flow of information.

Reason (R) : Effective free flow of information is the pre-requisite for knowledge society.

Codes:

(A) (A) is true, but (R) is false.

(B) (A) is false, but (R) is true.

(C) Both (A) and (R) are true.

(D) Both (A) and (R) are false

345. **Assertion (A) :** The total output of Indian publications is reflected in 'Indian National Bibliography'.

Reason (R) : A number of publishers in India are defaulters and do not deposit their publications as per Delivery of Books and Newspapers (Public Libraries) Act.

Codes:

(A) Both (A) and (R) are true.

(B) Both (A) and (R) are false.

(C) (A) is true, but (R) is false.

(D) (A) is false, but (R) is true.

346. **Assertion (A) :** No library is self sufficient in terms of resources even in electronic age.

Reason (R) : Resource sharing and consortia initiatives are essential to meet user needs.

Codes:

(A) (A) is true and (R) is false.

(B) (A) is false and (R) is true.

(C) Both (A) and (R) are true.

(D) Both (A) and (R) are false.

347. **Assertion (A) :** Interviewing is essential to supplement the research data collected through questionnaire.

Reason (R) : Interview is the most suitable technique to collect data as all respondents cooperate more during interview.

Codes:

(A) (A) is false, but (R) is true.

(B) Both (A) and (R) are true.

(C) Both (A) & (R) are false.

(D) (A) is true, but (R) is false.

348. **Assertion (A) :** Indexing and abstracting services fulfil the 4th Law of Library Science.

Reason (R) : These services serve as the substitute to the primary journals.

Codes:

(A) (A) is true, but (R) is false.

(B) Both (A) & (R) are false.

(C) Both (A) & (R) are true.

(D) (A) is false, but (R) is true.

349. **Assertion (A) :** All classification schemes adopt 'phase relations'.

Reason (R) : Subject formation by loose assemblage leads to complex subjects and isolates.

Codes:

(A) (A) is true, but (R) is false.

(B) Both (A) and (R) are true.

(C) Both (A) and (R) are false.

(D) (A) is false, but (R) is true.

350. **Assertion (A) :** RSS (Rich Site Summary) is considered as an alternate to the SDI Service.

Reason (R) : RSS Feeds enable us to syndicate data automatically.

Codes:

(A) Both (A) and (R) are true.

(B) Both (A) and (R) are false.

(C) (A) is false, but (R) is true.

(D) (A) is true, but (R) is false

351. **Assertion (A) :** Majority of academic libraries in India are lagging behind in switching over as technology-oriented service institutions.

Reason (R) : The apex academic bodies and library

Associations have not taken the lead role to devise standards and policies.

Codes:

(A) (A) is true, (R) is false.

(B) (A) is false, (R) is true.

(C) Both (A) and (R) is true.

(D) Both (A) and (R) are false.

352. **Assertion (A) :** In a particular study, we may reject the alternative hypothesis.

Reason (R) : In the same study the null hypothesis is not rejected.

Codes :

(A) (A) is true, but (R) is false.

(B) (A) is false, but (R) is true.

(C) Both (A) and (R) are true and (R) is the correct explanation of (A).

(D) Both (A) and (R) are true, but (R) is not the correct explanation of (A).

353. **Assertion (A) :** An electronic library may have both born digital and converted digital documents.

Reason (R) : A document stored in Unicode is same as storing the scanned image of the document.

Codes :

(A) (A) is false, but (R) is true.

(B) (A) is true, but (R) is false.

(C) Both (A) and (R) are true.

(D) Both (A) and (R) are false.

354. **Assertion (A) :** The diary technique enables the researcher to keep record of information activities of the users for a specified period of time.

Reason (R) : The diary technique is the most suitable technique of user studies over other techniques.

Codes:

(A) Both (A) and (R) are false.

(B) (A) is true, but (R) is false.

(C) Both (A) and (R) are true.

(D) (A) is false, but (R) is true.

355. **Assertion (A) :** Multilingual dictionaries provide equivalent words in three or more languages.

Reason (R) : They generally do not define the words but they give equivalent words in one or more foreign languages.

Codes :

(A) Both (A) and (R) are true.

(B) Both (A) and (R) are false.

(C) (A) is true, but (R) is false.

(D) (A) is false, but (R) is true.

356. **Assertion (A) :** Wikis have provided everybody an opportunity for authoring, editing and publishing.

Reason (R) : Web has provided very generic rules for creation, maintenance and development of Wikis.

Codes :

(A) (A) is true, but (R) is false.

(B) (A) is false, but (R) is true.

(C) Both (A) and (R) are true.

(D) Both (A) and (R) are false.

357. **Assertion (A) :** Webliographies are bibliographic tools for print and electronic documents.

Reason (R) : Webliography denotes an enumerative list of hypertext links surrounding a common subject following standard citation styles.

Codes :

(A) (A) is true, but (R) is false.

(B) (A) is false, but (R) is true.

(C) Both (A) and (R) are true.

(D) Both (A) and (R) are false.

358. **Assertion (A) :** An ISO 2709 : 2008 record structure and review format has 'Record Label', 'Directory', 'Data fields' and 'Record Separator'.

Reason (R) : ISO 2709 is a subset of MARC.

Codes :

(A) (A) is true, but (R) is false.

(B) (A) is false, but (R) is true.

(C) Both (A) and (R) are true.

(D) Both (A) and (R) are false.

359. **Assertion (A) :** Knowledge Management is an extension of conventional library management.

Reason (R) : Knowledge Management deals with elements like content, technology and culture.

Codes :

(A) (A) is true, but (R) is false.

(B) Both (A) and (R) are true.

(C) (A) is false, but (R) is true.

(D) Both (A) and (R) are false.

360. **Assertion (A) :** The plagiarism detection software implements a generic detection approach for all types of materials.

Reason (R) : There is no difference between text and source code plagiarism.

Codes :

(A) (A) is true, but (R) is false.

(B) (A) is false, but (R) is true.

(C) Both (A) and (R) are true.

(D) Both (A) and (R) are false.

361. **Assertion (A) :** UGC notification (2009) mandates submission of electronic theses and dissertations by the researchers in universities to facilitate open access.

Reason (R) : UGC wants to monitor the quality of research through open access.

Codes :

(A) (A) is true, but (R) is false.

(B) (A) is false, but (R) is true.

(C) Both (A) and (R) are true.

(D) Both (A) and (R) are false.

362. **Assertion (A) :** Bibliometric study is the popular area of research on which maximum number of Ph.D degree have been awarded in India.

Reason (R) : Bibliometric study adds to the extension of fundamental research.

Codes :

(A) Both (A) and (R) are true.

(B) (A) is true, but (R) is false.

(C) Both (A) and (R) are false.

(D) (R) is true, but (A) is false.

363. **Assertion (A) :** According to National Knowledge Commission, 'the library and information services sector in India has not kept pace with the paradigmatic changes taking place in society'.

Reason (R) : There is no proportionate growth in library resources.

Codes :

(A) Both (A) and (R) are true.

(B) (A) is true, but (R) is false.

(C) Both (A) and (R) are false.

(D) (A) is false, but (R) is true.

364. **Assertion (A) :** Federated search technique is an integral component of an information portal.

Reason (R) : 'Content Index' contains content that is find by the search server.

Codes :

(A) Both (A) and (R) are true.

(B) Both (A) and (R) are false.

(C) (A) is true but (R) is false.

(D) (A) is false but (R) is true.

365. **Assertion (A) :** A sample is the representation of a whole.

Reason (R) : The sample is subjected to observation and analysis.

(A) (A) is false but (R) is true.

(B) (A) is true but (R) is false.

(C) Both (A) and (R) are true.

(D) Both (A) and (R) are false.

366. **Assertion (A) :** Like social scientists, the natural scientists can also collect data by conducting experiments, interviewing/observing people and

reviewing literature.

Reason (R) : Social scientists cannot be as objective as can be natural scientists.

Codes :

(A) (A) is true, but (R) is false.

(B) (A) is false, but (R) is true.

(C) Both (A) and (R) are true.

(D) Both (A) and (R) are false.

367. **Assertion (A) :** Median is simply the middle value when the data have been arranged in ascending or descending order.

Reason (R) : Median refers to the middle value in a distribution.

Codes :

(A) Both (A) and (R) are true.

(B) (A) is true, but (R) is false.

(C) (A) is false, but (R) is true.

(D) Both (A) and (R) are false.

368. **Assertion (A) :** When the work is not protected by copyright, plagiarism may occur

Reason (R) : Plagiarism is the wrongful appropriation of another authors language, thoughts, ideas or expressions and the representation of them as once own.

Codes :

(A) (A) is true but (R) is false

(B) Both (A) and (R) are true

(C) (A) is false but (R) is true

(D) Both (A) and (R) are true, but (R) is not the correct explanation

369. **Assertion (A) :** Historical, Descriptive and Experimental Methods are scientific methods.

Reason (R) : A scientific method is one that adopts a logical and systematic procedure.

Codes:

(A) (A) is true but (R) is false.

(B) Both (A) and (R) are true

(C) (A) is false but (R) is true

(D) Both (A) and (R) are true but (R) is not the correct explanation

370. **Assertion (A) :** Research is a total process consisting of a series of steps.

Reason (R) : Sometimes several steps are carried out simultaneously.

Codes:

(A) Both (A) and (R) are True

(B) Both (A) and (R) are False

(C) (A) is true and (R) is false

(D) (R) is True and (A) is False

371. **Assertion (A) :** Action research is a form of interpretive research to study human actions and social practices for immediate application.

Reason (R) : Action research is an applied research, which is focussed on the solution to local problems, not to develop any theory for general application.

Code:

(A) (A) is true and (R) is false

(B) (R) is true and (A) is false

(C) Both (A) and (R) are false

(D) Both (A) and (R) are true

ANSWERS

1. (B)	2. (B)	3. (A)	4. (C)
5. (A)	6. (C)	7. (C)	8. (A)
9. (C)	10. (A)	11. (A)	12. (B)
13. (B)	14. (C)	15. (A)	16. (B)
17. (D)	18. (B)	19. (A)	20. (B)
21. (D)	22. (D)	23. (C)	24. (A)
25. (C)	26. (A)	27. (C)	28. (B)
29. (C)	30. (B)	31. (B)	32. (C)
33. (C)	34. (A)	35. (B)	36. (B)
37. (C)	38. (D)	39. (C)	40. (D)
41. (B)	42. (C)	43. (D)	44. (A)

45. (B)	46. (C)	47. (A)	48. (B)
49. (B)	50. (C)	51. (A)	52. (C)
53. (D)	54. (A)	55. (A)	56. (A)
57. (C)	58. (C)	59. (B)	60. (A)
61. (A)	62. (A)	63. (B)	64. (A)
65. (A)	66. (B)	67. (C)	68. (C)
69. (A)	70. (B)	71. (C)	72. (A)
73. (D)	74. (B)	75. (A)	76. (D)
77. (B)	78. (D)	79. (B)	80. (C)
81. (B)	82. (C)	83. (B)	84. (B)
85. (C)	86. (B)	87. (B)	88. (C)
89. (D)	90. (D)	91. (C)	92. (C)
93. (C)	94. (C)	95. (C)	96. (B)
97. (A)	98. (C)	99. (C)	100. (D)
101. (B)	102. (D)	103. (D)	104. (A)
105. (D)	106. (C)	107. (B)	108. (D)
109. (B)	110. (D)	111. (A)	112. (C)
113. (A)	114. (B)	115. (C)	116. (B)
117. (C)	118. (C)	119. (C)	120. (D)
121. (D)	122. (A)	123. (D)	124. (B)
125. (D)	126. (A)	127. (D)	128. (D)
129. (C)	130. (A)	131. (C)	132. (A)
133. (D)	134. (B)	135. (D)	136. (B)
137. (A)	138. (A)	139. (B)	140. (D)
141. (B)	142. (A)	143. (D)	144. (C)
145. (D)	146. (C)	147. (B)	148. (C)
149. (D)	150. (B)	151. (C)	152. (B)
153. (A)	154. (A)	155. (C)	156. (C)
157. (C)	158. (C)	159. (A)	160. (B)
161. (B)	162. (B)	163. (B)	164. (B)
165. (D)	166. (A)	167. (C)	168. (D)
169. (C)	170. (A)	171. (B)	172. (C)
173. (D)	174. (A)	175. (C)	176. (D)
177. (B)	178. (B)	179. (C)	180. (C)
181. (C)	182. (A)	183. (B)	184. (D)
185. (D)	186. (D)	187. (B)	188. (C)
189. (A)	190. (C)	191. (D)	192. (C)
193. (C)	194. (B)	195. (A)	196. (A)
197. (B)	198. (B)	199. (B)	200. (B)
201. (B)	202. (A)	203. (A)/C	204. (A)
205. (D)	206. (D)	207. (C)	208. (A)
209. (B)	210. (B)	211. (D)	212. (A)
213. (D)	214. (C)	215. (A)	216. (B)

217. (D)	218. (A)	219. (A)	220. (D)
221. (B)	222. (C)	223. (C)	224. (B)
225. (A)	226. (A)	227. (A)	228. (A)
229. (B)	230. (A)	231. (B)	232. (D)
233. (A)	234. (B)	235. (D)	236. (C)
237. (B)	238. (C)	239. (D)	240. (C)
241. (C)	242. (D)	243. (A)	244. (D)
245. (B)	246. (D)	247. (A)	248. (D)
249. (D)	250. (C)	251. (A)	252. (C)
253. (A)	254. (D)	255. (B)	256. (D)
257. (B)	258. (A)	259. (B)	260. (A)
261. (B)	262. (D)	263. (B)	264. (A)
265. (D)	266. (C)	267. (D)	268. (C)
269. (B)	270. (C)	271. (D)	272. (B)
273. (C)	274. (B)	275. (A)	276. (C)
277. (C)	278. (C)	279. (B)	280. (C)
281. (C)	282. (D)	283. (C)	284. (D)
285. (C)	286. (C)	287. (C)	288. (B)
289. (A)	290. (C)	291. (D)	292. (B)
293. (C)	294. (A)	295. (B)	296. (C)
297. (D)	298. (B)	299. (A)	300. (A)
301. (B)	302. (C)	303. (A)	304. (D)
305. (A)	306. (D)	307. (A)	308. (B)
309. (B)	310. (D)	311. (D)	312. (D)
313. (D)	314. (B)	315. (B)	316. (C)
317. (C)	318. (B)	319. (B)	320. (A)
321. (C)	322. (D)	323. (B)	324. (B)
325. (D)	326. (B)	327. (C)	328. (C)
329. (C)	330. (B)	331. (A)	332. (A)
333. (C)	334. (D)	335. (D)	336. (B)
337. (B)	338. (C)	339. (A)	340. (B)
341. (A)	342. (D)	343. (A)	344. (B)
345. (D)	346. (C)	347. (D)	348. (A)
349. (D)	350. (A)	351. (C)	352. (C)
353. (B)	354. (B)	355. (C)	356. (B)
357. (B)	358. (A)	359. (C)	360. (C)
361. (A)	362. (B)	363. (A)	364. (C)
365. (C)	366. (C)	367. (A)	368. (B)
369. (C)	370. (B)	371. (D)	

8
References

1. What type of document Conference proceedings are?
   (A) Conventional (B) Primary
   (C) Secondary (D) Tertiary
2. RSS feed is a tool of :
   (A) Graphic design (B) Web 1.0
   (C) Web 2.0 (D) Architecture
3. What is the source to find out an appropriate descriptive information ?
   (A) ????? (B) Directory
   (C) Encyclopedia (D) Dictionary
4. Glossary is a :
   (A) List of technical words with definitions
   (B) List of words in a language
   (C) List of thematically arranged words
   (D) Alphabetical index to passages of work
5. One of the following search engine is exclusively meant for scientific information :
   (A) Google (B) Yahoo
   (C) SCIRUS (D) Altavista
6. The author of 'Little Science Big Science' is
   (A) F. W. Lancaster (B) Blaise Cronin
   (C) Martia Bates (D) Derek De Solla Price.

7. Who among the following honoured with 'Nobel Prize' for his substantial contribution in Documentation ?
   (A) S. C. Bradford (B) Loosjes
   (C) Eric De Grolier (D) Henri La Fontaine
8. Non-bibliographic database contain which types of data?
   (A) Numeric data (B) Textual data
   (C) Visual data (D) All of the above
9. What is called that database which contains a mixure of textual and numerical data ?
   (A) Numerical database
   (B) Text-Numeric database
   (C) Numeric text database
   (D) None of these
10. COPSAT stands for:
   (A) Cooperative periodicals in science and technology
   (B) Current online periodicals in science and technology
   (C) Current online patent in science and technology
   (D) Contents of periodicals in science and technology
11. Who gave the concept of concretes and processes ?
   (A) Kaiser (B) H. P. Luhn
   (C) Derek Austin (D) S. R. Ranganathan
12. Who is the publisher of "Science Citation Index" ?
   (A) Emerald (B) Springer
   (C) Thomson (D) Elsevier
13. Which of the following is not true about e journals ?
   (A) They are distributed through digital methods
   (B) They also have editors or editorial boards
   (C) They are publications of serial nature
   (D) They are always free of cost
14. What is the meaning of 'Translation Pools' ?
   (A) Details about the names of translation experts
   (B) Details about the addresses of the translators
   (C) Agency of the names of translation experts
   (D) None of these.

15. 'Kinesis' is related to
    (A) communication (B) generation
    (C) storage (D) none of these.
16. The term 'Bibliophile' refers to
    (A) a Bibliographer (B) a Book Lover
    (C) a Publisher (D) a Book Binder.
17. MeSH is the name of a
    (A) Medical Library
    (B) C.S.I.R. Unit
    (C) Controlled Vocabulary
    (D) none of these.
18. Which record is the hub of the stack in a library ?
    (A) Accession register (B) Shelf list register
    (C) Book catalogue (D) Staff manual.
19. Who contributed on the systematic use of user's education ?
    (A) S.S.Green (B) Melvil Dewey
    (C) E. J. Coates (D) Patricia B. Knapp.
20. Which one is not the main property of a database ?
    (A) It permits shared access.
    (B) It permits finer granularity
    (C) It eliminates data duplication.
    (D) It enhances data dependence.
21. ISBN consists of
    (A) ten digits (B) thirteen digits
    (C) 8-bytes (D) there are no digits.
22. The concept of Selective Dissemination of Information (SDI) was introduced by
    (A) Kaiser (B) Luhn of IBM
    (C) S. R. Ranganathan (D) Derek Austin.
23. User education may be provided in four interrelated areas which are
    (A) user's awareness, user studies, library orientation, bibliographic instruction
    (B) user's awareness, library orientation, inter-profiling, bibliographic instruction

(C) aptitude test of the users, use of cataloguing, inter-profiling, user's awareness

(D) bibliographic instruction, library orientation, computer literacy, user's awareness.

24. Generally a reference service of a library in the conventional form is processed through the stages which are

(A) preparation, service, assimilation

(B) indexing, orientation, delivery of the query's reply

(C) orientation, user's study, photocopy supplied

(D) preparation, orientation, delivery of the query's reply.

25. There are a few basic factors which may be applied in winning the hearts of the readers. They are

(A) psychological factor, environmental factor, social factor

(B) self factor, psychological factor, service factor

(C) service factor, philosophical factor, self factor

(D) technological factor, service factor, self factor.

26. The marketing concepts in Library Service include

(A) analysis, planning, implementation and control

(B) advertising, planning, analysis and control

(C) distribution, control, analysis, implementation

(D) indexing, planning, control and implementation.

27. The first centre to use computer in the library and information activities in India is

(A) DESIDOC (B) INSDOC

(C) DRTC (D) UGC.

28. ISBN changed from 10 digits to 13 from

(A) January, 2007 (B) January, 2008

(C) January, 2006 (D) January, 2005

29. UNIMARC was developed under the umbrella of

(A) OCLC (B) IFLA

(C) UNESCO (D) None of the above

30. How different nodes in a network are connected and how they communicate are determined ?

(A) By Network Connectivity
(B) By Network Topology
(C) By Network Compatibility
(D) None of the above

31. WorldCat is maintained by
(A) Library of Congress
(B) Online Computer Library Center
(C) American Library Association
(D) None of the above

32. When a source referred to once in the footnote is referred to again and between themno other reference (i.e. citation) intervenes, then the footnote uses the abbreviation
(A) Ibid (B) Id
(C) Op.Cit (D) None of the above

33. Indexing system in which the coordination of terms is done at the search stage was first introduced by
(A) S.R. Ranganathan (B) Derek Austin
(C) Morfiner Taube (D) H.P. Luhn

34. Index Medicus is brought out as printed publication
(A) Quarterly (B) Monthly
(C) Weekly (D) Has ceased publication

35. Which publication was not authored by S.R. Ranaganathan ?
(A) Prolegomena to libraryclassification
(B) Reference Service
(C) Ramanujan : The man and the Mathematician
(D) Living with Books

36. JSTOR is an online system for archiving and accessing academic journals. It is located in
(A) Germany (B) UK
(C) USA (D) Budapest

37. What is Dublin Core ?
(A) Content management tool
(B) E- Library software
(C) Metadata standard
(D) Internet Protocol

38. Which one is the most important problem being faced by Institutional Repositories for archiving the documents ?
    (A) Availability (B) Rarity
    (C) Copyright issues (D) Author's resistance
39. INSDOC has been merged with NISCOM and is now known as
    (A) DELNET (B) NISCAIR
    (C) DESIDOC (D) NASSDOC
40. Bibliographical coupling is related to
    (A) Bibliometric studies
    (B) Bibliography compilation
    (C) Modes of subject formation
    (D) None of these
41. New Encyclopaedia Britannica is published from
    (A) London (B) New York
    (C) Paris (D) Chicago
42. 'Union List' is the record of
    (A) Library members living in a Union Territory
    (B) Periodicals available in a group of libraries
    (C) Library unions located in a Union Territory
    (D) List of Library
43. The term 'bibliometrics' was first used by
    (A) S. R. Ranganathan (B) Alan Pritchard
    (C) Allen Kent (D) A. C. Foskett
44. Databases mostly are prepared for ?
    (A) Periodicals
    (B) Books
    (C) Abstracting and Indexing periodicals
    (D) Patents and specifications.
45. 'Half-life' in Information Science relates to
    (A) Rate of obsolescence (B) Rate of growth
    (C) Degree of scatter (D) Information explosion
46. Which one is not the type of source databases ?
    (A) Numerical databases
    (B) Full Text databases

(C) Alphanumeric databases
(D) Explanatory databases.

47. The term 'Exponential growth' refers to
(A) Linear growth
(B) Normal mode of distribution
(C) Geometric Progression
(D) Arithmetic Progression

48. "Publishers' Weekly" is published by
(A) H. W. Wilson, New York
(B) R. R. Bowker, London
(C) American Library Association, Chicago
(D) Aslib, London

49. All Union Institute for Scientific and Technical Information (VINITI) was established in
(A) 1952 (B) 1953
(C) 1954 (D) 1956

50. Resources sharing among libraries was prompted by the factors
(A) Price escalation (B) Information explosion
(C) Both (A) and (B) (D) None of the above

51. Dublin core meta data consists of
(A) 15 elements (B) 10 elements
(C) 25 elements (D) 08 elements

52. A type of indexing where terms are coordinated prior to searching
(A) Post coordinate indexing
(B) Pre coordinate indexing
(C) Uniterm indexing
(D) None of the above

53. The University which telecasts interaction educational programmes through its ownchannel is
(A) Osmania University
(B) University of Pune
(C) Annamalai University
(D) Indira Gandhi National Open University (IGNOU)

54. Library Literature is a :
    (A) Primary source of information
    (B) Secondary source of information
    (C) Tertiary source of information
    (D) Literary source of information

55. Who has signed an MOU for Accreditation of Teacher Education Institutions in India?
    (A) NAAC and UGC (B) NCTE and NAAC
    (C) UGC and NCTE (D) NCTE and IGNOU

56. The frequency of Data India is :
    (A) Weekly (B) Fortnightly
    (C) Monthly (D) Bi-monthly

57. A.Borden introduced Open Access System in India B.The concept of "anamolous state of knowledge " was proposed by Dr.Ranganathan
    (A) A only Correct (B) B only correct
    (C) A&B are correct (D) None is correct

58. UNISIST is a
    (A) Software (B) A Programme
    (C) Welfare association (D) A committee

59. In which year the ISBN allocation office in India shifted from Kolkatta to Delhi?
    (A) 2009 (B) 2010
    (C) 2011 (D) 2012

60. Library Techology Report is a publication of
    (A) ALA (B) IASLIC
    (C) LA (D) ILA

61. ABGILA is a quarterly publication of
    (A) Assam Library Association
    (B) Andhra Desa Library Association
    (C) Indian Library Association
    (D) Raja Ram Mohun Roy Foundation

62. Encyclopedia of library and Information Science is published by :
    (A) H. W. Wilson (B) R. R. Bowker
    (C) Marcel Dekker (D) Andrew Deutsch

63. The secondary source of information comprised of:
    (A) Text books and research monographs.
    (B) Subject periodicals and encycyclopaedias
    (C) Indexing and Abstracting periodicals
    (D) Bibliography and patents
64. Who categorized information source into conventional, non conventional, neo conventional and micro documents :
    (A) Ranganthan (B) Bradford
    (C) Grogan (D) Henson
65. Article published in research journal are...
    (A) Reference sources (B) Secondary sources
    (C) Primary sources (D) Tertiary sources
66. What is the Thesaurus?
    (A) A collection of selected terminology
    (B) Synonymous terms
    (C) List of words
    (D) All of the above
67. World of learning is a what source of information
    (A) Primary source (B) Documentary source
    (C) Secondary source (D) Tertiary source
68. Indian books in Print are published from
    (A) Tamil nadu (B) Chennai
    (C) Bombay (D) New Delhi
69. Cumulative book index is published from
    (A) India (B) USA
    (C) Canada (D) Thailand
70. Statesman year book is published from
    (A) London (B) New york
    (C) Calcutta (D) Chicago
71. Word of learning is Published by
    (A) Asian events (B) Keesing's
    (C) Europa publication (D) Harper & Row
72. Who is the editor of "Library Herald"
    (A) Krishan Kumar (B) C. K. Sharma
    (C) S. R. Ranganathan (D) F.Monbray Volte

73. Who was Published the monthly Journal "The Library World'

(A) Krishankumar (B) J. D. Brown

(C) H. W. Wilson (D) K. Navlavi

74. Facts of File is weekly digest of

(A) Indian events (B) American events

(C) World events (D) England events

75. Who is the first editor of "Modern Librarian"?

(A) F.Monbrary Volte (B) Dr. S. R. Ranganathan

(C) J. D. Brown (D) Krishan Kumar

76. Indian national Bibliographical first appeared in

(A) 1947 (B) 1957

(C) 1967 (D) 1937

77. Who is the author of "Dictionary of anonymous and pseudonymous literature"

(A) S. Halkett& J. Laing (B) Robert Proctor

(C) Ralph De sols (D) Hanuman Sastri

78. Compton year book contains

(A) Political events (B) Cultural events

(C) Outstanding events (D) Economic events

79. Online Europa year book has a coverage since

(A) 1965 (B) 1975

(C) 1984 (D) 1985

80. Which of the following is a multi-subject gateway?

(A) Renardus (B) Humbul

(C) Sapling (D) EdWEb

81. Which of the following is a specialized information organization online tool?

(A) Mamma (B) Dogpile

(C) Vivisimo (D) Entireweb

82. Research periodicals are which category of sources?

(A) Primary (B) Secondary

(C) Tertiary (D) Non documentary.

83. Reference sources are those

(A) Which are large in size?

(B) Which are read at home easily?
(C) Which used to obtain particular information?
(D) Which are costly?

84. Who is the publisher of Encyclopedia of Library and information science?
(A) Boweker (B) H.W.Wilson company
(C) M.Dekker (D) H.W.Wilson

85. Retrospective search service is a type of
(A) Referral service (B) Responsive service
(C) CAS (D) SDI

86. Which part of new encyclopedia Britannica is useful for ready references?
(A) Macropaedia (B) Propaedia
(C) Micropaedia (D) Premedia

87. Year book are also known as
(A) Hand book (B) annual
(C) Directory (D) Dictionary

88. What is India: A reference annual?
(A) Year Book (B) Almonac
(C) Gide book (D) Hand book

89. What is Trade bibliography?
(A) List of Author Bibliography
(B) List of Special Bibliography
(C) List of books in print or for sale compiled by a publisher
(D) List of books of trade Library

90. Who publishes INIS Atom Index?
(A) INIS (Viena) (B) LC
(C) ICSU (D) AGRIS

91. What is the meaning of E-Documents?
(A) All Documents other than printed
(B) Non-Paper documents
(C) In electronic form such as Cassettes, CD-ROMs, etc.
(D) Audio visual tools

92. Which of the following is not the documents?
    (A) Manuscript (B) Book
    (C) Inscription (D) Periodical
93. Generally the information sources are divided mainly in to following categories?
    (A) Primary and secondary.
    (B) Reference and information sources.
    (C) Documentary and non-documentary
    (D) Books and periodicals
94. What are non- documentary sources?
    (A) Which are in printed form.
    (B) Which are in not printed form
    (C) Which are nor documents
    (D) None of these
95. Today which type of information sources is most useful?
    (A) Reference sources
    (B) Documentary source
    (C) Non- Documentary source
    (D) Both the Documentary and Non-Documentary sources
96. Cover to cover translation is treated as
    (A) Selective dissemination service
    (B) Current awareness services
    (C) On demand services
    (D) Anticipatory services
97. What is the suitable reference sources to know about the information of a particular place?
    (A) Directory (B) Gazetteer
    (C) Encyclopedia (D) Year book
98. What is the suitable reference sources to find out the list of historical monuments of Delhi?
    (A) Atlas (B) Gazetteer
    (C) Guide book (D) Globe
99. What do you call a collection of maps, tables, charts, etc.?

(A) Globe (B) Gazetteer
(C) Atlas (D) Map

100. How many volumes Micropaedia of new Encyclopedia Britannica is published?
(A) 2 (B) 10
(C) 19 (D) 12

101. Encyclopedia Americana consists of
(A) 20 Volumes (B) 25 Volumes
(C) 28 Volumes (D) 30 Volumes

102. Which of the following are not the secondary sources?
(A) Encyclopedia (B) Digest
(C) Thesis (D) Text book

103. What is the publication frequency of books in print?
(A) Monthly (B) Weekly
(C) Annually (D) Quarterly

104. What is National bibliography?
(A) List of books of National Library
(B) List of books published in a particular Nation
(C) List of books written by National government
(D) List of books on a nation

105. What is world of learning?
(A) Directory (B) Encyclopedia
(C) Dictionary (D) Year book

106. What is the frequency of I.N.B.?
(A) Quarterly (B) Monthly
(C) Weekly (D) Annual

107. 'Facts on File' is a
(A) Weekly list (B) Fortnightly
(C) Monthly (D) Quarterly

108. The term "Information Service" is an improvised name
(A) Administration (B) Documentation
(C) Bibliography (D) Reference service

109. Abstracting service provides...
(A) Abstract of articles
(B) Whole bibliographic description of articles

(C) Whole bibliographic description along with abstracts of article

(D) Whole bibliographic sources

110. Which service demands the creation of a 'user' profile?

(A) CAS (B) Information retrieval

(C) SDI (D) Reference service

111. "Reference service is the contact between the right reader and the right book in theright personal way" was stated by...

(A) D J Fockett

(B) S R Ranganathan

(C) James I Wyer

(D) A.L.A Glossary of library terms

112. CAS is defined as

(A) A process of dissemination of information

(B) A process of information

(C) A process of dissemination of current information

(D) A simple information service

113. Feedback mechanism is a part of which service?

(A) Reprography service (B) CAS

(C) Translation service (D) SDI

114. The person who provides reference service is called

(A) Chief librarian (B) Grade One Librarian

(C) Deputy Librarian (D) Reference Librarian

115. What are the sources of Information Gatekeepers ?

(A) documentary (B) human

(C) institutional (D) neo-conventional

116. Who categorises documents into three types such as primary, secondary and.tertiary?

(A) Grogan (B) Skeltor

(C) SR. Ranganathan (D) Hanson

117. Which is a legal document and can be used as a source of industrial information?

(A) Report (B) Law Review

(C) Patent (D) Specification

118. E-journals are accessed through:
   (A) Gopher and FTP (B) Telent and e-mail
   (C) Discussion list (D) All of these
119. ISBN stands for
   (A) Integrated Services Bibliographic Network
   (B) Indian Standard Book Number
   (C) International Standard Book Number
   (D) International Standard for Book and Non- book
120. Databases may be stored for ?
   (A) Periodicals
   (B) Books
   (C) Abstracting and indexing periodicals
   (D) Patents and specifications.
121. Which one of the following do not come in the group of source databases ? .
   (A) Numeric databases
   (B) Full text databases
   (C) Text Numeric databases
   (D) Referral databases
122. What is most important factor of evaluation of a reference source ?
   (A) Aims (B) Subject scope
   (C) Style (D) Arrangement.
123. E-journals are accessessed through:.
   (A) Gopher and FTP (B) Telnet and e-mail
   (C) Dicussion List (D) All of these
124. On which of the following technologies semantic web is not based?
   (A) RDF (B) Ontologism
   (C) Cloud seeding (D) URI
125. The term "Cyberspace" was first used by
   (A) Andrew Pollock (B) William Gibson
   (C) John Postal (D) Joe Flower
126. Raw, unevaluated, unprocessed and unorganized facts is known as:

(A) Data (B) Information
(C) Knowledge (D) Wisdom

127. INTERNET was initially developed by US Department of
(A) Commerce (B) Defense
(C) Interior (D) State

128. Information retrieval is fastest from
(A) Floppy Disk (B) Magnetic Tape
(C) Hard Disk (D) None of the above

129. In which of the following the term "Truncation" is used
(A) Budgeting (B) Search Formulation
(C) Coordination (D) Classified bibliography

130. Why the evaluation of reference source is essential for the libraries ?
(A) To know its usability and utility for the library.
(B) To observe the specific material contained in it.
(C) To check the scholarship and expertise of the authors.
(D) To know its merits and demerits.

131. PDA stands for:
(A) Personal Digital Assistance
(B) Personal Document Archive
(C) Personal Digital Archive
(D) Program Download Accessories

132. Pi is the e-book reading device by:
(A) Amazon (B) Sony
(C) Infibeam (D) Nokia

133. Following is an example of microblogging:
(A) Wordpress (B) Blogspot
(C) Livejournal (D) Twitter

134. Where ISDN was first started in 1990
(A) USA (B) UK
(C) India (D) Singapore

135. Now-a-days how many tipes of Protocol are used ?
(A) 5 (B) 4
(C) 3 (D) 2

136. Who publishes Annals of Library Science and documentation?
   (A) ILA (B) INSDOC
   (C) DRTC (D) IASLIC
137. What is full text e-Resource ?
   (A) JCCC (B) ISID
   (C) Science finder scholar(D) ACS
138. Which type of dictionary is just like an Encyclopedia ?
   (A) General dictionary (B) Subject dictionary
   (C) Language dictionary (D) Scientific dictionary
139. Which is the journal of Library and Information Science?
   (A) Abacus
   (B) Actanumerica
   (C) Interlending and Document supply
   (D) 4OR
140. The Electronic Library is.
   (A) A Magazine (B) A Journal Name
   (C) A Library (D) An Encyclopedia
141. What is e-prints ?
   (A) A catalogue (B) A journal
   (C) A repository Software (D) An encyclopedia
142. What is APS ?
   (A) A Search Engine?
   (B) A Full-text e-resource
   (C) Bibliographic database
   (D) Library Management Software
143. Which one is Library and Information Science Journal name?
   (A) Reference Reviews incorporating ASLIB Book Guide
   (B) Reference Reviews incorporating ASLIB Book journals
   (C) Reference Reviews incorporating ASLIB Book Review
   (D) Reference Reviews incorporating ASLIB E-Book

144. "Shodhganga" is a national level repository of:
    (A) E-Books (B) E-Journals
    (C) E-Theses (D) Journal Articles

145. "It is a library with little or no physical presence of books, periodicals, reading space or support staff, but are that disseminate disseminate selective information directly to distribute library customers, usually electronically". Said by whom?
    (A) Kay Gapen (B) Powell
    (C) Sherwell (D) H. G. Wells

146. "A library is a public institution or establishment charged with the care of collection of books, the duty of making them accessible to those who require the use of them and the task of converting every person in its neighborhood into a habitual library goers and reader of books."Quoted by whom?
    (A) Dr S R Ranganathan (B) K.N.Raj
    (C) C.A.Cutter (D) W.C.Sayers

147. "Special libraries serve a specialist clientele, located within a single establishment or group and all engaged in working towards one common purpose." Who said this
    (A) R.Astall (B) UNESCO
    (C) J.D.Brown (D) E.C.Richardson

148. When the second edition of Oxford English Dictioinary was published ?
    (A) In 1930 (B) In 1980
    (C) In 1960 (D) In 1989

149. What is geographical reference source Globe ?
    (A) Circular presentation of surface of the earth.
    (B) Photo of the earth
    (C) The map prepared on sphere
    (D) None of the above

150. NATIS stands for
    (A) National Information System
    (B) National Technical Information System
    (C) National Team for Information Science

(D) None of the above

151. POPSI was developed by
   (A) S.R. Ranganathan (B) Neelmeghan
   (C) B.S. Kesavan (D) G. Bhattacharya

152. The term 'Thesaurus' is associated with
   (A) Directory (B) Bibliography
   (C) Dictionary (D) None of the above

153. C.L.R.I (Central Leather Research Institute) is located at
   (A) Chennai (B) Calicut
   (C) Cochin (D) Cuttack

154. Which of the following combinations is wrong
   (A) PRECIS-Dreck Austin-BNB
   (B) KWIC-H.P. Luhn-Chemical titles
   (C) Citation Indexing-Eugene Garfield-SCI
   (D) Relational indexing-E.J. Coates-Biological Abstracts

155. Citation indexing was first developed in the field of
   (A) Science (B) Mathematics
   (C) Law (D) Social sciences

156. In a thesaurus, under an item "Internal Migration", which of the following lines would you expect to find
   (A) BT Migration
   (B) NT Rural-to-Urgan Migration
   (C) RT International Migration
   (D) All of the above

157. Among the different Boolean operators "AND" is used
   (A) to widen the search (B) to narrow the search
   (C) to begin the search (D) to end the search

158. Which of the following reference source will you consult to locate information on the Pokharn test?
   (A) Encyclopedia of Britannica
   (B) Asian Recorder
   (C) Commonwealth Universities Yearbook
   (D) Dictionary of National Biography

159. Information about Indian research studies on bakery and milling is input to IFIS through
    (A) The Central Rice Research Institute
    (B) Indian Agricultural Research Institute
    (C) National Institute of Nutrition
    (D) Central Food Technological Research Institute
160. Which of the following is not an example of Current Awareness Service (CAS)?
    (A) SDI (B) An Indexing Bulletin
    (C) Current Contents (D) A Reading List
161. Non-bibliographic Database contain
    (A) Numeric Data (B) Textual Data
    (C) Visual Data (D) All of the above
162. Indexing and abstracting sources are available in print, optical and online. Among the three formats there is usually
    (A) a difference in price, but not capability
    (B) no difference in price, but difference in capability
    (C) adifference both in price and in capability
    (D) no difference in price or capability
163. Which of the following research methods is useful in a study on measuring the active life of periodicals
    (A) Survey (B) Citation Analysis
    (C) Interview (D) Case study
164. SENDOC is the national documentation centre for
    (A) Science and Environment
    (B) Sociology and Economics
    (C) Sri Lanka
    (D) Small Scale Enterprise
165. Which of the following names are associated with Post-Coordinate indexing
    (A) Taube, Mooers, Batten
    (B) Taube, Austin, Coats
    (C) Taube, Austin, Garfield
    (D) Mooers, Taube, Garfield

166. The following is not an example of re-packaging of information
    (A) Trend report (B) Catalogue
    (C) Summary (D) Digest
167. The Indian National Bibliography does not include
    (A) Books published in India in English
    (B) Official reports
    (C) Books on India, published abroad
    (D) Books published in recognized Indian languages
168. The subject headings "Money" and "Inflation" are both used in a retrieval system
    (A) be linked by a "see also" reference
    (B) be linked by a "see" reference
    (C) be linked by both "see" and "see also" references
    (D) not be linked
169. The resource sharing strategy of a library may not include
    (A) joint acquisition (B) shared use
    (C) exchange of materials (D) restricted access
170. In KWIC index the keyword appears
    (A) at the beginning of each entry
    (B) at the centre of the line
    (C) as the highlighted word
    (D) at the end of the line
171. The relationship between the terms "Ship" and "Boats" is
    (A) syntactic relationship (B) semantic relationship
    (C) both (D) neither
172. Which of the following cannot be regarded as 'multimedia'
    (A) A tape-slide programme
    (B) A CD-ROM with text and visuals
    (C) Microfilm
    (D) A web page

173. The term "Information Service" is an improvised name.
    (A) Administration (B) Documentation
    (C) Bibliography (D) Reference service
174. Ready reference sources are those which are?
    (A) Publish annually.
    (B) Published annually and cover information about the whole year
    (C) Published annually and cover information about the previous year
    (D) Published annually and cover information about present year
175. Which of the following is the primary source of information?
    (A) Bibliography (B) Encyclopedia
    (C) Handwritten articles (D) Dictionary
176. "Reference service is the contact between the right reader and the right book in the right personal way" was stated by...
    (A) D J Fockett
    (B) S R Ranganathan
    (C) James I Wyer
    (D) A.L.A Glossary of library terms
177. What is the essential aspect of information service?
    (A) Retrieval of information
    (B) Storage of information
    (C) Collection of information
    (D) Communication of information
178. CAS, SDI, Indexing & Abstracting and Literature Searching Service
    (A) Bibliographical service
    (B) Reference Service
    (C) Indexing Service
    (D) None of the above
179. CAS is defined as
    (A) A process of dissemination of information_
    (B) A process of information

(C) A process of dissemination of current information
(D) A simple information service

180. Asian Recorder is published from where ?
(A) New Delhi (B) Islamabad
(C) Peeking (D) Colombo

181. What are the two parts of the annual report of the library
(A) Primary and Secondary
(B) Analytical and Systematic
(C) Upper and Lower
(D) Descriptive and Analytical.

182. A computer that connects one network to another for the purpose of file transfer is known as ...
(A) Highway (B) Search Engine
(C) Gateway (B) Super way

183. What is Bibliometry?
(A) Function of Library Network
(B) Information Management Service
(C) Information Management Tool.
(D) Library Service

184. The agency in India responsible for assigning ISSN is
(A) The National Library
(B) INSDOC (NASCAIR)
(C) INFLIBNET
(D) Raja Ram Mohan Roy Library Foundation

185. Which reference source is known as a store house of knowledge ?
(A) Dictionary (B) Encyclopedia
(C) Yearbook (D) Directory

186. 'Informatics' is a term which was first used for documentation in
(A) Britain (B) USA
(C) USSR/Russia (D) India

187. European Translation Centre is located at
(A) Italy (B) France
(C) Netherland (D) Germany

188. 'Micropaedia' is in how many volumes?
(A) 5 (B) 12
(C) 15 (D) 20

189. 'Facts on File' is published from
(A) India (B) Africa
(C) U.S.A (D) Europe

190. What is Bibliography
(A) A list of books published
(B) A list of books available in a library
(C) A list of books available in two libraries
(D) A list of Journals

191. Bibliographic service comes under
(A) Ready Reference Service
(B) Long Range Reference Service
(C) Referral Service
(D) None of the above

192. Mc-Graw Hill is a
(A) Author (B) Printer
(C) Publisher (D) Librarian

193. 'Indian Science Abstract' is published by
(A) INSDOC (B) ICSSR
(C) DST (D) DRTC

194. Library Week is celebrated on
(A) 10th November (B) 14th November
(C) 14th December (D) 25th December

195. Encyclopaedia Britannica is in how many parts
(A) Single (B) Two
(C) Three (D) Four

196. The author who defined Reference Service as the "Process of establishing contact between a reader and his documents in a personal way" is :
(A) WA. Katz (B) L. Shores
(C) M. Hutchins (D) S. R. Ranganathan

197. Identify the odd one :
(A) LISA (B) Psychological Abstracts
(C) Index Medicus (D) World of Learning

198. Which of the following is not correctly matched ?
   (A) DELNET - Telecommunication Network
   (B) Digital Library - Print Material
   (C) Thesaurus - List of Descriptors
   (D) ISBN - Serial Number

199. An entry in an Abstracting Journal consists of :
   (A) Bibliographic citation
   (B) An abstract and bibliographic citation
   (C) Annotation
   (D) Bibliographic citation, an abstract and initials of the abstractor

200. Technological Gatekeeper is :
   (i) An informal channel
   (ii) A term coined by T.J. Allen
   (iii) A formal channel
   (iv) A term coined by Derek De J. Solla Price

   Code:
   (A) (i) and (ii) are correct
   (B) (i) and (iii) are correct
   (C) (ii) and (iii) are correct
   (D) (iii) and (iv) are correct

201. Which of the following search devices will lead to an increase in the Recall output ?
   (A) Boolean 'And' (B) Boolean 'Not'
   (C) Proximity Operators (D) Truncation

202. Orientation of library users is a kind of :
   (A) Reference Service
   (B) Referral Service
   (C) Current Awareness Service
   (D) Selective Dissemination of Information Service

203. Which of the following are produced by Institute of Scientific Information :
   (i) Science Citation Index
   (ii) Current Contents
   (iii) Index Medicus
   (iv) Atom Index

Codes :

(A) (i), (ii) and (iii) (B) (i) and (ii) only

(C) (ii) and (iii) only (D) (i) and (iv) only

204. The term 'Precision'to measure the performance of Information Retrieval Systems,was suggested by :

(A) S.R. Ranganathan (B) F.W. Lancastere

(C) Cyril Cleverdon (D) H.P. Luhn

205. Which of the following would be the correct chronological sequence ?

(A) Bibliometrics, Informetrics, Librametry, Webometrics

(B) Librametry, Bibliometrics, Informetrics, Webometrics

(C) Librametry, Informetrics, Bibliometrics, Webometrics

(D) Bibliometrics, Informetrics, Webometrics, Librametry

206. Name of the President of the Royal society, can be found in

(A) World of Learning

(B) Commonwealth Universities Year Book

(C) International Who's Who

(D) Statesman's Year Book

207. Times Literary Supplement is most useful for

(A) book reviews

(B) news about Great Britain

(C) digest of newspapers

(D) library holding of U. K.

208. Information about Sahitya Academy Awards can be found in

(A) World of Learning

(B) Universities Handbook

(C) India: A Reference Annual

(D) Dictionary of National Biography

209. INB is published by

(A) National Library, Kolkata
(B) Central Reference Library, Kolkata
(C) INSDOC, New Delhi
(D) NASSDOC, New Delhi.

210. Library Herald is published from
(A) Denmark (B) Paris
(C) London (D) Delhi.

211. BBIP is a
(A) National bibliography
(B) trade bibliography
(C) universal bibliography
(D) none of the above.

212. The coverage of Cumulative Book Index is
(A) throughout the world (B) throughout USA
(C) throughout UK (D) throughout India.

213. British National Bibliography is published
(A) fortnightly (B) monthly
(C) bi-monthly (D) weekly.

214. Books In Print covers
(A) throughout the world (B) throughout India
(C) throughout Sri Lanka (D) throughout China.

215. Person(s) attempted to compile a universal bibliography is/are
(A) H. E. Bliss
(B) C. A. Cutter
(C) S. R. Ranganathan
(D) Paul Otlet and Henry LaFontain.

216. Subject encyclopedias are designed to satisfy the need of the
(A) beginners (B) subject specialists
(C) all types of users (D) none of these.

217. The persons associated with user education activities are
(A) S. R. Ranganathan& G. Bhattacharyya
(B) F. W. Lancaster & Blaise Cronin

(C) Louis Shores, Patricia B. Knapp & Thomas G. Kirk
(D) none of these.

218. One of the aspects of reference service useful to the freshman is
(A) user education
(B) initiation
(C) users behaviour study
(D) users information needs study.

219. For the bibliographical details of Fiedel Castro you will consult
(A) University Handbook
(B) Encyclopaedia Britannica
(C) Encyclopaedia Americana
(D) International Who's Who.

220. The author of 'National Library of India: A Critical Study' is
(A) P. N. Kaul (B) B. Guha
(C) S. R. Ranganathan (D) S. Seetharama.

221. 'India: A Reference Annual' is a
(A) Handbook (B) Yearbook
(C) Biography (D) Encyclopaedia.

222. The author of 'Penny Rate' is
(A) M. P. Satija (B) A. N. A. Raju
(C) Ramansu Lahiri (D) W. A. Munford.

223. The source of information for the quotation 'early to bed and early to rise, makes a man healthy, wealthy and wise' is
(A) Handbook of Quotations
(B) Encyclopaedia of Quotations
(C) Yearbook of Quotations
(D) Dictionary of Quotations.

224. Ulrich's International Periodicals Directory is a
(A) primary source (B) secondary source
(C) tertiary source (D) none of these.

225. User education was experimented for the first time by

(A) Monteith College (B) SNDT College
(C) Trinity College (D) Presidency College.

226. The name of Vice Chancellor of Karachi University can be found in
(A) Encyclopaedia Britannica
(B) Encyclopaedia Americana
(C) International Who's Who
(D) Commonwealth University Yearbook.

227. 'Putting Knowledge to Work' was authored by
(A) Franz Kafka (B) Leo Tolstoy
(C) Charles Dickens (D) Pauline Atherton.

228. The Publisher of 'Who's Who of Indian Writers' is
(A) EssEss Publications (B) Orient Longman
(C) S. Chand Publication (D) SahityaAcademy.

229. The first Library Science journal of the world 'Library Journal' was published in
(A) 1877 (B) 1878
(C) 1879 (D) 1876.

230. The 'New Encyclopaedia Britannica' is issued in
(A) 1 part (B) 2 parts
(C) 3 parts (D) 4 parts.

231. A 'Bibliography of Bibliographies' is a
(A) primary source (B) secondary source
(C) tertiary source (D) none of these.

232. 'Library and Information Science Abstract' is published by
(A) ALA (B) LA
(C) IFLA (D) ILA.

233. 'Referral Service' is
(A) the other name of Reference Service
(B) the other name of Indexing Service
(C) the other name of Abstracting Service
(D) directing the user to another institution/ individual where he can get the required information.

234. 'World of Learning' falls under the category of
(A) Yearbook (B) Handbook
(C) Directories (D) Encyclopaedia.

235. The document in any library entitled 'The Hindu' is a
(A) General Dictionary
(B) Dictionary of Quotations
(C) Thesaurus
(D) Yearbook.

236. The editors of Encyclopaedia of Library and Information Science are
(A) Leonard Montague & Robert Pelczar
(B) Robert Stryer& Allan Hopkinson
(C) Michael Ferreira & Robert Cock
(D) Allen Kent &HarrodLancour.

237. Recent arrangement of New Encyclopaedia Britannica is
(A) classified (B) alphabetical
C) alphabetical classed (D) none of these.

238. The source of information on current periodical publication in India is
(A) Press Trust of India (B) News Trust of India
(C) Press in India (D) none of these.

239. Bibliography of International Scientific and Technical Dictionarics was published by
(A) UNISIST (B) UNESCO
(C) IFLA (D) FID.

240. World Bibliography of Bibliographies edited by Alice F. Toomey was published from
(A) Prentice Hall (B) Orient Longman
(C) Willey Eastern (D) R. R. Bowker

241. Which of the following material would you not expect to find in a public library?
(A) Newspapers (B) Audio Cassettes
(C) Patents (D) Maps.

242. Which of the following is a union catalogue?

(A) Ulrich's International Periodical Directory
(B) New Serials Titles
(C) Press in India
(D) NUCSSI.

243. Which of the following is also available on CD-ROM?
(A) INB
(B) Indian Science abstracts
(C) National Union Catalogue of Scientific Serials in India
(D) Indian Books in Print.

244. Books in Print could be categorised as
(A) National Bibliography from India
(B) Trade Bibliography from India
(C) NationalBibliography from USA
(D) Trade Bibliography from USA.

245. Which of the following is not a secondary source of information?
(A) an encyclopaedia (B) a textbook
(C) a thesis (D) a statistical digest.

246. Concordance means
(A) an alphabetical index to a book or author's work
(B) a multi lingual dictionary
(C) Encyclopedia
(D) Glossary

247. Indian Library Science Abstract is published by
(A) ILA (B) IASLIC
(C) INSDOC (D) NASSDOC.

248. A "gazette" gives information about
(A) places to see
(B) history of places
(C) old records
(D) official announcementsand notifications.

249. Referral service means referring users to
(A) reference books
(B) other books in the collection

(C) sources outside theLibrary
(D) online search.

250. A special library has hand books, patents, research reports, manuals, technicaldigests. Which of the above are primary sources?
(A) manuals
(B) technical digests
(C) handbooks
(D) patents and research reports.

251. The NUCSSI is published by
(A) National Library, Kolkata
(B) Central Reference Library
(C) INSDOC
(D) DelhiPublic Library.

252. To answer the question 'Recent articles on Ethnic Problems in Sri Lanka' weuse
(A) Biological Abstract
(B) Sociological Abstracts
(C) Mathematical Abstracts
(D) Chemical Abstracts.

253. India: A Reference Annual is an example of
(A) periodical publication
(B) serial publication
(C) quarterly publication
(D) foreignpublication.

254. Her Majesty's Stationary Office (HMSO) is a publisher of
(A) British Government
(B) American Government
(C) Russian Government
(D) Indian Government.

255. Atlases form an important source of
(A) statistical information
(B) geographical information
(C) biographical information
(D) economic information.

256. Materials which are original in nature is known as
   (A) secondary sources (B) primary sources
   (C) tertiary sources (D) printed sources.
257. Sources consists of information that is distilled and collection of primary andsecondary sources is called as
   (A) Directory sources (B) Reference sources
   (C) Tertiary sources (D) Bibliographysources.
258. Which database supplement the existing card catalogues and can be consultedfor comprehensive searches?
   (A) DIALOG (B) OPAC
   (C) MEDLARS Database (D) OCLC.
259. A systematic summary of the knowledge that is most significant to mankind isknown as
   (A) Encyclopaedia (B) Directory
   (C) Yearbook (D) Handbook.
260. A well-organised list of written, printed or otherwise produced record ofcivilization e.g. of books, articles in periodicals, etc. is called as
   (A) Catalogue (B) Bibliography
   (C) Union Catalogue (D) Indexing Periodical.
261. An interactive system, using telephone lines and is available to subscribers onlyis denoted as
   (A) Teletext (B) Videotext
   (C) Online access (D) Dialog.
262. Yearbooks and annuals are
   (A) primary sources
   (B) ready reference sources
   (C) tertiary sources
   (D) bibliographic sources.
263. Bibliography deals with the study and detailed description of documents isknown as
   (A) Enumerative bibliography
   (B) Systematic bibliography
   (C) Analyticalbibliography
   (D) Descriptive bibliography.

264. Who is referred to as the father of encyclopaedias?
   (A) Johann HenrichAlsted
   (B) Aristotle
   (C) John Harris
   (D) Seville.
265. 'Indian Books in Print' is an example of
   (A) trade bibliography
   (B) national bibliography
   (C) universal bibliography
   (D) subject bibliography.
266. 'Chemical Abstracts' is published
   (A) fortnightly (B) yearly
   (C) monthly (D) weekly.
267. The State-of the –art reports can be grouped into three categories a) reviewsand survey b) advances and progresses and c)
   (A) trend reports
   (B) current awareness bulletins
   (C) yearbooks
   (D) researchreports.
268. To present consolidated information available in various forms and torepackage the same in a condensed form for users is the main purpose of the
   (A) Survey
   (B) Reviews
   (C) Trend Reports
   (D) State-of the-Art Reports.
269. Reviews are of two types 1) subject oriented and 2)
   (A) research oriented
   (B) topical
   (C) chronological
   (D) focusing in particularscientific or technical problem and its solution.
270. Which reference source provides an account of the general direction ofresearch in the subject based on a review of the documents on currentdevelopments?

(A) Current Contents (B) Trend Reports
(C) Reviews (D) Advances.

271. Glossary, Lexicon, Thesaurus, Vocabulary are some of the alternate names for
(A) bibliography (B) acronyms
(C) encyclopaedia (D) dictionaries.

272. Polygot refers to
(A) bilingual dictionaries
(B) multi-lingual dictionaries
(C) subject dictionaries
(D) language dictionaries.

273. The reference source often used for a stock of words and phrases with briefexplanations and meanings restricted to a single work or author is known as
(A) Lexicon (B) Thesaurus
(C) Vocabulary (D) Glossary.

274. 'Encyclopaedia of Library and Information Science' is published by
(A) Bowker and Saur
(B) Dekker
(C) Cambridge University Press
(D) McGraw Hill.

275. 'World Book Encyclopedia' is an example of
(A) generalencyclopedia
(B) subjectencyclopedia
(C) universalencyclopedia
(D) childrenencyclopedia.

276. The first edition of Encyclopedia Americana was published in
(A) 1920 (B) 1732
(C) 1829 (D) 1817.

277. 'University Handbook: India' is published by
(A) UGC
(B) AIU
(C) Ministry of Human Resource Development
(D) University of Delhi.

278. The ready reference sources are complementary as well as supplementarysources of
(A) dictionaries (B) encyclopaedias
(C) bibliographies (D) patents.

279. 'Famous First Facts' is an example of
(A) handbook (B) encyclopaedia
(C) yearbook (D) directory.

280. Almanacs are grouped into three categories namely a) Astronomical ii)Informational and c)
(A) National (B) International
(C) Physical (D) Topical.

281. 'National Register of Social Scientists in India' is an example of
(A) statistical sources (B) almanac
(C) directory (D) yearbook.

282. 'BIS Handbook' is a catalogue of around
(A) 20000 Indian standards with alphabetical index
(B) 13000 Indian standardswith alphabetical index
(C) 2000 Indian standards with alphabetical index
(D) 1,70,000 Indian standards with alphabetical index.

283. The Patent Information System (PIS) of India was set up in 1980 at
(A) New Delhi (B) Pune
(C) Nagpur (D) Chennai.

284. The International Patent Documentation Centre (INPADOC) is situated in
(A) Vienna (B) UK
(C) Russia (D) Australia.

285. 'Standards World Over' is a publication of
(A) ASTM (B) BIS
(C) ISO (D) IEO.

286. 'Gazetteer of India: The Indian Union' is published in
(A) 3 volumes (B) 4 volumes
(C) 2 volumes (D) 5 volumes.

287. 'Census Atlas National Volume' is an example of

(A) local atlas (B) historical atlas
(C) demographic atlas (D) anthropological atlas.

288. 'Current Geographical Publications' is published by
(A) Royal Geographic Society, London
(B) American Geographical Society
(C) The British Library
(D) Bowker – Saur.

289. 'International Who's Who' is published by
(A) Europa (B) Bowker – Saur
(C) Wilson (D) Marquis.

290. 'National Biographical Dictionary of India' is published by
(A) S.P.Sen (B) Durga Das
(C) Jagadis S. Sharma (D) Times of India.

291. 'Social Indicator of Development' is a publication by
(A) World Bank (B) UNESCO
(C) FAO (D) ILO.

292. 'World Tables' is a
(A) UNESCO publication (B) World Bank publication
(C) UN publication (D) IMFpublication.

293. 'Asian Recorder' covers
(A) 40 countries (B) 45 countries
(C) 50 countries (D) 55 countries.

294. 'Facts on File' is a
(A) current awareness service
(B) SDI service
(C) loose leaf service
(D) statisticalservice.

295. 'Data India' is published by
(A) PTI (B) Times of India
(C) INFA (D) HariSharanChhabra.

296. 'Summary of World Broadcast' is published by
(A) BBC (B) Chadwyek-Healey
(C) Doordarshan (D) CBS Television.

297. To deal with enquiries for information that could be answered through non-documentary sources, is generally known as
(A) bibliography centre (B) information centre
(C) reference centre (D) referralcentre.

298. Which institution was established to provide referral service globally, for allsources of environmental information?
(A) UNEP (B) UNESCO
(C) UNCTAD (D) UNICEF.

299. Which institutions are highly specialised types of information institutions thatemerged to provide critical, analytical and evaluated support services toinstitutions involved in high level research?
(A) IACs
(B) Libraries
(C) Documentation Centres
(D) Referral Centres.

300. Which persons are engaged in activities such as translations, printing,publishing, publishing, etc.?
(A) Information gatherers
(B) Information processors
(C) Information recorders
(D) Information generators.

301. Forms of communications that involve creativity, persuasion and impact of themassage carried by them is known as
(A) Multimedia (B) Public relation
(C) Mass media (D) Advertisement.

302. Which is a pervasive part of modern culture, a medium to build up images of asociety ?
(A) Mass media (B) Public relation
(C) Advertisement (D) Multimedia.

303. Among the print media that carry contents of mass communication whichoccupy the centre?
(A) daily newspapers (B) journals
(C) books (D) pamphlets.

304. Reference service is an example of
   (A) anticipatory service
   (B) current awareness service
   (C) on demand service
   (D) retrospective search service.
305. The information desk for the scientific and technological community whichdoes not provide enquirers with the information they need, but suggestssources likely to satisfy their needs is known as
   (A) Information Analysis Centre
   (B) Documentation Centre
   (C) Referral Centre
   (D) Data Centre.
306. Modern information services which are considered as extension of referenceservice place emphasis on
   (A) library oriented, need based reference service
   (B) information oriented, needbased reference service
   (C) user oriented, need based reference service
   (D) documentation oriented, need based reference service.
307. Bibliographies, indexes, abstracts and the like, answers the questions relatingto
   (A) persons
   (B) places
   (C) meaning of words/phrases
   (D) literature references.
308. Organising and presenting the collected information in the form of a report acceptable to the user is one of the step of
   (A) ready reference service
   (B) short range reference service
   (C) long range reference service
   (D) anticipatory information service.
309. Which programmes are aimed at developing skills in users in literature search,consulting different types of tools and preparing their personal informationfiles?

(A) User studies (B) User education
(C) Reference services (D) Informationservices.

310. Full form of SENDOC is
(A) Seminar on National Documentation
(B) Small Entrepreneurs DocumentationCentre
(C) Small Enterprises Documentation
(D) Small Enterprises NationalDocumentation Centre.

311. Biological Abstracts have five indexes viz. Generic, Basic, Cross, Bio-systematicand
(A) Editor (B) Compiler
(C) Series Editor (D) Author.

312. The method of deriving class index entries through chain procedure was devisedby
(A) Ganesh Bhattacharyya
(B) S. R. Ranganathan
(C) M. A. Gopinath
(D) P. N.Kaula.

313. 'Current Contents' is brought out by
(A) ILA
(B) IASLIC
(C) LA
(D) Institute for Scientific Information, Philadelphia.

314. BNB is at present deriving subject index entries according to
(A) POPSI (B) KWIC
(C) KWOC (D) PRECIS.

315. Headquarters of FID is located at
(A) India (B) Denmark
(C) Sweden (D) The Hague.

316. FID now stands for
(A) International Federation for Documentation
(B) International Federation forDatabase
(C) International Federation for Development
(D) InternationalFederation for Information and Documentat

317. NASSDOC is an organ of
    (A) INSDOC (B) SENDOC
    (C) DRTC (D) ICSSR.
318. POPSI was conceived by
    (A) Ganesh Bhattacharyya
    (B) S. R. Ranganathan
    (C) M. A. Gopinath
    (D) S.Seetharama.
319. Indian Science Abstracts is being published by
    (A) DRTC (B) ICSSR
    (C) INFLIBNET (D) INSDOC.
320. Konard Ganser is known as the father of ?
    (A) Documentation (B) Abstracting
    (C) Bibliography (D) Indexing.
321. The concept of co-ordinate indexing was developed by
    (A) Ganesh Bhattacharyya
    (B) Martia Bates
    (C) Blaise Cronin
    (D) Mortimer Taube.
322. In 'SDI' document characteristics are matched with
    (A) information needs profiles
    (B) information seeking behaviour profiles
    (C) information services profiles
    (D) user profiles.
323. The practice of consulting the colleagues and seeking information at the neededhour is known as
    (A) invisible information (B) invisible sights
    (C) invisible users (D) invisiblecolleagues.
324. Chemical Abstracts is published by
    (A) American Biological Society
    (B) American Sociological Society
    (C) AmericanAnthropological Society
    (D) American Chemical Society.
325. The basic difference between SDI and other modes of current awareness is thatSDI is

(A) directed towards the needs of a group of users
(B) directed towards the needsof all users
(C) directed towards the needs of an individual user/ project
(D) noneof these.

326. Routing of journals (Content by Journals) is related to
(A) Current Awareness Service
(B) Selective Dissemination of Service
(C) Abstracting
(D) Indexing.

327. In computer based system, commonly used indexing language is
(A) co-ordinate indexing language
(B) keyword indexing language
(C) freeindexing language
(D) none of these.

328. The union catalogue of Social Science Serials in India brought out by
(A) INSDOC (B) NASSDOC
(C) SENDOC (D) DRTC.

329. Non- conventional approach of subject indexing is
(A) pre-coordinate indexing
(B) post-coordinate indexing
(C) chain indexing
(D) citation indexing.

330. DRTC is located in
(A) Delhi
(B) Mumbai
(C) Kolkata
(D) Bangalore.

331. Science Citation Index is a publication of
(A) ALA
(B) American Chemical Society
(C) American Biological Society
(D) Institute for Scientific Information, Philadelphia (1964, 5 vols.).

332. 'Library Literature' is a
(A) abstracting periodical (B) indexing periodical
(C) serials (D) encyclopedia.

333. Paul Otlet and Henry La Fontain were instrumental for establishment of
(A) IFLA (B) FID
(C) ASLIB (D) ALA.

334. SENDOC aims at catering information needs of
(A) large scale industries (B) a community
(C) scholars (D) small scale industries.

335. The premier institution for prescribing standards in India is
(A) ISI (B) ANSI
(C) SSI (D) BIS.

336. Analytical bibliography deasl with ?
(A) Physical aspect of the book
(B) Analysis of subject.
(C) Classified list of books
(D) None of these.

337. Which kind of source INB is ?
(A) Primary source (B) Secondary source.
(C) Tartiary source (D) Other source

338. At present by which system B.N.B. derives subject Index Entries.
(A) Chain Indexing. (B) PRECIS
(C) POPSI (D) KWIC

339. CD-ROM version of Sciece Citation Index is being published since when ?
(A) Since 1965 (B) Since 1970
(C) Since 1975 (D) Since 1988

340. Periodicity of Chemical Abstract is
(A) fortnightly (B) monthly
(C) quarterly (D) weekly.

341. Secondary sources are created to facilitate access to information contents of

(A) secondary sources
(B) primary sources
(C) tertiary sources
(D) primary andsecondary sources.

342. Periodical articles are
(A) secondary sources (B) tertiary sources
(C) primary sources (D) none of these.

343. National Translation Services in India is located at
(A) NISSAT (B) INSDOC
(C) DESIDOC (D) NASSDOC.

344. The originator of 'Science Citation Index' is
(A) Eugene Garfield (B) Farradane
(C) H. P. Luhn (D) W.D.B. Sayers.

345. In which of the following types of Indexes are access points not derivedautomatically
(A) KWIC (B) Citation Indexing
(C) KWOC (D) POPSI.

346. KWIC indexing technique is based on
(A) Titles (B) Citations
(C) Abstracts (D) Full Text.

347. MESH is an example of
(A) classification scheme
(B) thesaurus
(C) abstracting journal
(D) classaurus.

348. A 'slanted abstract' is
(A) a critical evaluation of an article
(B) one that is written for a specific group ofusers
(C) an abstract of a biased article
(D) none of these.

349. Post co-ordinate indexes overcomes difficulties created by
(A) fixed citation order (B) synonymous terms
(C) time taken (D) inconsistencies.

350. Among the following which is a NISSAT sectoralcentre?

(A) National Chemical Laboratory
(B) National Information Centre
(C) Central Drug Research Institute
(D) Ahmedabad Textile Industries Research Association.

351. SENDOC is a documentation centre on
(A) steel enterprise (B) small scale industries
(C) stock exchange (D) sugarindustries.

352. "Half life" of information implies
(A) information is useful only half the time
(B) an information ages, it is used less
(C) the life of information is reduced
(D) dead information is not used.

353. "Grey literature" means
(A) documents which are bound in grey cloth
(B) literature which contains classified information
(C) literature which is semi-published
(D) literature whichis to be published in future.

354. Which of the following cannot be considered as a primary source ofinformation?
(A) an article describing original research
(B) a text book
(C) a patent
(D) a thesis

355. Conference proceedings are considered as
(A) conventional documents
(B) primary documents
(C) secondary documents
(D) tertiary documents.

356. Who divides documents into three types such as primary, secondary and tertiary?
(A) Grogan (B) J. S. Mills
(C) J. H. Shera (D) P. V. Young.

357. What type of information was provided by pamphlets?
(A) Obsolete (B) Current
(C) Traditional (D) Conventional.

358. ISI has been renamed as
   (A) NBT (B) BIS
   (C) ILA (D) ISO.

359. Which documents provide information on the processes and materials involvedin the manufacture of a product?
   (A) Patents (B) Standards
   (C) Specifications (D) Trade Literature.

360. Institutional and human resources are known as
   (A) biographical sources of information
   (B) government sources of information
   (C) documentary sources of information
   (D) non-documentary sources ofinformation.

361. What is the central character in Drury's principle of book selection?
   (A) staff (B) reader
   (C) library collection (D) building.

362. A critical evaluation of book is made through
   (A) book review (B) library review
   (C) newspaper (D) review digest.

363. A limited set of terms that must be used to index documents in a particularsystem refers to
   (A) Indexing (B) Indexing System
   (C) Vocabulary Control (D) Subject Heading.

364. The concept of 'Thesauro Facet' has been developed y
   (A) Derek Austin (B) Ganesh Bhattacharya
   (C) Ranganathan (D) Jean Atchison.

365. The indexing system in which coordination of terms in the index descriptionsare decided before any particular request is made, is known as
   (A) co-ordinate indexing system
   (B) post-coordinate indexing system
   (C) descriptive indexing system
   (D) pre-coordinate indexing system.

366. POPSI is an example of
   (A) post-coordinate indexing model
   (B) pre-coordinate indexing model

(C) naturalindexing model

(D) free indexing model.

367. The synonymous relationship between the terms is known as

(A) hierarchical relationship

(B) genus-species relationship

(C) associaterelationship

(D) equivalent relationship.

368. KWAC stands for

(A) Keyword Associate Context

(B) Keyword And Context

(C) KeywordAbbreviated Context

(D) Keyword And Context.

369. The type of user's approach in which a user may want to look all the informationthat have been published on a given topic is known as

(A) Everyday Approach (B) Current Approach

(C) Exhaustive Approach (D) Catching up Approach.

370. Which approach is essential to every active professional to keep abreast ofthe latest developments in his field and also to every researcher to avoidduplication of research effort?

(A) Everyday approach (B) Exhaustive approach

(C) Current approach (D) Catching up approach.

371. Which is essentially distinguishes between information source and resource?

(A) The idea of organization for reuse

(B) The idea of use of raw material

(C) Theidea of procuring the raw material

(D) The idea of dissemination of information.

372. The information services to the users can be grouped under

(A) two categories (B) three categories

(C) four categories (D) five categories.

373. When the reference personnel do the search on behalf of the user, it is known as

(A) direct search (B) delegated search
(C) self search (D) user search.

374. SDI stands for
(A) Selective Documentation of Information
(B) Subject Dissemination
(C) Specific Document of Information
(D) Selective Dissemination of Information.

375. SDI service is one form of
(A) current awareness service
(B) reference service
(C) literature search service
(D) referral service.

376. Which services do not aid the user to keep abreast of developments in anyspecific subject field, but enable him to find solution to a particular problem?
(A) Current awareness services
(B) Retrospective search services
(C) SDIservices
(D) Anticipatory search services.

377. IACs stands for
(A) Indian Abstracting Centres
(B) Information Addition Centres
(C) InformationAnalysis Centres
(B) Indian Analysis Centres.

378. Cambridge Crystallographic Data Centre is an example of
(A) Documentation centre
(B) Referral centre
(C) Reference centre
(D) Dataanalysiscentre.

379. Selection, evaluation, validation, standardization, summarisation, andsynthesis of information are the processes for
(A) abstracting (B) indexing
(C) literature search (D) information analysis.

380. Indian Institute of Science is located at
    (A) New Delhi (B) Mumbai
    (C) Kolkata (D) Bangalore.
381. The indexing and abstracting publication belong to the
    (A) primary publication group
    (B) secondary publication group
    (C) tertiarypublication group
    (D) reference publication group.
382. The National Translation Centre (USA)brings out
    (A) World Transindex
    (B) Translations Register-Index
    (C) Index Translationum
    (D) National Translation Index.
383. Document Delivery Service is sometimes referred to as
    (A) SDI service
    (B) Abstracting service
    (C) Back-up service
    (D) Literature searchservice.
384. Right Pages and Science Direct is a type of
    (A) abstracting service
    (B) altering service
    (C) document delivery service
    (D) publication service.
385. Newspaper clipping service is a type of
    (A) anticipatory information service
    (B) responsive information service
    (C) ondemand reference
    (D) retrospective information service.
386. Which files comprise of a complete documentation of information available injournals, reports, conference papers and similar publications in the subjectareas of projects?
    (A) Project specification (B) Project execution
    (C) Project information (D) Government project.

387. DELNET is a
   (A) wide area network (B) local area network
   (C) national network (D) regionalnetwork.

388. British Library Automated Information Services (BLAISE) is useful in the field of
   (A) Biochemistry (B) Biomedicine
   (C) Biophysics (D) Biology.

389. NICNET is a project sponsored by
   (A) Government of India (B) UGC
   (C) INFLIBNET (D) NISSAT.

390. AGRIS is mainly sponsored by
   (A) ICAR (B) IFLA
   (C) UNISIST & FAO (D) UNESCO.

391. INFLIBNET stands for
   (A) Informing Library Network
   (B) Information and Librarians Network
   (C) Information and Library Network
   (D) Indian National Frontier Library Network.

392. The library network mainly for university libraries in India is known as
   (A) CALIBNET (B) MALIBNET
   (C) INFLIBNET (D) DELNET.

393. National Information Centre on Chemistry and Chemical Technology(NICCHEM) is located at
   (A) Pune (B) Lucknow
   (C) Hyderabad (D) Bangalore.

394. NICDAP stands for
   (A) National Information Centre for Data Access Programmeming
   (B) NationalInformation Centre for Document Access Programmeming
   (C) NationalInformation Centre for Development and Programmeming
   (D) NationalInformation Centre for Drug and Pharmaceutical.

395. ERIC databases in USA covers the information regarding
    (A) education (B) energy
    (C) environment (D) mathematics.
396. NISSAT's sectoral information centre on drug is located at
    (A) Pune (B) Lucknow
    (C) New Delhi (D) Chennai.
397. The Library and Information Division of ICAR is the national centre for all
    (A) INIS activities (B) AGRIS activities
    (C) FAO activities (D) UNISIST activities.
398. NISSAT is responsible for rendering of information services in the field of
    (A) research and development
    (B) science and technology
    (C) agriculture
    (D) medicine.
399. INIS stands for
    (A) Indian Naval Information System
    (B) Indian Narcotics Information Service
    (C) International Nuclear Information System
    (D) Indian National InformationSystem.
400. BLAISE is operating in
    (A) Canada (B) U. K.
    (C) U. S. A. (D) India.
401. The library and information and information services division of BARC is thenationalcentre for
    (A) all UNISIST activities in India
    (B) all FAO activities in India
    (C) all INISactivities in India
    (D) all IFLA activities in India.
402. Grey literature means
    (A) external reports published as documents
    (B) internal rcports not published asdocuments
    (C) external reports not published as documents
    (D) internal reportspublished as documents.

403. The currently used full form of OCLC is
   (A) Ohio College Library Center
   (B) Online Computer Library Center
   (C) OnlineCatalogue of Library of Congress
   (D) none of these.
404. UBC stands for
   (A) Universal Bibliographic Control
   (B) Universal Bibliographic Classification
   (C) United Bibliographic Control
   (D) none of these.
405. RLIN is an information network functioning in
   (A) UK (B) Canada
   (C) Germany (D) USA.
406. The UAP stands for
   (A) Universal Advance Programmeming
   (B) Universal Academic Problems
   (C) Universal Academic Publication
   (D) Universal Availability of Publication.
407. A system contains
   (A) interrelated parts having a purpose
   (B) unrelated parts
   (C) unrelated partshaving different purpose
   (D) none of these.
408. INIS is an example of
   (A) distributed input and centralised output
   (B) centralised input and output
   (C) centralised input and distributed output
   (D) distributed input and output.
409. Which of the following network is not primarily for academic purposes?
   (A) ERNET (B) JANET
   (C) NICNET (D) INFLIBNET.
410. Transboarder data flow means
   (A) exchange of documents between countries
   (B) free flow of books betweencountries

(C) exchange of electronic information between countries
(D) none ofthese.

411. UAP is a programme of
(A) UNESCO (B) IFLA
(C) FID (D) British Library.

412. INFLIBNET is a programme sponsored by
(A) NISSAT
(B) Planning Commission
(C) Ministry of Electronics
(D) UGC.

413. The World Cat Service is provided by
(A) RLIN (B) OCLC
(C) LC (D) WLN.

414. Which is the World's largest and most comprehensive bibliographic database?
(A) First search (B) OCLC Access Service
(C) World Cat (D) Prompt Cat.

415. The Universal Bibliographic Control (UBC) programme (1974) was sponsored by
(A) FID (B) UNESCO
(C) IFLA (D) LC.

416. Information is a trinity consisting of content, conduit, and
(A) value (B) resource
(C) context (D) power.

417. The information services provided by utilizing telecommunication technologymay be categorized in
(A) two broad groups (B) three broad groups
(C) four broad groups (D) fivebroad categories.

418. Development Information System is maintained by
(A) UNESCO (B) UN
(C) INSDOC (D) UGC.

419. The name of S. C. Bradford is associated with
(A) occurrence of terms in a paragraph
(B) number of articles written by anauthor

(C) law of scattering
(D) citation of an article.

420. 'Recall' and 'Precision' are the terms used in
(A) reference service
(B) information retrieval system
(C) librarymanagement
(D) book selection.

421. PRECIS has been developed by
(A) E. J. Coates (B) Derek Austin
(C) S. R. Ranganathan (D) Mortimer Taube.

422. POPSI is a
(A) post co-ordinate indexing system
(B) keyword based indexing system
(C) preco-ordinate indexing system
(D) citation indexing.

423. Controlled vocabulary in indexing is called
(A) a thesaurus
(B) a language dictionary
(C) a dictionary of synonyms
(D) a list of subject headings.

424. The concept of 'Paperless Society' was first given by
(A) Derek Austin (B) F. W. Lancaster
(C) Jesse H. Shera (D) Maurice F. Taube.

425. The term 'Information Retrieval' was coined by
(A) B. C. Vickery (B) S. R. Ranganathan
(C) F. W. Lancaster (D) Calvin N.Mooers.

426. The effect of reduction in the level of specificity of indexing on informationretrieval is that it
(A) increases precision and decreases recall
(B) increases recall and decreasesprecision
(C) increases recall and precision both
(D) decreases recall andprecision both.

427. The process of retrieving detail / document relevant to a query from a catalogue/database adequately defines

(A) documentation
(B) acquisition
(C) information retrieval services
(D) cataloguingservices.

428. The term 'recall' is used in information retrieval to refer to
(A) recollect the documents
(B) the ability of a system to retrieve relevantDocuments
(C) to recollect the irrelevant documents
(D) to retrieve irrelevantdocuments.

429. B.N.B. uses which classification scheme ?
(A) DDC (B) UDC
(C) CC (D) LC

430. 'Truncation' is a technique used in
(A) cataloguing
(B) classification
(C) reference service
(D) online information retrieval.

431. The logic 'And', 'Or', and 'Not' was devised by
(A) F. W. Lancaster (B) George Boole
(C) S. R. Ranganathan (D) M. A. Gopinath.

432. Lotka's law is concerned with
(A) single number of paper per author
(B) two papers per author
(C) three papersper author
(D) average number of papers per author.

433. The mathematical theory of communication is associated with
(A) S. Ramanujan (B) S. R. Ranganathan
(C) I. N. Sengupta (D) Shannon andWeaver.

434. 'Bibliometrics' is a study of
(A) quantitative analysis of publications
(B) qualitative analysis of publications
(C) macro analysis of publications
(D) micro analysis of publications.

435. The Shanon –Weaver Model of Information as criticized for
    (A) being too mathematical
    (B) being unidirectional
    (C) being primarily suited toelectronic commission
    (D) all of the above.
436. There are a total number of 50 relevant documents in a collection response to aquery, only 30 documents are retrieved of these only 10 were relevant. What isthe recall percentage?
    (A) 20% (B) 33%
    (C) 40% (D) 60%.
437. The concept of 'Librametry' was developed by
    (A) S. C. Bradford (B) J. D. Bernal
    (C) D. J. Foskett (D) S. R. Ranganathan.
438. A retrieval system retrieves a total of 50 documents. Out of these 40 areirrelevant. Another 10 documents which were relevant but not retrieved. Theprecision percentage for that query would be
    (A) 40% (B) 20%
    (C) 60% (D) 80%.
439. The query on "Use of Audio Visual Aids in teaching Science at PrimarySchools" can be framed as
    (A) Audio Visual aids and Science and Primary Schools
    (B) Audio Visual aids orScience or Primary Schools
    (C) Audio Visual aids or Science and Primaryschools
    (D) Audio Visual aids and Science or Primary Schools.
440. Which of the following can be considered as formal channels ofcommunication?
    (A) Conferences, Research Reports, Theses
    (B) Research Reports,Correspondence, Books
    (C) Short Communication, Journals, E-Mail, Theses
    (D) Conversations, Electronic Journals, Research Reports.
441. A device for searching through a fragment of the search term so that it canmatch related terms starting with the same term is known as

(A) Boolean Search (B) Truncation
(C) Thesaurus (D) Indexing Language.

442. Venn diagram was developed by
(A) John Venn (B) Peter Venn
(C) Alfred Venn (D) Marlos Venn.

443. The merit of what type of searching is to offer the using of Boolean logic which allows limiting or expanding the search, as required?
(A) manual searching (B) online searching
(C) literature searching (D) referencesearching.

444. Which of the following is not a secondary source of information
(A) An encyclopedia (B) An annual review
(C) A thesis (D) A technical handbook

445. Identify the one that does not belong to the group
(A) MEDLARS (B) (B) CAS
(C) BIOSIS (D) BLAISE

446. Brenda Dervin and M.Kochen have researched on
(A) Information retrieval
(B) Information needs
(C) Computerized library system
(D) Classification

447. NICDRON is situated at
(A) Calcutta (B) Mumbai
(C) Chennai (D) Bangalore

448. The device that coverts analog signal to digital and vice versa is
(A) MODEM (B) Analog computer
(C) Digital computer (D) Digicom

449. A bibliography and an index are:
(A) similar, both are locating tools
(B) similar, they are arranged subjectwise
(C) not similar, bibliographies include books, indexes include journal articles
(D) not similar, a bibliography is prepared inhouse, an index is purchased

450. Which of the following combinations is wrong?
   (A) PRECIS-Derek Austin-BNB
   (B) KWIC-H.P.Luhn-Chemical Titles
   (C) Citation Indexing – Eugene Garfield-SCI
   (D) Relational Indexing-E.J.Coates-Biological Abstracts

451. Citation indexing was first developed in the field of
   (A) Science (B) Mathematics
   (C) Law (D) Social Sciences

452. In a thesaurus under a item "internal migration" – which of the following lines would you expect to find
   (A) BT Migration
   (B) NT Rural to Urban Migration
   (C) RT International Migration
   (D) All the above

453. Which of the following is not a secondary source of information
   (A) An encyclopedia
   (B) A text book
   (C) A biographical dictionary
   (D) Patents

454. Which of the following reference source will you consult to locate information on the Pokhran test?
   (A) Encyclopaedia Britannica
   (B) Asian Recorder
   (C) Commonwealth Universities Handbook
   (D) Dictionary of national Biography

455. Information about Indian research studies on bakery and milling is input to IFIS through
   (A) The Central Rice Research Institute
   (B) Indian Agricultural Research Institute
   (C) National Institute of Nutrition
   (D) Central Food Technological Research Institute

456. Which of the following is not an example of Current Awareness Service (CAS)?

(A) SDI (B) An Indexing Bull tin
(C) Current Contents (D) A Reading List

457. Non-bibliographic Database contain
(A) Numeric Data (B) Textual Data
(C) Visual Data (D) All of the above

458. Indexing and abstracting sources are available in print, optical and online. Among the three formats there is usually
(A) a different in price, but not in capability
(B) no difference in price, but difference in capability
(C) a difference both in price and in capability
(D) no difference in price or capability

459. In an empirical study on the impact of television viewing on violence, violence would be
(A) the dependent variable
(B) an independent variable
(C) an intervening variable
(D) not a variable at all

460. A big difference between the mean and median is an indication that
(A) There is a mistake in the calculation
(B) the calculation is correct
(C) there is a wide variation in the data
(D) None of the above

461. Which of the following research methods is useful in a study on measuring the active life of periodicals
(A) Survey (B) Citation Analysis
(C) Interview (D) Case Study

462. Which of the following networks does not have its own telecommunication infrastructure
(A) NICNET (B) ERNET
(C) INIS (D) EURONET

463. SENDOC is the national centre for
(A) Science and Environment
(B) Sociology and Economics
(C) Sri Lanka
(D) Small Scale Enterprise

464. Which of the following names are associated with post co-ordinate indexing
   (A) Taube, Mooers, Batten
   (B) Taube, Austin, Coates
   (C) Taube, Austin, Garfield
   (D) Mooers, Taube, Garfield

465. Indian National Bibliography does not include
   (A) Books published in India in English
   (B) Official reports
   (C) Books on India, published abroad
   (D) Books published in recognised Indian languages

466. The subject headings 'money' and 'inflation' are both used in a retrieval system
   (A) Be linked by a 'see also' reference
   (B) Be linked by 'see' reference
   (C) Be linked by both 'see' and 'see also' reference
   (D) Not be linked

467. The resource sharing strategy of a library may not include
   (A) Joint acquisition
   (B) Shared use
   (C) Exchange of materials
   (D) Restricted access

468. In KWIC index the keyword appears
   (A) At the beginning of each entry
   (B) at the centre of the line
   (C) as the highlighted word
   (D) at the end of the line

469. The relationship between the terms 'Ships' and "Boat" is
   (A) Syntactic relation (B) semantic relation
   (C) Both of them (D) Neither

470. What are bibliographical sources ?
   (A) Bibliography is presented in which
   (B) Which provide bibliographical informations.

(C) Which provide list of books
(D) Which provide bibliographical descriptions of the books.

471. The agency in India is responsible for assigning ISSN
(A) The National Library
(B) INSDOC
(C) INFLIBNET
(D) Raja Rammohan Roy Educational Resource Centre

472. Preparation, service, assimilation are the main stages involved in
(A) Initiation (B) User Education
(C) Reference Service (D) Bibliography

473. Desirableness of personal contact between reader and library material is stressed by
(A) H.P.Luhn (B) Derek Austin
(C) Samuel H.Green (D) S.C.Bradford

474. Identify the secondary source from the following
(A) Standards (B) Patents
(C) Journals (D) Directories

475. The procedures for chain indexing was developed by
(A) Jack Mills (B) C.A.Cutter
(C) S.R.Ranganathan (D) G.Bhattacharya

476. NATIS stands for
(A) National Information System
(B) National Technical Information System
(C) National Team for Information Science
(D) None of the above

477. Which type of service Mathematical Reviews is ?
(A) Indexing (B) Reprography
(C) Documentation (D) Abstracting

478. POPSI was developed by
(A) S.R.Ranganathan (B) A.Neelameghan
(C) B.S.Kesavan (D) G.Bhattacharya

479. Paul Otlet used the term 'Documentation' for the first time in a lecture at the International Congress at Brussels in

(A) 1905 (B) 1920
(C) 1931 (D) 1948

480. ISBN contains
(A) 6 digits
(B) 8 digits
(C) 10 digits
(D) 12 digits <presently 13 digits>

481. What was the title of LISA previously ?
(A) Libray Science Abstracts.
(B) Library and Information Science Academy.
(C) Library and Information Science Abstracts.
(D) Literature Search Academy.

482. European Translation Centre is located at
(A) Italy (B) France
(C) Netherland (D) Germany

483. Micropaedia is in how many volumes?
(A) 5 (B) 10
(C) 12 (D) 20

484. 'Facts on File' is published from
(A) India
(B) Africa
(C) USA
(D) Europe <leading publishers from 1941>

485. What is Bibliography
(A) A list of Books published
(B) A list of books available in a library
(C) A list of books available in two library
(D) A list of journals

486. Bibliographic service comes under
(A) Ready Reference Service
(B) Long Range Service
(C) Referral Service
(D) None of the above

487. McGraw-Hill is a
(A) Author (B) Printer
(C) Publisher (D) Librarian

488. 'Indian Science Abstract' is published by
   (A) INSDOC (presently NISCAIR)
   (B) ICSSR
   (C) DST
   (D) DRTC
489. Library week is celebrated on
   (A) 10th November (B) 14th November
   (C) 14th December (D) 25th December
490. Union Catalogue of Learned Periodicals in South Asia (Vol. 1) was complied and edited by :
   (A) Girija Kumar (B) N.M. Ketkar
   (C) S.R. Ranganathan (D) P.N. Kaula
491. Association is a
   (A) Personal Author (B) Pseudonymous Author
   (C) Periodical Publication (D) Corporate author
492. Lexicon refers to
   (A) Bibliography (B) Dictionary
   (C) Encyclopedia (D) Directory
493. To find an occurance of a term in a work which part of the work you refer
   (A) Contents (B) Chapters
   (C) Index (D) Title
494. The term 'thesaurus' is associated with
   (A) Directory (B) Bibliography
   (C) Dictionary (D) None of the above
495. CLRI (Central Leather Research Institute) is located at
   (A) Chennai (B) Calicut
   (C) Cochin (D) Cuttack
496. Census Atlas National Volume is an example of
   (A) Local (B) Historical
   (C) Demographic (D) Anthropologocal
497. COMPENDEX is the on-line Database on the subject:
   (A) Physics (B) Commerce and Export
   (C) Analytical Chemistry (D) Engineering
498. Routing of periodicals is:

(A) CAS (B) SDI
(C) Indexing Service (D) Abstracting Service

499. An indispensable function of Thesaurus is:
(A) Knowledge representation
(B) Problem solving
(C) Representation of relationship between concepts
(D) Knowledge engineering

500. Data about data is known as:
(E) Micro data (F) Database
(G) Metadata (H) Databank

501. The concept of Micro photography was developed by:
(E) Johan Gutenberg
(F) Chester cardson
(G) John Benjamin Dancer (1839)
(H) Ohi Battle

502. SSDC referred to the National Documentation Centre now known as:
(A) DESIDOC (B) SENDOC
(C) NISCOM (D) NASSDOC

503. Annual Convention of INFLIBNET organised to discuss the progress of the library automation and library services is known as:
(A) ISCON (B) NACLIN
(C) CALIBER (D) INFONET

504. Formulation of Research Hypothesis implies:
(E) Creating a legal basis for research
(F) Enunciation of Postulates
(G) Enumeration of canons
(H) Formation of tentative generalization

505. The study of Epistomology deals with:
(I) Modes of formation of subjects
(II) Classification of knowledge
(III) Cataloguing of composite books
(IV) Origin, source and nature of knowledge

In the type of items, there may be more than one answer. Identify the correct combination:

(A) I and II are correct
(B) II and III are correct
(C) I, II and III are correct
(D) II and IV are correct

506. Identify the correct chronological order in which they were setup:
(A) NASSDOC, RRRLF, DRTC, INSDOC
(B) RRRLF, INSDOC, NASSDOC, DRTC
(C) INSDOC(1952), DRTC (1962), NASSDOC (1970), RRRLF (1972)
(D) DRTC, INSDOC, NASSDOC, RRRLF

507. If two citations are called together, it is known as:
(A) Double citation (B) Twin citation
(C) Co-citation (D) Controlled citation

508. Grey literature means:
(A) The literature published by a publisher named as "Grey Publisher"
(B) The literature which is not published and is not available through normal book selling channels
(C) The literature published and made available in Grey shades
(D) The literature which is published and made available through special publishers

509. The smallest unit of data in a database is:
(A) Record (B) File
(C) Field (D) Table

510. Pre-coordinate indexing system is followed in:
(i) Chain Indexing (ii) POPSI
(iii) UNITERM (iv) PRECIS

Codes :
(A) (i) and (iv) are correct
(B) (i) (ii) and (iii) are correct
(C) (i) (ii) and (iv) are correct
(D) (ii) and (iv) are correct

511. ADONIS is a:
   (i) Bibliographic database only
   (ii) Numerical database only
   (iii) Full text database
   (iv) None of the above

   Codes :

   (A) (i) and (ii) are correct (B) (ii) and (iii) are correct
   (C) (iii) is correct (D) (iv) is correct

512. Primary sources include:
   (i) Thesis
   (ii) Patent
   (iii) Abstracting Periodical
   (iv) Periodical Article

   Codes :

   (A) (i) (ii) and (iii) are correct
   (B) (i) (iii) and (iv) are correct
   (C) (i) (ii) and (iv) are correct
   (D) (ii) (ii) and (iv) are correct

513. Select the right chronological sequence of information systems as per their year of establishment
   (A) INIS, AGRIS, NISSAT, Patent Information System (India)
   (B) AGRIS, NISSAT, INIS, Patent Information System (India)
   (C) Patent Information System (India), INIS, AGRIS, NISSAT
   (D) NISSAT, AGRIS, INIS, Patent Information System (India)

514. The author who defined Reference Service as the "Process of establishing contact between a reader and his documents in a personal way" is:
   (A) W.A.Katz (B) L.Shores
   (C) M.Hutchins (D) S.R.Ranganathan

515. Identify the odd one:
   (A) LISA (B) Psychological Abstracts
   (C) Index Medicus (D) World of Learning

516. Which of the following is not correctly matched?
    (A) DELNET – Telecommunication Network
    (B) Digital Library – Print Material
    (C) Thesaurus – List of Descriptors
    (D) ISBN – Serial Number

517. An entry in an Abstracting Journal consists of:
    (A) Bibliographic citation
    (B) An abstract and bibliographic citation
    (C) Annotation
    (D) Bibliographic citation, an abstract and initials of the abstractor

518. BNB adopted "Chain indexing" for the first time in:
    (E) 1950 (F) 1955
    (G) 1958 (H) 1970

519. Which of the following search devices will lead to an increase in the Recall output?
    (E) Boolean 'And' (F) Boolean 'Not'
    (G) Proximity Operators (H) Truncation

520. Orientation of library users is a kind of:
    (A) Reference Service
    (B) Referral Service
    (C) Current Awareness Service
    (D) Selective Dissemination of Information Service

521. Which of the following are produced by Institute of Scientific Information:
    (i) Science Citation Index
    (ii) Current Contents
    (iii) Index Medicus
    (iv) Atom Index

    Codes :
    (A) (i), (ii) and (iii) (B) (i) and (ii) only
    (C) (ii) and (III) only (D) (i) and (iv) only

522. The term 'Precision' to measure the performance of Information Retrieval Systems was suggested by:
    (A) S.R.Ranganathan (B) F.W.Lancaster
    (C) Cyril Cleverdon (D) H.P.Luhn

523. Which of the following would be the correct chronological sequence?
   (A) Bibliometrics, Informetrics, Librametry, Webometrics
   (B) Librametry, Bibliommetrics, Informetrics, Webometrics
   (C) Librametry, Informetrics, Bibliometrics, Webometrics
   (D) Bibliometrics, Informetrics, Webometrics, Librametry

524. Fundamental facts of research are available in
   (E) Primary sources
   (F) Secondary sources
   (G) Tertiary sources
   (H) None of the above

525. OCLC Project, MARC Project are the examples of:
   (E) Co-operative storage of materials
   (F) Co-operative acquisition of materials
   (G) Co-operative processing of materials
   (H) Co-operative stharing of materials

526. Dublin core is related to:
   (A) Metadata
   (B) MARC
   (C) ISBD
   (D) CCF

527. NICFOS is related to
   (A) Leather
   (B) Machine tools
   (C) Food Science
   (D) Atom

528. ISDN stands for:
   (A) International Standard Digital Network
   (B) International Standard Distributed Network
   (C) Integrated Services Digital Network
   (D) Integrated Services Distributed Network

529. The following is the search engine for scientific information only:
   (E) Google
   (F) SCIRUS
   (G) Yahoo
   (H) Alta Vista

530. OAI stands for:
   (E) Open Access Initiatives
   (F) Open Archives Initiatives

(G) On-line Archives Initiatives
(H) On-line Access Initiatives

531. "Search strategy is the mirror in the dark". Whose quotation is this?
(E) Kartz (F) Ranganathan
(G) Bliss (H) Cutter

532. INDEST is a
(E) Bibliography (F) Consortium
(G) Directory (H) Dictionary

533. Encyclopaedia of library and information science is published by:
(A) H.W.Wilson (B) R.R.Bowker
(C) Marcel Dekker (D) Andrew Deutsch

534. Arrange the following according to the work flow:
(I) Dissemination, Selection, Processing, Acquisition
(J) Selection, Processing, Acquisition, Dissemination
(K) Selection, Acquisition, Processing, Dissemination
(L) Processing, Acquisition, Dissemination, Selection

535. These documents are not primary sources:
(A) Thesis (B) Patents
(C) Conference Papers (D) Reference Books

536. World of Learning is:
(A) A Bibliography (B) An Abstract
(C) An Encyclopaedia (D) A Directory

537. Blog is a:
(E) Off-line Journal (F) Internet Journal
(G) Web Directory (H) Search Engine

538. This literature is not published and not available through normal book selling channels
(A) Grey Literature (B) Text Books
(C) Journals (D) None of the above

539. Library as a living system "takes a new matter, casts off old matter, changes in size and takes new shapes and term". Whose quotation is this?
(E) B.S.Kesavan (F) Melvil Dewey
(G) S.R.Ranganathan (H) W.C.B.Sayers

540. SCOPUS is a:
   (A) Full Text Database
   (B) Abstracts and Citation Database
   (C) Numerical Database
   (D) None of the above

541. Which of the following is not an Open Source Software?
   (E) Green Stone (F) D-Space
   (G) Plone (H) Delmark

542. NACLIN is sponsored by:
   (E) INFLIBNET (F) DELNET
   (G) AGRINET (H) CALIBNET

543. UNISIST, a project of UNESCO was launched in this year:
   (E) 1994 (F) 1972
   (G) 1958 (H) 2001

544. 'Dublin Core Metadata' consists of:
   (A) 11 elements (B) 13 elements
   (C) 10 elements (D) 15 elements

545. "The Wheat loan Educational Exchange Programme" was initiated in:
   (E) 1951 (F) 1972
   (G) 1981 (H) 1999

546. NISCAIR is a part of:
   (E) DST (F) ISRO
   (G) DSIR (H) CSIR

547. Use of Microfilming is considerably reduced due to:
   (A) Problems of preservation of microfilming
   (B) Need for use microfilm reader
   (C) Availability of better technology in the form of digitization
   (D) High cost involved in it.

548. Opaque paper is a:
   (E) Ultra-white paper (F) Ultra-white thin paper
   (G) Transparent paper (H) Non-Transparent paper

549. Which of the following is a public domain database:
    (A) INIS (B) AGRIS
    (C) Chemical Abstracts (D) MEDLINE
550. One of the following journal is published in UK:
    (A) Library Quarterly
    (B) Program
    (C) Libri
    (D) Herald of Library Science
551. Which of the following does not fall into the category of pre-coordinate indexing
    (A) Chain indexing
    (B) Uniform indexing
    (C) LCSH
    (D) Sear's List of Subject Headings
552. Which of the following is not associated with communication system?
    (A) Receiver (B) Sender
    (C) Channel (D) Entropy
553. Subject indexing systems were developed in the order as:
    (A) Chain indexing, Systematic indexing (Kaiser), PRECIS, COMPASS
    (B) Systematic indexing (1911), Chain indexing (1934), PRECIS (1969), COMPASS (1991)
    (C) Systematic indexing, PRECIS, Chain indexing, COMPASS
    (D) Systematic indexing, COMPASS, Chain indexing, PRECIS
554. Which is the primary source for finding out Indian periodicals in Agriculture?
    (A) Ulrich International Periodical Directory
    (B) Reference Asia
    (C) Press in India
    (D) INFA Yearbook
555. Which of the following indexes only papers presented in the conferences?

(A) LISA
(B) Current Research Abstracts
(C) Reseach-in-Progress
(D) ISTP

556. Recall and Precision ratios are used in the evaluation of
(A) Reference service
(B) Information retrieval
(C) Bibliographic service
(D) Document delivery service

557. Number of digits in ISBN now are
(A) 10 digits (B) 11 digits
(C) 12 digits (D) 13 digits

558. 'Emerald' is the database of
(A) Gems and jewelary literature
(B) Medical Science literature
(C) Library and Information Science literature
(D) Earth Science literature

559. A gazette gives information about
(A) Places of tourist interest
(B) History of places
(C) Official announcement and notification
(D) Old records

560. PRESTEL is an example of
(A) Teletext services (B) Videotext
(C) E-mail (D) OPAC

561. With which agency did UNESCO collaborate to establish UNISIST?
(A) ICSU (B) FID
(C) IFLA (D) ILA19.

562. Which university appointed the first full time university librarian?
(A) Delhi University (B) Punjab University
(C) Madras University (D) Calcutta University

563. Arrange according to year of establishment.

(A) Chemical Abstracts (1907), Biological Abstracts (1926), Science Citation index (1961), Indian Science Abstracts (1965)
(B) Chemical Abstracts, Science Citation Index, Indian Science Index, Indian Science Abstracts
(C) Biological Abstracts, Chemical Abstracts, Science Citation Index, Indian Science Abstracts
(D) Chemical Abstracts, Biological Abstracts, Indian Science Abstracts, Science Citation Index

564. The quotation "Where is the Wisdom, We Lost in Knowledge.." is by
(I) John Keats (J) M.P.Carter
(K) T.S.Eliot (L) Marshall McLuhan

565. Entropy is a measure of
(E) Degree of relevance of information
(F) Quantity of irrelevant information
(G) Degree of uncertainty in information
(H) Degree of certainty in information

566. An E-book which does not require an internet connection to access its contents is
(E) Web book (F) Palm book
(G) Electronic Ink e-book (H) Digital book

567. Emerald full text database is published from
(A) USA (B) Germany
(C) France (D) UK

568. Who propounded 'Conservative, moderate and liberal theories of reference service'?
(A) William A.Katz (B) S.R.Ranganathan
(C) James I. Wyer (D) R.Emery

569. The input centre for INIS in India is
(E) DRDO (F) DSIR
(G) TFIR (H) BARC

570. The Boolean operator 'AND' is related to
(E) Productive (F) Additive
(G) Logical Difference (H) None of the above

571. The simple Dublin Core Metadata Element Set (DCMES) consists of

(A) 10 elements (B) 15 elements

(C) 14 elements (D) 18 elements

572. 'Libraries as Gateways to Knowledge' is the title of the document

(E) National Information Policy, 1986

(F) Information Technology Act, 2000

(G) National Knowledge Commission on Libraries, 2007

(H) None of the above

573. Arrange the following bibliographies according to their date of origin:

(i) Indian National Bibliography

(ii) Cumulative Book Index

(iii) Book in Print

(iv) British National Bibliography

Codes:

(A) (iii) (iv) (i) (ii) (B) (ii) (iii) (iv) (i)

(C) (i) (ii) (iii) (iv) (D) (iv) (ii) (i) (iii)

574. Notification of new arrivals in the library is:

(A) SDI service

(B) Reference service

(C) Current awareness service

(D) Referral service

575. Who started Reference service in India for the first time

(A) B.S. Kesavan (B) M.A. Gopinath

(C) W.A.Bordan (D) S.R.Ranganathan

576. A type of indexing where terms are coordinated prior to searching

(A) Post coordinate indexing

(B) Pre coordinate indexing

(C) Uniterm indexing

(D) None of the above

577. Use of integrated circuits was made in

(E) First Generation Computers
(F) Secord Generation Computers
(G) Third Generation Computers
(H) Fourth Generation Computers

578. Arrange the following secondary publications according to the beginning of their publication in chronological order

(i) Biological Abstracts (1926)
(ii) Chemical Abstracts (1907)
(iii) LISA
(iv) Index Medicus

Codes:

(A) (i), (ii), (iii), (iv) (B) (i), (iii), (ii), (iv)
(C) (ii), (i), (iii), (iv) (D) (iii), (i), (iv), (ii)

579. ISBN changed from 10 digits to 13 from

(A) January, 2007 (B) January, 2008
(C) January, 2006 (D) January, 2005

580. WorldCat is maintained by

(A) Library of Congress
(B) Online Computer Library Center
(C) American Library Association
(D) None of the above

581. When a source referred to once in the footnote is referred to again and between them no other reference (i.e. citation) intervenes, then the footnote uses the abbreviation

(A) Ibid (B) Id
(C) Op.Cit. (D) None of the above

582. Indexing system in which the coordination of terms is done at the search stage was first introduced by

(A) S.R.Ranganathan (B) Derek Austin
(C) Mortimer Taube (D) H.P.Luhn

583. Index Medicus is brought out as printed publication

(A) Quarterly (B) Monthly
(C) Weekly (D) Has ceased publication

584. Which publication was not authored by S.R.Ranganathan?
    (A) Prolegomena to library classification
    (B) Reference Service
    (C) Ramanujan: The man and the Mathematician
    (D) Living with Books
585. JSTOR is an online system for archiving and accessing academic journals. It is located in
    (A) Germany (B) UK
    (C) USA (D) Budapest
586. NAPLIS document was prepared by a committee appointed by Department of ...., Govt. Of India.
    (A) Education
    (B) Information and Broadcasting
    (C) Culture
    (D) Information Technolgy
587. ALA Glossary of Library Terms defines the National Library as 'a library maintained by a ......
    (A) Province (B) Nation
    (C) County (D) State.
588. Dr. S. R. Ranganathan has grouped the users in to four categories such as i] general i] ordinary iii] freshman iv]........
    (A) students (B) specialist inquirer
    (C) public (D) researchers
589. Which is one of the indirect methods of knowing the user's needs.
    (A) Citatioinanalysis (B) Interviews
    (C) Field Survey (D) Using Statics
590. Introduction the user to the general methods of library usage and service is called
    (A) Orientation (B) Instruction
    (C) Initiation (D) Induction
591. Which one of the following is attemted to make user education programmes initiated in less developed Countries ?

(A) INIS (B) AGRIS
(C) NISSAT (D) UNISIST

592. The user profile is a
(A) List of descriptors
(B) List of useful citation
(C) List of records.
(D) Statement on user information neds.

593. 'Cyber Dewey' is an individual effort by
(A) David A. Mundie (B) Benjamin A Custer
(C) J.P. Comaromi (D) H.J. Ferguson

594. Atom Index is a computerised database developed by.
(A) MEDLARS (B) INIS
(C) AGRIS (D) DEVSIS

595. Which of the followings serves as a national centre for India to AGRIS:
(A) ARIC (B) ASIC
(C) PID (D) NISTAD

596. What is National bibliography?
(A) List of books of National Library
(B) List of books published in a particular Nation
(C) List of books written by National government
(D) List of books on a nation

597. What is the suitable reference sources to know about the information of a particular place?
(A) Directory (B) Gazetteer
(C) Encyclopedia (D) Year book

598. What is the suitable reference sources to find out the list of historical monuments of Delhi?
(A) Atlas (B) Gazetteer
(C) Guide book (D) Globe

599. The secondary source of information comprised of:
(A) Text books and research monographs.
(B) Subject periodicals and encyclopedias
(C) Indexing and Abstracting periodicals
(D) Bibliography and patents

600. Article published in research journal are...
   (A) Reference sources (B) Secondary sources
   (C) Primary sources (D) Tertiary sources
601. Generally the information sources are divided mainly in to following categories?
   (A) Primary and secondary.
   (B) Reference and information sources.
   (C) Documentary and non-documentary
   (D) Books and periodicals
602. In Sears List of Subject Headings 'XX' is use to denote.
   (A) See reference (B) See also reference
   (C) Cross reference (D) General reference
603. CAS is defined as
   (A) A process of dissemination of information
   (B) A process of information
   (C) A process of dissemination of current information
   (D) A simple information service
604. Today which type of information sources is most useful?
   (A) Reference sources
   (B) Documentary source
   (C) Non- Documentary source
   (D) Both the Documentary and Non-Documentary sources
605. World of learning is a what source of information
   (A) Primary source (B) Documentary source
   (C) Secondary source (D) Tertiary source
606. FAIRS, the retrieval system of US Federal Aviation agency was evaluated by
   (A) D.E. Berninger (B) C.W. Cleverdon
   (C) F.W. Lancaster (D) B.C. Vickery
607. The term "Information Service" is an improvised name
   (A) Administration (B) Documentation
   (C) Bibliography (D) Reference service
608. Which of the following is a specialized information organization online tool?

(A) Mamma (B) Dogpile
(C) Vivisimo (D) Entireweb

609. What is the Thesaurus?
(A) A collection of selected terminology
(B) Synonymous terms
(C) List of words
(D) All of the above

610. Research periodicals are which category of sources?
(A) Primary (B) Secondary
(C) Tertiary (D) Non documentary.

611. What are non- documentary sources?
(A) Which are in printed form?
(B) Which are in not printed form?
(C) Which are nor documents
(D) None of these

612. Reference sources are those
(A) Which are large in size?
(B) Which are read at home easily?
(C) Which used to obtain particular information?
(D) Which are costly?

613. Facts of File is weekly digest of
(A) Indian events (B) American events
(C) World events (D) England events

614. What is Trade bibliography?
(A) List of Author Bibliography
(B) List of Special Bibliography
(C) List of books in print or for sale compiled by a publisher
(D) List of books of trade Library

615. Compton year book contains
(A) Political events (B) Cultural events
(C) Outstanding events (D) Economic events

616. What is the meaning of E-Documents?
(A) All Documents other than printed
(B) Non-Paper documents

(C) In electronic form such as Cassettes, CD-ROMs, etc.

(D) Audio visual tools

617. Online Europa year book has coverage since

(A) 1965 (B) 1975
(C) 1984 (D) 1985

618. Which of the following is not the documents?

(A) Manuscript (B) Book
(C) Inscription (D) Periodical

619. What is the publication frequency of books in print?

(A) Monthly (B) Weekly
(C) Annually (D) Quarterly

620. Which part of new encyclopedia Britannica is useful for ready references?

(A) Macropaedia (B) Propaedia
(C) Micropaedia (D) Premedia

621. How many volumes Micropaedia of new Encyclopedia Britannica is published?

(A) 2 (B) 10
(C) 11 (D) 12

622. Year book are also known as

(A) Hand book (B) Annual
(C) Directory (D) Dictionary

623. Which of the following are not the secondary sources?

(A) Encyclopedia (B) Digest
(C) Thesis (D) Text book

624. What do you call a collection of maps, tables, charts, etc.?

(A) Globe (B) Gazetteer
(C) Atlas (D) Map

625. Encyclopedia Americana consists of

(A) 20 Volumes (B) 25 Volumes
(C) 28 Volumes (D) 30 Volumes

626. CAN SEARCH has been designed to provide access to literature for:

(A) X-ray Therapy (B) Lung Therapy
(C) Cancer Therapy (D) Drug Therapy

627. Feedback mechanism is a part of which service?
(A) Reprography service (B) CAS
(C) Translation service (D) SDI

628. The person who provides reference service is called
(A) Chief librarian
(B) Grade One Librarian
(C) Deputy Librarian
(D) Reference Librarian

629. Sci/Tech reference plus, CD-ROM data base is being brought out by
(A) Bowker-Saur (B) BLDSC
(C) OCLC (D) NLM

630. Where did Dr. S. R. Ranganathan put forth his five laws of library science?
(A) Meenakshi college, Annamalainagar
(B) Hindu College, New Delhi
(C) City College, Bangalore
(D) Christ College, Bangalore

631. CD-ROM' DXS is a data exchange standard developed by
(A) MacMillan (B) DIALOG
(C) Silver Platter (D) CD Plus

632. The internet search tool 'Archei' was developed by
(A) Univ. of Nevada (B) Univ. of Minnesota
(C) McGill Univ. (D) Colombia Univ.

633. Word of learning is a what source of information
(A) Primary source (B) Documentary source
(C) Secondary source (D) Tertiary source

634. Indian books in Print are published from?
(A) Tamil nadu (B) Chennai
(C) Bombay (D) Kolkata

635. Cumulative book index is published from?
(A) India (B) USA
(C) Canada (D) Thailand

636. Statesman year book is published from?
   (A) London (B) New york
   (C) Calcutta (D) Chicago

637. Thesaurus is used as a fool for
   (A) Abstracting (B) Cataloging
   (C) Classification (D) Indexing

638. "Reference service is the contact between the right reader and the right book in the right pers
   (A) D J Fockett
   (B) S R Ranganathan
   (C) James I Wyer
   (D) A.L.A Glossary of library terms

639. The person who expounded five principles of theasaurus construction was
   (A) A.S. Raizada (B) G.Bhattacharya
   (C) Salton (D) K.Ravi Chand Rao

640. Americana is an example of:
   (A) Distillation (B) Fusion
   (C) Custer (D) Agglomeration

641. In which year the ISBN allocation office in India shifted from Kolkatta to Delhi?
   (A) 2009 (B) 2010
   (C) 2011 (D) 2012

642. Who published the journal International classification?
   (A) IFLA (B) UNESCO
   (C) ISKO (D) ALA

643. Abstracting periodicals Who categorized information source into conventional, non conventional, neo conventional and micro documents?
   (A) Ranganthan (B) Bradford
   (C) Grogan (D) Henson

644. Who is the editor of "Library Herald" ?
   (A) Krishan Kumar (B) C. K. Sharma
   (C) S. R. Ranganathan (D) F.Monbray Volte

645. Who was Published the monthly Journal "The Library World'?

(A) Krishankumar (B) J. D. Brown

(C) H. W. Wilson (D) K. Navlavi

646. The process of collectionof things of the same kind and grounded together is known as

(A) Cluster (B) Fusion

(C) Fission (D) Agglomeration

647. Who is the first editor of "Modern Librarian"?

(A) F.Monbrary Volte

(B) Dr. S. R. Ranganathan

(C) J. D. Brown

(D) Krishan Kumar

648. Indian national Bibliographical first appeared in?

(A) 1947 (B) 1957

(C) 1967 (D) 1937

649. Who is the author of "Dictionary of anonymous and pseudonymous literature"?

(A) S. Halkett& J. Laing (B) Robert Proctor

(C) Ralph De sols (D) Hanuman Sastri

650. Reference Manual for Machine Readable Bibliographic Description was brought out in 1974 by :

(A) IFLA (B) FID

(C) UNESCO (D) ALA

651. The number of major components comprise in a bibliographic record of a document are

(A) Three (B) Four

(C) Six (D) Eight

652. Which of the following is a multi-subject gateway?

(A) Renardus (B) Humbul

(C) Sapling (D) EdWEb

653. What is India: A reference annual?

(A) Year Book (B) Almonac

(C) Gide book (D) Hand book

654. What is the suitable reference sources to know about the information of a particular place?

(A) Directory (B) Gazetteer

(C) Encyclopedia (D) Year book

655. What is the suitable reference sources to find out the list of historical monuments of Delhi?
(A) Atlas (B) Gazetteer
(C) Guide book (D) Globe

656. Pseudo series is the creation of:
(A) Publisher (B) CCC
(C) Author (D) AACR-2

657. Cranefield Project Phase 2 studied
(A) Indexing System (B) No. of Variables
(C) Classification System (D) Retrieval System

658. Roots Thesaurus was published by
(A) Two Volumes (B) Three Volumes
(C) Four Volumes (D) Five Volumes

659. UNCSCO/ PGI brought out 3rd edition of CCF in
(A) List of books of National Library
(B) List of books published in a particular Nation
(C) List of books written by National government
(D) List of books on a nation

660. In Which five year plan the INFLIBNET was established?
(A) Fourth five year plan (B) Fifth five year plan
(C) sixth five year plan (D) seventh five year plan

661. Who is the publishers of Sear's list of subject headings?
(A) Dr. S. R. Ranganathan
(B) Brown
(C) H. W. Wilson
(D) C. A. Cutter

662. Which one is E-Bibliographic database?
(A) Nature (B) Blackwell
(C) ISID (D) Springer

663. LANCET rules designed to be used in conjunction with AACR was published by
(A) ALA (B) CLA
(C) LA (D) L.C

664. The COS ATI Rules pertain to cataloguing of

(A) Social Science Rules
(B) Humanities Rules
(C) Technical Rules
(D) Scientific and Technical Rules

665. The famous "Ninety One Rules" for cataloguing was developed by
(A) C.C. Jewette (B) A. Panizzi
(C) C.A. Cutter (D) S. Lubctzky

666. The symbols NT, BT and RT are used in
(A) LCSH (B) PRECIS
(C) POPSI (D) KWOC

667. In which of the following the symbols UR and SA arc used.
(A) Roget's Thesaurus (B) LCSH
(C) Sear's List (D) Relative Index

668. Which national agency in India is responsible for assigning the ISBN?
(A) RRRLF
(B) BARC
(C) NCL
(D) National Library of India

669. What is full text e-Resource?
(A) JCCC
(B) ISID
(C) Science finder scholar
(D) American chemical society

670. Role of indicators are found in
(A) POPSI (B) KWIC
(C) KWOC (D) PRECIS

671. To derive class index entries fromm class number is known as
(A) Uniterm Indexing (B) Citation Indexing
(C) Coordinate Indexing (D) Chain Indexing.

672. UNO, UNIDO, FAO, WHO, UNSECO, are examples of:
(A) Committies (B) Commissions
(C) Institutions (D) Government bodies

673. Who is the publisher of Encyclopedia of Library and information science?

(A) Boweker (B) H.W.Wilson company

(C) M.Dekker (D) H.W.Wilson

674. Retrospective search service is a type of?

(A) Referral service (B) Responsive service

(C) CAS (D) SDI

675. Who is the publisher of Asian Recorder

(A) Academic Press (B) Bowker & Company

(C) Mc Millan & Co. (D) K.K.Thomas

676. What are bibliographical source?

(A) Bibliography is presented in which.

(B) Which provide bibliographical informations.

(C) Which provide list of books.

(D) Which provide bibliographical descriptions of the books.

677. Library Technology Report is a publication of?

(A) ALA (B) IASLIC

(C) LA (D) ILA

678. ABGILA is a quarterly publication of?

(A) Assam Library Association

(B) Andhra Desa Library Association

(C) Indian Library Association

(D) Raja Ram Mohun Roy Foundation

679. Which of the following are not the secondary sources?

(A) Encyclopedia (B) Digest

(C) Thesis (D) Text book

680. Match the following and choose the correct answer from the codes given below :

List A	**List B**
(1) World of learning	a. Alphabetical
(2) Sear's list of subject headings	b. Classified
(3) Roget's International Thesaurus	c. Geographical
(4) Indian National Bibliography	d. Topical.

Codes:	**(1)**	**(2)**	**(3)**	**(4)**
(A)	b	d	a	c
(B)	c	a	d	b
(C)	a	b	c	d
(D)	d	a	b	c

681. Match the following :

List – I	**List – II**
(A) Books in print	(i) Bibliography of periodicals
(B) Ulrich International Periodical Directory	(ii) Trade Bibliography
(C) World of Learning	(iii) Biographical source
(D) Who's Who in India	(iv) Directory

Codes:	**(a)**	**(b)**	**(c)**	**(d)**
(A)	(ii)	(i)	(iv)	(iii)
(B)	(i)	(ii)	(iii)	(iv)
(C)	(iii)	(i)	(iv)	(ii)
(D)	(i)	(iii)	(iv)	(ii)

682. Match the following :

List – I	**List – II**
(A) E.J. Coates	(i) KWIC
(B) H.P. Luhn	(ii) Things, Property, Material, Action
(C) Derek Austin	(iii) Concrete and process
(D) J. Kaiser	(iv) PRECIS

Codes:	**(a)**	**(b)**	**(c)**	**(d)**
(A)	(i)	(ii)	(iii)	(iv)
(B)	(ii)	(i)	(iv)	(iii)
(C)	(iii)	(ii)	(i)	(iv)
(D)	(iv)	(i)	(ii)	(iii)

683. Match the following :

List – I	**List – II**
(A) NTC	(i) UK
(B) ITC	(ii) India
(C) BLDSC	(iii) Netherlands
(D) NISCAIR	(iv) USA

Codes:	**(a)**	**(b)**	**(c)**	**(d)**
(A)	(iv)	(iii)	(i)	(ii)
(B)	(ii)	(i)	(iv)	(iii)
(C)	(i)	(iii)	(ii)	(iv)
(D)	(i)	(ii)	(iii)	(iv)

684. Match the following :

List – I	**List – II**
(A) Elements of Library Classification	(i) D.J. Desolla Price
(B) Little Science Big Science	(ii) S.R. Ranganathan
(C) Documentation	(iii) D.J. Fosket
(D) Subject Approach to Information	(iv) S.C. Bradford

Codes:	**(a)**	**(b)**	**(c)**	**(d)**
(A)	(ii)	(i)	(iv)	(iii)
(B)	(iii)	(ii)	(i)	(iv)
(C)	(iv)	(ii)	(iii)	(i)
(D)	(i)	(ii)	(iii)	(iv)

685. Match the following :

List – I	**List – II**
(A) SENDOC	(i) Social Sciences
(B) INPADOC	(ii) Sciences
(C) NASSDOC	(iii) Patents
(D) INSDOC (NISCAIR)	(iv) Small Scale Industries

Codes:	**(a)**	**(b)**	**(c)**	**(d)**
(A)	(ii)	(iii)	(iv)	(i)
(B)	(i)	(ii)	(iii)	(iv)
(C)	(iv)	(iii)	(i)	(ii)
(D)	(iii)	(iv)	(i)	(ii)

686. Match the following

List – I	**List – II**
(A) Books in Print	(i) Directory
(B) World of Learning	(ii) Trade bibliography
(C) Keesing's Record of World Events	(iii) Travel guide
(D) Fodor's Guide to India	(iv) Newspaper digest

Codes:	(a)	(b)	(c)	(d)
(A)	(ii)	(i)	(iv)	(iii)
(B)	(ii)	(iii)	(i)	(iv)
(C)	(iv)	(i)	(ii)	(iii)
(D)	(iii)	(ii)	(i)	(iv)

687. Arrange the following secondary publications according to the beginning of their publication in chronological order.

(i) Biological Abstracts
(ii) Chemical Abstracts
(iii) LISA
(iv) IndexMedicus

Codes :

(A) (i), (ii), (iii), (iv) (B) (i), (iii), (ii), (iv)
(C) (ii), (i), (iii), (iv) (D) (iii), (i), (iv), (ii)

688. Match the following :

List – I	**List – II**
(A) NASSDOC	(i) Defence Science
(B) DEVSIS	(ii) Social Sciences
(C) INIS	(iii) Development Science
(D) DESIDOC	(iv) NuclearScience

Codes:	(a)	(b)	(c)	(d)
(A)	(iv)	(ii)	(i)	(iii)
(B)	(ii)	(iii)	(iv)	(i)
(C)	(i)	(ii)	(iii)	(iv)
(D)	(iii)	(ii)	(i)	(iv)

689. Match the following :

List-I	**List-II**
(A) Search Engine	(i) Internet Explorer
(B) Subject Gateway	(ii) Dogpile
(C) Net Browser	(iii) FTP
(D) Meta Search Engine	(iv) SOSIG
	(v) Altavista

Codes:	**(a)**	**(b)**	**(c)**	**(d)**
(A)	(iv)	(iii)	(ii)	(i)
(B)	(v)	(iv)	(i)	(ii)
(C)	(v)	(i)	(ii)	(iii)
(D)	(v)	(i)	(iv)	(ii)

690. Match the following :

List-I	**List-II**
(A) Origin of a word	(i) World of Learning
(B) Synonyms for a word	(ii) Dictionary of Etymology
(C) How to install a gadget	(iii) Encyclopedia
(D) Address of Oxford University	(iv) Manual
	(v) Thesaurus

Codes:	**(a)**	**(b)**	**(c)**	**(d)**
(A)	(ii)	(v)	(iv)	(iii)
(B)	(v)	(iii)	(iv)	(i)
(C)	(v)	(iv)	(i)	(iii)
(D)	(ii)	(v)	(iv)	(i)

691. Match the following :

List-I	**List-II**
(A) IFLA	(i) Science Citation Index
(B) Unesco	(ii) First search
(C) OCLC	(iii) Patent Information
(D) ISI	(iv) Public Library Manifesto
	(v) Universal Availability of Publications

Codes:	**(a)**	**(b)**	**(c)**	**(d)**
(A)	(iii)	(iv)	(ii)	(i)
(B)	(iv)	(iii)	(i)	(ii)
(C)	(v)	(iv)	(ii)	(i)
(D)	(v)	(i)	(iv)	(ii)

692. Match the following :

List-I	**List-II**
(A) E-Mail	(i) Bulletin Board
(B) FTP	(ii) Remote Log In
(C) TELNET	(iii) Library Network
(D) USENET	(iv) Moving/Downloading Files
	(v) Exchanging Message

Codes:	**(a)**	**(b)**	**(c)**	**(d)**
(A)	(iv)	(iii)	(v)	(i)
(B)	(v)	(iv)	(ii)	(i)
(C)	(ii)	(iv)	(i)	(iii)
(D)	(v)	(i)	(iv)	(iii)

693. Match the following:

List-I (Abbreviation)	**List-II (Meaning)**
I. Ibid	a. See
II. Loc. Cit.	b. Previously cited
III. Op.cit.	c. Same reference cited immediately above
IV. Vide	d. The same place cited

Codes:

(A) I-a, II-b, III-C, IV-d

(B) I-b, II-a, III-d, IV-c

(C) I-c, II-d, III-b, IV-a

(D) I-d, II-c, III-a, IV-b

694. Match the following:

List-I (Types of users of information)	**List-II (Purpose of use of information)**
V. Students	a. Decision making
VI. Professionals	b. To impart knowledge
VII. Government Officials	c. To prepare for the course programme
VIII. Teachers	d. To pursue their respective vocation

Codes:

(A) I-c, II-d, III-a, IV-b

(B) I-d, II-a, III-b, IV-c

(C) I-c, II-b, III-d, IV-a

(D) I-b, II-b, III-c, IV-d

695. Match the following:

List-I (Database)	**List-II (Supplier)**
I. ERIC USA	a. American Chemical Society,
II. C.A.Search	b. Bowker& Saur London
III. Books in Print	c. R.R.Bowker USA
IV. LISA USA	d. National Institute of Education,

Codes:

(A) I-d, II-a, III-c, IV-b

(B) (B) I-d, II-b, III-a, IV-c

(C) (C) I-b, II-c, III-a, IV-d

(D) (D) I-a, II-d, III-b, IV-b

696. Match the following:

List-I	**List-II**
I. ILRC (Inter Library Resource Centre)	a. Science and Technology
II. NISSAT	b. Indexing Service
III. Journal of Librarianship	c. UK
IV. INIS Atomindex	d. Delhi

Codes:

(A) I-a, II-b, III-d, IV-c (B) I-b, II-c, III-a, IV-d

(C) I-d, II-a, III-c, IV-b (D) I-c, II-d, III-d, IV-a

697. Match the following:

List-I	**List-II**
I. POPSI	a. P.M.Roget
II. Citation Indexing	b. H.P.Luhn
III. Keyword Indexing	c. Eugene Garfield
IV. Thesaurus	d. G.Bhattacharyya

Codes:

(A) I-b, II-d, III-a, IV-c (B) I-c, II-d, III-a, IV-b

(C) I-d, II-c, III-b, IV-a (D) I-a, II-b, III-d, IV-c

698. Match the following:

List-I (Technical Terms)	**List-II (Meaning)**
I. Thesaurus	a. Collection of programmes for the Computer System
II. Windows	b. A revolving disc on which data is stored
III. Microprocessors	c. A graphical user interface created as DOS Extension by Microsoft
IV. Software	d. A multi user Operating System
	e. A classified dictionary of synonyms

Codes:

(A) I-b, II-d, III-c, IV-a
(B) I-c, II-e, III-a, IV-d
(C) I-e, II-c, III-b, IV-a
(D) I-c, II-d, III-a, IV-b

699. Match the following:

List-I	**List-II**
I. Browser	a. Google
II. Operating System	b. 'C'
III. Programming language	c. Internet Explorer
IV. Search Engine	d. Windows

Codes:

(A) I-a, II-c, III-b, IV-d
(B) I-c, II-b, III-d, IV-a
(C) I-c, II-d, III-b, IV-a
(D) I-d, II-b, III-c, IV-a

700. Match the following:

List-I	**List-II**
I. INIS	a. Ohio
II. AGRIS	b. Delhi
III. OCLC	c. Vienna
IV. NICNET	d. Rome

Codes:

(A) I-c, II-a, III-b, IV-d (B) I-b, II-d, III-c, IV-a

(C) I-d, II-c, III-a, IV-b (D) I-c, II-d, III-a, IV-b

701. Match the following:

List-I	**List-II**
(a) Translation Service	(i) BLDSC
(b) Information Repackaging Services	(ii) DELNET
(c) Document Delivery Service	(iii) ITC
(d) Library Networking Centre (IAC)	(iv) Information Analysis
(v) DRTC	

Codes:	**(a)**	**(b)**	**(c)**	**(d)**
(A)	(ii)	(iv)	(i)	(iii)
(B)	(iii)	(iv)	(i)	(ii)
(C)	(v)	(iv)	(ii)	(i)
(D)	(iii)	(v)	(iv)	(ii)

702. Match the following

List-I	**List-II**
(a) Z39.50	(i) Standard for Document Description
(b) ISO 9000	(ii) Standard for Library Building
(c) ISO 2709	(iii) Information Retrieval
(d) ISBD (G)	(iv) Quality Related Standards
	(v) Bibliographic Record Structure

Codes:	**(a)**	**(b)**	**(c)**	**(d)**
(A)	(iii)	(iv)	(v)	(i)
(B)	(iv)	(v)	(ii)	(iii)
(C)	(v)	(iv)	(ii)	(i)
(D)	(iv)	(iii)	(v)	(ii)

703. Match the following:

List-I	**List-II**
(a) Classarus	(i) Jean Aitchinson
(b) Relative Index	(ii) J.L.Ferradane
(c) Thesauro facet	(iii) S.R.Ranganathan
(d) Relational Indexing	(iv) G.Bhattacharya
(v) Melville Dewey	

Codes:	**(a)**	**(b)**	**(c)**	**(d)**
(A)	(iii)	(i)	(ii)	(v)
(B)	(iv)	(v)	(i)	(ii)
(C)	(ii)	(v)	(i)	(iii)
(D)	(iii)	(ii)	(i)	(v)

704. Match the following:

List-I	**List-II**
(e) CCF	(i) OCLC
(f) UNIMARC	(ii) American Library Association
(g) DUBLIN CORE	(iii) Library of Congress
(h) USMARC	(iv) Unesco
(v) IFLA	

Codes:	**(a)**	**(b)**	**(c)**	**(d)**
(A)	(v)	(iv)	(i)	(iii)
(B)	(iv)	(v)	(i)	(ii)
(C)	(iii)	(v)	(iv)	(ii)
(D)	(ii)	(iv)	(v)	(i)

705. Match the following:

List-I (Publication)	**List-II (Institution/System)**
(a) AGRINDEX	(i) INSPEC
(b) ATOMINDEX	(ii) National Library of Medicine
(c) Physical Abstracts	(iii) AGRIS
(d) INDEX MEDICUS	(iv) INIS

Codes:	**(a)**	**(b)**	**(c)**	**(d)**
(A)	(iv)	(i)	(iii)	(ii)
(B)	(i)	(iii)	(iv)	(ii)
(C)	(iii)	(iv)	(i)	(ii)
(D)	(i)	(ii)	(iii)	(iv)

706. Match the following:

List-I (Contribution)	**List-II (Organisation)**
(a) Public Library Manifesto	(i) DRTC
(b) POPSI	(ii) Library of Congress
(c) UDC	(iii) UNESCO
(d) MARC	(iv) FID

Codes:	**(a)**	**(b)**	**(c)**	**(d)**
(A)	(i)	(ii)	(iii)	(iv)
(B)	(ii)	(i)	(iii)	(iv)
(C)	(iii)	(i)	(iv)	(ii)
(D)	(iv)	(ii)	(iii)	(i)

707. Match the following:

List-I	**List-II**
(a) Origin of a word	(i) World of Learning
(b) Synonyms for a word	(ii) Dictionary of Etymology
(c) How to install a gadget	(iii) Encyclopedia
(d) Address of Oxford University	(iv) Manual
(v) Thesaurus	

Codes:	**(a)**	**(b)**	**(c)**	**(d)**
(A)	(ii)	(v)	(iv)	(iii)
(B)	(v)	(iii)	(iv)	(i)
(C)	(v)	(iv)	(i)	(iii)
(D)	(ii)	(v)	(iv)	(i)

708. Match the following:

List-I	**List-II**
(a) Biological Abstracts	(i) H.W.Wilson
(b) Statesman Yearbook	(ii) NISCAIR
(c) Indian Science Abstracts	(iii) Institute of Scientific Information
(d) Cumulative Book List	(iv) U N Statistical Office

Codes:	**(a)**	**(b)**	**(c)**	**(d)**
(A)	(i)	(iii)	(iv)	(ii)
(B)	(iii)	(iv)	(ii)	(i)
(C)	(iv)	(ii)	(iii)	(i)
(D)	(ii)	(iii)	(i)	(iv)

709. Match the following:

List-I	**List-II**
(a) NISCAIR	(i) MINISIS
(b) DESIDOC	(ii) LibSys
(c) IDRC	(iii) Granthalaya
(d) INFOTEK	(iv) Sanjay
(v) SLIM	

Codes:	**(a)**	**(b)**	**(c)**	**(d)**
(A)	(ii)	(v)	(iii)	(iv)
(B)	(i)	(ii)	(v)	(iv)
(C)	(iii)	(ii)	(i)	(v)
(D)	(iii)	(iv)	(i)	(ii)

710. Match the following:

List-I	**List-II**
(a) Journal of Librarianship	(i) Delhi
(b) Herald of Library Science	(ii) London
(c) Library Herald	(iii) New York
(d) Library Literature	(iv) Lucknow
	(v) Canada

Codes:	**(a)**	**(b)**	**(c)**	**(d)**
(A)	(ii)	(iv)	(i)	(iii)
(B)	(iv)	(iii)	(i)	(v)
(C)	(iii)	(ii)	(v)	(iv)
(D)	(ii)	(i)	(iv)	(iii)

711. Match the following:

List-I	**List-II**
(a) INIS	(i) 1950
(b) AGRIS	(ii) 1970
(c) INPADOC	(iii) 1972
(d) OCLC	(iv) 1974
	(v) 1967

Codes:	**(a)**	**(b)**	**(c)**	**(d)**
(A)	(iv)	(iii)	(ii)	(v)
(B)	(ii)	(iv)	(iii)	(v)
(C)	(i)	(iv)	(ii)	(iii)
(D)	(ii)	(iii)	(v)	(iv)

712. Match the following:

List-I	**List-II**
(a) Subject indexing	(i) P.M.Rogget
(b) Keyword indexing	(ii) H.P.Luhn
(c) Automated indexing	(iii) H.Ohlman
(d) SLIC indexing	(iv) M.E.Sears
	(v) S.L.McNold

Codes:	**(a)**	**(b)**	**(c)**	**(d)**
(A)	(iii)	(ii)	(iv)	(i)
(B)	(iv)	(i)	(ii)	(iii)
(C)	(ii)	(i)	(v)	(iv)
(D)	(v)	(iii)	(iv)	(ii)

713. Match the following:

List-I	**List-II**
(a) INIS	(i) Institute of Electrical Engineering, UK
(b) AGRIS	(ii) International Atomic Energy Agency, Vienna
(c) MEDLINE	(iii) Agricultural Organization of UN, Rome
(d) INSPEC	(iv) National Library of Medicine, USA

Codes:	**(a)**	**(b)**	**(c)**	**(d)**
(A)	(iii)	(ii)	(i)	(iv)
(B)	(ii)	(iii)	(iv)	(i)
(C)	(iv)	(ii)	(iii)	(i)
(D)	(ii)	(i)	(iii)	(iv)

714. Match the following:

List-I	**List-II**
(a) Paul Otlet	(i) List of Subject Heading
(b) Fermont Rider	(ii) Role operators
(c) George Boole	(iii) National Library
(d) Minie Sears	(iv) International Classification

(v) Universal Decimal Classification

Codes:	**(a)**	**(b)**	**(c)**	**(d)**
(A)	(iii)	(i)	(v)	(iv)
(B)	(v)	(iv)	(ii)	(i)
(C)	(iv)	(v)	(i)	(ii)
(D)	(i)	(iv)	(iii)	(v)

715. Match the following:

List-I	**List-II**
(a) BLAISE project	(i) Library of Congress
(b) MARC project	(ii) Intel
(c) Union Catalogue project	(iii) INSDOC
(d) Microchip	(iv) British Library

Codes:	**(a)**	**(b)**	**(c)**	**(d)**
(A)	(iii)	(ii)	(iv)	(i)
(B)	(i)	(ii)	(iii)	(iv)
(C)	(iv)	(i)	(iii)	(ii)
(D)	(ii)	(iii)	(i)	(iv)

716. Match the following:

List-I	**List-II**
(a) P.Wassermann	(i) Line of thinking
(b) P.Atherton	(ii) Foundation of Education for Librarianship
(c) J.H.Shera	(iii) New Librarianship
(d) Maurice B.Line	(iv) Putting knowledge to work

Codes:	**(a)**	**(b)**	**(c)**	**(d)**
(A)	(i)	(ii)	(iii)	(iv)
(B)	(ii)	(i)	(iii)	(iv)
(C)	(iv)	(iii)	(i)	(ii)
(D)	(iii)	(iv)	(ii)	(i)

717. Match the following items given in List I and List – II

List-I	**List-II**
(A) Bibliographic description	(i) Current Awareness Service
(B) Short-range reference service	(ii) Post Coordinating Indexing
(C) SDI	(iii) Abstract
(D) Uniterm	(iv) Ready Reference Source

Codes:	**(a)**	**(b)**	**(c)**	**(d)**
(A)	(iii)	(iv)	(i)	(ii)
(B)	(ii)	(i)	(iii)	(iv)
(C)	(iv)	(i)	(ii)	(iii)
(D)	(ii)	(iii)	(iv)	(i)

718. Match the following:

List-I	**List-II**
(a) SHE	(i) Nuclear Energy
(b) MESH	(ii) Education
(c) ERIC	(iii) Medicine
(d) INIS	Iv) Engineering

Codes:	**(a)**	**(b)**	**(c)**	**(d)**
(A)	(i)	(iii)	(ii)	(iv)
(B)	(iv)	(iii)	(ii)	(i)
(C)	(ii)	(iii)	(i)	(iv)
(D)	(i)	(ii)	(iii)	(iv)

719. Match the following:

List-I	**List-II**
(a) Bradford's law	(i) Author's production
(b) MESH	(ii) Citation indexing
(c) ERIC	(iii) Word frequency
(d) INIS	(iv) Scattering

Codes:	**(a)**	**(b)**	**(c)**	**(d)**
(A)	(i)	(ii)	(iv)	(iii)
(B)	(iii)	(iv)	(ii)	(i)
(C)	(iv)	(ii)	(i)	(iii)
(D)	(iv)	(i)	(ii)	(iii)

720. Match the following:

List-I	**List-II**
(a) Mission Oriented	(i) Patent Information System
(b) Social Science Oriented	(ii) DESIDOC
(c) ERIC	(iii) NISSAT
(d) INIS	(iv) NASSDOC

Codes:	**(a)**	**(b)**	**(c)**	**(d)**
(A)	(iii)	(iv)	(ii)	(i)
(B)	(iv)	(iii)	(ii)	(i)
(C)	(i)	(ii)	(iii)	(iv)
(D)	(ii)	(iii)	(iv)	(i)

721. Match the following:

List-I	List-II
(a) Little Science, Big Science	(i) S.C.Bradford
(b) Documentation	(ii) William Martin
(c) The third Wave	(iii) Eric J de Solla Price
(d) The Information Society	(iv) Alwin Toffler

Codes:	**(a)**	**(b)**	**(c)**	**(d)**
(A)	(i)	(ii)	(iii)	(iv)
(B)	(iii)	(i)	(iv)	(ii)
(C)	(iv)	(iii)	(ii)	(i)
(D)	(ii)	(i)	(iv)	(iii)

722. Match the following:

List-I	List-II
(a) Key Word Indexing	(i) J.R.Sharp
(b) Citation Indexing	(ii) H.P.Luhn
(c) Uniterm Indexing	(iii) E.Garfield
(d) SLIC Indexing	(iv) M.Taube

Codes:	**(a)**	**(b)**	**(c)**	**(d)**
(A)	(ii)	(iii)	(iv)	(i)
(B)	(iii)	(iv)	(i)	(ii)
(C)	(iv)	(i)	(iii)	(ii)
(D)	(i)	(iii)	(ii)	(iv)

723. Match the following:

List-I	List-II
(a) Web Navigation Element	(i) Telecommunication
(b) Shift+Tab	(ii) SQL
(c) ANSI Standard	(iii) Hyperlink
(d) TELNET	(iv) Select the previous link

Codes:	**(a)**	**(b)**	**(c)**	**(d)**
(A)	(i)	(ii)	(iii)	(iv)
(B)	(iv)	(iii)	(ii)	(i)
(C)	(iii)	(iv)	(ii)	(i)
(D)	(ii)	(iii)	(i)	(iv)

724. Match the following:

List-I	**List-II**
(a) Macfee	(i) DOAJ
(b) Directory	(ii) Antivirus
(c) Personal Web pages	(iii) Vendor on Internet
(d) Amazon.com	(iv) Blogs

Codes:	**(a)**	**(b)**	**(c)**	**(d)**
(A)	(ii)	(i)	(iv)	(iii)
(B)	(i)	(iv)	(iii)	(ii)
(C)	(ii)	(iii)	(iv)	(i)
(D)	(iv)	(iii)	(ii)	(i)

725. Match the following:

List-I	**List-II**
(a) Theory of Knowledge	(i) Farmington Plan
(b) IS: 1553-1960	(ii) Metadata Format
(c) Resource Sharing	(iii) Library Building
(d) TEI	(iv) Epistomology

Codes:	**(a)**	**(b)**	**(c)**	**(d)**
(A)	(i)	(iii)	(ii)	(iv)
(B)	(ii)	(iii)	(i)	(iv)
(C)	(iv)	(iii)	(i)	(ii)
(D)	(iii)	(i)	(ii)	(iv)

726. Match the following:

List-I	**List-II**
(a) NASSDOC	(i) Defence Science
(b) DEVSIS	(ii) Social Sciences
(c) INIS	(iii)Development Science
(d) DESIDOC	(iv) Nuclear Science

Codes:	**(a)**	**(b)**	**(c)**	**(d)**
(A)	(iv)	(ii)	(i)	(iii)
(B)	(ii)	(iii)	(iv)	(i)
(C)	(i)	(ii)	(iii)	(iv)
(D)	(iii)	(ii)	(i)	(iv)

727. Match the following:

List-I	List-II
(a) CLRI	(i) Hyderabad
(b) SENDOC	(ii) New Delhi
(c) NASSDOC	(iii) Mumbai
(d) BARC	(iv) Chennai

Codes:	**(a)**	**(b)**	**(c)**	**(d)**
(A)	(ii)	(i)	(iv)	(iii)
(B)	(iv)	(iii)	(i)	(ii)
(C)	(iv)	(i)	(ii)	(iii)
(D)	(iii)	(i)	(iv)	(ii)

728. Match the following:

List-I	List-II
(a) Fumigation	(i) Acquisition
(b) Building library collection	(ii) Preservation
(c) Kardex	(iii) Reference service
(d) Information desk	(iv) Registration of Periodicals

Codes:	**(a)**	**(b)**	**(c)**	**(d)**
(A)	(ii)	(iii)	(i)	(iv)
(B)	(ii)	(iii)	(iv)	(i)
(C)	(iii)	(ii)	(i)	(iv)
(D)	(ii)	(i)	(iv)	(iii)

729. Match thc following:

List-I	List-II
(a) Books in print	(i) Bibliography of periodicals
(b) Ulrich International Periodical Directory	(ii) Trade Bibliography
(c) World of Learning	(iii) Biographical source
(d) Who's Who in India	(iv) Directory

Codes:	**(a)**	**(b)**	**(c)**	**(d)**
(A)	(ii)	(i)	(iv)	(iii)
(B)	(i)	(ii)	(iii)	(iv)
(C)	(iii)	(i)	(iv)	(ii)
(D)	(ii)	(i)	(iv)	(iii)

730. Match the following:

List-I	**List-II**
(a) E.J.Coates	(i) KWIC
(b) H.P.Luhn	(ii) Things, Property, material, Action
(c) Derek Austin	(iii) Concrete and process
(d) J.Kaiser	(iv) PRECIS

Codes:	**(a)**	**(b)**	**(c)**	**(d)**
(A)	(i)	(ii)	(iii)	(iv)
(B)	(ii)	(i)	(iv)	(iii)
(C)	(iii)	(ii)	(i)	(iv)
(D)	(iv)	(i)	(ii)	(iii)

731. Match the following:

List-I	**List-II**
(a) NTC	(i) UK
(b) ITC	(ii) India
(c) BLDSC	(iii) Netherlands
(d) NISCAIR	(iv) USA

Codes:	**(a)**	**(b)**	**(c)**	**(d)**
(A)	(iv)	(iii)	(i)	(ii)
(B)	(ii)	(i)	(iv)	(iii)
(C)	(i)	(iii)	(ii)	(iv)
(D)	(i)	(ii)	(iii)	(iv)

732. Match the following:

List-I (Subjects)	**List-II (Modes of Formation)**
(a) India	(i) Agglomeration
(b) Agriculture of Wheat	(ii) Lamination
(c) Biochemistry	(iii) Fusion
(d) Biological Sciences	(iv) Denudation

Codes:	**(a)**	**(b)**	**(c)**	**(d)**
(A)	(iv)	(ii)	(iii)	(i)
(B)	(i)	(iii)	(ii)	(iv)
(C)	(iv)	(iii)	(i)	(ii)
(D)	(ii)	(iv)	(iii)	(i)

733. Match the following:

List-I	List-II
(a) Elements of Library Classification	(i) D.J.DeSolla Price
(b) Little Science big Science	(ii) S.R.Ranganathan
(c) Documentation	(iii) D.J.Fosket
(d) Subject Approach to Information	(iv) S.C.Bradford

Codes:	**(a)**	**(b)**	**(c)**	**(d)**
(A)	(ii)	(i)	(iv)	(iii)
(B)	(iii)	(ii)	(i)	(iv)
(C)	(iv)	(ii)	(iii)	(i)
(D)	(i)	(ii)	(iii)	(iv)

734. Which one of the following is not correctly matched?
(A) Books in Print – Trade Bibliography
(B) Cummulative Book Index – Books published in English language
(C) British Books in Print – R.R.Bowker
(D) National Bibliography – INB

735. **Assertion (A) :** Primary source is one in which information is original.

Reason (R) : Secondary sources repack the original information.
(A) Both (A) and (R) are true.
(B) (A) is true but (R) is false.
(C) (A) is false but (R) is true.
(D) Both (A) and (R) are false.

736. **Assertion (A) :** Indexing periodical retrieves information, which includes briefsummary of the article.

Reason (R) : It provides list of articles along with the title, authors and other bibliographicdetails.

Codes :
(A) Both (A) and (R) are true.
(B) Both (A) and (R) are false.
(C) (A) is true, but (R) is false.
(D) (A) is false, but (R) are true.

737. **Assertion (A) :** Data base is a collection of interrelated data stored together.

Reason (R) : It is an organised, integrated collection of data.

Codes :

(A) Both (A) and (R) are false.

(B) (A) is false, but (R) is true.

(C) Both (A) and (R) are true.

(D) (A) is true, but (R) is false.

(E) Both (A) and (R) are false

738. **Assertion (A) :** Reference service is the hub of all library activities.

Reason (R) : It is provided in the shortest possible time.

Codes :

(A) (A) is true, but (R) is false

(B) (R) is true, but (A) is false

(C) Both (A) and (R) are true, but (R) is not the right explanation of (A)

(D) Both (A) and (R) are true, and (R) is the right explanation

739. **Assertion (A) :** Users can have access to large number of E-journals through consortia.

Reason (R) : Users are not aware of using web-resources.

Codes :

(A) (A) is false and (R) is true

(B) (A) is true and (R) is false

(C) Both (A) and (R) are true, but (R) is not the right explanation of (A)

(D) Both (A) and (R) are false

740. **Assertion (A):** Libraries have no scope for the growth and development in future.

Reason (R): E-resources can be used anywhere anytime.

Codes:

(A) Both (A) and (R) are true
(B) Both (A) and (R) are false
(C) (A) is false but (R) is true
(D) (A) is true but (R) is false

741. **Assertion (A) :** Several methods can be devised for assisting librarians to keep abreast of developments in his field to maintain efficiency.

Reason (R) : Seminars, conferences, workshops can solve the purpose.

Codcs:

(A) Both (A) and (R) are true but (R) is not the correct explanation of (A).
(B) Both (A) and (R) are true and (R) is the correct expression of (A). (
(C) (A) is true but (R) is false.
(D) (A) is false but (R) is true

742. **Assertion (A) :** As thc level of recall increases, precision tends to decrease.

Reason (R) : Recall and precision tend to vary inversely

Codes:

(A) Both (A) and (R) are true
(B) (A) is true but (R) is false
(C) Both are partially true
(D) (R) is true but (A) is false

743. **Assertion (A) :** Operators using 'AND', 'OR' and 'NOT' are mostly used in online IR.

Reason (R) : User interfaces cannot transform the natural language input into Boolean search query

Codes:

(A) Both (A) and (R) are true
(B) (A) is true but (R) is false
(C) (R) is true but (A) is false
(D) Both (A) and (R) are false

744. **Assertion (A) :** User profile is an essential component of SDI service.

Reason (R) : SDI is a personalized current awareness service.

Codes:

(A) Both (A) and (R) are true

(B) Both (A) and (R) are false

(C) Both are partially true

(D) (A) is true but (R) is false

745. **Assertion (A) :** Document transfer and information transfer are not the same.

Reason (R) : Assimillation of the content of the document by the user constitutes information transfer.

Codes:

(A) (A) is true and (R) is false

(B) (R) is true but (A) is false

(C) Both (A) and (R) are true

(D) Both (A) and (R) are false

746. **Assertion (A) :** Consortia cannot provide an effective strategy to increase the buying power of individual libraries.

Reason (R) : Consortia arrangement saves the funds of the libraries in developing their information sources.

Codes :

(A) (A) is false but (R) is true

(B) (A) is true but (R) is false

(C) Both (A) and (R) are false

(D) Both (A) and (R) are true

747. **Assertion (A) :** Classification and indexing have always been of central intellectual interest in IR

Reason (R) : Conceptual analysis of the content of the queries and documents are essential input to an IR system.

Codes :

(A) (A) is true and (R) is false

(B) (R) is true and (A) is false

(C) Both (A) and (R) are true

(D) (A) and (R) both are partially true

748. **Assertion (A) :** Any change in the environment of the subject can not affect the state of the subject

Reason (R) : A subject can be viewed as a system consisting of a set of interacting component ideas.

Codes :

(A) (A) is true and (R) is false

(B) (R) is true and (A) is false

(C) Both (A) and (R) are true

(D) Both (A) and (R) are false

749. **Assertion (A) :** PRECIS is not based upon any particular system of classification.

Reason (R) : PRECIS is not built around any theoretical ideas on classification.

Codes :

(A) (A) is true but (R) is false

(B) (A) is false but (R) is true

(C) Both (A) and (R) are true

(D) Both (A) and (R) are true

750. **Assertion (A) :** INDEST conceived J-Gate as a customized gate for e-journals subscribed by the member libraries

Reason (R) : J-Gate provides a common access platform for all its members to search and share resources subscribed by the member libraries.

Codes :

(A) Both (A) and (R) are true and (R) is the correct explanation

(B) Both (A) and (R) are true but (R) is not the correct explanation

(C) (A) is true but (R) is false

(D) (A) is false but (R) is true

751. **Assertion (A) :** Measuring the Internet and in particular the web is a difficult task.

Reason (R) : Web is considered as a new publishing medium with inadequate editorial process.

Codes :

(A) Both (A) and (R) are true and (R) is the correct explanation.

(B) Both (A) and (R) are true and (R) is not the correct explanation

(C) (A) is true but (R) is false.

(D) (A) is false but (R) is true

752. **Assertion (A) :** Ann indexing language is an artificial language as it uses controlled vocabulary.

Reason (R) : It provides different relationships between terms.

Codes :

(A) Both (A) and (R) are false.

(B) Both (A) and (R) are true.

(C) (A) is true but (R) is false.

(D) (A) is false but (R) is true.

753. **Assertion (A) :** With large collection of documents, recall can be measured properly.

Reason (R) : The proper estimation of maximum recall for a query requires detailed knowledge of all the documents in the collection.

Codes :

(A) Both (A) and (R) are true.

(B) Both (A) and (R) are true and (R) is not the correct explanation.

(C) (A) is true but (R) is false.

(D) (A) is false but (R) is true

754. **Assertion (A) :** The development of Institutional Repositories in India is at a slow pace.

Reason (R) : This can be attributed to the non-availability of open source software and lack of interest among the LIS professionals.

Codes :

(A) Both (A) and (R) are true.

(B) Both (A) and (R) are false.

(C) (A) is true but (R) is partially true.

(D) (A) is false and (R) is true

755. **Assertion (A) :** Subject gateways offer the users an alternative to 'vacuum Cleaner' type of search engines, such as Google, Infoseek, Alta Vista etc.

Reason (R) : Subject gateways hold manually created records, rich resource description containing relevant information.

Codes:

(A) Both (A) and (R) are true.

(B) Both (A) and (R) are true and (R) is not the correct explanation

(C) (A) is true but (R) is false

(D) (A) is false but (R) is true

756. **Assertion (A) :** An indexing language is much more than a list of index terms that are acceptable to users.

Reason (R) : An indexing language helps users discriminate between terms and reduces ambiguity in the language.

Codes:

(A) Both (A) and (R) are true and (R) is not the correct explanation.

(B) Both (A) and (R) are true and (R) is the correct explanation.

(C) (A) is false but (R) is true

(D) (A) is true but (R) is false

757. **Assertion (A) :** SDI is a user oriented current information service.

Reason (R) : It is an alerting service directed towards groups.

Codes:

(A) Both (A) and (R) are true

(B) (A) is true, but (R) is false

(C) (A) is false but (R) is true

(D) Both (A) and (R) are false.

758. **Assertion (A) :** Indexing periodical retrieves information, which includes brief summary of the article.

Reason (R) : It provides list of articles alongwith the title, authors and other bibliographic details.

Codes:

(A) Both (A) and (R) are true

(B) Both (A) and (R) are false

(C) (A) is true, but (R) is false

(D) (A) is false but (R) are true

759. **Assertion (A) :** Database is a collection of interrelated data stored together

Reason (R) : It is an organised, integrated collection of data

Codes:

(A) Both (A) and (R) are false

(B) (A) is false but (R) is true

(C) Both (A) and (R) are true

(D) (A) is true but (R) is false

760. **Assertion (A) :** A bibliographic utility is an organization that offers bibliographic

Reason (R) : Library of Congress is a bibliographic utility.

Codes :

(A) (A) is true, but (R) is false.

(B) (A) is false, but (R) is true.

(C) Both (A) and (R) are true.

(D) Both (A) and (R) are false.

761. **Assertion (A) :** LISA is a primary source of information.

Reason (R) : All primary sources provide original information.

Codes :

(A) (A) is false, but (R) is true.

(B) (A) is true, but (R) is false.

(C) Both (A) and (R) are false.

(D) Both (A) and (R) are true.

762. **Assertion (A) :** Information Literacy provides training to use maximum resourcesavailable in a library.

Reason (R) : Information Literacy always aims at specific group of users.

Codes :

(A) (A) is false, but (R) is true.

(B) Both (A) and (R) are false.

(C) Both (A) and (R) are true.

(D) (A) is true, but (R) is false.

763. **Asertion (A) :** Arrangement of documents by subject will satisfy more users.

Reason (R) : Many users search for documents by title.

Codes :

(A) Both A and R are true and R is the correct explanation

(B) Both A and R are true and R is not the correct explanation

(C) A is true but R is false

(D) A is false but R is true

764. **Assertion (A) :** Information can be obtained from several sources other than the libraries.

Reason (R) : Library science is narrower in scope than information science

Codes :

(A) (A) is false and (R) are true

(B) (R) is false and (A) is true

(C) Both (A) and (R) are false

(D) Both (A) and (R) are true

765. **Assertion (A) :** Reference service is the hub of all library activities.

Reason (R) : It is provided in the shortest possible time.

Codes:

(A) (A) is true but (R) is false.

(B) (R) is true but (A) is false.

(C) Both (A) and (R) are true, but (R) is not the right explanation of (A).

(D) Both (A) and (R) are true and (R) is the right explanation

766. **Assertion (A) :** SDI is a user oriented current information service.

Reason (R) : It is an alerting service directed towards groups.

Codes :

(A) Both (A) and (R) are true.

(B) (A) is true, but (R) is false.

(C) (A) is false, but (R) is true.

(D) Both (A) and (R) are false.

767. **Assertion (A) :** Maximization of the use of documents is the motto of the library.

Reason (R) : Maximization of the use of documents is the motto of the library.

Codes:

(A) Both (A) and (R) are true

(B) Both (A) and (R) are false

(C) (A) is true but (R) is false

(D) (R) is true but (A) is false

768. **Assertion (A) :** Users can have access to large to large number of E-journals through consortia.

Reason (R) : Users are not aware of using web resources.

Codes:

(A) (A) is false and (R) is true

(B) (A) is true and (R) is false

(C) Both (A) and (R) are true but (R) is not the right explanation of (A)

(D) Both (A) and (R) are false

ANSWERS

1. (B)	2. (C)	3. (C)	4. (A)
5. (C)	6. (D)	7. (D)	8. (D)
9. (B)	10. (B)	11. (A)	12. (C)
13. (D)	14. (C)	15. (A)	16. (B)
17. (C)	18. (B)	19. (D)	20. (D)
21. (B)	22. (B)	23. (A)	24. (B)
25. (A)	26. (D)	27. (B)	28. (A)
29. (B)	30. (C)	31. (A)	32. (C)

33. (D)	34. (B)	35. (D)	36. (C)
37. (C)	38. (C)	39. (B)	40. (A)
41. (A)	42. (B)	43. (C)	44. (C)
45. (A)	46. (D)	47. (D)	48. (A)
49. (A)	50. (C)	51. (A)	52. (B)
53. (D)	54. (D)	55. (A)	56. (A)
57. (A)	58. (B)	59. (C)	60. (A)
61. (C)	62. (C)	63. (B)	64. (A)
65. (C)	66. (D)	67. (C)	68. (D)
69. (B)	70. (A)	71. (C)	72. (A)
73. (B)	74. (C)	75. (A)	76. (B)
77. (A)	78. (C)	79. (D)	80. (A)
81. (C)	82. (A)	83. (C)	84. (C)
85. (A)	86. (B)	87. (B)	88. (A)
89. (C)	90. (A)	91. (C)	92. (C)
93. (C)	94. (B)	95. (C)	96. (B)
97. (B)	98. (C)	99. (C)	100. (D)
101. (D)	102. (D)	103. (C)	104. (B)
105. (A)	106. (B)	107. (A)	108. (D)
109. (C)	110. (C)	111. (B)	112. (C)
113. (D)	114. (D)	115. (B)	116. (A)
117. (C)	118. (D)	119. (C)	120. (C)
121. (D)	122. (B)	123. (D)	124. (C)
125. (B)	126. (A)	127. (B)	128. (C)
129. (B)	130. (A)	131. (A)	132. (C)
133. (D)	134. (A)	135. (B)	136. (B)
137. (D)	138. (B)	139. (C)	140. (B)
141. (C)	142. (B)	143. (A)	144. (C)
145. (B)	146. (A)	147. (A)	148. (D)
149. (A)	150. (A)	151. (D)	152. (C)
153. (A)	154. (D)	155. (A)	156. (D)
157. (A)	158. (B)	159. (D)	160. (B)
161. (D)	162. (C)	163. (B)	164. (D)
165. (D)	166. (B)	167. (B)	168. (D)
169. (A)	170. (B)	171. (A)	172. (A)
173. (D)	174. (C)	175. (C)	176. (B)
177. (D)	178. (A)	179. (C)	180. (A)
181. (D)	182. (C)	183. (C)	184. (B)
185. (B)	186. (D)	187. (D)	188. (B)
189. (D)	190. (A)	191. (A)	192. (C)
193. (A)	194. (B)	195. (D)	196. (D)
197. (D)	198. (B)	199. (B)	200. (D)
201. (A)	202. (A)	203. (B)	204. (B)

205. (C)	206. (C)	207. (A)	208. (C)
209. (B)	210. (D)	211. (B)	212. (A)
213. (D)	214. (A)	215. (D)	216. (B)
217. (C)	218. (B)	219. (D)	220. (A)
221. (B)	222. (D)	223. (D)	224. (C)
225. (A)	226. (D)	227. (D)	228. (D)
229. (D)	230. (D)	231. (C)	232. (B)
233. (D)	234. (C)	235. (D)	236. (D)
237. (B)	238. (C)	239. (B)	240. (D)
241. (C)	242. (D)	243. (B)	244. (D)
245. (C)	246. (A)	247. (B)	248. (D)
249. (C)	250. (D)	251. (C)	252. (B)
253. (B)	254. (A)	255. (B)	256. (B)
257. (C)	258. (B)	259. (A)	260. (B)
261. (B)	262. (C)	263. (C)	264. (A)
265. (A)	266. (D)	267. (A)	268. (C)
269. (D)	270. (B)	271. (D)	272. (B)
273. (C)	274. (B)	275. (D)	276. (A)
277. (B)	278. (B)	279. (A)	280. (D)
281. (C)	282. (B)	283. (C)	284. (A)
285. (B)	286. (B)	287. (C)	288. (B)
289. (A)	290. (C)	291. (A)	292. (B)
293. (B)	294. (C)	295. (A)	296. (A)
297. (D)	298. (A)	299. (A)	300. (C)
301. (D)	302. (C)	303. (A)	304. (C)
305. (C)	306. (C)	307. (D)	308. (C)
309. (B)	310. (D)	311. (D)	312. (B)
313. (D)	314. (D)	315. (D)	316. (D)
317. (D)	318. (B)	319. (D)	320. (C)
321. (D)	322. (D)	323. (D)	324. (D)
325. (C)	326. (A)	327. (D)	328. (B)
329. (D)	330. (D)	331. (D)	332. (B)
333. (B)	334. (D)	335. (D)	336. (A)
337. (B)	338. (B)	339. (D)	340. (D)
341. (B)	342. (C)	343. (B)	344. (A)
345. (D)	346. (A)	347. (B)	348. (B)
349. (A)	350. (C)	351. (B)	352. (A)
353. (C)	354. (B)	355. (B)	356. (A)
357. (B)	358. (B)	359. (A)	360. (D)
361. (B)	362. (A)	363. (C)	364. (D)
365. (D)	366. (B)	367. (D)	368. (B)
369. (A)	370. (C)	371. (A)	372. (A)
373. (B)	374. (D)	375. (A)	376. (C)

377. (C) 378. (D) 379. (D) 380. (D)
381. (B) 382. (C) 383. (C) 384. (C)
385. (A) 386. (C) 387. (A) 388. (B)
389. (B) 390. (C) 391. (C) 392. (C)
393. (A) 394. (D) 395. (A) 396. (B)
397. (B) 398. (B) 399. (C) 400. (B)
401. (C) 402. (B) 403. (B) 404. (A)
405. (D) 406. (D) 407. (A) 408. (C)
409. (C) 410. (C) 411. (B) 412. (D)
413. (B) 414. (C) 415. (C) 416. (C)
417. (B) 418. (A) 419. (C) 420. (B)
421. (B) 422. (C) 423. (A) 424. (B)
425. (D) 426. (B) 427. (C) 428. (B)
429. (A) 430. (D) 431. (B) 432. (D)
433. (D) 434. (A) 435. (D) 436. (B)
437. (D) 438. (B) 439. (A) 440. (A)
441. (B) 442. (A) 443. (B) 444. (C)
445. (B) 446. (B) 447. (D) 448. (A)
449. (A) 450. (D) 451. (A) 452. (D)
453. (D) 454. (B) 455. (D) 456. (B)
457. (D) 458. (C) 459. (A) 460. (C)
461. (B) 462. (C) 463. (D) 464. (A)
465. (B) 466. (A) 467. (D) 468. (A)
469. (A) 470. (D) 471. (D) 472. (D)
473. (A) 474. (D) 475. (C) 476. (B)
477. (D) 478. (D) 479. (C) 480. (D)
481. (A) 482. (C) 483. (C) 484. (C)
485. (A) 486. (A) 487. (C) 488. (A)
489. (B) 490. (C) 491. (D) 492. (B)
493. (C) 494. (C) 495. (A) 496. (C)
497. (D) 498. (A) 499. (C) 500. (C)
501. (C) 502. (D) 503. (C) 504. (D)
505. (D) 506. (C) 507. (C) 508. (B)
509. (A) 510. (C) 511. (C) 512. (C)
513. (C) 514. (A) 515. (D) 516. (D)
517. (B) 518. (A) 519. (D) 520. (A)
521. (B) 522. (B) 523. (B) 524. (A)
525. (C) 526. (A) 527. (A) 528. (C)
529. (B) 530. (A) 531. (A) 532. (B)
533. (C) 534. (C) 535. (D) 536. (A)
537. (C) 538. (A) 539. (C) 540. (A)
541. (D) 542. (B) 543. (B) 544. (D)
545. (A) 546. (D) 547. (B) 548. (D)

549. (A)	550. (B)	551. (B)	552. (D)
553. (B)	554. (C)	555. (D)	556. (B)
557. (D)	558. (C)	559. (C)	560. (B)
561. (A)	562. (C)	563. (A)	564. (C)
565. (C)	566. (D)	567. (A)	568. (A)
569. (D)	570. (B)	571. (B)	572. (C)
573. (A)	574. (C)	575. (D)	576. (B)
577. (C)	578. (C)	579. (A)	580. (B)
581. (A)	582. (C)	583. (B)	584. (D)
585. (B)	586. (C)	587. (B)	588. (B)
589. (D)	590. (A)	591. (C)	592. (D)
593. (A)	594. (B)	595. (A)	596. (B)
597. (B)	598. (C)	599. (C)	600. (C)
601. (C)	602. (B)	603. (C)	604. (C)
605. (C)	606. (A)	607. (D)	608. (C)
609. (D)	610. (A)	611. (B)	612. (C)
613. (C)	614. (C)	615. (C)	616. (C)
617. (D)	618. (C)	619. (C)	620. (C)
621. (D)	622. (B)	623. (C)	624. (C)
625. (D)	626. (C)	627. (D)	628. (D)
629. (A)	630. (A)	631. (C)	632. (C)
633. (D)	634. (D)	635. (B)	636. (A)
637. (D)	638. (B)	639. (C)	640. (C)
641. (C)	642. (C)	643. (A)	644. (A)
645. (B)	646. (A)	647. (A)	648. (B)
649. (A)	650. (C)	651. (B)	652. (A)
653. (A)	654. (B)	655. (C)	656. (B)
657. (B)	658. (B)	659. (A)	660. (D)
661. (C)	662. (C)	663. (C)	664. (D)
665. (B)	666. (A)	667. (B)	668. (A)
669. (D)	670. (D)	671. (D)	672. (C)
673. (C)	674. (B)	675. (D)	676. (D)
677. (A)	678. (C)	679. (C)	680. (D)
681. (A)	682. (B)	683. (A)	684. (A)
685. (C)	686. (A)	687. (C)	688. (B)
689. (B)	690. (D)	691. (C)	692. (B)
693. (C)	694. (A)	695. (A)	696. (C)
697. (C)	698. (C)	699. (C)	700. (D)
701. (B)	702. (A)	703. (B)	704. (B)
705. (C)	706. (C)	707. (D)	708. (B)
709. (D)	710. (D)	711. (B)	712. (B)
713. (B)	714. (B)	715. (C)	716. (C)
717. (A)	718. (B)	719. (D)	720. (A)

721. (B)	722. (A)	723. (C)	724. (A)
725. (C)	726. (B)	727. (C)	728. (D)
729. (A)	730. (B)	731. (A)	732. (A)
733. (A)	734. (C)	735. (A)	736. (A)
737. (C)	738. (C)	739. (C)	740. (C)
741. (A)	742. (B)	743. (A)	744. (A)
745. (A)	746. (A)	747. (C)	748. (B)
749. (C)	750. (A)	751. (B)	752. (B)
753. (C)	754. (C)	755. (B)	756. (B)
757. (A)	758. (D)	759. (C)	760. (C)
761. (A)	762. (D)	763. (B)	764. (D)
765. (B)	766. (A)	767. (C)	768. (C)

9

Miscelleneous

1. Which part of computer can be used as both Input/ output devices?

   (A) Joystick (B) Monitor

   (C) Printer (D) Keyboard

2. Which one of the following is not a "Search Engines".

   (A) Altavista (B) Web Crawler

   (C) Excite (D) Netscape Navigator

3. DSL stands for:

   (A) Direct Service Locator

   (B) Digital Subscriber Line

   (C) Digital Service Line

   (D) None of these.

4. CAT-5 is a kind of:

   (A) Unshielded twisted wring

   (B) Optical fibre

   (C) Shielded twisted wiring

   (D) Electrical wiring

5. Which one of the following is not a layer described by OSI in communication process?

   (A) Data Link Layer (B) Network Layer

   (C) Sender Layer (D) Physical Layer.

6. Layer 1-3 deals with
   (A) Data transmission
   (B) End-to-end communication.
   (C) Data receiving
   (D) None of these
7. If a network, cable ends are not joined then is:
   (A) Bus topology (B) Mesh topology
   (C) Star topology (D) Ring topology
8. Telephone is an example of:
   (A) Uni-directional communication
   (B) Bi- directional communication
   (C) Both (A) & (B)
   (D) None of these.
9. Packet switching is used in:
   (A) Library software development.
   (B) Library database development.
   (C) Making communication between two computers.
   (D) All of the above
10. Which one of seven-layer is first layer in data transport?
   (A) Layer 1 (B) Layer 7
   (C) Layer 3 (D) Layer 6
11. AND, OR and NOT are types of operations:
   (A) Simple alphabetic terms
   (B) Qualifying operators of PRECIS.
   (C) Computer operators
   (D) Boolean operators
12. How far a satellite is placed above earch in Satellite Communication?
   (A) 22,300 (B) 11,000
   (C) 20,600 (D) 11,600
13. ENVIS network is located at:
   (A) Department of Electronics, Govt. Of India.
   (B) Department of Electrical Engineering, University of Delhi
   (C) Department of Environment, Govt. of India
   (D) Department of Environment, Govt. of U.K.

14. In which of MARC a URL is stored ?
    (A) 800 (B) 830
    (C) 856 (D) 956
15. The publisher of index of conference proceding received is
    (A) LC (B) BL
    (C) Bowker (D) Willson.
16. Which part of computer system is known as "Brain of Computer".
    (A) Motherboard (B) CPU
    (C) Memory (D) Hard Disk Drive (HDD)
17. Who is the originator of ETHERNET?
    (A) Robert Metcalfe. (B) Lancaster
    (C) Richard Metcalfe (D) Vickerey
18. MEDLARS is a service provided by:
    (A) National Library of Medicine, USA
    (B) National Medical Library, New Delhi
    (C) National Science Library, New Delhi
    (D) Library of Congress, USA.
19. Apache is a kind of
    (A) Open Source Software
    (B) Licensed software
    (C) Both of these
    (D) None of these
20. SIRNET stands for:
    (A) Sri Lankan Information Network
    (B) Scientific Information Network
    (C) Subjective Information Network
    (D) Scientific and Industrial Research Network
21. Which one of the following Biblometric laws deals with frequency of occurrence of words in a text?
    (A) Lotka's Law (B) Ziff's Law
    (C) Brandford's Law (D) Pritchard's Law

22. Ahmadabad, City of India is having:
    (A) Headquarters of ILA
    (B) Headquarters of NISSAT
    (C) Information Centre of ISRO
    (D) Information & Library Network (INFLIBNET)
23. Which one of the following protocol is used in transferring file over Internet?
    (A) FTP (B) SMTP
    (C) POP (D) TCP/IP
24. VIKRAM, a data network is established by:
    (A) Department of Electronics.
    (B) Department of Telecommunications.
    (C) Informatics (India) Ltd.
    (D) Ministry of Defense.
25. "NISCAIR" an organization of CSIR is created by
    (A) An Independent body under the UNESCO Grant.
    (B) Combining INSDOC and NISCOM.
    (C) Combining INSDOC and NISTAD of CSIR.
    (D) Bifurcating UGC.
26. The term "Automation" was first time used by:
    (A) Lancaster (B) H.P. Luhn
    (C) Pascal (D) D.S. Harder
27. SENDOC is located at
    (A) Kolkata (B) Pune
    (C) Hyderabad (D) Nagpur
28. "METRON" is a:
    (A) International Library Network
    (B) IACE Publication.
    (C) International Information System in Medicine
    (D) Current Awareness Journal Published by INSPEC.
29. INFLIBNET was made operational under:
    (A) Seventh Plan (B) Eight Plan
    (C) Sixth Plan (D) Fifth Plan
30. Which one of the following is National Centre for India in INIS?

(A) BARC, Trombay (B) NISCAIR, New Delhi
(C) DISIDOC, New Delhi (D) ISRO, Bangalore

31. Which one of the following is commercial network?
(A) VIKRAM (B) ERNET
(C) INDONET (D) NICENET

32. NICENET has its regional centers at:
(A) Pune (B) Bhubaneswar
(C) Hyderabad (D) All of the above.

33. What is full form of BHEL?
(A) Birla Heavy Equipment Limited.
(B) Bharat Heavy Electricals Limited.
(C) Bangalore Hardware Engineering Lab.
(D) Bombay Heavy Engineering Limited.

34. Which one of the following system acts as "World Science Information System"?
(A) ISORID (B) OCLC
(C) PGI (D) UNISIST

35. National Information Centre for Crystallography (NICRYS) is located at:
(A) Chennai (B) Mysore
(C) Pune (D) Bangalore

36. UNIST is served by information from India through:
(A) NISCAIR (B) National Library
(C) NISTADS (D) NISSAT

37. Which NISSAT, sectoral centre is located at Lucknow:
(A) NICFOS (B) NICRYS
(C) NICDAP (D) NICMAP

38. BRS is a search service of:
(A) NASA (B) NML
(C) INIS (D) CIA

39. Which one of the following is member of POPIN in India?
(A) Ministry of Health (B) National Medical Library
(C) NIHFW (D) National Science Library

40. National Information Centre for Food Science (NICFOS) is located at:

(A) Chennai (B) Pune
(C) Mysore (D) New Delhi

41. PIPIN network is related to:
(A) Poverty Information.
(B) Physics Information
(C) Political Science Information.
(D) Population Information.

42. Dublic core is used to:
(A) Exchange Information
(B) Catalog web resources
(C) Transport data over optical fibres
(D) None of these.

43. Which city out of the following does not have NISSAT regional centre?
(A) Lucknow (B) New Delhi
(C) Chennai (D) Pune

44. Which one of the following is Indian input centre for ISDS:
(A) Central Secretariat Library
(B) IARI
(C) National Library
(D) NISCAIR

45. International Standards Information Network (ISONET) is in:
(A) Geneva (B) Hague
(C) Chicago (D) Paris.

46. DIALOG is a software originally developed for:
(A) NML (B) NSL
(C) NASA (D) CIA

47. In BLCMP, the letter 'B' denotes.
(A) British (B) Bombay
(C) Birmingham (D) Banaras

48. "MINISAS" is developed by:
(A) UNESCO (B) NISSAT, India
(C) Libsys, India. (D) IDRC, Canada

50. First Search is a service of:
    (A) DIALOG (B) OCLC
    (C) DRBIT (D) LISA
51. Food Science and Technology Abstracts (FSTA) is published from:
    (A) India (B) USA
    (C) Paris (D) U.K.
52. "TRAILS" is a system for:
    (A) Document organization in INSDOC.
    (B) Document organization in SENDOC
    (C) Internet Surfing Software
    (D) Indexing techniques
53. Which studies showed that "worker's actions are influenced by the group".
    (A) Studies of Taylor
    (B) Studies of Elton Mayo
    (C) Studies of Luther Gullick
    (D) Studies of Mary Follett.
54. "Time-Rate method" is used in:
    (A) Job-Analysis (B) Job-Evaluation
    (C) Wage-determination (D) Staff-promotion
55. What are the steps involved in MBO?
    (A) Finding the objectives
    (B) Setting the objectives
    (C) Controlling and reporting the status of the objectives
    (D) All of the above.
56. Self-Actualising theory was propounded by:
    (A) Abraham Maslow (B) Peter Drucker
    (C) Douglas McGregor (D) Henri Fayol
57. The Thematic Apperception Test (TAT) was conducted by:
    (A) Abrahm Maslow (B) Elton Mayo
    (C) Herbert Simon (D) McClelland
58. Which process examines one's productivity with other institutions of same kind?

(A) Benchmarking (B) Cost-benefit analysis
(C) MBD (D) TQM

59. Who is associated with Leadership Grid formation?
(A) Rensis Likert (B) Robert R. Blake
(C) Kurt Lewin (D) All of the above

60. Which study is considered pioneer in showing the importance of the human begins in organizations?
(A) Manto Carlo techniques
(B) Peter & Drucker Studies
(C) Hawthorne Studies
(D) Abraham Maslow Studies

61. Who has written "The Wealth of Nations"?
(A) Taylor (B) Maslow
(C) Adam Smith (D) Lancaster

62. Cost Accounting is being done:
(A) To estimate the financial requirement of next year.
(B) To have an idea of past performance.
(C) To have an idea of cost involved in providing a service
(D) To keep a check on proper use of accounts.

63. In McClelland's theory, which need is drive to succeed:
(A) Need for power (B) Need for affiliation
(C) Need for achievement (D) None of these.

64. Path-Goal theory is related to:
(A) Management styles (B) Organisation structures
(C) Theory of Leadership (D) None of these.

65. Which analysis shows that cost of providing a service is greater than or less that the value of service
(A) Cost-effectiveness analysis.
(B) Cost-benefit analysis
(C) MBD
(D) TQM

66. What type of organizations are not found on the organization chart?

(A) Formal organizations
(B) Informal organizations
(C) Government Organizations
(D) Non- Government Organizations.

67. What are the major categories of human needs according to McCelland's need theory?
(A) Four (B) Five
(C) Three (D) Two

68. Another name of "Estimate of income & expenditure":
(A) Annual Report (B) Budget
(C) Committee's Report (D) Balance Sheet.

69. Grapevine is a type of
(A) Oral communication
(B) Formal communication
(C) Informal communication
(D) Is a type of fruit

70. Sold lines in an organization charts shows:
(A) Authority (B) Staff
(C) Authority & Staff (D) None of these

71. Which theory supports that "Leaders are born", not made
(A) Trait approach theories
(B) Ohio state studies
(C) Behavioral approach theories
(D) University of lowa studies.

72. Which one of the following charging system is named after the place where it was devised?
(A) Dickman Book Charging System
(B) Gaylord Charging system
(C) Scotch Tape Tabs system
(D) Newark Charging System.

73. A minimum amount per head of population is fixed in:
(A) Proportion Method (B) Per capital Method
(C) Browne Method (D) Methods of details

74. Intelligence Tests were suggested by:
    (A) Alfred Binot (B) H.P. Luhn
    (C) Mayo (D) R.N. Anthony
75. Which one of the following is generally last step in financial administration?
    (A) Auditing (B) Budgeting
    (C) Wage distribution (D) Budget Estimation
76. "Easy methods" are used in an organization.
    (A) In place or interview methods
    (B) In writing complains about staff
    (C) In writing complaints of staff
    (D) As employee appraised
77. Who identified the eight central value of librarianship.
    (A) Margaret Mann (B) Michael Gorman
    (C) D. Hume (D) S.R. Ranganathan
78. Who propounded the Goal-Setting theory?
    (A) McGregor (B) McClelland
    (C) B.F. Skinner (D) Edwin Locke
79. Which one is not part of Job Analysis?
    (A) To find out what is to be done.
    (B) To find the best method of doing it.
    (C) To fix the money value for it.
    (D) To determine qualification needed by worker to do it.
80. What type of performance appraisal methods are most commonly used?
    (A) Essay methods
    (B) Rating Scales
    (C) Forced distribution methods
    (D) Graphic rating scale
81. Information is key to the process of:
    (A) Policy formation (B) Decision making
    (C) Budget making (D) Annual Report writing
82. The UNIMARK came into existence in:
    (A) 1967 (B) 1977
    (C) 1978 (D) 1968

83. CC 6thd. Uses phase relation indicator:
    (A) Anpersand (B) Color
    (C) Zero (D) Dot.

84. The terms NT, BT and RT are used in
    (A) Vocabulary Control Devises
    (B) Classified Catalogue Code
    (C) Classified Schedules.
    (D) Library Statistics Maintenance

85. Common isolates in UDC are:
    (A) Special & Common auxiliaries
    (B) ACI & PCI
    (C) Form divisions & view points
    (D) Space CI & Time CI

86. A list which shows the arrangement of documents in the library?
    (A) Accession List (B) Shelf List
    (C) Call Number (D) Class Number.

87. The first step in cost analysis is to define the unit of, service
    (A) measurement (B) Specification
    (C) Overhead (D) Service

88. How many levels of phase relations are in colon classification?
    (A) Six (B) Four
    (C) One (D) Three

89. Which one of the followings says "Notation is merely a set of symbols sanding in the place of terms".
    (A) Ranganathan (B) Lancaster
    (C) Richardson (D) Sayers

90. UNIBID is related to:
    (A) Biographical description
    (B) Biological description
    (C) Bibliographic description
    (D) Bibliographic data system.

91. "Nothing before something" filling method is also known as:

(A) Letter by letter (B) Word by word
(C) Both of the above (D) None of the above

92. Which one indicates inner form of the catalogue?
(A) Classified catalogue (B) Book catalogue
(C) Card catalogue (D) Shelf list

93. The "Medicine" in CC 6th Ed. Follows:
(A) Principle of Bottom Upwards
(B) Principle of Top down words
(C) Principle of Later-in-time
(D) Principle of later in evolution.

94. How many categories of Indexing languages are common?
(A) Two (B) Five
(C) Six (D) One

95. The Botany in DDC is arranged according to:
(A) Principle of Later in Evolution
(B) Principle of Earlier in Evaluation
(C) Principle of Later in Time
(D) Principle of Earlier in Time

96. Thesaurus is a kind of indexing languages:
(A) Natural (B) Controlled
(C) Free (D) All the above

97. UNIBID is an agency associated with:
(A) Biographic Description
(B) Bibliographic Description
(C) Classification Schemes
(D) Subject headings list.

98. The sequence of steps taken in Analytic synthetic classification schemes are:
(A) Facet Synthesize – Facet Sequence – Facet Analyses
(B) Facet Analysis – Facet Numbering – Facet Sequence
(C) Facet Analysis – Facet Sequence
(D) None of the above

99. "Clustering" is a term associated with:
    (A) Modes of subject formation
    (B) Modes of Information Storage
    (C) Modes of communication
    (D) Modes of knowledge dissemination.

100. Recall and Relevance are related to:
    (A) Cataloguing
    (B) Classification
    (C) Natural Language Indexing
    (D) Information Retrieval

101. "Principle of Inversion" is followed in
    (A) Subject Headings derivation
    (B) Indexing of scientific periodicals
    (C) Abstracting of Social Science periodicals
    (D) Classifying and arranging of documents.

102. According to 7th Edition of colon classification contains the number of Basic Subjects are
    (A) 669 (B) 679
    (C) 769 (D) 779

103. Dynamic Theory of Library classification is associated with?
    (A) Dr. S. R. Ranganathan
    (B) Lancaster
    (C) W.B. Sayers
    (D) Melvil Dewey

104. Postulation approach to classification gives principles for:
    (A) Facet Analysis and Synthesis
    (B) Selecting terminology of index terms
    (C) Rendering subject headings in a catalogue
    (D) Arranging documents on shelves.

105. Canon of context is related to:
    (A) Idea plane (B) Verbal plane
    (C) Notational plane (D) None of these

106. In colon classification "Homeopathy" is taken as -
    (A) Subject Bundles (B) Specials
    (C) Aqatomerates

107. Library of Congress uses:
    (A) Non-faceted notation (B) Pure notation
    (C) Roman Smalls (D) Indo-Arabic notation
108. Place value of 6 in 0.635 is:
    (A) 6000 (B) 600
    (C) 7/1000 (D) 6/10
109. What is "Base" in a Notational System?
    (A) A paper which have digits written on it.
    (B) Total digits available in a notational system.
    (C) A set of digits used by a notational system.
    (D) None of these.
110. Thc "Cycle Indexing" is developed by
    (A) S.R. Ranganathan (B) Lancaster
    (C) D.J. Forskett (D) M.E. Sears
111. "Minor Authors" initially used in DDC was removed due to the effect of:
    (A) Canon of Reference (B) Canon of Performance
    (C) Canon of context (D) Canon of currency
112. Designer of Classification Scheme is:
    (A) Classifier (B) Classificationist
    (C) Classes (D) Class
113. ISBD (M) is associated with bibliographic description of:
    (A) Motion pictures (B) Maps
    (C) Monographs (D) Monograms
114. Which punctuation sign will be used before subtitle AACR-2?
    (A) Colon (B) Semi-colon
    (C) Dash (D) Dot
115. AACR-1 defines series as:
    (A) A list of documents published by a publisher in a year
    (B) A number of separate books published in succession and related to one another by a collective title.
    (C) Proceedings of government legislatures
    (D) None of the above

116. Chain procedure divides links into:
    (A) Significant links (B) Insignificant links
    (C) Bothe of the above (D) None of the above
117. The residual class in DDC is denoted by digit:
    (A) 9 (B) 8
    (C) 0 (D) None of these
118. "Three dots" are used in AARC-2
    (A) After Indian Authors name in main entry.
    (B) Indicates Omissions
    (C) Inserted after parallel titles
    (D) Inserted after each element in the tracing.
119. Which classification scheme is used in classifying ISA?
    (A) LC (B) CC
    (C) UDC (D) DDC
120. Which one of the following author's name is not inverted?
    (A) English names (B) Name of female authors
    (C) Ethiopian names (D) Indic names
121. In AACR-2, what is used before the first statement of responsibility that comes after the title?
    (A) Comma (B) Semi-colon
    (C) Diagonal Slash (D) Two dots
122. Entry element is defined as:
    (A) Word or groups of words occurring first in the heading.
    (B) Name/Title under which main entry is made.
    (C) Name of the catalogue, who has made its entry.
    (D) It is a concept in documents which have fancy titles.
123. AACR-2 provides how many types of levels of descriptions?
    (A) Four (B) Two
    (C) Three (D) One
124. Which punctuation sign is used when author's name is inverted?

(A) Comma (B) Semi-colon
(C) Colon (D) Dot

125. Which one of the following catalogue is used in stock verification?
(A) Inventory catalogue (B) Union catalogue
(C) Card catalogue (D) MARC form catalogue

126. In ISBD (G) the alphabet (G) stands for:
(A) Graphs (B) Geometrical
(C) Geographical (D) General

127. Transliteration of any author name helps in:
(A) It's cataloging by the non-English knowing catalogues.
(B) It's understands by a common library user.
(C) It's alphabetical arrangement.
(D) None of the above

128. Double colon in UDC is used to show:
(A) Simple relation (B) Sub grouping
(C) Order fixing (D) Coordination

129. In CCC, CIE and CRIE are described in:
(A) Part A to D (B) Part G
(C) Part K & L (D) Part S-W

130. Which edition of colon classification is freely faceted classification?
(A) Edition-1 (B) Edition-2
(C) Edition-6 (D) Edition-7

131. C.C.C. is divided into:
(A) 26 parts (B) 2 parts
(C) 21 parts (D) 20 parts

132. In CCC, entry can be made in title only when:
(A) It is a government publication
(B) When there are more than three author?
(C) When there is no author or collaborator.
(D) Entry can never be in title of document.

133. In a classification system we are not bothered about:

(A) Place value of digit
(B) Ordinal value of digit
(C) Coordinal value of digit
(D) Semantic value of digit.

134. C.C.C. (5th ed) is divided on the basis of:
(A) Five Criteria (B) Three Criteria
(C) Six Criteria (D) Two Criteria

135. In AACR-2, entry can be in the name of collaborator, if:
(A) Here are more collaborators than its authors.
(B) The collaborators are of high repute
(C) If the document is government publication
(D) It can never be in the name of collaborator.

136. Which one of the following is not a criterion in division of CCC (5th Ed)?
(A) Normative principles and theory
(B) Cataloging operations
(C) Types of entries
(D) Rules of choice of access points.

137. In CCC, anonymous work is entered under:
(A) Title of the document
(B) Name of the publisher
(C) Name of the collaborator
(D) No clear roles are there

138. "See" reference entry is related to:
(A) CCC (B) AACR-2
(C) Both of the above (D) None of the above

139. If the title page of the document docs not gives the name of personal author, which one of the following will be used first in main entry heading?
(A) Title of the document
(B) Name of the joint collaborators
(C) Name of the collaborator
(D) Name of the publisher

140. In AACR-2, a reference entry is to be make when:

(A) Author of a document is not ascertained
(B) There are anonymous editions of works whose authors have been ascertained
(C) When there is a government publication
(D) When document is in machine readable form.

141. In CCC "A tale of tub (published anonymously, by J.Swift" will be entered under Title
(A) Swift, J
(B) Swift, J, with Reference entry under title
(C) None of the above

142. In AACR-2, entry is made under title when?
(A) Document is produced by three authors.
(B) Document is a Non-book material
(C) Document is having fancy title
(D) Document is a sacred scripture

143. Which of the following international document initially uses chain procedure?
(A) INB
(B) Sear's list of subject heading
(C) INSPEC
(D) BNB

144. How many zones have been identified by Dr. Ranganathan in an array?
(A) 3 (B) 5
(C) 6 (D) 4

145. Subject analytical entry is known in CCC as:
(A) CIE (B) BIE
(C) CRIE (D) CRE

146. All through alphabetization is also known as:
(A) Letter by letter (B) Word by word
(C) Both of these (D) None of these

147. Which one of the following visible indexes uses cards in it?
(A) Lindex (B) Chaindex
(C) Stripdex (D) Kardex

148. "Portability" is a characteristic while studying:
   (A) During choice of subject headings.
   (B) Comparison of AACR-2 and CCC
   (C) Inner form of Catalogue
   (D) Physical form of catalogue
149. Ranganathan does not five emphasis on Imprint & Collation because:
   (A) Ranganathan was not aware of these terms.
   (B) Ranganathan cannot give attention to terms
   (C) Ranganathan gives emphasis on closed access.
   (D) Ranganathan considered that catalogue of open access does not need such sections.
150. In CCC, short form for 'Editor' is:
   (A) Ed. (B) Edit
   (C) ed. (D) None of the above
151. In using chain procedure, the classification scheme should have:
   (A) Indo-Arabic Notation
   (B) The lower link in it must be a sub-division of its above link
   (C) It should have any type of facet sequence.
   (D) It should be purely enumerative scheme.
152. Which one of the following uses words of tiles in deriving subject headings?
   (A) KWIC (B) KWAC
   (C) KWOC (D) All of the above
153. Which one of the following term is given by Ranganathan?
   (A) Cooperative cataloguing
   (B) Centralized cataloguing
   (C) Literary Warrant
   (D) Pre-natal cataloguing
154. Canon of Ascertainability is proposed by:
   (A) Antony Panizzi (B) S.R. Ranganathan
   (C) C.A. Cutter (D) H.P. Luhn

155. According to AACR-2, if a person is known by different names, then main entry will be in:
   (A) Latest name
   (B) Name that appears most frequently in his/her works
   (C) Both of these will be considered
   (D) None of these
156. Unsought links are those links:
   (A) Which represents relationship isolates
   (B) Which are used by readers in searching documents
   (C) Which represents subjects but not sought by readers
   (D) None of the above
157. Which one of the following journal was published by Ranganathan?
   (A) Annals of Library Science
   (B) Library science with a slant to documentation
   (C) Journal of Lib. & Inf. Science
   (D) None of the above
158. Library of Congress initiated the following programme:
   (A) Pre-natal cataloguing
   (B) Cataloguing-in-publication
   (C) Both of the above
   (D) None of the above.
159. Links representing connecting symbols is known as:
   (A) False links (B) Missing links
   (C) Sought links (D) Unsought links
160. Which edition of AACR gives more illustration examples?
   (A) AACR-I
   (B) AACR-II
   (C) Both gives similar emphasis
   (D) Nonc gives any examples.
161. AACR-I was divided into:
   (A) Is a single document (B) Three parts
   (C) Two parts (D) Six parts.

162. AACR-2 is divided into:

(A) Is a single document (B) Three parts

(C) Two parts (D) Six parts

163. 'Part M' in CCC is most important because of:

(A) It gives theoretical aspects of cataloguing

(B) It is related to non-book materials

(C) It given Ranganathan's biography

(D) Rules for choice & rendering of main entries.

164. Chapter-I (Part-I) in AACR-2 is related to:

(A) Descriptive cataloguing applicable to non-book materials.

(B) Descriptive cataloguing applicable to any kind of lib. Material

(C) Both of the above

(D) None of the above.

165. In AACR-2 "Choice of Access points" is dealt at

(A) Part-I (B) Part-II

(C) Both have its rules (D) None of these.

166. Chapter 2-13 (Part-I) in AACR-2 are related to:

(A) Descriptive cataloguing of Government publications.

(B) Descriptive cataloguing of conference proceedings.

(C) Descriptive cataloguing of specific types of library materials.

(D) None of the above

167. While choosing main entry heading, what is main difference in AACR-2 and CCC

(A) In AACR-2 information can be taken from outside source

(B) In CCC, information can be sought from other sources.

(C) Both of the above

(D) No difference in AACR-2 and CCC

168. Which canon says that heading in a catalogue entry should not be subjected to change?

(A) Canon of Individualisation
(B) Canon of context
(C) Canon of currency
(D) Canon of Performance

169. "Geographic Names" in AACR-2 is dealt at:
(A) Chapter-12 (B) Chapter-13
(C) Chapter-21 (D) Chapter-23

170. Which one of the following canon was added in 1968?
(A) Canon of context
(B) Canon of Sought headings
(C) Canon of currency
(D) Canon of Recall value.

171. Which canon prescribes that the current usage term should be used in describing subject in subject entries?
(A) Canon of sought headings
(B) Canon of permanence
(C) Canon of context
(D) Canon of currency

172. Since when BNB has started using PRECIS in its subject heading derivations:
(A) 1958 (B) 1967
(C) 1971 (D) 1978

173. How many normative principles are related to cataloguing?
(A) Three (B) Four
(C) Nine (D) Six

174. In Canon of Recall value, Recall value means.
(A) Word which a documents repeats in its title.
(B) Word which a user uses in its day-to-day life.
(C) Word that is most likely toe back to the memory by a user
(D) None of the above.

175. Which Canon describes that the most important word group should be used as the entry element?

(A) Canon of Permanence
(B) Canon of Sought Headings
(C) Canon of Currency
(D) Canon of Prepotency

176. In AACR-2, Part-I is further sub-divided into:
(A) 3-chapters (B) 6-chapters
(C) 13-chapters (D) 20-chapters

177. AACR-2 is based on the following principles:
(A) Principle of Authorship
(B) Principle of Literary units
(C) Both of the above
(D) None of the above

178. CODATA is associated with:
(A) Information Retrieval
(B) Bibliographic description
(C) Indexing system
(D) Data compilation

179. Out of the four ISBN components which one is not from it?
(A) Group Identifier (B) Year Identifier
(C) Publisher Identifier (D) Title Identifier

180. Who is the developer of SLIC index?
(A) E.J. Coates (B) J. Kaiser
(C) A.C. Foskett (D) J.R. Sharp

181. Ideas of E.J. Coates can be seen in the following document:
(A) Atom index
(B) Current Technology Index
(C) Index Medicos
(D) POPSI

182. Standard Book Numbers were used in:
(A) U.K (B) U.S.A
(C) China (D) India

183. The elementary categories used in POPSI are written as (in sequence)

(A) D, E, A, P (B) D, A, E, P

(C) P, D, A, E (D) P, E, D, A

184. In AACR-2. Series area begins after:
    (A) Physical description area
    (B) Tracing Area
    (C) ISSN Area
    (D) Year of Publication.
185. Which one of the following is Kaiser's dual category in indexing system?
    (A) Action (B) Property
    (C) Process (D) Entity
186. Optical coincidence system is a type of:
    (A) Pre-coordinate indexing
    (B) Post-coordinate indexing
    (C) Is not related to indexing system
    (D) None of the above.
187. Which National Library is associated with AACR-I:
    (A) National Library of India
    (B) British Museum
    (C) Library of Congress
    (D) State Lenin Library
188. The basic difference between thesaurus and list of subject headings is:
    (A) List of subject headings provide example listing.
    (B) List of subject headings is for post coordinate indexing.
    (C) Thesaurus list terms in a helpful order.
    (D) Thesaurus is done to pre-coordinate indexing need.
189. Which one of the following is Recall oriented device?
    (A) Coordination (B) Links
    (C) Roles (D) Synonym Control
190. Problem of Homonyms is related to:
    (A) Artificial Language (B) Natural Language
    (C) Machine Language (D) Controlled Language
191. The full form of TEST is:

(A) The Engineering science thesaurus
(B) Thesaurus of Engineering and Scientific terms
(C) Thesaurus of Scientific & Technology information
(D) The English subject thesaurus.

192. "Precision ratio" is a term used in:
(A) Indexing system
(B) Evaluation of indexing system
(C) Information storage devices
(D) None of these

193. Ranganathan uses (-irt) is his indexes for:
(A) Information retrieval techniques
(B) Information recall technology
(C) In relation to
(D) In relation for

194. Which one of the following is Recall Oriented device?
(A) Coordination (B) Links
(C) Roles (D) Synonym control

195. (RT) is thesaurus is used for:
(A) Related term (B) Right term
(C) Referred term (D) Received term

196. Illustrative material of document is given in:
(A) Imprint section
(B) Collection section
(C) GMD section
(D) Physical description section

197. Which one of the following is a post-coordinate indexing system?
(A) PRECIS (B) POPSI
(C) KWIC (D) UNITERM system

198. Which of the following principles are related to static theory of classification?
(A) Richardson's criteria
(B) Bliss's principles
(C) Berwick Sayer's canons
(D) All of the above

199. Which indexing technique uses keywords outside the title of the document?
    (A) KWIC (B) KWOC
    (C) PRECIS (D) KWAC

200. Accession Number in AACR-2 is written:
    (A) Along with call number
    (B) At fourth horizontal line from above
    (C) At fourth horizontal line from below
    (D) It not written at all.

201. Subject headings along with their relationships are defined in :
    (A) Subject headings list
    (B) Encyclopedias
    (C) Dictionaries
    (D) Thesaurus

202. Tracing of an entry is done in CCC.
    (A) in the last lines of the card
    (B) in the reverse side of the entry
    (C) In both the places
    (D) Not done in CCC.

203. If we say 9-Apples, then the digit 9 has:
    (A) Ordinal value (B) Cardinal value
    (C) Semantic Value (D) Place value

204. How many indentions are there in AACR-2?
    (A) Three (B) Two
    (C) One (D) Four

205. Which canon of classification says that the arrangement of classes in an array of classes should be helpful to the uses?
    (A) Canon of Relevant succession
    (B) Canon of consistent succession
    (C) Canon of consistent sequence
    (D) Canon of Helpful sequence

206. Macro-subject can be defined as:
    (A) A subject with huge literature on it.
    (B) A subject having very important aspect.
    (C) A subject whose name is very long
    (D) A subject with great extension and small intensions.
207. Which one of the following is not a metal faculty on which Francis Bacon divides his scheme?
    (A) Memory (B) Intuition
    (C) Imagination (D) Reason
208. Which canon of classification says that the characteristic applied for division of a universe should completely divided it?
    (A) Canon of consistent succession
    (B) Canon of Exclusiveness
    (C) Canon of Exhaustiveness
    (D) Canon of Consistent sequence.
209. "Child marriage" is a type of subject:
    (A) Basic subject (B) Compound subject
    (C) Complex subject (D) All of the above.
210. Bodlein library initially uses the classification scheme of:
    (A) Melvil Dewey (B) S.R. Ranganathan
    (C) Francis Bacon (D) K.V. Gesner
211. Problem of homonym occurs in:
    (A) Idea plane (B) Verbal plane
    (C) National plane (D) Both (A) & (B)
212. The totality of the ideas consumed by human is called:
    (A) Idea (B) Array
    (C) Knowledge (D) Subject
213. A generic term used to denote any component of a compound subject.
    (A) Facet (B) Idea
    (C) Focus (D) Chain

214. J.C. Brunet belongs to:
(A) France (B) London
(C) New York (D) Russia

215. "Kama" is the division of knowledge in
(A) Comte's classification
(B) Baconian classification
(C) Greek classification
(D) Vedic classification

216. Who publishes his classification scheme in "Advancement of Human Learning?"
(A) Francis Bacon (B) Melvil Dewey
(C) S.R. Ranganathan (D) C.A. Cutter

217. Callimachus is associated with:
(A) Information retrieval (B) Classification
(C) Cataloguing (D) Library administration.

218. Which classification scheme follows inverted Baconian classification scheme?
(A) Bliss Classification (B) Colon Classification
(C) Library of Congress (D) DDC

219. Name of the replacement which use at the time place of publication is not given in AACR-2,?
(A) S.n. (B) S.l.
(C) Three dots (D) Left blank

220. Who said that "Knowledge classification" is the basis of "Library classification?"
(A) W.C. Berwick Sayers (B) S.R. Ranganathan
(C) August Comte (D) Herbert Spenser

221. Which of the following classification scheme have no logical basis?
(A) Beconian system
(B) Konrad Von Gesner Scheme
(C) Gabriel Naude's bibliographic classification.
(D) Melvil Dewey's DDC.

222. In the glossing of CCC (rirt) stands for:
(A) Right in relation to (B) Related in right term
(C) Referred in relation to (D) None of these

223. The entry element is written in CAPITAL letter in :
    (A) AACR-I (B) AACR-2
    (C) CCC (D) None of these
224. In AACR-2, the conference proceeding entry will be
    (A) Title (No. of Conf.: Year: Place)
    (B) Title (Year: Place: NO. of Conf.)
    (C) Title only.
    (D) (Year: Place: NO. of Conf.) Title.
225. Which one of the following is correct AACR-2 entry?
    (A) India, Human Resource Development, Ministry of
    (B) India, Ministry of Human Resource Development
    (C) India, Parliament of, MHRD
    (D) Any, one of these
226. Which indic names are to entered in their first part of the name?
    (A) Sikhs (B) Muslims
    (C) Bengalis (D) North Indians
227. If more than one place of publication is given for a document, then in entry-
    (A) Place of international repute will be written
    (B) S.N. will be written
    (C) First place of publication will be written
    (D) None of these will be used.
228. North Indian name is to be entered under the family name in:
    (A) AACR-2
    (B) CCC
    (C) In both AACR-2 & CCC
    (D) None of them
229. Call Number of a book consist of:
    (A) Class Number (B) Book Number
    (C) Collection Number (D) All of the above
230. Which one of the following is not a kind of subject?
    (A) Simple Subject (B) Complex subject
    (C) Compound subject (D) Duplex subject

231. From which edition DDC is available online:
   (A) 19th Ed. (B) 20th Ed.
   (C) 22nd Ed. (D) 24th Ed.

232. "Term Card" is associated with
   (A) Pre-coordinate Indexing system
   (B) Post- coordinate indexing system
   (C) Development of Classification Schemes
   (D) Cataloguing of Rare-documents.

233. The type of notation used in colon classification is:
   (A) Pure Roman (B) Mixed Notation
   (C) Indo-Arabic Numerals (D) None of these.

234. "Niti-Niti principle" is used to identify:
   (A) Personality (B) Matter
   (C) Space (D) Energy

235. Colon was the only connecting symbol in colon classification upto:
   (A) 6th Ed. (B) 2nd Ed.
   (C) 1st Ed. (D) 3rd Ed.

236. What term is used in colon classification for "INDEX".
   (A) Bibliography. (B) Not used at all
   (C) Dictionary (D) Concordance

237. Which of the following is fully enumerative classification scheme?
   (A) Colon classification
   (B) Universal Decimal classification
   (C) Dewey Decimal classification
   (D) Library of Congress classification.

238. Margaret Mann is associated with.
   (A) Classification
   (B) Cataloguing
   (C) Information storage & Retrieval
   (D) Public Library Movement in USA

239. Which of the following devices are used to increase the capacity of a notational system?
   (A) Octave device (B) Sector device
   (C) Packeted notation (D) All of the above.

240. Which type of source of information is Trade Literature?
 (A) Primary (B) Secondary
 (C) Tertiary (D) None of these.

241. University of Illinois publishes
 (A) Journal of Documentation
 (B) Journal of Information Science
 (C) Library Trends
 (D) Library Quarterly

242. An incident of Afghanistan will get more coverage in:
 (A) Facts of File
 (B) Keesing's record of world events
 (C) Asian recorder
 (D) None of these.

243. Main aim for publishing Trade Bibliographies is:
 (A) To help users (B) To do business
 (C) To help library staff (D) All of the above

244. Pamphlet is a document of a few printed pages, usually less than:
 (A) 5 pages (B) 10 pages
 (C) 49 pages (D) 60 pages

245. According to Ranganathan, "PATENT" is a document classed under
 (A) Tertiary document
 (B) Neo-conventional document
 (C) Non-conventional document
 (D) Informal source of information.

246. The frequency of SCI is:
 (A) Monthly (B) Quarterly
 (C) Bimonthly (D) Weekly

247. "Current contents" is published by
 (A) Institute of Scientific Information (Philadelphia)
 (B) Indian Institute of Science
 (C) University of Illinois
 (D) National Medical Library

248. Meta-document is a term given by:

(A) Denis Grogan (B) C.W. Hanson
(C) S.R. Ranganathan (D) Paul Otlet

249. Science Citation Index consists of:
(A) One index (B) Two indexes
(C) Four indexes (D) Three indexes

250. Which open of the following is National Input Centre for UNESCO's Index Translatonium?
(A) National Science Library
(B) National Library
(C) Parliament Library
(D) Defence Science Library

251. The term GILA is associated with:
(A) Indexing system
(B) Information Storage System
(C) Directory of Govt. of India Libraries
(D) None of these.

252. During Vedic period, knowledge was divided into one of the following branches:
(A) Moksha (B) Poesy
(C) Logic (D) Concrete

253. "Traite de Documentation" was published by:
(A) Henri La Fontaine (B) Paul Otlet
(C) F.W. Lancaster (D) C.A. Cutter

254. ISO recommendation for abbreviation of periodical titles as:
(A) ISO/R690-1968 (B) ISO/TC-46
(C) ISO/DR-1278 (D) ISO/R4-1953

255. When were Five Laws of library science first conceived and published in?
(A) 1927;1929 (B) 1923;1925
(C) 1945;1948 (D) 1930;1931

256. Indira Gandhi National Centre for Arts (IGNCA) was established in:
(A) 1981 (B) 1945
(C) 1986 (D) 1976

257. ISO recommendation for bibliographical references is?
(A) ISO/R690-1968 (B) ISO/DR-1278
(C) ISO/TC-46 (D) ISO/R4-1953

258. Which one of the following is intermediary between information user and its generation?
(A) Reprographic System (B) Information System
(C) Indexing System (D) Abstracting System

259. Which one of the following is not a characteristic of knowledge?
(A) It is infinite (B) It is fragmented
(C) It is dynamic (D) It is coherent

260. Year 1930 is an important landmark in Indian Librarianship because:
(A) National Public Library Act was passed.
(B) Dr. S.R. Ranganathan was awarded 'Bharat Ratna'
(C) ILA was established
(D) None of these.

261. In the name of S.R.Ranganathan, "Shiyali" is the name of
(A) His wife (B) His mother
(C) His elder sister (D) His village

262. Who was first Chairman of UGC?
(A) Dr. C. D. Deshmukh (B) Dr. S.R. Ranganathan
(C) Dr. Kothari (D) Dr. Manmohan singh

263. What is the correct sequence of the following according to their decrease in coverage?
(A) Law-Principle-Cannon
(B) Canon-law-principal
(C) Law-Canon-Principle
(D) Law-Canon-Principle- Hypothesis

264. Mass media is a kind of communication Channel:
(A) Formal Channel
(B) AR Entertainment media
(C) Two- way channel
(D) Informal channel

265. In which year 49th FID conference was held:
    (A) 1998 at Delhi (B) 1996 at Jaipur
    (C) 1989 at Shimla (D) 1981 at Delhi
266. Library Day is celebrated in :
    (A) 14th February (B) 14th July
    (C) 20th December (D) 5th September
267. Which one of the following is not essential element of communication system?
    (A) Communication (B) Message
    (C) Interpreter (D) Recipient
268. Ranganathan gets an idea about analytics-synthetic classification scheme by seeing
    (A) Library of Congress (B) British Museum
    (C) BHU library (D) Meceano set
269. Which one of the following is barrier to communication?
    (A) Lack of interest
    (B) Lack on need
    (C) Lack of understanding or foreign language document.
    (D) None of the above.
270. Any process where there is "An exchange and exact application of thoughts feeling, facts belies and ideas between and among the individuals" is known as:
    (A) Communication Process
    (B) Information Retrieval Techniques
    (C) Vocabulary control techniques
    (D) Knowledge conservation technique.
271. ISLA is an
    (A) Indexing journal
    (B) Dept.of Library & information Science Journal
    (C) Current Information Source
    (D) Abstracting journal
272. Who is known as Ranganathan of Pakistan":
    (A) Mazid Ali Khan (B) Mohd K Ahmad
    (C) Dr Hameed (D) J.D. Brown.

273. Which one of the following chairperson of University Library Committee.

(A) Librarian (B) Registrar

(C) Vice- Chancellor (D) None of the above.

274. Library cess is a source of income for:

(A) School Library (B) Private Library

(C) Public Library (D) University Library

275. "Library of Congress" (USA) is equivalent to:

(A) Parliament Library in India

(B) National Science Library of India

(C) National Achieves of India

(D) Central Secretariat Library of India

276. The first true Public Libraries Act of UK was passed in:

(A) 1849 (B) 1850

(C) 1854 (D) 1852

277. National Institute of Oceanography is located at:

(A) Chennai (B) Hyderabad

(C) Goa (D) Mumbai

278. Kenyon Committee was set up for Library development in:

(A) UK (B) Kenya

(C) Paris (D) Nigeria

279. There is no separate Department of Public libraries in:

(A) Andhra Pradesh (B) Uttar Pradesh

(C) Tamil Nadu (D) Karnataka

280. What is date of birth of Dr. S. R. Ranganathan?

(A) 14th August, 1901 (B) 16th August, 1901

(C) 25th August, 1901 (D) 15th August, 1901

281. Library of ISRO (India) comes under the category of:

(A) Academic Library (B) Full-Automated Library

(C) Defence Library (D) Special Library.

282. Special Library is maintained through:

(A) Govt. Grant (B) Public fund

(C) Library Cess (D) None of the above

283. CDRI is located at:
   (A) Lucknow (B) Haridwar
   (C) Pune (D) New Delhi

284. Who was teacher of Dr. Ranganathan in London?
   (A) Anthony Pannizi (B) W.C.B Sayers
   (C) H.E.Bliss (D) J.D. Brown

285. ILSA is an
   (A) Indexing journal
   (B) Dept. of Library & Information Science Journal
   (C) Current Information Source
   (D) Abstracting journal

286. Standardisation bodies are mainly concerned with three topics, which of the following is one of it?
   (A) Abstracting (B) Transliteration
   (C) Translation (D) None of the above

287. The first mobile library was started in:
   (A) Karnataka (B) Kerala
   (C) Haryana (D) Tamil Nadu

288. Who had authored 'Putting Knowledge to work'?
   (A) Jesse H. Shera (B) S.R.Ranganathan
   (C) A.J.wells (D) Pauline Atherton

289. The concept of 'Librametry' was developed by:
   (A) A.W. Gouldner (B) S. R. Ranganathan
   (C) M. Murphy (D) G. R. Lyle

290. To resolve the conflict between two Canons, an appeal can be made to:
   (A) Postulates (B) Principles
   (C) The Five Laws (D) None of the above

291. The term 'Library Science' was first used by:
   (A) J. Mills (B) W.C. Berwick Sayers
   (C) Melvil Dewey (D) S.R. Ranganathan.

292. Name given by S.R. Ranganathan for Book Mobiles is:
   (A) Janitor (B) Mobile Van
   (C) Library on Wheels (D) Librachine

293. Ranganathan was appointed as National Research professor in Library Science by Government of India in:
    (A) 1965 (B) 1966
    (C) 1967 (D) 1968
294. The first Indian book on Library Science entitled 'Primer of Librarianship' was written by:
    (A) S.R. Ranganathan (B) D.N. Marshall
    (C) Asa Don Dickenson (D) None of the above
295. Which honour was awarded to Dr.Ranganathan by Government of India in recognition of his services in the field of Library Science and Librarianship.
    (A) Rao Sahib (B) D. Litt
    (C) Padmashri (D) Padma Bhushan
296. The term "Informatics" is used in France for:
    (A) Information Retrieval
    (B) Indexing System
    (C) Machine processing of data
    (D) Manually retrieval of information
297. "INFOTERM Series" is published by":
    (A) INFLIBNET, Ahmedabad
    (B) INFONET, New Delhi
    (C) ISALIC, Kolkata
    (D) INFOTERM, Paris.
298. Main three types of information requirement given by:
    (A) Mikhailov (B) Melvin Voigt
    (C) Vickery (D) S.C. Bradford
299. ANSI headquarters is located at:
    (A) Chicago (B) New Jersey
    (C) New York (D) Washington, DC
300. ICIREPAT is an international organizations associated with:
    (A) Information Retrievals
    (B) Standards
    (C) Patents
    (D) Information Exchange.

301. Which one of the following technical committee was set up for standardization work in documentation field.
   (A) ISA-46 (B) ISA-33
   (C) ISA-39 (D) ISA-40
302. In which of the information approach, the need of information is continuous one?
   (A) Exhaustive approach
   (B) Current approach
   (C) Catching-up approach
   (D) Everyday approach
303. "Informatologia Yugoslavica" is name of a
   (A) A periodical
   (B) An Institute
   (C) A documentation Centre
   (D) A Society
304. Which one of the following information need requires almost all relevant information documents to users?
   (A) Exhaustive approach
   (B) Everyday approach
   (C) Brusting-up approach
   (D) Current approach.
305. Which one of the information gathering technique uses direct contact with user?
   (A) Interview method (B) Questionnaire method
   (C) Diary method (D) Observation by self
306. Which one of the following is not an approach to information?
   (A) Current approach
   (B) Everyday approach
   (C) Catching-up approach
   (D) Leisure approach
307. New name of "American Documentation Institute" is:
   (A) American Documentation Centre
   (B) United States Centre of Documentation
   (C) American Information Resource Centre
   (D) Knowledge & Learning Centre.

308. When communication takes place without bringing the lien of Authority in consideration, It is called?
   (A) Informal communication
   (B) One-way communication
   (C) It is not a communication process
   (D) Diagonal communication.
309. ISO is associated with:
   (A) Information storage
   (B) Information Standardization
   (C) Intellectual system organization
   (D) Standardization Agency.
310. Which one of the following is related to development of team "informatics"?
   (A) Calvin Mooers (B) Mikhailov
   (C) Paul Otlet (D) Henri La Fontaine
311. The term 'Recall' is used in information retrieval to refer to the ability of a system to:
   (A) Withhold irrelevant documents
   (B) Respond to a query without loss of time
   (C) Retrieve relevant documents
   (D) Recall a specific document.
312. An instrument which is defined as "Government grant of exclusive privilege of making/selling the new inventions" is known as:
   (A) Power of Attorney (B) Specifications
   (C) Patents (D) Standards
313. The basic difference between SDI and other modes of Current Awareness is that SDI is:
   (A) Directed towards the needs of an individual user/ project
   (B) A computer based information service
   (C) Provided only at the local level
   (D) Provided only to the top managers.
314. Biggest consumers of information are:
   (A) Students (B) Researchers
   (C) Teachers (D) All the above

315. Who suggested to impost bibliographical control one big journal is sufficient"
   (A) J.D. Bernal (B) S.R. Ranganathan
   (C) Weston Devis (D) Alvin Weignberg.
316. Who suggested that one big library is the basic factor for bibliographical control:
   (A) Weston Devis (B) D.J. Foskett
   (C) J.D. Bernal (D) Alvin Wiegnberg
317. Among the following which is not a NISSAT Sectoral Center:
   (A) National Chemical Laboratory
   (B) National Informatics Center
   (C) Central Drug Research Institute
   (D) ATIRA
318. Which one of the following is not the feature of an information retrieval system:
   (A) Relevance (B) Recall
   (C) Precision (D) Perception
319. Which one is the barrier for information communication?
   (A) Classification (B) Censorship
   (C) Indexing(D) Weeding out.
320. Growth of information beyond manageable limit is known as:
   (A) Information growth (B) Information dynamics
   (C) Exponential growth (D) Information explosion
321. The first director of DRTC was:
   (A) P.N. Kaula (B) S.R. Ranganathan
   (C) A. Neelameghan (D) B.S. Kesavan
322. Size to size reproduction of documents is called:
   (A) Reduction (B) Enlargement
   (C) Facsimile (D) None of the above.
323. World Science Information System refers to
   (A) UNISIST (B) NATIS
   (C) DEVSIS (D) ISDS

324. The concept of 'Technological Gatekeepers' was first proposed by:
    (A) Allen (B) Diana Crane
    (C) Solla Price (D) B. Guha
325. In which of the following types of indexes are access points not derives automatically:
    (A) KWIC (B) Citation Indexing
    (C) KWOC (D) POPSI
326. What is routing of journals:
    (A) Reference service
    (B) Information service
    (C) Current Awareness service
    (D) Selective Dissemination of Information.
327. Free indexing language is commonly used in:
    (A) Citation indexes
    (B) Computer-based system
    (C) Pre-coordinate indexing system
    (D) Post-coordinate indexing system.
328. What is the function of Referral Centre?
    (A) Which directly gives information
    (B) Which provides information directly to the enquirer
    (C) Which does not provide information directly to the enquirer
    (D) Which does not provide information directly to the enquirer but suggest sources
329. 'GISTRNIC' is a part of:
    (A) SIRNET (B) INFLIBNET
    (C) DELNET (D) NICNET
330. The direct method of electrostatic photocopying is known as:
    (A) Zerography (B) Electrography
    (C) Thermography (D) Electrofax
331. ASLIB Cranfield Research Project was mainly concerned with:
    (A) Classification and cataloguing
    (B) Information retrieval

(C) Evaluation of indexing system

(D) Selective Dissemination of Information.

332. Notification of new arrivals in the library is a:

(A) SDI service (B) CAS service

(C) Reference service (D) Information service

333. ISR stands for:

(A) Information Source Retrieval

(B) Indexing, sorting and Retrieval

(C) Indexing system of research methods

(D) Information storage and retrieval.

ANSWERS

1. (B)	2. (D)	3. (B)	4. (C)
5. (C)	6. (A)	7. (A)	8. (B)
9. (C)	10. (B)	11. (D)	12. (A)
13. (C)	14. (C)	15. (B)	16. (B)
17. (A)	18. (A)	19. (A)	20. (D)
21. (B)	22. (D)	23. (A)	24. (B)
25. (B)	26. (D)	27. (C)	28. (D)
29. (B)	30. (A)	31. (C)	32. (D)
33. (B)	34. (D)	35. (A)	36. (D)
37. (D)	38. (D)	39. (C)	40. (C)
41. (D)	42. (B)	43. (A)	44. (D)
45. (A)	46. (C)	47. (C)	48. (D)
49. (D)	50. (B)	51. (D)	52. (B)
53. (B)	54. (C)	55. (D)	56. (A)
57. (D)	58. (A)	59. (B)	60. (C)
61. (C)	62. (C)	63. (C)	64. (C)
65. (B)	66. (B)	67. (C)	68. (B)
69. (C)	70. (A)	71. (A)	72. (D)
73. (B)	74. (A)	75. (A)	76. (D)
77. (B)	78. (D)	79. (C)	80. (D)
81. (B)	82. (B)	83. (C)	84. (A)
85. (A)	86. (B)	87. (A)	88. (D)
89. (D)	90. (C)	91. (B)	92. (A)
93. (A)	94. (A)	95. (B)	96. (B)
97. (B)	98. (C)	99. (A)	100. (D)
101. (D)	102. (D)	103. (A)	104. (A)
105. (B)	106. (A)	107. (A)	108. (D)
109. (C)	110. (C)	111. (A)	112. (B)
113. (C)	114. (A)	115. (B)	116. (C)

117. (A)	118. (B)	119. (C)	120. (C)
121. (C)	122. (A)	123. (C)	124. (C)
125. (A)	126. (D)	127. (C)	128. (C)
129. (C)	130. (D)	131. (C)	132. (C)
133. (C)	134. (A)	135. (D)	136. (D)
137. (C)	138. (C)	139. (C)	140. (B)
141. (A)	142. (D)	143. (B)	144. (B)
145. (D)	146. (A)	147. (D)	148. (D)
149. (D)	150. (A)	151. (B)	152. (D)
153. (D)	154. (B)	155. (C)	156. (C)
157. (B)	158. (A)	159. (A)	160. (B)
161. (B)	162. (C)	163. (D)	164. (B)
165. (B)	166. (C)	167. (A)	168. (D)
169. (D)	170. (D)	171. (D)	172. (C)
173. (D)	174. (C)	175. (D)	176. (C)
177. (C)	178. (D)	179. (B)	180. (D)
181. (B)	182. (A)	183. (A)	184. (A)
185. (A)	186. (A)	187. (C)	188. (C)
189. (D)	190. (B)	191. (B)	192. (B)
193. (C)	194. (D)	195. (B)	196. (D)
197. (D)	198. (D)	199. (D)	200. (C)
201. (D)	202. (B)	203. (B)	204. (A)
205. (D)	206. (D)	207. (B)	208. (C)
209. (B)	210. (C)	211. (D)	212. (C)
213. (A)	214. (A)	215. (D)	216. (A)
217. (B)	218. (D)	219. (B)	220. (A)
221. (C)	222. (C)	223. (C)	224. (A)
225. (B)	226. (A)	227. (C)	228. (B)
229. (D)	230. (D)	231. (B)	232. (B)
233. (B)	234. (A)	235. (B)	236. (D)
237. (D)	238. (B)	239. (A)	240. (A)
241. (C)	242. (C)	243. (B)	244. (C)
245. (B)	246. (C)	247. (A)	248. (D)
249. (D)	250. (B)	251. (C)	252. (A)
253. (B)	254. (C)	255. (D)	256. (C)
257. (A)	258. (B)	259. (B)	260. (C)
261. (D)	262. (A)	263. (C)	264. (A)
265. (A)	266. (C)	267. (C)	268. (D)
269. (C)	270. (A)	271	272. (A)
273. (C)	274. (C)	275. (A)	276. (B)
277. (C)	278. (A)	279. (C)	280. (A)
281. (D)	282. (D)	283. (A)	284. (B)
285. (D)	286. (B)	287. (D)	288. (D)

289. (D)	290. (C)	291. (D)	292. (C)
293. (A)	294. (C)	295. (C)	296. (C)
297. (D)	298. (C)	299. (C)	300. (C)
301. (A)	302. (B)	303. (A)	304. (A)
305. (A)	306. (D)	307. (A)	308. (C)
309. (D)	310. (B)	311. (C)	312. (C)
313. (A)	314. (B)	315. (A)	316. (A)
317. (B)	318. (D)	319. (B)	320. (D)
321. (B)	322. (C)	323. (A)	324. (A)
325. (D)	326. (C)	327. (B)	328. (D)
329. (D)	330. (D)	331. (C)	332. (B)
333. (D)	334. (C)	335. (C)	336. (A)
337. (C)	338. (B)	339. (C)	340. (B)
341. (B)	342. (A)	343. (A)	344. (A)
345. (A)	346. (C)	347. (A)	348. (B)
349. (D)	350. (C)	351. (C)	352. (C)
353. (A)	354. (C)	355. (C)	356. (C)
357. (C)	358. (C)	359. (C)	360. (B)
361. (B)	362. (A)	363. (B)	364. (A)
365. (A)	366. (A)	367. (C)	368. (D)
369. (C)	370. (A)	371. (B)	372. (A)
373. (B)	374. (B)	375. (A)	376. (C)
377. (A)	378. (A)	379. (D)	380. (D)
381. (C)	382. (D)	383. (D)	384. (B)
385. (B)	386. (C)	387. (C)	388. (C)
389. (B)	390. (C)	391. (C)	392. (D)
393. (C)	394. (A)	395. (C)	396. (B)
397. (A)	398. (A)	399. (A)	400. (C)
401. (A)	402. (D)	403. (B)	404. (B)
405. (B)	406. (D)	407. (D)	408. (A)
409. (A)	410. (C)	411. (A)	412. (D)

10
Fill in the Blanks

1. The Head Quarters of IFLA is located at............ (The Hague, Brussels, Amsterdam)
2. Incunabula are the kinds of books printed before .... (12th Century, 15th B.C., 15th Century A.D.)
3. The periodicity of "University News" is .... (Fortnightly, Monthly, Quarterly)
4. American Library Association was established in the year .... (1876, 1877, 1895)
5. The UGC was formally establish by an executive order in the year .... (1955, 1956, 1561)
6. Indian Library Association was established in the year .... (1934, 1933, 1929)
7. Newark System is a method of ....and ....books (Charging and Discharging, Inter-library Loans and Reservation, Reservation and Charging)
8. Diamond Jubilee of the ILA was celebrated in the year............ (1993, 1994, 1992)
9. The Educational Commission(1964-66) recommends allocation of ....% of the total budget of the University for its library.(10, 25, 15).
10. The University Education Commission (1948) was headed by .... (Kothari, Radhakrishnan, Ranganathan)

11. AVRC's and EMRC's set by the .... are part of countrywide class room transmission programme. (UGC, ISOR, INFLIBNET)
12. There are ....Public Libraries in India which were granted privilege of "Legal Deposit" by the Act of 1954. (Three, Four, Five)
13. The word "Library" is derived from ....word ....meaning .... (Latin, liber, a book; Greek, Library, Book; Greek, liber, a book)
14. The forth law of library science is .... (Library is a Growing Organism, Save the Time of the Reader, Every Reader His/ Her Book)
15. The third revision of UNESCO Manifesto (Public Library) was released in the year .... (1995, 1994, 1996)
16. The main objective to established FID was to prepare............ (UDC, Revise DDC, Documentation)
17. The Network for the exchange of information in science and technology for Asia and Pacific is known as .... (DEVIVSA, ASTINFO, APINESS)
18. The "Books for all' is corollary to the .... Law of Library science.(Second, First, Third)
19. The .... Library is the "legal deposit" Library of the southern Region

    (Connemara Public, State Central, Saraswathi Mahal).
20. The Department/ .wings of UNESCO dealing with libraries affairs is known as .... (Science Division; Documentation, Bibliography and Archives; NATIS)
21. The (Revised) Indian Copyright Act (After Independence) was brought out in the year............ (1954,1957,1956)
22. The FID was founded in Brussels in the year .... (1890,1895,1897)
23. In India the "Delivery of Books and News Papers (Public Libraries) Act is generally termed as .... (Copyright Act, Censorship Act, Legal Deposit Act)
24. The First Law of Library Science "Books are for Use" is

a concept that replaced the old Concept .... (Books are for posterity, Books are for preservation, Books are for Library)

25. The Special, University and Public Libraries in general are distinguishable in respect of three factors ....(Books, Journals and User ; Reading Materials, User and Services ;Organizations, Users and Services)
26. The Ewart Bill, the First Public Library Bill was brought in .... (UK, USA, France)
27. The mankind's first ever written book of Sumerians is called a/an............ (Epic, Rosetta Stone, Gilgamesh)
28. British Museum Library was established in .... (1875,1753,1573)
29. The Calcutta University Commission appointed in 1917 was headed by .... (Michael Sadler, Maurice Guwyer, Lord Chemsford)
30. The cooperative acquisition plan for University Libraries in 1948 was pioneered by............ (Scandia Plan, Dealer Library Plan, Farmington Plan)
31. The famous Clay Tablet Library of kindg Ashurbanipal an Assyrian king was found in .... (Babylonia, Nineveh, Mesodonia)
32. The Library Association(UK) was founded in the year ....(1876,1875, 1877)
33. The first University to start a University level course in Library Science in India was the .... (University of Lahor, Banaras Hindu University, University of Madras)
34. The book "Five Laws of Library Science" by Ranganathan was first published in the year............ (1933, 1931, 1924)
35. The Parry Committee in the United Kingdom was appointed to review the .... Libraries. (Special, University, Public)
36. The early Egyptian books were made up of .... (Papyrus Rolls, Palm Leaf, Vellum)

37. If University and Public Libraries provided documents, whereas the special libraries emphasise on .... (Lending Services, Information Services, Extension Services).
38. The UBC and UAP are the two complementary programmers' of .... (UNESCO, FID, IFLA)
39. Dr. Ranganathan was appointed as Librarian of University of Madras in .... (1924,1923,1925)
40. The term Documentation was used by Paul Otlet as early as in .... (1896, 1905, 1876)
41. The former name of ASIS was .... (Aslib, American Documentation Institute, Special Librarics Association)
42. The components of Translation service are ...., ..., ... (Translation Pools, Panels, Banks; Translation Centers, Translators, Translations; Translation Centers, Pools and Panels)
43. The term Information Science was first used in .... (1956, 1954, 1959)
44. The Russian equivalent of the term information Science is .... (Documentation, Informatics, Scientometrics)
45. The term Informatics was proposed by .... (Garfield, Mikhailov, Borko)
46. The data that can perceive, understand and put together as knowledge is called .... (Document, Information, Wisdom)
47. Information is .... data (Raw, Processed, New)
48. The first printed book by Gutenberg is known as .... (Movable type, Printed Book, Gutenberg Bible)
49. Cybernetics is the study of communication between .... and ....(Man and Machine, Machine and Computer, Hardware and Software)
50. The language barrier is overcome by .... service. (Translation, Extension, Reference)
51. The two channels of communication are .... and .... (Documentary and Formal, Conventional and

Non-formal, Formal and Informal)

52. .... is both producer and consumer of information (Library, User, Researcher)

53. Quantitative growth of literature, where literature gets doubled every few years is termed as .... (Literature growth, Information Explosion, Exponential growth)

54. The term Information Retrieval was coined by .... in 1950 (H.P.Luhn, Calvin Mooers, D.A.Kemp)

55. 'Data' is a series of .... facts and observations (Organised, Unorganised, Disconnected)

56. A Period predominantly centered on information activities is known as............ (Information age, Information Span, Information Explosion)

57. Data may be converted into information by .... (Observation, Experiment, Analysing)

58. The Mathematical Theory of communication is the contribution of .... (Lasswell, Shannon, Berlo)

59. The word 'Data' Latin in origin used in its plural form is derived form the word ....(Datum, Codata, Metadata)

60. Complete the Quotation "Where is wisdom we have lost in .... (Wisdom, Data, Information)

61. Barriers to communication and information flow are Language, Jargon and .... (Style, Media, Presentation)

62. Communication process consists of at least three basic elements, and the first element is............(Massage, Source, Media)

63. Machlup epitomizes information science broadly as a cluster of many .... (Science, Disciplines, Derivatives)

64. The term Communication originates from the .... word .... (Latin, Greek, French; Communis, Community, Commute)

65. The concept of Information Explosion also characterized

by the measures like, Scatter, Seepage and .... (Drainage, Doubling, Obsolescence)

66. The earliest use of the term 'Documentation' is found in the year............ (1905,1920,1932)
67. The International Organisation for Standardisation (ISO) is located at............(New York, Paris, Geneva)
68. The data can be first categoriesed on the basis of .... (Occuranes, Disciplines, Countries)
69. The term 'Cybernetics' was coined by ....(Norbert Weiner, Shannon, Warren Weaver)
70. The Apex Organisation of India Statistical System is .... (CSO, NSS, NIC)
71. The Asiatic Society was founded in Calcutta in the year .... (1788,1784,1780)
72. In communication process the information is transferred from receiver (User, Generator, Originator)
73. The Bureau of Indian Standards was earlier known by abbreviated name .... (ISO, ISI, IIS)
74. The first International Conference on Scientific Communication held in 1948 was organized by ....(Royal Society, American Documentation Institute, American Library Association)
75. The Weinberg report which deals with the key issue of International Science was also responsible for the establishment of ....(COSATI, OSTI, VINITI)
76. Aristotle's idea of communication process is dealt in his work entitled ....(The State, Democracy, Rhetoric).
77. One of the proponents of cognitive Paradigm of Information Science was ....(Mooers, Garfield, Belkin).
78. The Technical Committee of ISO relating to Libraries, Information Centres, Documentation and others is denoted by............(ISO/TC46,ISO/TC37, ISO/TC97).
79. The Noise in the communication process can be reduced by ....(Interpersonal Communication,

Feedback, Formal Communication Media).

80. The concept of Information Society implies growing proportion of workers in .... activities (Data, Knowledge, Information).

81. The author of the book entitled "DOCUMENTATION" published in the year 1948 was .... (Eugene, Garfield, S.C.Bardford, B.C. Vickery).

82. The growth of information is characterized as to follow .... Progression. (Arithmetic, Trigonometric, Geometric).

83. Harold Lasswell's communication consists of .... components (5, 6, 7).

84. Information is considered as a .... resource (Third, Fourth, Fifth).

85. The Primary data is normally categorized as data with reference to .... (Mode of generation, Time Factor, Terms of Expression).

86. The Information transfer model consists of Source, Message .... And Recipient (Link, Need. Channel).

87. Communication Media is broadly classified as Print media and .... (Magnetic Media, Electronic Media, Microform).

88. The article entitled "As we may think" published in 1945 which made a beginning for the study of information Science was written by .... (Vannever Bush, Ralph Shaw, Robert hayes).

89. The ISO Committee on Standardisation of Technology is designated as .... (ISO/TC37, ISO/TC46, ISO/TC97).

90. The acronym POSDCORB was coined by .... (Peter Gulick, Frederik Taylor, Peter Drucker).

91. F.W.Tatlor is usually regarded as Father of .... (Classical Management, Scientific management, Behavioural school of Thought).

92. Maslow's theory is one of the .... theories of management (Leadership, Classical, Human Behaviour

and Motivation).

93. Father of Modern Management is .... (Henry Koontz, Peter Drucker, Henry Ford).
94. Fayol evolved .... principles (Administrative, Management, Business).
95. Operation Research is also called .... (Operation Management, Research on Operations, None).
96. Management by Objectives was originally developed by .... (Henry Feyol, Reathlisberger, Abraham Maslow).
97. PPBS stands for .... (Programme, Planning and Budgeting System; Performance Budgeting System; Planning and Performance Budgeting System).
98. Time, space, material and product budget enumerated by .... (Ranganathan, Koontz, Kotlar).
99. The delegation of authority is closely related to the concept of .... and .... (Control and Management; Coordination and Strategic Leadership; Cooperation and Planning).
100. Hawthorne experiment was conducted by .... (mayo, Reathlisberge, Dickinson, Mayo, Evans, Fayol; Koontz, Argyis, Drucker).
101. Max Weber was acknowledge for .... (Personnel Organisation, Bureaucratic Organisation, Administrative Theory).
102. Esprit DeCrops is one of the .... of .... (Function of Management, Laws of Administration, Principle of Management).
103. Theory X and theory Y was conceived by .... (Maslow, McGregor, Machlup).
104. Unique feature of MIS is to provide information in hierarchical pattern is mostly in decision levels namely to .... (Middle Management, Lower Management, Top Management).
105. Staff formula for personnel estimation was devised by .... (Ranganathan, Dewey, Keshavan).

106. Feedback mechanism is one of the characteristic of .... system (Monitoring, Supervisory, Control).
107. Abraham Maslow was associated with .... school of thought. (Classical, Behavioural, Neo-classical)
108. .... considered as the founding father of General systems theory. (Peter Drucker, Ackoff, Ludwig vonBartlanfly)
109. The concept of ZBB is a financial statement of the revenue and .... for a given period. (Expenditure, Income, Receipts)
110. The classical theory of management was expounded by .... (F.W.Taylor, Henry Fayol, Peter Drucker)
111. Brainstorming is one of the technique for the management/technique of .... (Quality, Quantity, Monitoring)
112. MBO stands for .... (Management, Business, Organisation; Management by Object ; Management Before Objectives)
113. The .... methods of financial estimation for Library are the percent age based on the total education Budget of the Government. (Proportional, Per Capital, Methods of Details)
114. Maslow's theory is called theory of .... needs (Levels of, Hierarchical of, Estimation of)
115. The last letter of POSTCORB stands for .... (Brainstorming, Barcode Processing, Budgeting)
116. The path-goal theory of leadership was developed by .... House and Evans, Mayo and Evans, Dickinson and Mcgregor)
117. The method of determining quantum of Library stuff evolved by S.R.Ranganathan is popularly known as the .... (Personnel Planning, Stuff Planning, Stuff Formula)
118. The four elements of Total Quality are; System, Management, Process and .... (Material, Machine, People)

119. Gnatt was responsible for developing a charting system like .... (CPM & PART, Boolean Logic, Flow Charting)

120. The most powerful Library Committee is .... committee. (Advisory, Self-Perpetuating, Executive)

121. Managerial Grid Style of leadership was proposed by .... (Blake and Houton, Blake and Brown, Houton and House)

122. Among the methods of financial estimation the .... method is fixed on the per head of population (Methods of Details, Proportional, Per Capita)

123. In the acquisition of periodicals, the methods largely followed by libraries is by .... (Subscription, Membership, Exchanged)

124. "Esteem" need is .... level in Maslow's hierarchy of needs (2,3,5)

125. PPBS is one of the methods of .... (Planning, Budgeting, Controlling)

126. The motto of Library Rules is guided by the axiom; If "rights imply duties, vigilance is the price of ...." (Freedom, Regulation, Privileges)

127. Japanese Philosophy and style of participative management is denoted by the term .... (Negotiating, Inter-personal Communication, Quality Circles)

128. Time and Motion Study was enunciated by .... (Frank Evans, Frank & Littian Gilbreth, Harrington Emerson)

129. The Unified Concept of Management was developed by .... (Henry Fayol, F.W.Taylor, Abraham Maslow)

130. Likert System of .... is a behavioural approach theory of Leadership (Laissz-faire,Trait-Theory,1, 2, 3 & 4)

131. For managers and decision makers .... technique helps make better forecasts (System, Delphi, MIS)

132. The Libraries in the context of Managements Theories

account for .... Organisation (Non-Profit Making, Profit Making, Service Oriented)

133. The explanatory/factual statement of a specific job is termed as .... (Job Description, Job Analysis, Job Specification)
134. Macro Evaluation aims at evaluation of the total evaluation performance.(Financial, Manpower, System)
135. The modern approach to management of Libraries and Information Centres is perceived to be a .... Centered.(Document, User, Media).
136. Early management in characterized as "............" period. (Autocratic, Bureaucratic, Renaissance).
137. The Karnataka Public Libraries Act provides for collecting cess on .... as source for financing city libraries (Land and Building, Corporation tax, Entertainments tax).
138. The Quality Circle is a small group consisting of .... people (Two to three, three to twelve, two to five).
139. The type of organisation structure when all the workers are responsible direct to the head is called .... (Line type, Chain type, Stuff type).
140. The methods of Details in financial estimation for Libraries implied on .... (Details of Material, Equipment, staff).
141. The hybrid variety of management was introduce by .... (David Dawden, K.Masuda, Kaoru Ishikawa).
142. For solving space problems in Libraries the .... storage/stacks method is found to be suitable (Compact, Rolling, Tower).
143. In India .... regularly announces the Foreign Exchange rates to enable Academic Libraries to decide of exchanges rates of foreign books purchased.(NPC, GOC, UGC)
144. A Budget is an estimate of Revenue and .... for the coming year (Income, Receipt, Expenditure)

145. Library building, reading materials and equipments are to be guarded against six enemies, namely; Dust, Dirt and Cobweb, Water, Vermin, Fire and .... (Humans, Reptiles, Animals)
146. Quality circles are considered as new channels of .... management. (Motivational, Participative, Organizational)
147. .... propounded the concept of ZBB (Peter Pkyhrr, Peter Drucker, Robert Erickson)
148. One of the major sources of finance for Academic (University) Libraries is form .... (State Govt., Central Govt., UGC)
149. PERT and CPM are the techniques adopted in the .... system management (Complex, Network, Computer)
150. The catalogue of information sources on the INTERNET/INTRANET is known as ....(IRC, IRNET, IPC)
151. Micropaedia is a volume dealing with .... facility (Outline of Knowledge, Ready Reference, Knowledge in Depth)
152. Propaedia is a volume dealing with .... facility. (Ready Reference, Outline of Knowledge, Knowledge in Depth).
153. Patent is a .... source of information (Neo-documentary, Non-Documentary, Primary).
154. The title of the first Encyclopaedia is .... (Encyclopaedia Britannica, Historia Naturalis, Speculum majus)
155. The publishers of world of learning are .... (Europa, R.R.Bowker, H.W.Wilson)
156. The New Encyclopaedia of Britannica is in .... parts. (4,3,6)
157. Science Citation Indexing is in .... (5,7,3)
158. The electronic source of information on Biomedical literature available through Elsevier science publishers

is known as .... (CINAHL, EMBASE, OVID)

159. Guide to Indian Periodical Literature is published .... (Bi-weekly, Monthly, Quarterly)

160. The first Edition of Encyclopaedia Britannica was published in the year .... (1768, 1771, 1773)

161. "Keesing Record of World Events" is an example of .... (Newspaper Digest, Newspaper Index, Index of Individual Newspaper)

162. The electronic Journals (Pages on contents) services provided by Elsevire is known as .... (ESTOC, EJIS, LSDA)

163. The URL of online version of the Encyclopaedia Britannica is .... (www.britannica.com, www. Eb.gov, www.eb.edu)

164. Indian Dissertation Abstracts is published by .... (ICAR, ICSSR, UGC)

165. The source which give original and nascent information are termed as .... sources (Primary , Documentary, Tertiary)

166. The major source of information on Indian Biomedical literature is available through .... (NICNET.Indian Medlars, RENNIC, IndMed)

167. The Universities Handbook is published by .... (Association of Indian Universities, UGC, ICSSR)

168. The Science Directory is the product of .... for Electronic Journals (Academic, Elsevier Science, Blackwell Scientific)

169. "International Who's Who" is a .... biographical source (Current/Universal, Retrospective/Universal, Retrospective/ National)

170. The first edition of Encyclopaedia Britannica was in .... volumes. (2,3,4)

171. The British National Bibliography was started in the year .... (1945, 1965, 1950)

172. Yearbook covers .... information of a particular year whereas Almanac cover both .... and

.... (Current, Current and Retrospective; Current Retrospective and Old ; Retrospective, Current, Old)

173. Handbook deal with .... knowledge (Current, Established, Revised)
174. One of the main advantages of the Electronic Journals is .... (Access, Storage, Reference)
175. Glossary explains the technical terms of a particular .... (Country, Subject, Individual)
176. Dictionaries are regarded as .... Reference/ Information sources (Ready, Tertiary, Retrospective)
177. The name of the individual who coined the word "Atlas" is known as .... (R.A.Skelton, M.O.wcbstcr, Mercator)
178. Yearbook and Almanacs are known as .... and .... Sources. (Trends and Facts, Current and Retrospective, Digest and Summary)
179. Advances and progresses are compiled from .... sources. (Secondary, Tertiary, Primary)
180. Statistical sources provide .... and .... statistics than any other ready reference sources (Accurate & Reliable; Revised and Reviewed; Known and Analysed)
181. The word Encyclopaedia is derived from .... word enkyklios paideia. (Greek, Latin, Spanish)
182. International yearbook include all information about all .... of the .... (Countries and Nations, Countries and World, None)
183. "India Economic Diary" is an example of a .... (National Digest, Subject Digest, Subject Index)
184. Atlases cover statistical information about .... of various countries. (Economic and Agriculture etc., Political and Social, Educational and Technical)
185. The main objective and function of the supplement to Encyclopaedia is to .... main encyclopaedia (Complement, Supplement, Revise)
186. Statistical information is the outcome of the ....

and .... of numerical data.(Collection and Classification; Collection and Dissemination; Storage and Retrieval)

187. The Cumulative Book Index is a publication of .... (H.W.Willson, R.R.Bowker, Pergamon)
188. Yearbook are group in different categories according to their .... and .... (Date and publisher, scope and authority, Scope and coverage)
189. Oxford English Dictionary and Webster's Third New International Dictionaries fall in the category of .... dictionaries. (Prescriptive, Descriptive, Abridged)
190. Journals constitute major categories of .... sources (Secondary, Reference, Primary)
191. The "Gazetteer of India" is in .... volumes. (10,4,6)
192. Pamphlets come under the category of .... documents. (Primary, Secondary, Tertiary)
193. A review is a survey of primary literature and indicates .... (Research trend, Information growth and development, what has been published)
194. For the dissemination of the research results, the .... is the primary source. (House Bulletin, Periodicals, News Letter)
195. Serials are those that are published on .... basis (Formal, Informal, Continuing)
196. The name of the Medical Dictionary that has gone Online is .... (onMed, OEM, Dorland's MedicalOn)
197. The Bell and Howell information is the new name for .... International (EBSCO, University Microfilms, Universal Microfilms)
198. Indian Books In Print is a publication of .... (National Library of India, Indian Bureau of Bibliographies, INSDOC)
199. Atlapaedia is an online site for .... (Hamonds' Atlas, Reader's Digest Atlas, Maps and Atlases)
200. The name of new Web Catalogue of National Library of

Madicine is .... (LOCATOR, DIALOG Plus, Medline-Plus)

201. The American Psychological Association's Abstracting Journal is now available as .... (APAlist, PsychoInfo, PsycLit)
202. JURIX a Judicial and Legal Database on CD is of .... origin. (USA, Indian, Japan)
203. World Patent Index is Produced by .... (KoMPAS, US Petent Office, Derwent)
204. A Systematic bibliography is also known as .... bibliography. (Enumerative, Classified, Descriptive)
205. The .... is the Encyclopaedia brought out by Micro Soft in Electronic form (Encarta, Funk-Wagnalls, Britannica Online)
206. Library and Information Science Abstract is a .... publication (Monthly, Bimonthly, Quarterly)
207. LISA print and CD version is published by .... (Aslib Publication, Library Association Publication, British Library)
208. Special Encyclopaedias are .... to more expended research (Accurate Sources, Stepping Stone, flag-post)
209. General Encyclopaedia help in enriching .... knowledge of a common individual (General, Specific, Curricular)
210. Encyclopaedia Britannica follows .... revision procedure (Continuous, Periodical, Publication of Yearbook)
211. The Bibliographic database on CD produced by CMTI, Bangalore is called .... (Buyer's Guide, MTech OnCD, VAPIS)
212. The CD-ROM version of J. of Economic Literature is Known as .... (EcoLit, JELit, Sociofile)
213. The name of the contributors that prefixes with the title Encyclopaedia of Chemical Technology is .... (Kirk-Othmer, Mark-Ulleman, Chapman-Hall)
214. .... is the Medical Encyclopaedia that is available

on INTERNET (Infomedical, Kaiser Permanenete, Medscape)

215. The issue of .... rights that often confronts the Electronic sources of information (Technological, Legal, Economical)
216. AGRICOLA is a bibliographic database is created by .... (National Agricultural Library, IARI, FAO)
217. Sociofile's equivalent of Print media is known as .... (Sociology Index, Sociological Abstracts, Social Science Index)
218. The "Gazetteer of India" is an abridged version of the .... (Gazetteer of East India Company, Burma Gazetteer, Imperial Gazetteer of India)
219. The URL of the newspaper 'Deccan Herald' is .... (www.deccan.com, www.heralddeccan.com, www.deccanherald.com)
220. The Biosystemetic Index is the part of .... (Index Medicus, Biomedical Index, BIOSIS.
221. Ranganathan conceived the idea of synthesis in classification from a .... he observed while in London. (Mechano Set, Chess Board, Toys).
222. The scheme of classification devised by Cutter is known as .... (Expansive Classification, Subject Classification, International Classification)
223. Econometrics is a .... Basic Subject (Distilled, Fused, Fissioned)
224. When a scheme of classification employs more than one species of digit the notation is known as .... notation. (Mixed, Pure, Complex)
225. As per W. Holme the classification should be based on .... (Subject Approach, Literary Warrant, One Place Theory)
226. The notational based of the DDC follows .... notation. (Mixed, Decimal Fraction, Simple)
227. Ranganathan recognized .... planes of work. (Two, Four, Three)

228. The structure of main classes in DDC is an inversion of .... method of classification (Francis Bacon, Immanuel Kant, Hegel)
229. The approach that is always found helpful for the arrangement of books in libraries is .... (Author, Subject, Title)
230. The types of Common Isolates in Colon Classification assigned to approach documents are ....(ACI, PCI, Common Personality Isolates)
231. The Call Number of a document consists of three elements, namely Class Number, ... & Collection Number (Accession Number, Cardinal Number, Book Number)
232. H. E. Bliss's idea of subject arrangement in close proximity is known as .... (Collation, Collocation, Connotation)
233. The name DDC and Relative Index was first used from .... edition(Third, Second, First)
234. Table 2 of DDC auxiliaries is pertaining to ....(Area, Persons, Language)
235. The new type of phase relation introduce in CC Ed.7 is named .... (Method Phase, Tool Phase, Technique Phase)
236. There are .... Table of Common Auxiliaries in UDC (5,6,7)
237. The term Classification was derived from the .... andd ....(Greek and Liber, Latin/Liber, French/ Libra)
238. The facet formula for 'O: Literature' in CC is .... (P1,P2,P3,P4; P,E;P,E cum2P)
239. The rounds and levels are the .... of fundamentals categories (Principles, Canon, Manifestation)
240. A .... subject is one with a Basic Subject and with one or more isolate ideas (Fused Basic, Compound, Complex)

241. The work in the Idea plane is to deal with enumeration of .... and to show their interrelations (Universe of Subjects, Names of Subjects, notation)

242. The well known synthetic device used in DDC from the beginning as "Divide Like" is now known as .... (Centred Heading, Divide as, Add to)

243. The BBK Classification originated from .... (Russia, Germany, France)

244. The new addition to CC7, which hither-to-before not part of any CC editions is the enumeration of .... (Environment Division, Common Personality Isolates, Space Isolates)

245. Since 1988 the publishing ownership of DDC has changed from Forest press to .... (IFLA, FID, OCLC)

246. 'Time' is considered as the .... element 9Most concrete, Least concrete, More concrete)

247. The mapping of subjects in CC follow the law of .... (Parsimony, Symmetry, Osmosis)

248. The best example of a classification system devised as a Switching Language is the .... (SRC, UDC, BSO)

249. The proportion of listing of concepts in different versions of UDC from full Abridge version is found to be approximately in the Ratio of .... (30:1, 10:1, 50:1)

250. The Apex committee under FID which undertakes the revision and development of UDC is denoted by .... (FID/CR, FID/CD, FID/CCC)

251. The body that is created to revise the Bliss's Bibliographic Classification is headed .... (D.J.Fosket, Jack Mills, E.G.Coates)

252. The isolates of 'Religion' is CC are arranged as per the Principle of .... (Later in Evolution, Filiatory Sequence, Later in Time)

253. One of the organizations which has been associated

with devising special Classification systems is the .... (CRJ, DRTC, ASLIB)

254. The UDC is published in three versions, they are Full, Abridged and .... (Condensed, Medium, Subject Specials)

255. The parts of a Plant in Botany schedule of CC are arranged as per the Principle of .... (Bottom Upwards, Centre to Periphery, Top Downwards)

256. The first international French edition of UDC was published in the year .... (1920,1905,1897)

257. The Phase Relation for example "Mathematics for Engineers" implies .... (Tool, Bias, Difference)

258. The ideas of "Gradation by Speciality " is evolved by .... (Sayers, Bliss, brown)

259. Maximum Synthesis in UDC is achieved by the use of............ (Combinations, Extension, Auxiliaries)

260. Citation order in CC is derived from a process termed as .... (Facet Analysis, Facet Formula, Facet Sequence)

261. The first English Edition of UDC was prepared with the contribution of .... (B.C. Vickery, S. C. Bradford, D.J.Foscate)

262. The Fundamental Category Personality has both Rounds and Levels, whereas for Energy has only/or .... (Rounds, Levels, Rounds and Levels too)

263. The two Classification System which are widely used in OPAC's are .... (LC & DDC, DDC & UDC, LC & UDC)

264. The changes proposed for UDC revision are circulated by FID as .... (P-Notes, R-Notes, PN-Notes)

265. Among the trends in research in Classification, the establishment of .... is considered to be latest landmark.(UNISIS,CRG,ISKO)

266. The well know Special Classification System devised US Department of Health Library in the field Health Science is known as .... Classification.(NML,NLM,

John Hopins University)

267. UDC and DDC are usually consider as .... Classification Systems. (Aspect, Concept, Faceted)

268. The word 'Thesaurus' was derived from Greek and Latin word that means .... (a Treasury, a Terminology, a Vocabulary)

269. The National Information Standards Organisation for searching database appointed a committee to develop .... (Common Commu7nication Format, SQL, Common Command Language)

270. In PRECIS the Chain is referred to as a/an .... (Array, Entry, String)

271. The control device that was used in Coordinate indexing also finds application in PRECIS is .... (Roles, Links, Analysis)

272. The Chain of POPSI represents the mode of .... (Class Number, Facet Structure, Facet Analysis)

273. The particulars about publisher, place and year of the publication together is known as .... (Collation, Imprint, Physical Description).

274. The project of unique identification of all serial constituted was .... (ISDS, ISSN, CODEN).

275. If ISBN is for books, and ISSN is for serials, what STRN is for (Patents, Reports, Sound Recordings)

276. The last section of main entry as per CCC is .... Section (Accession, Note, Tracing)

277. .... was used for subject indexing in British National Bibliography (POPSI, PRECIS, SLIC)

278. The specific implementation of ISO 2709 is visualized with the use of .... (UNIMARC, MARC, CCF)

279. Recall and Precision Evaluation Parameters of Indexing systems are evolved from the ....Project (SMART, Aslib-Cranfield, Medlars)

280. The Semantics of PRECIS is controlled by .... (RIN & SIN, Indicators, Weights)

281. The system of coordinate Indexing developed by Mortimer Taube is known as .... System. (WADEX, KWIC, Uniterm Indexing)
282. The point of access to an entry is identified by the Canon of .... (Recall Value, Sought Heading, Context)
283. The methods of deriving indexing entries in KWIC is by .... (Chain Procedure, Permutation of Title, Coordination)
284. PRECISE has adopted .... line entry format(Two, Four, Five)
285. MARC is thc acronym that stands for .... (Machine Readable Coordination, Machine Readable Cataloguing, Machine Readable Catalogue)
286. Ranganathan devised .... for deriving subject headings from class numbers(Subject Catalogue, Dictionary Catalogue, Chain Procedure)
287. .... was the first to use the term Thesaurus in the Information Retrieval Context. (H.P.Luhn, Helen Bownson, A.C. Fosket)
288. The idea of citation indexing was propounded by............ (E. Garfild, S.Price, Gerald Salton)
289. Hierarchical relations in a thesaurus is the relation between .... and .... (Broader Term and Narrower Term, Broader Term and Related Term, Related Term and Narrower Term)
290. The KWIC version augmented with author name is known as .... (KWOC,KWAC, WADEX)
291. ISBN was introduced in the year .... (1959, 1969, 1979)
292. MARC was developed for computer produced catalogue by .... (Library of Congress, ALA, BLA)
293. The point of access in subject in a catalogue is determined by thc canon of .... (Recall value, Sought Heading, Prepotence)
294. The Human Level of PRECIS is to assign the roles, while

the computer level is to generate .... (Author Entries, Class Number, Subject Index)

295. The developments in general cataloguing have profound influence of .... Principle 1961 (Paris, The Hague, Vienna)

296. The KWIC indexing was developed by .... (Gerald Salton, H.P.Luhn, E. Garfield)

297. A Thesaurus links the user query from a unpreferred term to a .... term (Hierarchical, Synonymus, Preferred)

298. In BNB .... was used as subject indexing system (Chain Indexing, PRECIS, SLIC)

299. In Hierarchical relationship super-ordinate relationships are denoted by .... (BT & NT, BT & RT, RT & NT)

300. The National Library of India before Independence was called............ (British Library, National Library of UK, Imperial Library).

301. The Head Quarters of IASLIC is located at .... (Calcutta, Mumbai, New Delhi)

302. Bibliotheque Nationale is the National Library of .... (Australia, France, Poland)

303. The Karnataka Public Library Act was passed in the year .... (1966, 1965, 1967)

304. The National Medical Library of India is located at .... (New Delhi, Calcutta, Bangalore)

305. UNESCO statement on Public Library is Known as .... (Declaration, Manifesto, Statute)

306. The orientation of Library Building should be .... (North-South, South-East, East-West)

307. The Library Building planning team should consist of ...., ... and .... (Librarian, Dy. Librarian, Principle; Librarian, Architect, Management; Architect, Engineer, Management)

308. The purpose of book selection is .... (To buy book, To buy best books at lest cost, To seek permission to

order books)

309. The kardex is used mainly for the inventory control of .... (Books, Periodicals, Standards)
310. The 'Best reading for the largest at the least cost' is the principle given by .... (Melvil Dewey, John Drury, Ranganathan)
311. PRECIS was developed by Derek Austin for use in the .... (BNB, INB, ISBD)
312. A skillful method of providing means mechanism and structural elements to. streamline organizational work is known as .... (Strategic planning, Role analysis, Work culture)
313. DOI is web resources is equivalent to .... of book. (ISBN, Statement of responsibility, Call Number, Accession Number).

ANSWERS

1. The Hague
2. 15th Century A.D.
3. Fortnightly
4. 1876
5. 1956
6. 1933
7. Charging and Discharging
8. 1992
9. 10
10. Radhakrishnan
11. UGC
12. Four
13. Latin, liber, a book
14. Save the Time of the Reader
15. 1994
16. UDC
17. ASTINFO
18. Second
19. Connemara Public
20. Documentation, Bibliography and Archives
21. 1957
22. 1895
23. Legal Deposit Act
24. Books are for preservation
25. Reading Materials, User and Services
26. UK
27. Gilgamesh
28. 1753
29. Michael Sadler
30. Farmington Plan
31. Nineveh
32. 1877
33. University of Madras
34. 1931
35. University
36. Papyrus Rolls
37. Information Services

38. IFLA
39. 1924
40. 1905
41. American Documentation Institute
42. Panels, Banks; Translation Centers
43. 1959
44. Informatics
45. Mikhailov
46. Information
47. Processed
48. Gutenberg Bible
49. Man and Machine
50. Translation
51. Formal and Informal
52. Researcher
53. Information Explosion
54. Calvin Mooers
55. Organised
56. Information Span
57. Analysing
58. Shannon
59. Datum
60. Information
61. Presentation
62. Source
63. Disciplines
64. Latin, Communis,
65. Obsolescence
66. 1905
67. Geneva
68. Disciplines
69. Norbert Weiner
70. CSO
71. 1784
72. Generator
73. ISI
74. Royal Society
75. COSATI
76. Rhetoric
77. Belkin.
78. ISO/TC46
79. Feedback
80. Information
81. S.C.Bardford
82. Geometric
83. 5, 6, 7.
84. Fourth
85. Mode of generation
86. Channel
87. Electronic Media
88. Vannever Bush
89. ISO/TC37
90. Peter Gulick
91. Scientific management
92. Human Behaviour and Motivation.
93. Peter Drucker
94. Management
95. Research on Operations
96. Reathlisberger
97. Programme, Planning and Budgeting System
98. Kotlar.
99. Coordination and Strategic Leadership
100. mayo, Reathlisberge, Dickinson
101. Bureaucratic Organisation
102. Principle of Management
103. McGregor
104. Top Management
105. Ranganathan

106. Control
107. Behavioural
108. Ludwig von Bartlanfly
109. Expenditure
110. Henry Fayol
111. Quality
112. Management by Object
113. Proportional
114. Hierarchical of
115. Budgeting
116. House and Evans
117. Stuff Formula
118. People
119. CPM & PART
120. Executive
121. Blake and Houton
122. Per Capita
123. Subscription
124. 2
125. Budgeting
126. Freedom
127. Quality Circles
128. Frank & Littian Gilbreth
129. Henry Fayol
130. 1, 2, 3 & 4
131. Delphi
132. Non-Profit Making
133. Job Description
134. System
135. User
136. Autocratic
137. Corporation tax
138. two to five
139. Line type
140. staff
141. Kaoru Ishikawa
142. Compact
143. GOC
144. Expenditure
145. Humans
146. Participative
147. Peter Pkyhrr
148. UGC
149. Network
150. IRC
151. Ready Reference
152. Outline of Knowledge
153. Primary.
154. Historia Naturalis
155. Europa
156. 3
157. 3
158. EMBASE
159. Quarterly
160. 1771
161. Newspaper Digest
162. ESTOC
163. www.britannica.com
164. ICSSR
165. Primary
166. IndMed
167. Association of Indian Universities
168. Elsevier Science
169. Current/Universal
170. 3
171. 1950
172. Current, Current and Retrospective
173. Established
174. Access
175. Subject
176. Ready
177. Mercator
178. Trends and Facts

179. Primary
180. Accurate & Reliable
181. Greek
182. Countries and World
183. Subject Digest
184. Economic and Agriculture etc.,
185. Supplement
186. Collection and Classification
187. H.W.Willson
188. Scope and coverage
189. Descriptive
190. Primary
191. 4
192. Primary
193. Research trend
194. Periodicals
195. Continuing
196. onMed
197. University Microfilms
198. Indian Bureau of Bibliographies
199. Maps and Atlases
200. LOCATOR
201. PsycLit
202. Indian
203. Derwent
204. Classified
205. Encarta
206. Quarterly
207. Library Association Publication
208. Stepping Stone
209. General
210. Publication of Yearbook
211. MTech OnCD
212. EcoLit
213. Kirk-Othmer
214. Medscape
215. Legal
216. National Agricultural Library
217. Sociological Abstracts
218. Imperial Gazetteer of India
219. www.deccanherald.com
220. BIOSIS.
221. Mechano Set
222. Expansive Classification
223. Fused
224. Mixed
225. Literary Warrant
226. Decimal Fraction
227. Three
228. Francis Bacon
229. Subject
230. ACI
231. Book Number
232. Collocation
233. Second
234. Area
235. Tool Phase
236. 5
237. Latin/Liber
238. P1,P2,P3,P4
239. Manifestation
240. Compound
241. Universe of Subjects
242. Add to
243. Russia
244. Environment Division
245. OCLC
246. Least concrete

247. Symmetry
248. BSO
249. 30:1
250. FID/CCC
251. Jack Mills
252. Later in Timc
253. CRJ
254. Medium
255. Bottom Upwards
256. 1905
257. Bias
258. Bliss
259. Auxiliaries
260. Facet Analysis
261. S.C.Bradford
262. Rounds
263. DDC & UDC
264. P-Notes
265. ISKO
266. NLM
267. Aspect
268. a Treasury
269. Common Command Language
270. String
271. Roles
272. Facet Analysis
273. Imprint
274. ISDS
275. Reports
276. Tracing
277. PRECIS
278. CCF
279. Aslib-Cranfield
280. RIN & SIN
281. Uniterm Indexing
282. Recall Value
283. Permutation of Title
284. Two
285. Machine Readable Cataloguing
286. Chain Procedure
287. Helen Bownson
288. E. Garfild
289. Broader Term and Narrower Term
290. WADEX
291. 1969
292. Library of Congress
293. Sought Heading
294. Subject Index
295. Paris
296. H.P.Luhn
297. Preferred
298. PRECIS
299. BT & NT
300. Imperial Library
301. Calcutta
302. France
303. 1965
304. New Delhi
305. Manifesto
306. North-South
307. Librarian, Architect, Management
308. To buy best books at lest cost
309. Periodicals
310. Melvil Dewey
311. BNB
312. Strategic Planning
313. ISBN